Business Intelligence Roadmap

Addison-Wesley Information Technology Series
Capers Jones and David S. Linthicum, Consulting Editors

The information technology (IT) industry is in the public eye now more than ever before because of a number of major issues in which software technology and national policies are closely related. As the use of software expands, there is a continuing need for business and software professionals to stay current with the state of the art in software methodologies and technologies. The goal of the **Addison-Wesley Information Technology Series** is to cover any and all topics that affect the IT community. These books illustrate and explore how information technology can be aligned with business practices to achieve business goals and support business imperatives. Addison-Wesley has created this innovative series to empower you with the benefits of the industry experts' experience.

For more information point your browser to www.awprofessional.com/itseries

Sid Adelman, Larissa Terpeluk Moss, *Data Warehouse Project Management.* ISBN: 0-201-61635-1

Sid Adelman et al., *Impossible Data Warehouse Situations: Solutions from the Experts.* ISBN: 0-201-76033-9

Wayne Applehans, Alden Globe, and Greg Laugero, *Managing Knowledge: A Practical Web-Based Approach.* ISBN: 0-201-43315-X

David Leon Clark, *Enterprise Security: The Manager's Defense Guide.* ISBN: 0-201-71972-X

Frank P. Coyle, *XML, Web Services, and the Data Revolution.* ISBN: 0-201-77641-3

Kevin Dick, *XML, Second Edition: A Manager's Guide.* ISBN: 0-201-77006-7

Jill Dyché, *e-Data: Turning Data into Information with Data Warehousing.* ISBN: 0-201-65780-5

Jill Dyché, *The CRM Handbook: A Business Guide to Customer Relationship Management.* ISBN: 0-201-73062-6

Patricia L. Ferdinandi, *A Requirements Pattern: Succeeding in the Internet Economy.* ISBN: 0-201-73826-0

David Garmus and David Herron, *Function Point Analysis: Measurement Practices for Successful Software Projects.* ISBN: 0-201-69944-3

John Harney, *Application Service Providers (ASPs): A Manager's Guide.* ISBN: 0-201-72659-9

International Function Point Users Group, *IT Measurement: Practical Advice from the Experts.* ISBN: 0-201-74158-X

Capers Jones, *Software Assessments, Benchmarks, and Best Practices.* ISBN: 0-201-48542-7

Ravi Kalakota and Marcia Robinson, *e-Business 2.0: Roadmap for Success.* ISBN: 0-201-72165-1

Ravi Kalakota and Marcia Robinson, *Services Blueprint: Roadmap for Execution.* ISBN: 0-321-15039-2

Greg Laugero and Alden Globe, *Enterprise Content Services: Connecting Information and Profitability.* ISBN: 0-201-73016-2

David S. Linthicum, *B2B Application Integration: e-Business-Enable Your Enterprise.* ISBN: 0-201-70936-8

David S. Linthicum, *Enterprise Application Integration.* ISBN: 0-201-61583-5

David S. Linthicum, *Next Generation Application Integration: From Simple Information to Web Services.* ISBN: 0-201-84456-7

Sergio Lozinsky, *Enterprise-Wide Software Solutions: Integration Strategies and Practices.* ISBN: 0-201-30971-8

Anne Thomas Manes, *Web Services: A Manager's Guide.* ISBN: 0-321-18577-3

Larissa T. Moss and Shaku Atre, *Business Intelligence Roadmap: The Complete Project Lifecycle for Decision-Support Applications.* ISBN: 0-201-78420-3

Bud Porter-Roth, *Request for Proposal: A Guide to Effective RFP Development.* ISBN: 0-201-77575-1

Ronald G. Ross, *Principles of the Business Rule Approach.* ISBN: 0-201-78893-4

Dan Sullivan, *Proven Portals: Best Practices for Planning, Designing, and Developing Enterprise Portals.* ISBN: 0-321-12520-7

Karl E. Wiegers, *Peer Reviews in Software: A Practical Guide.* ISBN: 0-201-73485-0

Ralph R. Young, *Effective Requirements Practices.* ISBN: 0-201-70912-0

Bill Zoellick, *CyberRegs: A Business Guide to Web Property, Privacy, and Patents.* ISBN: 0-201-72230-5

Business Intelligence Roadmap

The Complete Project Lifecycle for Decision-Support Applications

Larissa T. Moss, Shaku Atre

✦ Addison-Wesley

Boston • San Francisco • New York • Toronto • Montreal
London • Munich • Paris • Madrid
Capetown • Sydney • Tokyo • Singapore • Mexico City

The publisher offers discounts on this book when ordered in quantity for bulk purchases and special sales. For more information, please contact:

U.S. Corporate and Government Sales
(800) 382-3419
corpsales@pearsontechgroup.com

For sales outside of the U.S., please contact:

International Sales
(317) 581-3793
international@pearsontechgroup.com

Visit Addison-Wesley on the Web: www.awprofessional.com

Library of Congress Cataloging-in-Publication Data

Moss, Larissa Terpeluk.
   Business intelligence roadmap : the complete project lifecycle for decision-support applications / Larissa T. Moss, Shaku Atre.
       p.   cm.
   Includes bibliographical references and index.
   ISBN 0-201-78420-3 (pbk. : alk. paper)
   1. Business intelligence 2. Decision support systems. I. Atre, S., 1940– II. Title.

HD38.7 .M67 2003
658.4'03—dc21

2002026196

Text printed on recycled and acid-free paper.

ISBN 0201784203

3 4 5 6 7 8 PH   07 06 05 04

3rd Printing   September 2004

DEDICATION

To my soul mate, Donald P. Sherman,
whose love and support have encouraged me to
achieve goals that once seemed unreachable and
to face life's events that at times seemed unbearable.

—*Larissa T. Moss*

To Tante Lisel, and to my mother.

—*Shaku Atre*

Contents

About the Authors

Larissa T. Moss

Ms. Moss is president of Method Focus, Inc. She consults, lectures, and speaks at conferences worldwide on the topics of business intelligence, data warehousing, customer relationship management, information quality, data integration, and cross-organizational application development. She has coauthored the books *Data Warehouse Project Management* (Addison-Wesley, 2000) and *Impossible Data Warehouse Situations* (Addison-Wesley, 2002). She publishes white papers through the Cutter Consortium and articles in *TDWI Journal of Data Warehousing*, *DM Review*, *Cutter IT Journal*, *The Navigator*, and *Analytic Edge*. She is a member of the IBM Gold Group and a senior consultant of the Cutter Consortium. She is a contributing member to the "Ask the Experts" forum of *DM Review*. She was a part-time faculty member at the Extended University of California Polytechnic University, Pomona, and an associate of the Codd & Date Consulting Group. Ms. Moss can be reached at *lmoss@methodfocus.com*.

Shaku Atre

Ms. Atre is president of Atre Group, Inc., specializing in business intelligence, data warehousing, and DBMS. She is on the board of AtreNet, Inc., a Web agency in Santa Cruz, CA. Ms. Atre was a partner with PriceWaterhouseCoopers. She held a wide variety of management and technical positions at IBM. She is a renowned expert, consultant, and a speaker in business intelligence, data warehousing, end-user computing, and "Politics and IT." She has taught graduate-level courses in databases at New York University. Ms. Atre lectures on these topics worldwide. She is a columnist with Computerworld. Her articles are available at *http://www.atre.com*. Ms. Atre is the author of five books, including *Data Base: Structured Techniques for Design, Performance and Management,* and *Distributed Databases, Cooperative Processing & Networking*. Ms. Atre holds a master's degree in statistics and has done research at the University of Heidelberg, Germany, in mathematics. She can be reached at *shaku@atre.com*.

Foreword

In today's highly competitive and increasingly uncertain world, the quality and timeliness of an organization's "business intelligence" (BI) can mean not only the difference between profit and loss but even the difference between survival and bankruptcy.

In helping senior executives and information technology (IT) managers, Moss and Atre's greatest contribution, I believe, is the comprehensive nature of their "roadmap"; as the subtitle of their book promises, they have provided a complete project lifecycle for the development of such systems. Because BI and decision-support systems ultimately rely on a rich treasure trove of data, there is a significant emphasis in *Business Intelligence Roadmap* on various technical aspects of data: meta data, data mining, data warehousing, multidimensional data analysis (online analytical processing [OLAP]), data security, and so on. But there is also significant emphasis on the business justification, project planning, analysis, implementation, and deployment details of BI systems. In addition to the more traditional details of systems analysis, Moss and Atre also provide practical advice on the structure and organization of the project team, as well as the skills and talents of the human resource roles required for such project teams. And, because of the importance of building enterprise-wide BI systems, the authors also describe the lifecycle activities that must be carried out in a cross-organizational fashion.

Anyone planning to lead a BI project initiative, as well as the data analysts, systems architects, and other senior IT professionals involved in such an initiative, should definitely read *Business Intelligence Roadmap* from cover to cover. It wouldn't hurt senior executives to read the entire book, too, for then they might have a better appreciation for the careful planning and disciplined project organization required to make a BI project succeed. But Moss and Atre have wisely recognized that many senior executives are too busy, or too technophobic, to read the entire book; for such people, they have provided an "at a glance" section of the book that concludes with a final chapter summarizing dos, don'ts, and tips for each of the project lifecycle steps that they discuss in detail. For example, the penultimate tip, in the final chapter of the book, advises the reader to

> Implement your BI applications using the release concept. It is much better to deliver high-quality, partially functioning application releases over time than to deliver a low-quality, completed application that is fraught with many defects and with dirty data. If the first release is successful, new requirements will emerge as the business people get used to the iterative development process.

Edward Yourdon
New York City
September 2002

Preface

Many organizations are already well equipped to implement successful business intelligence (BI) decision-support applications, such as data warehouses, data marts, and other business analytics applications. However, during our consulting and teaching engagements, we have encountered many ill-equipped organizations as well. We observed some common factors among them, which we address in this book:

- Lack of understanding of the complexity of BI decision-support projects
- Lack of recognizing BI decision-support projects as cross-organizational business initiatives and not understanding that cross-organizational initiatives are different from stand-alone solutions
- Unavailable or unwilling business representatives
- Unengaged business sponsors or business sponsors who have little or no authority due to their low-level positions within the organization
- Lack of skilled and available staff as well as suboptimum staff utilization
- Inappropriate project team structure and dynamics
- No software release concept (no iterative development method)
- No work breakdown structure (no methodology)
- Ineffective project management (only project administration)
- No business analysis and no standardization activities
- No appreciation of the impact of dirty data on business profitability
- No understanding of the necessity for and the usage of meta data
- Too much reliance on disparate methods and tools (the "silver bullet" syndrome)

BI project managers and project teams can use this book to improve their project life cycles. They can also use it to obtain the appropriate recognition for their BI projects from the business community and to solicit the required support from their executive management. BI project team members and the business representatives assigned to them can use this book to gain a better understanding of the development effort required to build and deploy successful BI decision-support applications.

THE PURPOSE OF THIS BOOK

Business Intelligence Roadmap is a guide for developing BI decision-support applications. The two main purposes of this book are to

1. Explain the complexity of BI decision-support projects
2. Present a step-by-step guide for the entire BI project lifecycle

Complexity

In order to give you an appreciation of the complexity of BI decision-support projects, we describe all of the components that go into a BI decision-support development effort. For example:

- You should know what makes a BI decision-support application different from a traditional decision-support system so that you can avoid costly mistakes.
- You should understand the infrastructure components of your new BI decision-support application, such as the tools available (for development and for access and analysis).
- You should be able to recognize items that could impair the success of your new BI decision-support application.
- You should determine how many resources you need and what type of resources, both technical and human.
- You should decide on the design or architecture of your BI decision-support application, such as designing for multidimensional reporting or ad hoc querying.

Step-by-Step Guide

Our step-by-step guide across the breadth of a complete development lifecycle includes activities, deliverables, roles and responsibilities, dos and don'ts, and entry and exit criteria, plus tips and rules of thumb to lead you to a successful BI decision-support implementation. For example:

- You should choose which steps you ought to perform on your BI project because no two BI decision-support projects are exactly alike.
- You should know whether to start with a cross-organizational decision-support solution or a tailored departmental solution with the basis for expansion.
- You should understand the sequence in which to perform development activities, that is, which ones can be performed in parallel tracks and which ones have a strong dependency on one another.

In contrast to topic-specific materials available on BI, this book is a *single-source development guide* written specifically for BI decision-support applications. The guidelines presented in this book are based not only on our personal experiences but also on some of the best practices covered in topic-specific books, articles, and Web sites.

HOW THIS BOOK IS ORGANIZED

All software development projects are complicated engineering projects, as demonstrated by the breadth of topics covered in this book. Chapter 0, Guide to the Development Steps, explains the general organization of the development guidelines in *Business Intelligence Roadmap*, which is as follows:

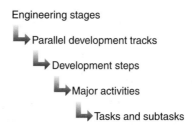

This book is organized into two major parts. Part I, Stages and Steps, describes the 16 development steps, which are introduced in Chapter 0. Part I gives you a broad understanding of the development effort involved in BI decision-support projects. Part II, At a Glance, supplements the text contained in the first part of the book with several matrices that should be used together as a reference guide for all BI decision-support projects.

Part I: Stages and Steps

Part I begins with Chapter 0, Guide to the Development Steps, and is followed by 16 development chapters. Each of the 16 development chapters is dedicated to one unique development step and describes the effort required to perform the activities of that step.

Guide to the Development Steps (Chapter 0) describes the general layout of the development guidelines presented in this book, contrasting those guidelines with a traditional development methodology. It discusses the six engineering stages as well as the three parallel development tracks, and it groups the applicable development steps under both. Chapter 0 explains the application release concept and shows how to organize a BI project with the appropriate roles and responsibilities for the core team and the extended team.

Each of the *development steps* (Chapters 1–16) begins with an individual chapter overview followed by a section called Things to Consider. These are general questions BI project teams usually contemplate when deciding which activities need to be performed under each development step. These questions are merely presented as "food for thought" and are not necessarily explored in the chapters; nor are they all-inclusive. Each chapter discusses the main topics applicable to the development step covered by that chapter. Some topics apply to more than one development step, such as testing or product evaluation. However, to avoid redundancy these common topics are covered in only one chapter and are only briefly referenced in the other chapters.

Each of the 16 chapters contains a list of major activities for that development step, accompanied by a figure showing what activities could be performed concurrently. The list of activities is followed by descriptions of the deliverables resulting from these activities and the roles involved in performing these activities. Each chapter concludes with a brief discussion of risks to weigh in case you decide not to perform that step on your project. Do not interpret the risks of not performing the step to mean that every BI project team must perform every development step exactly as suggested. Instead, use the risk section to determine whether the activities in that development step are—or should be—mandatory on your project. If they are not, you may decide not to perform some or all of those activities after discussing the risks with the business sponsor.

Part II: At a Glance

Part II contains the following matrices.

- The *Human Resource Allocation Matrix* (Chapter 17) lists all the vital roles involved in performing the step activities, tasks, and subtasks. The roles listed in this matrix need to be assigned to project team members. In order to help you discover and avoid potential resource allocation problems, the steps that can be performed in parallel and their appropriate roles are listed together.

- The *Entry & Exit Criteria and Deliverables Matrix* (Chapter 18) indicates the prerequisites, results, and deliverables for each development step. Not every BI project team will need to perform all activities for all development steps. This matrix should help you determine whether you can skip a step or incorporate some of its activities into other steps.

- The *Activity Dependency Matrix* (Chapter 19) is a collection of activity dependency charts for the development steps. This matrix shows at a glance which activities in each step can be performed concurrently. It should be used to determine workflow and task assignments for project team members.

- The *Task/Subtask Matrix* (Chapter 20) itemizes all pertinent tasks, and in some cases subtasks, for all the major activities under each step. This matrix should be used to prepare the work breakdown structure for the project plan. You can customize (expand or reduce) the tasks and subtasks on an as-needed basis for individual projects.

- The *Practical Guidelines Matrix* (Chapter 21) presents three subsections for each development step: Dos, Don'ts, and Tips and Rules of Thumb. Dos point out best practices for the development steps, and Don'ts instruct you how to avoid traps and pitfalls. Tips and Rules of Thumb are our personal collection of experiences over several decades of developing cross-organizational decision-support applications.

HOW TO USE THIS BOOK

We suggest that all core members of the BI project team make use of this book as follows.

1. First, read all the chapters in Part I to gain an overall understanding of all the components of BI decision-support development.

2. Next, compare your own BI project scope and requirements to the topics in the book. Use the discussions in the chapters to decide which specific development steps apply to your project.

3. Go to Chapter 18 and look up the entry and exit criteria for the steps you selected. Be sure that you have the prerequisites to implement your development approach and that you have a clear understanding of what it takes to move forward.

4. Put your project plan together for the steps you have chosen by consulting the activity dependency flow charts in Chapter 19 and by using the tasks and subtasks listed in Chapter 20. To kick-start your project, you may want to copy and customize the work breakdown structure provided on the CD included with this book to fit your needs. The work breakdown structure on the CD is a Microsoft Project file that already includes the step dependencies (shown in Figure 0.6 in Chapter 0) and the activity dependencies (shown in the flow charts in Chapter 19). In addition, the work breakdown structure contains some basic mandatory task dependencies.

5. Use the matrices in Part II as a quick reference to help guide your development work throughout the project.

WHO SHOULD READ THIS BOOK

Segments of this book should be read and referenced by every member of the BI project team, including business representatives. It is important that *all* project participants understand "the big picture" and how they and their roles fit into it. This also applies to third-party consultants, who can fill any technical role on the project team. Understanding this larger view of the project and its development effort is essential in maintaining a level of enthusiasm and cooperation necessary for the team.

Below we spotlight team members' roles and provide lists of the most useful and applicable chapters for each specific role.

Business Representatives

Although the development steps are technical in nature, business representatives involved in BI projects must understand what activities need to occur during the development effort. Business representatives are expected to participate as full-time members of the project core teams, and some of the activities described in this book will be assigned to them. Table P.1 lists chapters of particular interest to business representatives.

Table P.1: Chapters for Business Representatives

Chapter	Title
0	Guide to the Development Steps
1	Step 1: Business Case Assessment
2	Step 2: Enterprise Infrastructure Evaluation (especially Section B, Nontechnical Infrastructure Evaluation)
3	Step 3: Project Planning
4	Step 4: Project Requirements Definition
5	Step 5: Data Analysis
6	Step 6: Application Prototyping
7	Step 7: Meta Data Repository Analysis
9	Step 9: Extract/Transform/Load Design
13	Step 13: Data Mining
16	Step 16: Release Evaluation

Business Sponsors

Although business sponsors are not directly involved in the daily development effort, they should make frequent checks on the health of the project as well as the project team. In order to do this, business sponsors

Table P.2: Chapters for Business Sponsors

Chapter	Title
0	Guide to the Development Steps
1	Step 1: Business Case Assessment
2	Step 2: Enterprise Infrastructure Evaluation (especially Section B, Nontechnical Infrastructure Evaluation)
3	Step 3: Project Planning
4	Step 4: Project Requirements Definition
5	Step 5: Data Analysis
13	Step 13: Data Mining
16	Step 16: Release Evaluation

must have a comprehensive, high-level understanding of the effort. Table P.2 lists the chapters recommended for business sponsors.

Project Managers

The project manager is responsible for the entire development effort and must therefore be intimately familiar with all development steps. He or she must read all chapters in the book and use the matrices in Part II as an ongoing reference guide, as shown in Table P.3.

 BI projects are not for inexperienced project managers. A thorough understanding of project management principles is required.

Table P.3: Chapters for Project Managers

Chapter	Title
0	Guide to the Development Steps
1–16	Part I: Stages and Steps
17–21	Part II: At a Glance

Technicians

Various types of technicians work on BI projects. Some technicians are assigned to the core team on a full-time basis, such as a lead developer; others are on the extended team supporting the development activities on an as-needed basis, such as a security officer. (For an itemized list of roles assigned to the core team and to the extended team, refer to Chapter 0.)

- **Core team technicians** should read all the chapters in the book and use the matrices as an ongoing reference guide, as shown in Table P.4.
- **Extended team technicians** should read, at a minimum, the chapters listed in Table P.5. However, these technicians would gain a greater understanding of the BI decision-support development process if they read all the chapters in the book.

Table P.4: Chapters for Core Team Technicians

Chapter	Title
0	Guide to the Development Steps
1–16	Part I: Stages and Steps
17–21	Part II: At a Glance

Table P.5: Chapters for Extended Team Technicians

Chapter	Title
0	Guide to the Development Steps
2	Step 2: Enterprise Infrastructure Evaluation (especially Section A, Technical Infrastructure Evaluation)
3	Step 3: Project Planning
4	Step 4: Project Requirements Definition
16	Step 16: Release Evaluation
	Additional chapters on an as-needed basis (For example, an ETL developer should read Step 9: Extract/Transform/Load Design, Step 11: Extract/Transform/Load Development, and Step 15: Implementation.)

COMMENTS

Despite the large collection of topic-specific BI material, we observed a strong need by project teams for a unified plan or method to follow. Therefore, we started this book with the notion of writing a complete development methodology for BI decision-support projects. We quickly realized that to meet such a goal we would have to produce a multivolume work—something not feasible for most project managers and project team members to read. Our original plan quickly gave way to a general roadmap that would serve as an umbrella for all the major development steps, topics, considerations, and activities of a BI project. In addition, at the end of each chapter we provide a list of references that are most applicable to the topics of the chapter.

We also wanted to share with project managers, project teams, and business representatives our personal discoveries about what works and what doesn't work on BI projects. Therefore, the information we present in the matrices in Part II is an accumulation of our own personal observations, experiences, and judgments.

Finally, to enhance the readability of this complex technical material, we broke up the text with as many tables, graphs, pictures, and other visuals as possible. We hope these visual aids make this book easier to read in addition to clarifying the topics presented.

Acknowledgments

Writing this all-encompassing development guide for BI decision-support applications required extensive knowledge of traditional as well as current information technology (IT) development disciplines. While we have over 50 years of combined IT experience, many colleagues and friends contributed their expertise and time to this book.

Our special appreciation goes to Melvin Rusakoff, who came out of retirement to help us jump-start the book. We want to thank him for all of his contributions, in particular on testing and peer reviews. His extensive knowledge of methodologies provided a benchmark for quality assurance of our book.

We thank Sid Adelman and Florence Alcorn for their extensive and merciless critiques of our first draft. Their input profoundly changed the scope and content of this book.

We are grateful to David Marco for his early contribution on meta data repositories. Our appreciation also goes to Mike Schmitz for his database suggestions, to Joyce Bischoff for her ETL comments, and to Herb Edelstein and Arun Swami for their data mining remarks.

The extensive critiques provided by two IT journalists, Paul Gillin and Peter Krass, made our technical jargon more comprehensible. We are indebted to John Tiglias who, based on his high-level management experience, provided us valuable insights into the needs of CIOs and gave us suggestions for addressing them.

We are also very thankful for the real-life comments from the "trenches" provided by Tom McCullough, Ross Armstrong, Bill Tillman, Majid Abai, Pat Higgs, and Jane Aubol.

Our special thanks go to Ed Yourdon for taking time out of his very busy schedule and for giving us encouragement from the very beginning of this long project to the very end. We are also very thankful to Bill Inmon for reviewing our manuscript on very short notice.

We are indebted to Info-Edge Inc. for working with us on this project. We also want to thank Anthony Ianniciello and Tushar Atre of AtreNet, Inc. for helping us with the cover design.

Our sincere appreciation goes to our executive editor, Mary O'Brien, at Addison-Wesley, who displayed extraordinary patience while accommodating our every out-of-the-ordinary book-formatting request. In addition, we thank the many Addison-Wesley team members for their individual contributions to making our book a success, in particular Brenda Mulligan for coordinating all aspects of the editorial process, Simone Payment and Jacquelyn Doucette for managing the production process, Chrysta Meadowbrooke for copyediting, and Curt Johnson and Chanda Leary-Coutu for their tireless efforts in marketing.

Our special gratitude goes to Donald P. Sherman, who spent an extraordinary amount of his time editing and cross-checking the book multiple times to ensure consistency and readability. We also thank Blanca Eusse-Patino for being our liaison and for providing assistance to meet our deadlines.

Finally, we thank our families for putting precious family time on hold while the book was in the making. They have been the main pillars of support for our professional endeavors.

—*Larissa T. Moss and Shaku Atre*

PART I

Stages and Steps

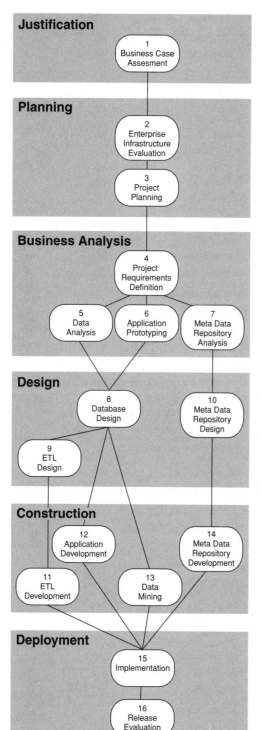

Justification
- 1 Business Case Assessment

Planning
- 2 Enterprise Infrastructure Evaluation
- 3 Project Planning

Business Analysis
- 4 Project Requirements Definition
- 5 Data Analysis
- 6 Application Prototyping
- 7 Meta Data Repository Analysis

Design
- 8 Database Design
- 9 ETL Design
- 10 Meta Data Repository Design

Construction
- 11 ETL Development
- 12 Application Development
- 13 Data Mining
- 14 Meta Data Repository Development

Deployment
- 15 Implementation
- 16 Release Evaluation

Guide to the Development Steps

CHAPTER OVERVIEW

This chapter covers the following topics:

- Business intelligence (BI), with a focus on BI decision-support applications, such as sales forecasting

- The need for and the structure of *Business Intelligence Roadmap* as a development guide

- The 16 development steps applicable to BI decision-support projects

- The three parallel development tracks usually followed by BI project teams

- Project team structure, including the roles and responsibilities assigned to the core team members and the extended team members

- A brief justification for using *Business Intelligence Roadmap* as your development guide for BI decision-support projects

BUSINESS INTELLIGENCE DEFINITION

BI is neither a product nor a system. It is an architecture and a collection of integrated operational as well as decision-support applications and databases that provide the business community easy access to business data. *Business Intelligence Roadmap* specifically addresses *decision-support* applications and databases.

BI decision-support applications facilitate many activities, including those listed below:

- Multidimensional analysis, for example, online analytical processing (OLAP)
- Click-stream analysis
- Data mining
- Forecasting
- Business analysis
- Balanced scorecard preparation
- Visualization
- Querying, reporting, and charting (including just-in-time and agent-based alerts)
- Geospatial analysis
- Knowledge management
- Enterprise portal implementation
- Mining for text, content, and voice
- Digital dashboard access
- Other cross-functional activities

Examples of BI decision-support databases include the following:

- Enterprise-wide data warehouses
- Data marts (functional and departmental)
- Exploration warehouses (statistical)
- Data mining databases
- Web warehouses (for click-stream data)
- Operational data stores (ODSs)
- Operational marts (oper marts)
- Other cross-functional decision-support databases

Business Intelligence Roadmap is primarily a project lifecycle guide for developing BI decision-support applications using *structured* data. For BI applications with specialized requirements, such as using unstructured data (e.g., mining for text, content, and voice), building an enterprise portal, or incorporating XML-enabled features and services, you will need to expand the activities and roles in the relevant development steps. Consult the topic-specific references listed at the end of each chapter.

BI DECISION-SUPPORT INITIATIVES

BI decision-support initiatives are expensive endeavors. Disparate business data must be extracted and merged from online transaction processing (OLTP) systems, from batch systems, and from externally syndicated data sources. BI decision-support initiatives also call for new technology to be considered, additional tasks to be performed, roles and responsibilities to be shifted, and analysis and decision-support applications to be delivered quickly while maintaining acceptable quality.

A staggering 60 percent of BI projects end in abandonment or failure because of inadequate planning, missed tasks, missed deadlines, poor project management, undelivered business requirements, or poor quality deliverables. Project managers need to know the *dos* and *don'ts* of BI implementations based on reliable hands-on experience.

 What is needed is a new, proven method for understanding and implementing the processes required in the successful deployment of BI decision-support applications.

DEVELOPMENT APPROACHES

Almost every kind of engineering project—structural engineering as well as software engineering—goes through six stages between inception and implementation, as illustrated in Figure 0.1.

As the arrow in Figure 0.1 indicates, engineering processes are iterative. Once deployed, a product is continually improved and enhanced based on the feedback from the business community that uses the product. Each iteration produces a new product release (version) as the product evolves and matures. (This release concept is explained in detail in Step 16, Release Evaluation.)

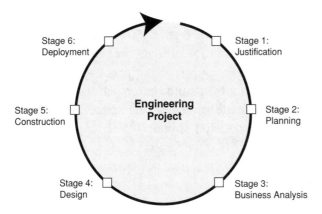

Figure 0.1: Engineering Stages

Stage 1. Justification: Assess the business need that gives rise to the new engineering project.

Stage 2. Planning: Develop strategic and tactical plans, which lay out how the engineering project will be accomplished and deployed.

Stage 3. Business analysis: Perform detailed analysis of the business problem or business opportunity to gain a solid understanding of the business requirements for a potential solution (product).

Stage 4. Design: Conceive a product that solves the business problem or enables the business opportunity.

Stage 5. Construction: Build the product, which should provide a return on investment within a predefined time frame.

Stage 6. Deployment: Implement or sell the finished product, then measure its effectiveness to determine whether the solution meets, exceeds, or fails to meet the expected return on investment.

The Traditional Development Approach

Since BI is an enterprise-wide *evolving environment* that is continually improved and enhanced based on feedback from the business community, the system development practices of the past are inadequate and inappropriate.

In the past, systems were never designed or built with integration in mind. Every system had a beginning and an end, and every system was designed to solve only one isolated problem for one set of business people from one line of business. The old "single-swim-lane" development practices were suitable for such static stand-alone systems. However, they are not well suited for integrated BI initiatives because the old practices do not include any cross-organizational activities necessary to sustain an enterprise-wide decision-support environment. In the past, cross-organizational activities were not only deemed unnecessary but were also perceived to stand in the way of progress because they slowed down the projects.

For nonintegrated system development, conventional waterfall methodologies are sufficient. They provide enough guidance for planning, building, and implementing stand-alone systems. However, these traditional methodologies do not cover strategic planning, cross-organizational business analysis, or evaluation of new technologies with every project; nor do they embrace the concept of application releases. Traditional methodologies typically start with a functional business need, then concentrate on design and development, and finally end in maintenance, as illustrated in Figure 0.2.

Unlike static stand-alone systems, a dynamic, integrated BI decision-support environment cannot be built in one big bang. Data and functionality must be

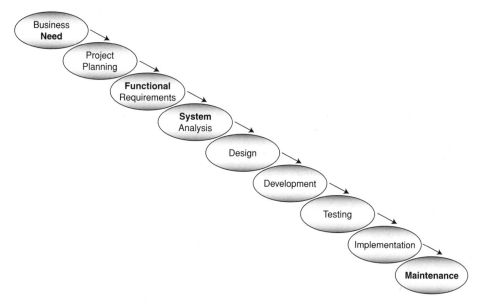

Figure 0.2: Conventional Waterfall Deployment

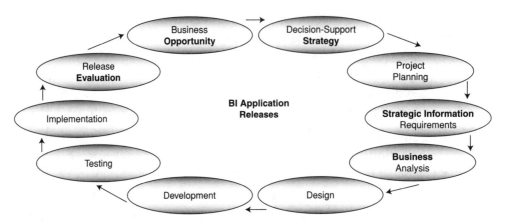

Figure 0.3: The BI Application Release Concept

rolled out in iterative releases, and each deployment is likely to trigger new requirements for the next release, as shown in Figure 0.3.

Figure 0.3 highlights other major differences between BI applications and stand-alone systems.

- BI applications are mostly driven by business *opportunity* rather than business need.
- BI applications implement a cross-organizational decision-support *strategy* rather than departmental decision-support silos.
- BI decision-support requirements are mostly *strategic information* requirements rather than operational functional requirements.
- Analysis of BI projects emphasizes *business* analysis rather than system analysis, and analysis is the most important activity when developing a BI decision-support environment.
- Ongoing BI application release evaluations promote iterative development and the *software release* concept rather than big-bang development.

The Cross-Organizational Development Approach

With the expansion of e-business comes an increasing demand for cross-organizational integration. This integration does not refer merely to bridging old systems across different platforms using enterprise application integration (EAI) middleware. Instead, it refers to:

- Information consolidation
- Information integration
- Information integrity
- Seamless business functionality
- Streamlined organizational business processes

Moving an organization from a "single-swim-lane" development approach to a cross-organizational, "cross-swim-lane" development approach requires organizational changes, including a culture shift. No other initiative demonstrates this as vividly as customer relationship management (CRM). If organizations would implement more cross-organizational BI operational applications (front-office as well as back-office) like CRM, they could significantly reduce their construction efforts on BI decision-support applications.

Although in *Business Intelligence Roadmap* we do not address organizational changes and culture shifts, we do define the necessary BI project activities that support an integrated enterprise-wide infrastructure. Both technical infrastructure and nontechnical infrastructure are required core competencies for cross-organizational integration. In addition to defining project activities, we identify the roles and responsibilities to be assigned to project team members for each development step.

The development steps outlined in this book form an engineering roadmap that provides a framework for developing different kinds of BI decision-support projects. The flexible entry and exit points of this framework allow you to start with any step as long as you meet the "entry criteria" outlined in the Entry and Exit Criteria and Deliverables Matrix. We also designed these steps to be agile and adaptive so that you can organize and manage the development of a BI application as multiple subprojects, each going through several of its own iterations or releases. For example, Figure 0.4 shows two iterations each for the Extract/Transform/ Load (ETL), Application, and Meta Data Repository subprojects.

The approach presented in *Business Intelligence Roadmap* encourages the use of parallel development tracks (subprojects) so that multiple development steps can be performed simultaneously and multiple project activities can occur concurrently. Some project teams may choose to roll up project activities from multiple development steps into one step, while other project teams may not need to perform some steps or activities at all. Figure 0.5 illustrates the dynamics of a typical BI decision-support project, showing several steps running simultaneously

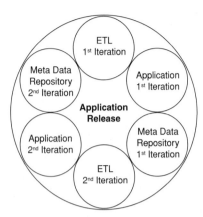

Figure 0.4: Iterative Subprojects of an Application Release

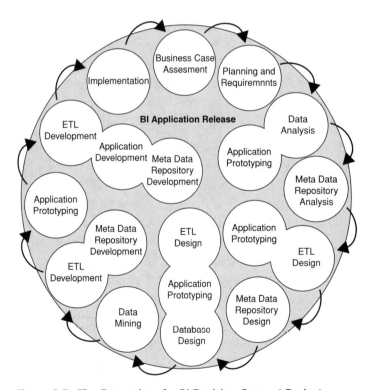

Figure 0.5: The Dynamics of a BI Decision-Support Project

(such as Step 5, Data Analysis, and Step 6, Application Prototyping) and multiple iterations of the same step (such as Step 9, ETL Design).

ENGINEERING STAGES AND THE DEVELOPMENT STEPS

BI projects are organized according to the same six stages common to every engineering project. Within each engineering stage, certain steps are carried out to see the engineering project through to its completion. *Business Intelligence Roadmap* describes 16 development steps within these stages, as outlined below.

The Justification Stage

Step 1: Business Case Assessment

The business problem or business opportunity is defined and a BI solution is proposed. Each BI application release should be cost-justified and should clearly define the benefits of either solving a business problem or taking advantage of a business opportunity.

The Planning Stage

Step 2: Enterprise Infrastructure Evaluation

Since BI applications are cross-organizational initiatives, an enterprise infrastructure must be created to support them. Some infrastructure components may already be in place before the first BI project is launched. Other infrastructure components may have to be developed over time as part of the BI projects. An enterprise infrastructure has two components:

1. **Technical infrastructure**, which includes hardware, software, middleware, database management systems, operating systems, network components, meta data repositories, utilities, and so on.

2. **Nontechnical infrastructure**, which includes meta data standards, data-naming standards, the enterprise logical data model (evolving), methodologies, guidelines, testing procedures, change-control processes, procedures for issues management and dispute resolution, and so on.

Step 3: Project Planning

BI decision-support projects are extremely dynamic. Changes to scope, staff, budget, technology, business representatives, and sponsors can severely impact the success of a project. Therefore, project planning must be detailed, and actual progress must be closely watched and reported.

The Business Analysis Stage

Step 4: Project Requirements Definition

Managing project scope is one of the most difficult tasks on BI decision-support projects. The desire to have everything instantly is difficult to curtail, but curtailing that desire is one of the most important aspects of negotiating the requirements for each deliverable. Project teams should expect these requirements to change throughout the development cycle as the business people learn more about the possibilities and the limitations of BI technology during the project.

Step 5: Data Analysis

The biggest challenge to all BI decision-support projects is the quality of the source data. Bad habits developed over decades are difficult to break, and the damages resulting from bad habits are very expensive, time consuming, and tedious to find and correct. In addition, data analysis in the past was confined to the view of one line of business and was never consolidated or reconciled with other views in the organization. This step takes a significant percentage of the time allotted to the entire project schedule.

Step 6: Application Prototyping

Analysis of the functional deliverables, which used to be called system analysis, is best done through prototyping so it can be combined with application design. New tools and programming languages enable developers to relatively quickly prove or disprove a concept or an idea. Prototyping also allows business people to see the potential and the limits of the technology, which gives them an opportunity to adjust their project requirements and their expectations.

Step 7: Meta Data Repository Analysis

Having more tools means having more technical meta data in addition to the business meta data, which is usually captured in a computer-aided software engineering (CASE) modeling tool. The technical meta data needs to be mapped to the business meta data, and all meta data must be stored in a meta data repository. Meta data repositories can be licensed (bought) or built. In either case, the requirements for what type of meta data to capture and store should be documented in a logical meta model. When licensing a meta data repository product, the requirements documented on this logical meta model should be compared to the vendor's meta model, if one is provided. In addition, the requirements for delivering meta data to the business community have to be analyzed (e.g., online help function).

The Design Stage

Step 8: Database Design

One or more BI target databases will store the business data in detailed or aggregated form, depending on the reporting requirements of the business community. Not all reporting requirements are strategic, and not all of them are multidimensional. The database design schemas must match the information access requirements of the business community.

Step 9: Extract/Transform/Load Design

The ETL process is the most complicated process of the entire BI decision-support project. It is also the least glamorous one. ETL processing windows (batch windows) are typically small, yet the poor quality of the source data usually requires a lot of time to run the transformation and cleansing programs. Finishing the ETL process within the available batch window is a challenge for most organizations.

Step 10: Meta Data Repository Design

If a meta data repository is licensed, it will most likely have to be enhanced with features that were documented on the logical meta model but are not provided by the product. If a meta data repository is being built, the decision must be made whether the meta data repository database design will be entity-relationship based or object oriented. In either case, the design has to meet the requirements of the logical meta model.

The Construction Stage

Step 11: Extract/Transform/Load Development

Many tools are available for the ETL process, some sophisticated and some simple. Depending on the requirements for data cleansing and data transformation developed during Step 5, Data Analysis, and Step 9, ETL Design, an ETL tool may or may not be the best solution. In either case, preprocessing the data and writing extensions to supplement the capabilities of the ETL tool is frequently required.

Step 12: Application Development

Once the prototyping effort has firmed up the functional requirements, true development of the access and analysis application can begin. Developing the application can be a simple matter of finalizing an operational prototype, or it can be a more involved development effort using different, more robust access and analysis tools. In either case, the front-end application development activities are usually performed in parallel with the activities of back-end ETL development and meta data repository development.

Step 13: Data Mining

Many organizations do not use their BI decision-support environment to the fullest extent. BI applications are often limited to prewritten reports, some of which are not even new types of reports but replacements of old reports. The real payback comes from the information hidden in the organization's data, which can be discovered only with data mining tools.

Step 14: Meta Data Repository Development

If the decision is made to build a meta data repository rather than to license one, a separate team is usually charged with the development process. This becomes a sizable subproject in the overall BI project.

The Deployment Stage

Step 15: Implementation

Once the team has thoroughly tested all components of the BI application, the team rolls out the databases and applications. Training is scheduled for the business staff and other stakeholders who will be using the BI application and the meta data repository. The support functions begin, which includes operating the help desk, maintaining the BI target databases, scheduling and running ETL batch jobs, monitoring performance, and tuning databases.

Step 16: Release Evaluation

With an application release concept, it is very important to benefit from lessons learned from the previous projects. Any missed deadlines, cost overruns, disputes, and dispute resolutions should be examined, and process adjustments should be made before the next release begins. Any tools, techniques, guidelines, and processes that were not helpful should be reevaluated and adjusted, possibly even discarded.

You do not need to perform the development steps in sequence; most project teams will likely perform them in parallel. However, because there is a natural order of progression from one engineering stage to another, certain dependencies exist between some of the development steps, as illustrated in Figure 0.6. Steps stacked on top of each other in the diagram can be performed simultaneously, while steps that appear to the right or left of each other are performed relatively linearly (with less overlap) because of their dependencies.

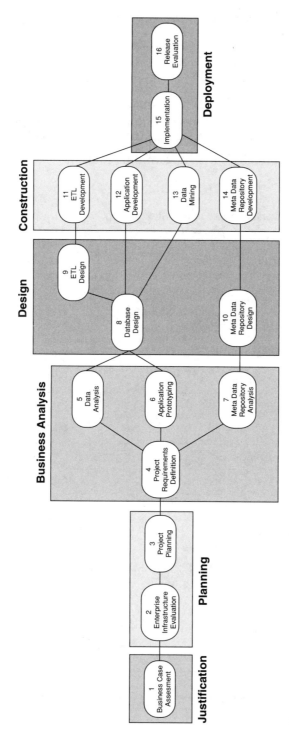

Figure 0.6: Development Step Dependencies

While some development steps are clearly project-specific, most development steps must be performed from a cross-organizational perspective. Thus the focus of those project activities takes on a cross-functional dimension, and the reviewers of those activities should include business representatives from other lines of business. The main task for the business representatives from the other lines of business is to validate and ratify the strategies, policies, business rules, and standards either being used or being developed during the BI project. Table 0.1 indicates which steps are project-specific and which ones are cross-organizational.

Table 0.1: Project-Specific versus Cross-Organizational Steps

Development Step	*Project-Specific versus Cross-Organizational*
1. Business Case Assessment	Cross-organizational
2. Enterprise Infrastructure Evaluation (technical and nontechnical)	Cross-organizational
3. Project Planning	Project-specific
4. Project Requirements Definition	Project-specific
5. Data Analysis	Cross-organizational
6. Application Prototyping	Project-specific
7. Meta Data Repository Analysis	Cross-organizational
8. Database Design	Cross-organizational
9. ETL Design	Cross-organizational
10. Meta Data Repository Design	Cross-organizational
11. ETL Development	Cross-organizational
12. Application Development	Project-specific
13. Data Mining	Cross-organizational
14. Meta Data Repository Development	Cross-organizational
15. Implementation	Project-specific
16. Release Evaluation	Cross-organizational

PARALLEL DEVELOPMENT TRACKS

As illustrated in Figure 0.7, every BI decision-support project has at least three development tracks running in parallel after the project requirements have been defined and before implementation.

1. **The ETL Track**

   The ETL track is often referred to as the *back end*. The purpose of this development track is to design and populate the BI target databases. The ETL track is the most complicated and important track of a BI decision-support project. The fanciest OLAP tools in the world will not provide major benefits if the BI target databases are not designed properly or if they are populated with dirty data. The team working on the ETL track is usually staffed with knowledgeable business analysts, experienced database administrators, and senior programmers.

2. **The Application Track**

   The Application track is often referred to as the *front end*. The purpose of this development track is to design and build the access and analysis applications.

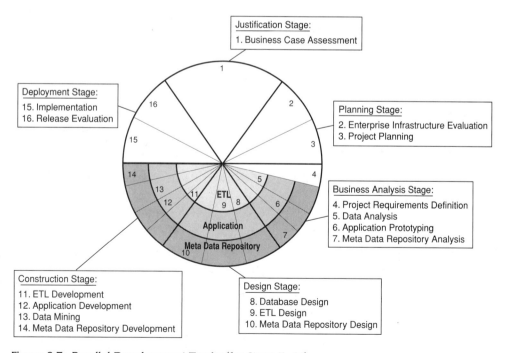

Figure 0.7: Parallel Development Tracks (for Steps 5–14)

After all, the key reasons for building a BI decision-support environment are to:

- Deliver value-added information
- Provide easy, spontaneous access to the business data

The team for the Application track is usually staffed with subject matter experts, "power users," and programmers who know Web languages, can effectively use OLAP tools, and have experience building client/server-based decision-support applications that incorporate graphical user interfaces.

3. The Meta Data Repository Track

Meta data is a mandatory deliverable with every BI application. It can no longer be shoved aside as *documentation* because it must serve the business community as a *navigation* tool for the BI decision-support environment. Therefore, the purpose of this development track is to design, build, and populate a meta data repository. The team members are responsible for designing and building the access interfaces as well as the reporting and querying capabilities for the meta data repository. The team working on the Meta Data Repository track is usually staffed with a meta data administrator and developers who have experience with building client/server-based interfaces and are knowledgeable about Web applications.

Table 0.2 maps the *Business Intelligence Roadmap* stages and steps across these three development tracks.

These three parallel tracks can be considered major subprojects of a BI project. Each will have its own team members and its own set of activities after the project requirements have been formalized. Discoveries made in one track can (and often do) impact the other tracks. Figure 0.8 shows the interaction of the three tracks across the development steps.

Each development track has specific deliverables that contribute to the overall BI project objectives.

- The ETL track delivers loaded BI target databases.
- The Application track delivers the BI reports and queries.
- The Meta Data Repository track delivers the meta data.

Table 0.2: Stages and Steps across Development Tracks

Stages Steps	ETL Track	Application Track	MDR Track
Justification			
Business Case Assessment	✓	✓	✓
Planning			
Enterprise Infrastructure Evaluation	✓	✓	✓
Project Planning	✓	✓	✓
Business Analysis			
Project Requirements Definition	✓	✓	✓
Data Analysis	✓		
Application Prototyping	✓	✓	
MDR Analysis			✓
Design			
Database Design	✓	✓	
ETL Design	✓		
MDR Design			✓
Construction			
ETL Development	✓		
Application Development		✓	
Data Mining		✓	
MDR Development			✓
Deployment			
Implementation	✓	✓	✓
Release Evaluation	✓	✓	✓

Abbreviations: ETL, extract/transform/load; MDR, meta data repository.

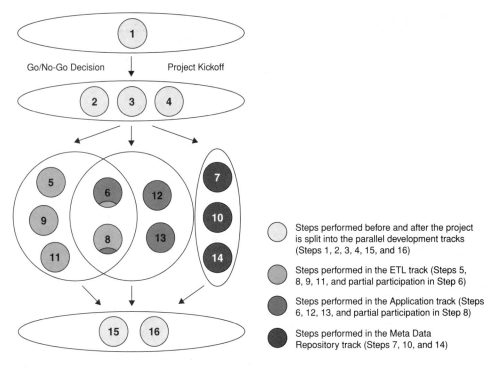

Figure 0.8: Steps Performed in Parallel Development Tracks

BI PROJECT TEAM STRUCTURE

Every BI project team must have a complementary skill set to perform the necessary activities for the three development tracks. Although each track will have its own subproject team members, from the overall BI project management perspective the BI project team structure contains only two types of teams:

1. The core team
2. The extended team

The Core Team

The core team can be thought of as a SWAT team. A project SWAT team is a self-organizing team—the members redistribute the workload among themselves, peer-review each other's task deliverables, make decisions together, brainstorm together, and co-lead the project. The core team has permanent *project* core team members and permanent *step* core team members.

- **Permanent project core team members** must be available 100 percent of their time from beginning to end of the BI project to perform project activities applicable to the roles assigned to them. More importantly, they must *co-lead* the project. The optimum size for this team is four or five people, never exceeding seven people. This team should be staffed with:
  - One project manager (not an administrator)
  - One representative from the business side
  - One business analyst from the information technology (IT) department (either a data administrator or a business liaison)
  - One technical person from the IT department (either a senior systems analyst or a senior programmer)

 The business person's full-time availability is a critical success factor for all BI projects. If the business executives resist releasing one business person full-time, it indicates that they neither view nor support the BI project as a critical cross-organizational strategic business initiative.

- **Permanent step core team members** must be available 100 percent of their time from beginning to end of those development steps that require their full-time involvement. For example, the ETL lead developer must be fully dedicated to lead the activities of the ETL track.

All core team members brainstorm together, assign work to each other, review each other's deliverables, resolve issues, and make project-related decisions together.

 Each person on the core team can and probably will be assigned multiple roles, regardless of whether they are permanent project core team members or permanent step core team members.

Table 0.3 lists the core team roles (in alphabetical order) and their major responsibilities.

 The business representative role on the core team is usually assigned to the primary business person representing the business community for whom the BI application is being developed. He or she participates on the project as a full-time member of the project core team. If necessary or desired, this role can be assigned to more than one business person, with the stipulation that every business person will dedicate 100 percent of his or her time to the BI project.

Table 0.3: Core Team Roles and Responsibilities

Role	*Major Responsibilities*
Application lead developer	Designing and overseeing the development of the access and analysis application (e.g., reports, queries)
BI infrastructure architect	Establishing and maintaining the BI technical infrastructure (in some organizations, overseeing the nontechnical infrastructure as well); usually reports to the strategic architect on the extended team
Business representative	Participating in modeling sessions, providing data definitions, writing test cases, making business decisions, resolving disputes between business units, and improving the data quality under the control of the business unit represented by this role
Data administrator	Performing cross-organizational data analysis, creating the project-specific logical data models, and merging the logical data models into an enterprise logical data model
Data mining expert	Choosing and running the data mining tool; must have a statistical background
Data quality analyst	Assessing source data quality and preparing data-cleansing specifications for the ETL process
Database administrator	Designing, loading, monitoring, and tuning the BI target databases
ETL lead developer	Designing and overseeing the ETL process
Meta data administrator	Building or licensing (buying), enhancing, loading, and maintaining the meta data repository
Project manager	Defining, planning, coordinating, controlling, and reviewing all project activities; tracking and reporting progress; resolving technical and business issues; mentoring the team; negotiating with vendors, the business representative, and the business sponsor; has overall responsibility for the project
Subject matter expert	Providing business knowledge about data, processes, and requirements

Some roles can be combined and some are mutually exclusive. For example, one person can perform one of the following combinations of roles:

- Application lead developer and ETL lead developer (assuming the person has the different skill sets required for both)
- Data administrator, data quality analyst, and meta data administrator (assuming the person has the required technical skills)
- Data quality analyst, subject matter expert, and business representative

Mutually exclusive roles, which should never be assigned to the same person, are listed below.

- Data administrator and database administrator: The data administrator produces process-*independent* logical data models, while the database administrator produces process-*dependent* physical data models (logical database designs). It would be difficult for one person to perform these bipolar activities on the same project, even if the person had the skills to do both.
- Project manager and any nonlead role: Managing a BI decision-support project is a full-time job and cannot be put in second position to any development work. One person will simply not have time to both manage the project and do the work.

The Extended Team

The extended team members also have responsibilities on the BI project, but for these members the BI project is not their main priority during the entire project schedule. These members have to schedule time to work with the full-time core team members. They can also be called into sessions when their expertise is needed to resolve a problem or to help make a decision.

Each member on the extended team can be assigned one or multiple roles and is responsible for the activities performed under each assigned role. Table 0.4 lists the extended team roles (in alphabetical order) and their major responsibilities.

As on the core team, some roles on the extended team can be combined and some are mutually exclusive. For example, one person can perform one of the following combinations of roles:

- Application developer, ETL developer, and meta data repository developer (assuming the person has the different skill sets required for the three development tracks)
- Web developer and Web master

Table 0.4: Extended Team Roles and Responsibilities

Role	Major Responsibilities
Application developer(s)	Coding the report programs, writing query scripts, and developing the access and analysis applications
BI support (help desk staff)	Mentoring and training the business staff
Business sponsor	Championing the BI initiative and removing business-related roadblocks for the BI project team
ETL developer(s)	Coding the ETL programs and/or preparing the instructions for the ETL tool
IT auditor or QA analyst	Determining the risks and exposures of the BI project due to internal lack of controls or external forces
Meta data repository developer(s)	Coding the meta data repository migration programs to load the meta data repository database; providing meta data reports and an online help function
Network services staff	Maintaining the network environment
Operations staff	Running the batch processes for the ETL cycles, the access and analysis application, and the meta data repository
Security officer	Ensuring that security requirements are defined and that security features are tested across all tools and databases
Stakeholders (other business representatives or IT managers)	Handling limited responsibilities on the BI project, such as reviewing and ratifying the cross-organizational standards and business rules the BI project team uses or develops
Strategic architect	Managing the overall technical Infrastructure for the organization, including the BI technical infrastructure
Technical services staff	Maintaining the hardware infrastructure and the operating systems

(Continued)

Table 0.4: *(Continued)*

Role	Major Responsibilities
Testers	Testing programming code created by the developers from the ETL, Application, and Meta Data Repository tracks
Tool administrators	Installing and maintaining the developer tools and the access and analysis tools
Web developer(s)	Designing the Web site and creating the Web pages for displaying reports and queries on the intranet, extranet, or Internet
Web master	Setting up the Web server and Web security

Mutually exclusive roles, which should never be assigned to the same person, are:

- Developer (of any type) and tester: A developer testing his or her own programs is like the fox guarding the henhouse. Even if the developer were motivated to break his or her own code, it is unlikely that he or she would think of all the possible test cases and carry out an objective test plan. However, a developer can take on the role of a tester for another developer's programs, as done in peer reviews and integration testing.

Additional Limited Roles

Other roles participate on the BI project on a limited, as-needed basis.

- *Data owners* are the major stakeholders in any BI initiative. They are responsible for the quality of business data under their ownership and for validating the business meta data.
- The *facilitator* is a third-party participant during post-implementation reviews. His or her responsibility is to lead the review meetings.
- The *scribe* is also a third-party participant during post-implementation reviews. He or she is responsible for taking notes and documenting the meeting minutes and the resulting action items.

The BI Arbitration Board

The discussion on roles and responsibilities cannot end without mention of the BI arbitration board. On cross-organizational BI projects, technical as well as business disputes will arise that neither the core team nor the extended team will be able to resolve. A dispute resolution procedure should be established with guidelines for handling these types of disputes. If a resolution cannot be achieved through other prescribed means, the project team must have access to a body of executives with the authority to be the tiebreaker. This body of executives is the BI arbitration board, sometimes known as the BI steering committee.

BI arbitration boards can be organized in a variety of ways. A BI arbitration board can be a newly created group whose members include the business sponsor, the chief technology/information officer (CTO/CIO), IT managers, the chief operating officer (COO), the chief financial officer (CFO), and line-of-business managers. In some smaller organizations, even the chief executive officer (CEO) could be a member of this board.

In other organizations, the BI arbitration board can be an existing committee. Most organizations already have some official or unofficial executive committee. For example, the CTO/CIO typically meets monthly with the employees who report directly to him or her, and the CEO typically meets monthly with line-of-business executives, the CFO, and the COO. If a separate BI arbitration board cannot be established, then the BI project teams must have access to the existing executive committees.

JUSTIFICATION FOR USING THIS PROJECT LIFECYCLE GUIDE

It has been said in the industry that "a paper airplane can be constructed with little forethought, but a jet airplane cannot." Similarly, a stand-alone system that has only a handful of business people using it can get by without a set of carefully planned and executed project activities, but a cross-organizational BI initiative certainly cannot.

As the BI decision-support environment evolves over time, it is imperative that a strong foundation exists to support such expansion. To build a strong foundation, many things have to be considered and many tasks have to be performed by many people. It is irresponsible to casually "make up" who does what and when along the way. That type of ad hoc development approach would put the organization's large investment at risk and would pose an even bigger risk for losing business opportunities. There are quite a few casualties in the trenches of lost opportunities!

The question is not whether or not a set of formalized guidelines must be used but what type of guidelines to use. A waterfall methodology is not suitable for the iterative releases of BI decision-support applications, but an agile and adaptive development guide specifically geared toward BI decision-support applications is. *Business Intelligence Roadmap* is such a guide.

BIBLIOGRAPHY AND ADDITIONAL READING

Adelman, Sid, and Larissa Terpeluk Moss. *Data Warehouse Project Management.* Boston, MA: Addison-Wesley, 2000.

Beck, Kent. *Extreme Programming Explained: Embrace Change.* Boston, MA: Addison-Wesley, 2000.

Humphrey, Watts S. *Winning with Software: An Executive Strategy.* Boston, MA: Addison-Wesley, 2002.

Inmon, William H., Claudia Imhoff, and Ryan Sousa. *Corporate Information Factory.* New York: John Wiley & Sons, 1997.

Zachman, John. *The Zachman Framework: A Primer for Enterprise Engineering and Manufacturing.* La Canada, CA: Zachman International, 2002.

DM Review: http://www.dmreview.com

Journal of Data Warehousing: http://www.dw-institute.com

Glossaries: *http://www.techweb.com/encyclopedia* and *http://www.ncits.org/tc_home/k5htm/ANSDIT.htm*

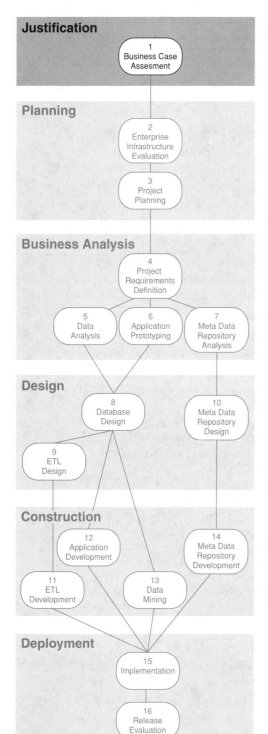

CHAPTER ONE

Step 1: Business Case Assessment

CHAPTER OVERVIEW

This chapter covers the following topics:

- Things to consider during a business case assessment

- The importance of developing a business justification and a business strategy for BI decision-support initiatives

- Business drivers and strategic business goals, rather than new technology, as the motivating forces behind every BI project

- Business analysis issues such as defining the organization's information needs, identifying data sources, and analyzing the current and desired quality of data

- The use of cost-benefit analyses to demonstrate how (and how soon) a return on investment (ROI) can be achieved

- Risk assessment and the six major risk categories of technology, complexity, integration, organization, project team, and financial investment

- Brief descriptions of the activities involved in business case assessment, the deliverables resulting from those activities, and the roles involved

- The risks of not performing Step 1

THINGS TO CONSIDER

Access to Information

✓ Where do we get the information we need for making decisions today?
✓ What information do we already have? What additional information do we need?

Business Drivers and Sponsorship

✓ What are the business drivers for an overall BI decision-support initiative?
✓ What are the specific business drivers for this BI application?
✓ Who could be a potential business sponsor?
✓ Do we already have a business sponsor for this BI application?

Readiness Assessment

✓ Are we ready for a BI decision-support environment?
✓ Have we performed a readiness assessment?
✓ What do we need to do to get ready? Buy hardware? Acquire tools? Establish standards? Hire more staff?

Risks

✓ What are the risks of building a BI decision-support environment?
✓ What are the risks of *not* building a BI decision-support environment?

Cost Justification

✓ Is it worth building this BI application, or will it cost more than we can justify?
✓ Do we know what all the BI project costs will be?
✓ Will we have to buy new hardware? Upgrade our network? Buy new tools? Hire consultants?

Return on Investment

✓ How will we measure ROI? For example:
  • Will the BI application have an effect on our customer service?
  • Will it help us increase customer satisfaction?
  • Will it help us increase our revenue?
  • Will it help us make strategic decisions that will lead to increased profits?
  • Will it help us reduce our costs?
  • Can we expect to gain a bigger market share as a result of the BI application?

Although BI has captured the imagination of many organizations, the industry is still challenged to quantify benefits accurately, especially since an organization cannot buy a BI product off the shelf and expect it to provide a complete solution to the business needs. "Business intelligence," or intelligence about the business, is unique to every organization, as are the policies and business rules governing the organization's business practices. This uniqueness should be explored for competitive advantage. Buying an off-the-shelf product, which was not built around the unique features of an organization, reduces the likelihood for competitive advantage.

BUSINESS JUSTIFICATION

Since it usually costs millions of dollars to create a BI environment, an organization considering such an initiative needs a BI strategy and a business justification to show the balance between the costs involved and the benefits gained. A BI decision-support initiative provides numerous benefits—not only tangible benefits such as increasing the sales volume but also intangible benefits such as enhancing the organization's reputation. Many of these benefits, especially the intangible ones, are difficult to quantify in terms of monetary value. Nevertheless, you should prepare an itemized and detailed list of benefits in order to measure them against the high cost of a BI implementation. Although the general benefits of BI decision-support initiatives are documented widely, they cannot justify your BI initiative unless you can associate these benefits to your organization's specific business problems and strategic business goals.

Justification for a BI decision-support initiative must always be business-driven and not technology-driven. It would not be wise to set up an expensive BI decision-support environment only to experiment with new technology. Therefore, each proposed BI application must reduce measurable "business pain" (problems affecting the profitability or efficiency of an organization) in order to justify building the application.

It is best to start the business justification process by identifying the organization's strategic business goals. The BI decision-support initiative as a whole, and the proposed BI application specifically, should support those strategic business goals. This enables the ongoing viability of the BI decision-support environment. If BI applications are built without a good business justification, management will most likely not support the effort.

The business representative should be primarily responsible for determining the business value of the proposed BI application. The information technology (IT) department can become a solution partner with the business representative and can help explore the business problems and define the potential benefits of the BI application. IT can also help clarify and coordinate the different needs of the varied groups of business people (knowledge workers, business analysts, business executives). For example, there could be different requirements for:

- Ease of use
- Level of data granularity
- Timeliness
- Data quality
- Security
- Amount of external data
- Historical requirements
- Tool capabilities

With the business representative leading the business case assessment effort, IT staff can assist with the four business justification components (Figure 1.1).

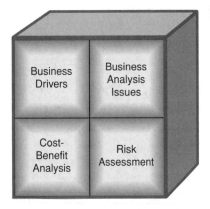

Figure 1.1: Business Justification Components

- **Business drivers:** Identify the business drivers, strategic business goals, and BI application objectives. Ensure that the BI application objectives support the strategic business goals.

- **Business analysis issues:** Define the business analysis issues and the information needed to meet the strategic business goals by stating the high-level information requirements for the business.

- **Cost-benefit analysis:** Estimate costs for building and maintaining a successful BI decision-support environment. Determine the ROI by assigning monetary value to the tangible benefits and highlighting the positive impact the intangible benefits will have on the organization.

- **Risk assessment:** Assess the risks in terms of technology, complexity, integration, organization, project team, and financial investment.

The next four sections in this chapter explore each of these components.

BUSINESS DRIVERS

Without strong business drivers and without an alignment with the strategic business goals of the organization, the BI decision-support initiative may falter. For example, let us assume that the organization wants to increase revenue by decreasing time to market. This translates into building BI applications as fast as possible, no matter what other effects this might have (for example, as speed goes up, quality goes down). Further, let us assume that the BI application objective is to decrease operating costs by increasing productivity. This leads to building BI applications that deliver business process improvements no matter what it takes (for example, as quality goes up, speed goes down). In this example, the organization's strategic goal and the BI application objective are both worthy business drivers for building a BI solution. However, because the strategic goal and the BI application objective are not compatible in terms of speed and quality issues, it will be difficult to get management's support for this BI application.

This example illustrates the importance of understanding the organization's strategic business goals as well as the IT strategic plan and ensuring that the BI application objectives support both. This may be more difficult to do than it appears. Even some of the most sophisticated organizations often do not have easily accessible or well-articulated strategic business goals statements. Become a "detective" and review the organization's annual report, public statements, newspaper coverage, syndicated articles, and internal memos for valuable information.

Substantiate your business justification. Do not invent a business case where one does not exist just to get the BI project approved. Interview senior managers to confirm the organization's strategic goals, and interview business managers and business analysts to validate the BI application objectives.

Let us discuss an example of a valid business justification. An automobile manufacturer was rated near the bottom of a study on customer satisfaction and product quality. This hurt the manufacturer in two ways.

1. The warranty costs were much higher than those of an average automobile manufacturer. These measurable costs were directly impacting the organization's bottom line.

2. Unsatisfied customers spread the word about the manufacturer: "I'll never buy another car from that company—and I'll tell all my friends." The costs of damaged customer confidence and lost sales were immense but much more difficult to measure than the costs of warranty.

In this example, the strategic business goals were to retain the customers and to reduce the expenses on warranty costs. In order to achieve these two goals the automobile manufacturer had to be able to communicate the information about malfunctioning parts to the parts makers on a timely basis. If a parts maker did not improve the quality of a part, the automobile manufacturer would have to buy that part from a different parts maker. The automobile manufacturer also needed information about the customers who were returning the malfunctioning cars in order to contact them for "damage control."

This automobile manufacturer justified building a BI application to measure manufacturing quality and to relate the quality measures to loss of sales, customer complaints, and customer defection. Quality measures were to be captured at the time of assembly as well as from the warranty data. Since a major portion of overall product quality is based on the quality of the parts that go into the automobile, the quality measures were to be provided to the parts makers through secure Web access. By giving the parts makers this information, the automobile manufacturer believed the parts makers would be able to improve the quality of their parts, which, in turn, would improve the overall quality of the assembled automobile. In this case, the BI application objectives directly supported the strategic business goals.

Business justification is an iterative process. As difficult as it might be to justify the business case, realize that business managers are aware of the buzz about BI and would like to take advantage of any competitive benefit they can get. Reiterating the benefits will help crystallize the business justification and make everyone feel comfortable about funding the BI decision-support project.

Once the strategic business goals and BI application objectives are verified and matched, you can define the business analysis requirements for the BI application that will allow the organization to meet its strategic business goals.

BUSINESS ANALYSIS ISSUES

In most organizations, business analysis issues usually revolve around unmet information needs from current heterogeneous data sources and poor quality of the source data.

Information Needs

With the help of business analysts, formulate the business issues that need to be resolved by each BI application objective. Determine what results you want to obtain from the business analysis, for example, answers to such questions as, "Why are we losing 50 percent market share to ABC Company in New England?" Then define the information requirements for the business issues at hand. Determine the subject areas, timing, level of detail, granularity of data, and even what external data you need to answer the business questions. Identify the associated business roles (e.g., senior business management, business analyst, and so on) that would be active in the various decision-support functions.

Identify possible data sources where the required information could reside. Data sources can be internal as well as external, and business insights often lie buried in the relationships among the multiple data sources.

Types of Data Sources

One of the challenges in building a BI decision-support environment is to merge data from different types of data sources. There are three major types of data sources: operational, private, and external (Figure 1.2).

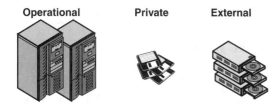

Figure 1.2: Three Major Data Sources

Operational Data

Online transaction processing (OLTP) and batch systems provide internal operational data about subject areas, such as the following:

- Financial
- Logistics
- Sales
- Order entry
- Personnel
- Billing
- Research and engineering

Private Data

This internal departmental data usually comes from the desktops and workstations of business analysts, knowledge workers, statisticians, and managers. Examples include the following:

- Product analysis spreadsheets
- Regional product usage spreadsheets
- Prospective customer databases

External Data

Organizations often purchase external data from vendors that specialize in collecting industry-specific information available in the public domain, such as the following:

- Health care statistics
- Customer profile information
- Customer catalog-ordering habits
- Customer credit reports

  External data is usually clustered around the following categories:

- *Sales and marketing data:* lists of prospective customers
- *Credit data:* individual credit ratings, business viability assessments
- *Competitive data:* products, services, prices, sales promotions, mergers, takeovers

- *Industry data:* technology trends, marketing trends, management science, trade information
- *Economic data:* currency fluctuations, political indicators, interest rate movements, stock and bond prices
- *Econometric data:* income groups, consumer behavior
- *Demographic data:* age profiles, population density
- *Commodity data:* raw material prices
- *Psychometric data:* consumer profiling
- *Meteorological data:* weather conditions, rainfall, temperature (especially for agricultural and travel industries)

Source Data Quality

Merging and standardizing data is usually a requirement of every BI application but one that is not so easy to accomplish. One of the difficulties in merging and standardizing data from different types of data sources is that the data is stored in different file structures on different platforms. What makes the process even more difficult is that the keys for the same objects on different data sources usually do not match, the definitions for the same apparent data are often inconsistent, and the values are often missing or conflicting. In addition, different people in the organization have authority to determine business rules and policies for data from different types of data sources, and resolving data conflicts among them or getting clarification is often all but impossible.

Standardizing data from internal operational data sources is difficult enough, but standardizing data from private and external data sources is a major challenge and could be costly. This cost should be calculated and included in the cost-benefit analysis.

COST-BENEFIT ANALYSIS

A common complaint is that BI projects are hard to cost-justify. That can be true if there is no obvious business problem to solve. One of the most difficult aspects in building a business case for a BI application is to show an adequate ROI. Despite the difficulty, you must demonstrate how, by analyzing and mining the information in the BI decision-support environment, the organization can more effectively maneuver and adapt to an increasingly changing marketplace.

Benefits are usually harder to quantify than costs, and it will take many high-valued benefits to offset the costs. A very effective method for justifying the expenditure of a BI application is to tie it directly to a business problem of measurable proportion. For example, let us assume an organization is losing $5 million each year because it cannot curb insurance fraud due to insufficient and unreliable data about its underwriting practices. If the proposed BI application can resolve that specific business problem, it will be relatively easy to justify. Therefore, be as detailed as possible when identifying the benefits, even if it is difficult to quantify a precise ROI. This way you can gain the confidence of business executives and win approval for the BI project.

Note that not all business problems need a BI solution. For example, the types of problems that do not require a BI application because they can be solved in more economical and less complicated ways are:

- Provide easier online access to a flat file
- Archive operational data
- Merge two operational files for operational processing
- Separate the operational reporting function from the operational update function

Sometimes all you need to do to solve an operational problem is to buy a better reporting tool or move the data into a relational database; neither should be interpreted as a need for a BI solution. However, if the business problem hinges on an inability to analyze integrated cross-functional data or to extract from the operational systems hidden intelligence needed to make strategic business decisions, then a BI decision-support initiative is probably the right solution.

The results of the cost-benefit analysis should succinctly state how the BI application would solve a business problem or enable a business opportunity. It should also state what type of information will be available, how that information can be used to make better business decisions, and when and how the information will be presented to the business community (e.g., monthly reports, ad hoc access through online analytical processing [OLAP] tools). Once you have clearly stated the business need and outlined the benefits, the next step is to estimate and compare the detailed costs and benefits so you can produce the projected ROI, which provides the justification for the BI project.

All BI decision-support initiatives should fulfill at least one of the five benefit categories listed below (Figure 1.3).

Figure 1.3: Benefit Categories

1. **Revenue increase,** possibly in the form of:
   - Identification of new markets and niches
   - More effective suggestive selling
   - Faster opportunity recognition
   - Faster time to market
2. **Profit increase,** including possibilities for:
   - Better targeted promotional mailings
   - Early warning of declining markets
   - Identification of under-performing product lines or products
   - Identification of internal inefficiencies
   - More efficient merchandise management
3. **Customer satisfaction improvement** through:
   - Improved understanding of customer preferences
   - Improved customer-to-product matching
   - Up-selling to customers
   - Increased repeat business
   - Faster resolution of customer complaints
4. **Savings increase** through:
   - Reduction in wasted or out-of-date merchandise
   - Reduction in requests for customized reporting

5. **Market share gain** through:
   - Increased numbers of customers who defect from the competition
   - Much higher customer retention rate as compared with previous years and with the competition

In addition to determining ROI, a business case assessment must include an appraisal of risk. Any project is bound to involve some risks and, given the high costs of BI projects, performing a risk assessment is a high priority.

RISK ASSESSMENT

Risks are factors or conditions that may jeopardize a project. Risks should be assessed for the following six major variables:

1. The *technology* used for implementing the project
2. The *complexity* of the capabilities and processes to be implemented
3. The *integration* of various components and of data
4. The *organization* and its financial and moral support
5. The *project team* staff's skills, attitudes, and commitment levels
6. The *financial investment* in terms of ROI

Table 1.1 depicts a basic risk assessment matrix for these six variables, using the colors of a traffic light to indicate the severity of the risk:

Green = low risk—go ahead with the project

Yellow = medium risk—caution, proceed slowly

Red = high risk—stop, reevaluate before proceeding

Each organization should develop its own appropriate variables and risk conditions for analyzing the risks most likely to impact its BI project. In developing that detailed risk assessment matrix for your organization, expand on the questions listed below.

- **Technology risk**
  - How mature are the selected technologies within the marketplace?
  - How mature are the selected technologies within the organization?
  - How many different technologies will co-exist?
  - Do we have incompatible operating systems?
  - Do we have incompatible database management systems (DBMSs)?

Table 1.1: Basic Risk Assessment Matrix

	Level of Risk		
Variable	*Green (Low)*	*Yellow (Medium)*	*Red (High)*
Technology	Experienced with mature technology	Minimal experience with technology	New technology, little experience
Complexity	Simple, minimal workflow impact	Moderate, some workflow impact	Mission critical, will require extensive reengineering
Integration	Stand-alone, no integration	Limited integration required	Extensive integration required
Organization	Solid internal support	Supportive to a large extent	Little internal support
Project team	Business experience, business-driven, talented, great attitude	Some business experience, business-driven, talented, fair attitude	No business experience, only technology-driven, limited talent, bad attitude
Financial Investment	Possible ROI within a very short time	Possible ROI within a moderate time frame	Possible ROI after a few years

- **Complexity risk**
  - How complex is the overall IT environment?
  - How complex is the BI application itself?
  - How extensively will workflow have to change? Will it have to be completely reengineered?
  - How many sites will be supported?
  - What is the degree of distribution of data, processes, and controls?
- **Integration risk**
  - How many interfaces will the BI application have?
  - Are there external interfaces?
  - How much source data redundancy exists?
  - Can the primary keys from various data sources be matched?

- Do we have incompatible standards? No standards?
- Do we have "orphan" records as a result of referential integrity problems?

• **Organization risk**
- How much risk will business management tolerate?
- How much risk will IT management tolerate?
- How much financial and moral support can we expect when the project encounters hurdles?

• **Project team risk**
- How much experience does the team have with successful implementations of BI applications?
- How broadly based is that experience?
- How well balanced is the team?
- How is team morale?
- How likely is it that we may lose one or more team members?
- Do our team members' skills cover all the basic disciplines?
- Will the business representative be an active player?
- How strong is the project manager?

• **Financial investment risk**
- How fast can ROI be expected?
- How likely is it that the costs will outweigh the benefits?
- Can financial risk be mitigated by using only proven technologies?

 The combination of high complexity and greater integration often results in a higher risk of failure to the organization.

Expand each of these risk categories with organization-specific detailed variables and detailed conditions for each of the three severity rankings (low, medium, high). Table 1.2 shows an example of a detailed risk assessment matrix taken from a case study.

The managers for the organization in this case study listed the detailed risk variables. Then for each variable, they described the conditions for each of the three risk severity rankings. For example, in the category for business workflow support:

- Low risk = Supports business workflow seamlessly
- Medium risk = Requires some manual intervention
- High risk = Requires significant manual intervention

Table 1.2: Case Study: A Detailed Risk Assessment Matrix

	Level of Risk		
Variable	*Green (Low)*	*Yellow (Medium)*	*Red (High)*
Project requirements: ad hoc reporting	Supports every critical ad hoc reporting requirement	Supports most critical ad hoc reporting requirements	Fails to support critical ad hoc reporting requirements
Project requirements: AS/400	Supports every key business requirement	Supports most key business requirements	Fails to support key business requirements
Business workflow support	Supports business workflow seamlessly	Requires some manual intervention	Requires significant manual intervention
Architecture evaluation	Well-architected application	Existence of some architectural issues	Poorly architected application
Extensibility into subsequent releases	Fully extensible into subsequent releases	Extensible for most requirements	Not extensible into subsequent releases
Logical data model: completeness	All information requirements met	Most information requirements documented	Significantly missing information requirements
Logical data model: extensibility	Fully extensible	Some extensibility issues	Not extensible
Meta data (business and technical)	Complete and easily maintainable	Incomplete or not easily maintainable	Not incorporated
Physical data model: completeness	Complete and tuned	Complete but not tuned	Incomplete, cannot be evaluated
Physical data model: extensibility for new product types	Fully extensible for new product types	Limited product type extensibility	Incomplete, cannot be evaluated

(Continued)

Table 1.2: *(Continued)*

Variable	Level of Risk		
	Green (Low)	**Yellow (Medium)**	**Red (High)**
Physical data model: source system feeds	Acceptable design support for source systems	Performance or timing concerns	Incomplete, cannot be evaluate
Interfaces (external and internal)	Supports external and internal interfaces	Limited support for external and internal interfaces	Poor support for external and internal interfaces
Analysis dimensions and measures: adding new product lines	Easy to add	Can be added, but requires significant cube reconstruction	Cannot be evaluated at the current time
Analysis dimensions and measures: adding new tools for data analysis	Proposed cubes and set of dimensions sufficient to support the business analysts	Proposed cubes and set of dimensions provide minimum sufficiency	Proposed cubes and set of dimensions insufficient
Use of meta data repository	Fully developed	Limited meta data support	No meta data support
Loading of the BI target databases	Load procedures established and perform well	Load procedures poorly documented or perform poorly	Load procedures not developed, cannot be evaluated
Physical database issues	Effective and efficient physical database design	Minor issues with physical database design	Physical database design incomplete, cannot be evaluated
Performance issues	Conforms to stated performance requirements	Some performance issues	Cannot be evaluated at this time
Systems management issues: maintenance	Support procedures well established and documented	Limited support documentation	No support procedures

(Continued)

Table 1.2: *(Continued)*

Variable	Level of Risk		
	Green (Low)	**Yellow (Medium)**	**Red (High)**
Support issues	Backup and disaster recovery procedures developed and installed	Backup and disaster recovery procedures developed but not installed	No thought given to backup and disaster recovery procedures
Security implementation	Satisfies application needs and is easy to maintain	Difficult to maintain	Security design incomplete, cannot be evaluated

The managers then selected the applicable risk severity ranking for each variable by highlighting the description that most accurately portrayed the condition of their BI project using the colors green, yellow, and red. Out of 21 variables, they rated only two variables low risk, six variables medium risk, and thirteen variables high risk. The managers decided that the overall risk for this BI project was *high*.

Having a realistic assessment of the severity of potential risks will help the project team create realistic estimates and expectations for the BI project. Conversely, unidentified and unmanaged risks can result in project failure or even jeopardize the entire BI initiative.

BUSINESS CASE ASSESSMENT ACTIVITIES

The business case assessment activities do not need to be performed linearly. Figure 1.4 indicates which activities can be performed concurrently. The list below briefly describes the activities associated with Step 1, Business Case Assessment.

1. **Determine the business need.**
   Justification of a BI project is difficult only if there is no obvious business reason for the BI application. There must be a clearly defined business information need that cannot be satisfied with traditional decision-support methods. The business need should be tied to a financial consequence for the organization, either as cost overruns or lost revenue. The financial consequence could

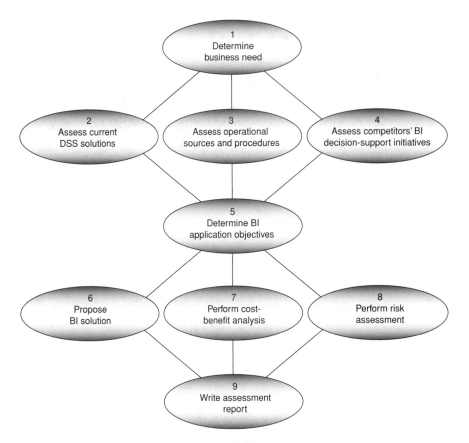

Figure 1.4: Business Case Assessment Activities

be the result of a lost business opportunity (e.g., lack of access to vital information) or a business problem (e.g., reporting inconsistencies or reliance on
dirty data). In either case, you must quantify the business need as a monetary
expression (e.g., $5 million lost annually to the competition because of an
inability to cross-sell to current customers).

2. **Assess the current decision-support system solutions.**
Examine the current decision-support system (DSS) solutions and determine
their deficiencies. If the current solutions do not provide the information
needed to mitigate the business problem, the reasons have to be understood.
If the necessary information is not being delivered, it could be due to
resource shortages and long backlogs in IT's workload. Other reasons could

include difficulty accessing and merging source data because of different key structures, missing keys, or data redundancy and inconsistencies.

3. **Assess the operational sources and procedures.**

   While assessing the current DSS solutions, give special attention to the operational source data and operational procedures. The business problem could exist because the business people cannot trust the information being delivered to them. Data quality problems may be the result of poor data entry practices, lack of edits, defective program code, or lack of training. A solution to the business problem may be to tighten those procedures.

4. **Assess the competitors' BI decision-support initiatives.**

   Staying ahead of the competition is extremely important in today's economy. In order to stay ahead, you must know what your competitors are doing. It would be helpful to know about the competitors' successes and failures with their BI decision-support initiatives and whether they have achieved higher sales or introduced innovative products.

5. **Determine the BI application objectives.**

   Once you define the business problem and understand the deficiencies of the current environment, you can clearly state the BI application objectives. These objectives must be compared to the organization's strategic business goals to ensure that they are in synch.

6. **Propose a BI solution.**

   Using the BI application objectives and the analysis results of the current environment, including the current DSS solutions, you can now propose a BI solution. The business problem may be too complicated to address all at once, in which case you will need to devise an iterative release approach. Unfulfilled requirements from previous BI projects must be evaluated and the decision must be made whether or not to include them in this release.

7. **Perform a cost-benefit analysis.**

   Determine the projected BI application costs. In addition to new hardware, software, and tools, include ongoing maintenance fees and training costs. Remember to account for the costs of new employees if you need to hire more staff to administer the new tools or to perform new business activities, such as data mining. Determine the benefits of the BI application, both the tangible and intangible ones. Itemize how the BI application will solve the business problem and save the organization money or increase the organization's profit margin. Finally, calculate the ROI and indicate the time frame in which it will be realized.

8. **Perform a risk assessment.**

   List all the possible risks for your project and create a risk assessment matrix. If you do not have sufficient information to produce a detailed risk assessment matrix at this time, use the six basic risk categories: technology, complexity, integration, organization, project team, and financial investment. Determine the severity of each risk: low, medium, or high. Also determine how likely it is that each risk will materialize and what impact it would have on the BI project.

9. **Write the assessment report.**

   Describe the business need (whether it is a business problem or a business opportunity), and suggest one or more BI decision-support solutions. Include the results of the costs-benefit analysis and the risk assessment. Add a short summary to the report, and deliver it to the business sponsor as well as executive management.

DELIVERABLE RESULTING FROM THESE ACTIVITIES

1. **Business case assessment report**

   The business case assessment report should document the following:
   - Strategic business goals of the organization
   - Objectives of the proposed BI application
   - Statement of the business need (business problem or business opportunity)
   - Explanation of how the BI application will satisfy that need (proposed BI solution)
   - Ramifications of *not* addressing the business need and not committing to the proposed BI solution
   - Cost-benefit analysis results
   - Risk assessment
   - Recommendations for business process improvements to the operational systems or to the operational business processes and procedures

   The assessment report should also have a one- or two-page executive overview that summarizes the details of the report.

ROLES INVOLVED IN THESE ACTIVITIES

◆ **Business representative**
The business representative is the business person who will directly benefit from the BI application and who will participate as a full-time member on the project core team. He or she should complete the benefits portion of the cost-benefit analysis and should assist the project manager with the risk assessment.

◆ **Business sponsor**
The business sponsor is the person holding the "purse strings." He or she ensures that proper objectives for the BI application are established and that those objectives support the strategic business goals of the organization. He or she approves the business case assessment and helps set and negotiate the BI project scope to meet the stated BI application objectives.

◆ **Data quality analyst**
The quality of the source data is always overestimated. In reality, source data quality is much worse than anyone can imagine. The data quality analyst has to be able to estimate the time, effort, and cost associated with finding the dirty data and cleansing it.

◆ **Project manager**
The project manager should have experience as a systems integrator. The BI decision-support environment requires the management and integration of multiple types of software as well as hardware. In addition, the project manager needs skills in managing the staff, the project, and the expectations of the business community.

◆ **Subject matter expert**
Expertise in the business is mandatory, and the subject matter expert brings that expertise to the BI project. He or she should also have an understanding of the competition and of the trends in the industry.

RISKS OF NOT PERFORMING STEP 1

One of the major risks of not performing this step is that you may end up building a BI decision-support solution that has no strong business driver and does not support a strategic business goal. This can lead to a disappointed business community and an unhappy management group at the end of the project. No matter how valuable the BI application is from an IT perspective, it may not meet the expectations of the business community. If the business people are not content with the information provided to them, they might reject other BI solutions proposed by IT to solve other business problems.

BIBLIOGRAPHY AND ADDITIONAL READING

Adelman, Sid, and Larissa Terpeluk Moss. *Data Warehouse Project Management.* Boston, MA: Addison-Wesley, 2000.

Bischoff, Joyce, and Ted Alexander. *Data Warehouse: Practical Advice from the Experts.* Upper Saddle River, NJ: Prentice Hall, 1997.

DeMarco, Tom. *Slack: Getting Past Burnout, Busywork, and the Myth of Total Efficiency.* New York: Broadway Books, 2001.

Devlin, Barry. *Data Warehouse: From Architecture to Implementation.* Reading, MA: Addison-Wesley, 1997.

Dyché, Jill. *e-Data: Turning Data into Information with Data Warehousing.* Boston, MA: Addison-Wesley, 2000.

English, Larry P. *Improving Data Warehouse and Business Information Quality: Methods for Reducing Costs and Increasing Profits.* New York: John Wiley & Sons, 1999.

Hackney, Douglas. *Understanding and Implementing Successful Data Marts.* Reading, MA: Addison-Wesley, 1997.

Inmon, William H., Claudia Imhoff, and Greg Battas. *Building the Operational Data Store.* New York: John Wiley & Sons, 1996.

Inmon, William H., Claudia Imhoff, and Ryan Sousa. *Corporate Information Factory.* New York: John Wiley & Sons, 1997.

Inmon, William H., John A. Zachman, and Jonathon G. Geiger. *Data Stores, Data Warehousing and the Zachman Framework: Managing Enterprise Knowledge.* New York: McGraw-Hill, 1997.

Jarke, Matthias, Maurizio Lenzerini, Yannis Vassiliou, and Panos Vassiliadis. *Fundamentals of Data Warehouses.* New York: Springer, 2000.

Kuan-Tsae, Huang, Yang W. Lee, and Richard Y. Wang. *Quality Information and Knowledge Management.* Upper Saddle River, NJ: Prentice Hall, 1998.

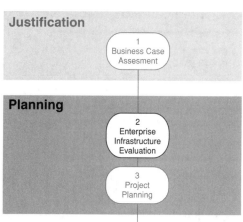

Justification
1 Business Case Assesment

Planning
2 Enterprise Infrastructure Evaluation
3 Project Planning

Business Analysis
4 Project Requirements Definition
5 Data Analysis
6 Application Prototyping
7 Meta Data Repository Analysis

Design
8 Database Design
10 Meta Data Repository Design
9 ETL Design

Construction
12 Application Development
14 Meta Data Repository Development
11 ETL Development
13 Data Mining

Deployment
15 Implementation
16 Release Evaluation

CHAPTER TWO

Step 2: Enterprise Infrastructure Evaluation

CHAPTER OVERVIEW

An enterprise infrastructure is to BI applications what a transportation infrastructure is to automobile owners. In order to safely and comfortably travel with an automobile, there must be a physical infrastructure, such as roads, bridges, traffic lights, and traffic signs, as well as nonphysical infrastructure, such as standardized traffic rules and their interpretation. For example, without the universal interpretation of the rule that "Green means go, red means stop," traffic lights would be of no use. Similarly, an enterprise infrastructure consists of two major components:

1. Technical infrastructure, such as hardware, middleware, and database management systems (DBMSs)

2. Nontechnical infrastructure, such as standards, meta data, business rules, and policies

Accordingly, this chapter is divided into two sections—Step 2, Section A, Technical Infrastructure Evaluation, and Step 2, Section B, Nontechnical Infrastructure Evaluation. The first section covers the following topics:

■ Things to consider about technical infrastructure

■ The importance of scalability for the hardware platform

■ Middleware, with emphasis on DBMS gateways since they are one of the most important middleware components for BI applications

■ DBMS requirements for the specific functionality needed to support BI applications

■ Brief descriptions of the technical infrastructure activities, the deliverables resulting from those activities, and the roles involved

■ The risks of not performing Step 2, Section A

The second section, on nontechnical infrastructure, covers the following topics:

- Things to consider about nontechnical infrastructure

- Bad practices and old habits that lead to stovepipe development (automation silos)

- The need for a nontechnical infrastructure to enable an integrated BI decision-support environment

- The enterprise architecture components: business function model, business process model, business data model, application inventory, and meta data repository

- Enterprise standards for such things as data naming, data quality, and testing

- Brief descriptions of the nontechnical infrastructure activities, the deliverables resulting from those activities, and the roles involved

- The risks of not performing Step 2, Section B

Step 2, Section A: Technical Infrastructure Evaluation

THINGS TO CONSIDER

Hardware

✓ What hardware platforms do we already have or use?

✓ On which platform should we implement the BI application?

✓ Do we need new hardware? What will it cost?

✓ Will we need more staff to maintain the new hardware?

✓ Will the new hardware integrate with our existing platforms?

✓ How will the new hardware scale to accommodate ever-increasing loads of processing and volumes of data?

Network

✓ What type of local area network (LAN) are we using?

✓ What type of wide area network (WAN) are we using?

✓ Is the bandwidth of our WAN sufficient to grow?

Middleware

✓ What type of middleware do we already have or use?

✓ Do we have the necessary middleware to retrieve the source data from heterogeneous platforms and transfer it to the BI decision-support environment?

✓ What is the operational source architecture? (e.g., enterprise resource planning [ERP], legacy files)

✓ Do we need new middleware? What will it cost?

✓ Will the connection be permanent between the source files (or source databases) and the BI target databases?

✓ Which of our hardware, software, and middleware is proprietary? Have we purchased it? Or are we leasing it?

Database Management Systems

✓ What DBMSs do we already have?

✓ Will we need to buy a new DBMS? What will it cost?

✓ Will the new DBMS be compatible with our operating system(s)?

✓ What software tools can run with it?

✓ Does our staff have the skills to use and administer the new DBMS?

✓ Will we have to hire more database administrators?

Tools and Standards

✓ How are the business analysts currently analyzing the data? What reporting and querying tools do they use?

✓ What additional tools and utilities do we need?

✓ What other software do these tools need to interact with?

✓ Do we know of any major problems with our technical infrastructure?

✓ What are our technical standards for compatibility and access?

The development efforts of early BI applications, such as the early data warehouses, were relatively slow, labor-intensive, risky, and expensive. Extraction and transformation of operational data into a data warehouse frequently involved creating new, custom-written application code. The target databases were either based on proprietary DBMSs or were using proprietary hardware platforms. There was also a shortage of tools to administer, control, and expand the new decision-support environment. The lesson learned from the early BI days was that in order to reach the best performance results for data access and retrieval, a comprehensive application platform must be chosen. Therefore, it is important to select the appropriate hardware, middleware, and DBMS and to ensure that these components are implemented properly.

THE HARDWARE PLATFORM

For adequate report and query performance, it is very important to have sufficient "horsepower" with the hardware platform. Scalability is of utmost importance.

Controlled Chaos

Do not despair if your computer environment looks like the one in Figure 2.1. This is more often the case than not in organizations of any size. What exists can at best be described as controlled chaos!

Accompanying the hardware chaos are usually a huge portfolio of disparate software and a large staff with only enough skills to support the existing systems. In order to minimize the chaos, most organizations implementing a BI decision-

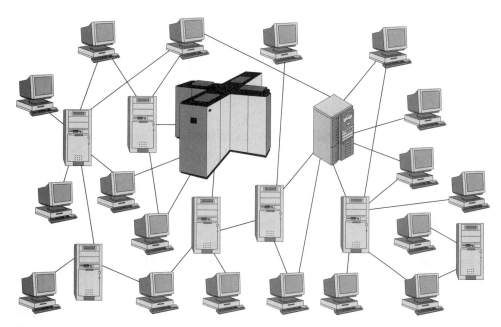

Figure 2.1: Controlled Hardware Chaos

support environment have to consider at least four imperatives in hardware platform selection.

1. New hardware platforms have to fit into the existing hardware configuration.
2. The DBMS on the selected hardware platform must perform well as database access and usage grow. Scalability is therefore one of the major issues to be addressed.
3. Platform selection is restricted by the need for interoperability between various hardware platforms (if required).
4. Cost and return on investment (ROI) for the previous three qualifiers are controlling factors.

Hardware Platform Requirements

The hardware must have sufficient power to handle complex access and analysis requirements against large volumes of data. It has to support not only predefined, simple queries on summary data but also ad hoc complex queries on detailed data. It must also be scalable because rapid changes will occur in:

- Data volumes
- Updating frequencies
- Data access patterns
- Number of reports and queries
- Number of people accessing the BI target databases
- Number of tools running against the BI target databases
- Number of operational systems feeding the BI target databases

It is useful to think of a BI decision-support environment in terms of a three-tier computing architecture (Figure 2.2). First, the extract/transform/load (ETL) engine extracts, cleanses, and transforms operational data. Then, using middleware, the BI target databases are populated. Finally, when data is requested, it is mapped into suitable representations for the business community at the interface level for running queries, reports, and online analytical processing (OLAP) applications. The interface level can be a customized graphical user interface (GUI) application, an enterprise portal, or Extensible Markup Language (XML) Web services.

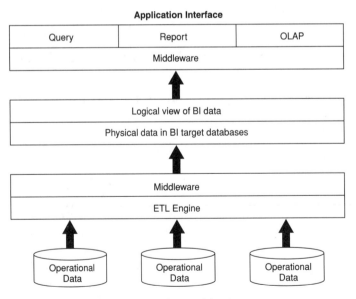

Figure 2.2: Three-Tier Computing Architecture

THE MIDDLEWARE PLATFORM

The term *middleware* refers to runtime system software, which is layered between the application programs and the operating system. It acts as a bridge to integrate application programs and other software components in an environment with multiple network nodes, several operating systems, and many software products. Middleware is needed to run client/server architectures and other complex networked architectures in a distributed computing environment. Therefore, the middleware should support directory services, message-passing mechanisms, and database gateways.

Most middleware falls into two major categories:

1. *Distributed logic middleware* supports program-to-program communication between two pieces of custom-written application code.

2. *Data management middleware* connects an application or DBMS on one platform with a DBMS running on another platform.

Middleware can also be used to enable "reach-through" queries from summaries in the BI target databases to the underlying detail data held in operational systems. To keep the cost to a minimum, a number of organizations are already using gateways to transfer data from multiple heterogeneous sources of server data to client workstations, as illustrated in Figure 2.3.

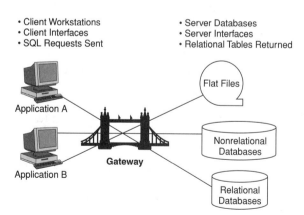

Figure 2.3: Gateway Example

DBMS Gateways

DMBS gateways, a form of middleware, are generally required to connect the different network architectures of desktop computers, remote clients, or small enterprise servers to industrial-strength enterprise servers.

Gateways fall into four major categories.

1. *Point-to-point gateways* provide access to only one type of DBMS. Vendors market each point-to-point gateway as a different product. A point-to-point gateway is easy to implement because it handles only one DBMS at a time. It is also a less expensive solution compared with the other three gateway solutions. However, when the organization requires access to multiple DBMSs, it needs multiple gateways. In that case, point-to-point gateways may not be a less expensive solution than using a universal gateway.

2. *Gateways that can be used universally* provide access to different types of databases on various platforms. Universal gateways require extensive effort to implement and maintain. As a result, these gateways become expensive.

3. *Gateways using Structured Query Language* (SQL) can access only "real" relational databases, not simulated ones. The SQL gateway translates the client request into the native SQL syntax used by the server's relational DBMS.

4. *Gateways based on application programming interfaces* (APIs) are driven by vendor specifications. One of the major gateways of this type is open database connectivity (ODBC). A number of ODBC vendors provide drivers for accessing databases residing on various servers.

Organizational data is distributed across multiple DBMS platforms, cooperating across a network with different instruction sets from multiple vendors. ODBC-enabled applications can access multiple distributed data sources concurrently via ODBC's common interface approach (Figure 2.4).

Modules called *database drivers* can be added to link the applications to the DBMS of their choice. Database drivers consist of dynamic link libraries (DLLs) that applications can invoke on demand.

THE DBMS PLATFORM

The database infrastructure changes with the size of the BI decision-support environment, which in turn influences the selection of the DBMS, as shown in Figure 2.5. A small departmental data mart application may reside on a local file

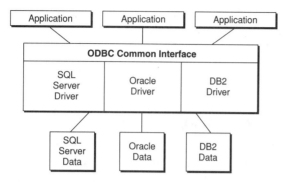

Figure 2.4: ODBC-Enabled Applications

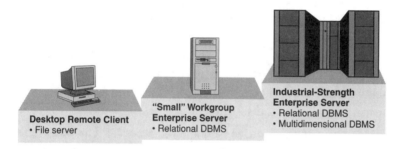

Figure 2.5: Database Infrastructures

server, but a larger BI application may need the infrastructure support of an enterprise server, and very large enterprise-wide BI solutions may need to use a mainframe.

Criteria for Selecting a DBMS

The following functions are important and necessary attributes of a DBMS for handling the workload of a large BI target database or very large database (VLDB):

- Degree of parallelism in handling queries and data loads
- Intelligence in handling dimensional data models and optimizers
- Database scalability
- Internet integration
- Availability of advanced index schemes
- Replication on heterogeneous platforms
- Unattended operations

A DBMS is a sophisticated piece of software and consists of a number of features that need to be evaluated. Features to look for in a DBMS for BI applications are listed below.

- *Network support* provided by the DBMS should be compatible with the organization's data communications standards.

- *Dimensional capability* in the form of seamless support for fast and easy loading and maintenance of precompiled summaries is important.

- *Adequate state-of-the-art triggers and stored procedures* can be used as "event alerters," which trigger an action in response to a given set of circumstances.

- *Administrative support features* should provide for:
  - Maintenance of consistent historical data
  - Support for archiving (e.g., dropping the oldest week's data when adding the data for a new week)
  - Controls for implementing resource limits to display a warning when a query that consumes excessive resources is about to be terminated
  - Workload tracking and tuning mechanisms
  - Careful monitoring of activity and resource utilization

- *Location transparency across the network* must allow the access and analysis tools to retrieve data from multiple BI target databases from a single workstation.

- *Future usage explosion* must be supported by:
  - Effective caching and sharing of data to minimize input/output (I/O) bottlenecks
  - Effective management of task switching while running many queries concurrently
  - Compatibility with multiple processors

- *Scalability* requires that the DBMS has the capability to support:
  - Advanced functions for sorting and indexing
  - Fault tolerance for uninterrupted processing
  - Uninterrupted maintenance operations, such as unload, backup, and restore
  - Checkpoints, recovery, and rapid restart of interrupted operations

- *Query performance optimization* should address aspects of query processing (such as JOINs, sorting, and grouping) that require intensive use of the central processing unit (CPU).

- *Load process and performance* must address:
  - Data obtained directly from a variety of feeds, including disk files, network feeds, mainframe channel connections, and magnetic tapes

– Complete data loading and preparation, including format conversion, integrity enforcement, and indexing

• The *security system* must support unique passwords, password protection, and the authorization constraints necessary for specific persons and for specific tables of the database. The system administrator should provide restricted access to the views and virtual tables.

• The *data dictionary* should feed into a meta data repository, and the database objects should be linked to all data objects described in the enterprise logical data model.

Selecting and reevaluating the appropriate hardware, middleware, and DBMS components of the technical infrastructure are some of the most important activities on BI projects because they ensure the continued scalability and high performance of the BI applications.

TECHNICAL INFRASTRUCTURE EVALUATION ACTIVITIES

The technical infrastructure evaluation activities do not need to be performed linearly. Figure 2.6 indicates two activities that can be performed concurrently. The list below briefly describes the activities associated with Step 2, Section A, Technical Infrastructure Evaluation.

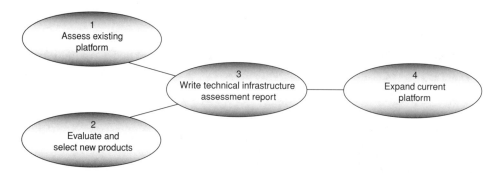

Figure 2.6: Technical Infrastructure Evaluation Activities

1. Assess the existing platform.

Review the existing platform in terms of hardware, middleware, DBMS, and tools. It is important to evaluate the interdependence of the tools for their various purposes, such as the interdependence between a multidimensional reporting tool and an ad hoc querying tool. In addition, review the existing network architecture. One of the biggest bottlenecks today, especially in organizations with decentralized applications, is the lack of bandwidth coupled with a limited capacity for network growth.

2. **Evaluate and select new products.**
   After assessing the existing platforms, identify which types of new hardware, software, or networking components you must acquire. If the existing hardware platform appears to be sufficient, be sure to determine that it will be able to provide the productivity and performance the organization expects from it. Engage business representatives and stakeholders in the decision-making process by including them in peer reviews during the selection process.

3. **Write the technical infrastructure assessment report.**
   Compile all findings about the existing platform into a report. Explain the strengths and weaknesses of the current hardware, middleware, DBMS, and tools, and provide a list of missing technical infrastructure components necessary to meet the project requirements.

4. **Expand the current platform.**
   Once you have determined which new products need to be acquired, you can begin the process of evaluating, selecting, ordering, installing, and testing them.

DELIVERABLES RESULTING FROM THESE ACTIVITIES

1. **Technical infrastructure assessment report**
   This report should itemize the scalability and limitations of the hardware, middleware, DBMS, and tool platform and should cover the following items:
   – Servers
   – Client workstations
   – Operating systems
   – Middleware (especially DBMS gateways)
   – Custom interfaces
   – Network components and bandwidth
   – DBMS functionality and utilities (backup and recovery, performance monitoring)
   – Development tools such as computer aided software engineering (CASE) and ETL tools
   – Access and analysis tools such as OLAP tools and report writers
   – Meta data repository

Include a gap analysis section and provide recommendations for upgrading the platform. Incorporate the product evaluation and selection results, listing the weighted requirements and the product features you evaluated. The product and vendor evaluation and selection process is described in more detail in Step 10, Meta Data Repository Design.

2. **Installation of selected products**

   If you identified new products to purchase, write a request for proposal (RFP) or a request for information (RFI) and send it to the vendors on the short list. After selecting a product, order, install, and test it.

ROLES INVOLVED IN THESE ACTIVITIES

◆ **BI infrastructure architect**

The BI infrastructure architect is responsible for developing the capacity plans for the hardware, middleware, DBMS, and network in order to ensure the scalability needed by the BI decision-support environment. The BI infrastructure architect and the database administrator have to work side by side while evaluating the current environment, determining the appropriate future platforms, and implementing the selected technologies.

◆ **Database administrator**

The database administrator has to evaluate the current DBMS platform on the current hardware. The database administrator also has to evaluate the tools and the middleware as they relate to the DBMS. He or she has to determine the future DBMS requirements and should participate in performing the technical infrastructure gap analysis.

RISKS OF NOT PERFORMING STEP 2, SECTION A

In order to provide adequate performance in a growing BI decision-support environment, it is mandatory to assess the hardware, middleware, DBMS, and tools from time to time. If you do not perform this part of Step 2, technical performance could degrade to such an extent that the BI decision-support environment becomes unusable. It is also necessary to stay current with the existing technology. Technology advances occur every few months. Not staying current and not taking advantage of new and improved features can turn the BI decision-support environment into an extinct dinosaur in a very short time.

Step 2, Section B: Nontechnical Infrastructure Evaluation

THINGS TO CONSIDER

Logical Data Model

✓ Do we already have logical data models for the source systems? If not, who is responsible for creating a logical data model for this BI project?

✓ Who are the data owners and business people who have to participate in the validation of the logical data model and the business meta data?

✓ How many trained data administrators do we have? Will we have to hire more?

✓ Who will integrate our logical data model into the enterprise logical data model?

✓ Who will validate the expanded enterprise logical data model?

✓ What CASE tool do we have for logical data modeling? Will we need to license (buy) one?

Meta Data

✓ Do we already have a meta data repository? Will we need to license (buy) or build a meta data repository?

✓ If we have one, how easy is it for the business people to access and navigate through the meta data repository? Do we need to enhance it?

✓ Who is responsible for capturing all the meta data components? Who is responsible for loading the meta data into the meta data repository?

✓ How will we merge the new business meta data from the CASE tool with the new technical meta data from the ETL tool and the OLAP tool?

Standards, Guidelines, and Procedures

✓ Are our current standards too lax or too stringent?

✓ Where are the standards documented? Are they being followed?

✓ How effective are our data quality guidelines for measuring dirty data and and triaging data cleansing?

✓ Are our change-control procedures easy to use? Do we have a template?

✓ Do we have a template for an issue log?

✓ What are our testing standards?

✓ Are we habitually testing too much or too little? Are we testing the right things?

✓ How are we currently resolving technical and business disputes?

✓ Do we need to create or change our dispute resolution procedure?

✓ What are the roles and responsibilities that will be assigned to the core team members?

✓ Is our current team structure effective?

Enterprise-wide nontechnical infrastructure is a critical success factor for a BI decision-support environment. Without a cross-organizational infrastructure, BI applications would only contribute to the existing chaos of stovepipe applications and databases.

THE EFFECTS OF STOVEPIPE DEVELOPMENT

In the past, the mental model for providing an automated information technology (IT) solution to a business problem has been to "divide and conquer."

1. Divide a large problem into smaller "digestible" pieces, that is, prioritize and separate the deliverables.

2. Conquer the problem by working on each piece individually, that is, build each deliverable separately.

This approach works very well for reducing risk by breaking a complex problem into small, manageable chunks. However, this approach also has a severe drawback when applied without a nontechnical infrastructure. Namely, it produces stovepipe systems (automation silos). The effects of stovepipe systems are lost business knowledge and lost cross-organizational business view, which severely impact business analytics and data mining activities.

Most businesses are very complex, and as organizations mature, their business complexity increases. As business complexity is broken apart into smaller and less complex components, the interrelationships among those individual components are lost. Much of the business intelligence is contained in these lost interrelationships, and that is a problem for BI applications. Most BI applications,

Figure 2.7: Fundamental Business Questions

and especially data mining applications, expect to find "golden nuggets" of business wisdom embedded in these complex interrelationships.

Although business managers can answer most questions about the business functions of their own departments, when asked a question spanning two or three lines of business (where complex interrelationships have been lost), those managers must scramble for weeks to piece together the answer. Fundamental business questions, such as the ones illustrated in Figure 2.7, present multimillion-dollar problems to large organizations.

The answers to these and many other questions do exist in the real business world. We have just been neglecting to design our systems in a cross-functional manner that would allow us to find these answers quickly.

The Need for Nontechnical Infrastructure

An organization needs to create a nontechnical infrastructure to prevent the BI decision-support environment from becoming as fragmented as the operational and traditional decision-support environments, from which cross-organizational questions cannot be answered. Creating this infrastructure involves cross-organizational activities such as those listed below.

- *Conduct an extensive business analysis* involving business people from many lines of business. During this activity, define or redefine the lost complex interrelationships among business functions and business data.

- *Adopt a system of peer reviews* to support cross-organizational attendance and evaluation of business analysis activities.

- *Resolve age-old disputes* about data definitions and domains (valid data contents).

- *Standardize data names and data values* to reflect true business rules and business policies.

- *Get agreement from the business people* on the business rules and business policies in the first place.

- *Create a regular forum* for business people to maintain and review the standards, business rules, and business policies on an ongoing basis.

- *Over time, create one consolidated, nonredundant data architecture* for the entire enterprise to reflect the complex reality of the business; that is, create an enterprise logical data model. This model documents the data inventory of an organization. It is also the primary vehicle for mapping the inventory of operational data to the inventory of BI data.

- *Create a meta data repository* and populate it with nonredundant meta data.

- *Create an inventory of source data* and map it to the applicable BI target databases. Also create an inventory of other system components, such as programs, reports, screens, and so on, thereby identifying the reusability of data and process components.

- *Create and manage* one *expanding central staging area* (per load periodicity) for the ETL processes. Do not allow independent ETL processes for each data mart solution.

Enterprise infrastructure activities, technical as well as nontechnical, are strategic cross-organizational activities. A central enterprise architecture group (Figure 2.8) must manage and coordinate these activities. Many large organizations have a strategic enterprise architecture group whose charter is to integrate and manage the IT infrastructure components as assets of an organization. These infrastructure components are inventories or models of business functions, business processes, business data, meta data, applications, and other technical implementation elements. If an organization does not have an enterprise architecture group, then data administration can perform the information architecture subfunction,

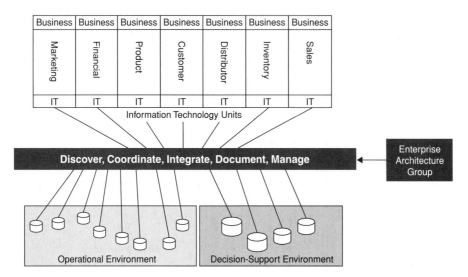

Figure 2.8: Enterprise Architecture Group

which includes creating and managing the enterprise logical data model and the meta data repository. If the organization has a separate meta data administration, the information architecture responsibilities would be divided between those two groups (data administration and meta data administration).

ENTERPRISE ARCHITECTURE

An enterprise architecture is comprised of a set of pictorial representations (models) of the organization in terms of business functions, business processes, and business data. Each enterprise architecture model is supplemented with supporting meta data, such as standard definitions, business rules, and policies. The purpose of these models is to document the set of business actions performed on any real-world object in the course of conducting business. In other words, enterprise architecture models describe the actual business in which the organization engages.

Every active organization has an enterprise architecture by default, even if it is not documented. With undocumented architecture, the organization's business actions and business objects are most likely not consistently understood by everyone in the organization. The goal of documenting the architecture is to avoid

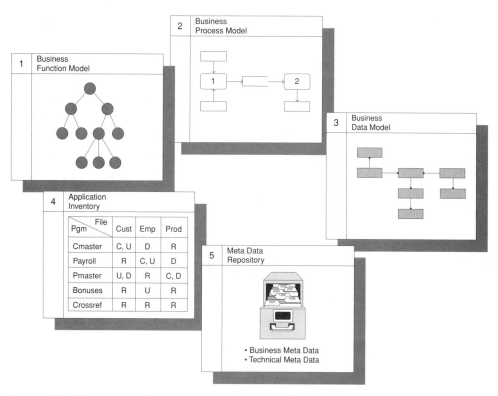

Figure 2.9: Enterprise Architecture Components

abusing, misusing, or redundantly recreating unique processes or data about business objects, which can lead to losing sight of the cross-organizational picture.

A fully documented enterprise architecture includes at least five architectural components (Figure 2.9). The following subsections describe these components.

The Business Function Model

This model depicts the hierarchical decomposition of an organization's nature of business; it shows *what* the organization does. This model is instrumental for organizing or reorganizing the structure of an organization into its lines of business. Usually one vertical line of business supports a major business function on this model. Two examples of such an alignment are the loan-origination division and the loan-servicing division of a mortgage-lending institution.

The Business Process Model

This model depicts the processes implemented for the business functions; it shows *how* the organization performs its business functions. This model is essential for business process reengineering as well as business process improvement initiatives, which often result from BI projects. For example, a business process model could be analyzed to determine whether it is possible to streamline a current business process called loan payment processing because customers have complained about the long delays in posting their loan payments while their loans continue to accrue interest.

The Business Data Model

This model, which is commonly called the *enterprise logical data model* or *enterprise information architecture*, shows *what data* is part of the organization's business activities. This model depicts the following:

- Data objects participating in a business activity
- Relationships among these objects as they exist in the actual business activities
- Data elements stored about these objects
- Business rules governing these objects

Since data objects and data elements are all unique, they appear in the real world only once. Therefore, they are documented in the business data model only once, regardless of the numbers of physical files and databases used for their storage. There is only one business data model for an organization. This model and the meta data repository are the two most important nontechnical infrastructure components for an evolving BI decision-support environment.

The Application Inventory

The application inventory is an accounting of the physical implementation components of business functions, business processes, and business data (objects as well as data elements). It shows *where* the architectural pieces reside in the technical architecture. Application inventory entries include the relationships among the physical implementation components, such as programs, job streams, databases, or files.

Organizations should always identify, catalog, and document their applications as well as the business rules about their business data as part of the development work on *every* project—but they seldom do. Such inventories are paramount for performing impact analysis. Remember the colossal efforts of Y2K impact analysis without such an inventory!

The Meta Data Repository

Although "a picture is worth a thousand words," business models without words are not worth much. The descriptive details about the models are called *meta data*. Business meta data is collected during business analysis, and technical meta data is collected during design and construction. The two types of meta data are linked to each other and made available to the business community of the BI decision-support environment. Meta data is an essential navigation tool. Some examples of meta data components include the following:

- Column name
- Column domain (allowable values)
- Table name
- Program name
- Report name
- Report description
- Data owner
- Data definition
- Data quality metrics

ENTERPRISE STANDARDS

Organizations must establish architectural standards for their BI decision-support environments in the same way they set up standards for their Web sites. An organization would never consider building its Web site with a different look and feel for each Web page. In the same vein, no organization should build a BI decision-support environment in which each BI application had a different look and feel. Therefore, all BI applications must adhere to the same enterprise standards within an organization. Figure 2.10 lists the categories of standards to develop, which are briefly described below.

Figure 2.10: Enterprise Standards

Development Approach

Business Intelligence Roadmap provides a complete list of all the major activities and tasks that are appropriate for BI projects. However, since scope and deliverables of BI projects can vary widely, not every BI project team has to perform every single activity in every step. Some BI projects may justifiably skip activities within a step, combine activities from different steps into one, or skip entire steps. However, no BI project should be developed ad hoc. Organizations should have some guidelines that list the minimum number of activities required (minimum work breakdown structure), the mandatory deliverables, sign-off requirements, and workflow dependencies in order to control the project risks.

Data Naming and Abbreviations

Data naming and abbreviation standards for BI applications provide consistency and a common look and feel useful for both developers and business people. Proven standards can be applied (such as the convention of name compositions using prime, qualifier or modifier, and class words), or new organization-specific standards can be created. The data administration group usually has been trained in the various industry-standard naming conventions.

Abbreviations are part of naming standards, but they apply only to physical names (e.g., column names, table names, program names), not to business names. The organization should publish a standard enterprise-wide abbreviations list that includes industry-specific and organization-specific acronyms. Every BI project team should use these abbreviations and acronyms.

Meta Data Capture

Meta data is a world unto itself. Large amounts of descriptive information can be collected about business functions, business processes, business data objects, business data elements, business rules, data quality, and other architectural components. The organization needs standards or guidelines that govern who captures which meta data components and how, when, and where to capture them. The meta data repository should be set up in such a way that it supports the standards for meta data capture and usage.

Logical Data Modeling

Logical data modeling is a business analysis technique (not to be confused with logical database design). Every business activity or business function uses or manipulates business data in some fashion. A logical data model documents those logical data relationships irrespective of how the functions or the data are implemented in the physical databases and applications.

Project-specific logical data models should be merged into one cohesive, integrated enterprise logical data model. This activity usually is—and should be—included in the job description for the data administration department, which may be part of the enterprise architecture group. The enterprise logical data model is the baseline business information architecture into which physical systems (operational or decision-support, including BI applications) are mapped. The organization should establish standards for creating the project-specific logical data models for BI projects and for merging the models into the enterprise logical data model.

Data Quality

Information can be only as good as the raw data on which it is based. Most organizations have a lot of dirty data—too much to cleanse it all. Each organization must establish guidelines about triaging (categorizing and prioritizing) dirty data for cleansing. In addition, the organization must create standards that define acceptable quality thresholds and specify how to measure data quality during database loads. Instructions for error handling and suspending dirty data records should also be part of the standards.

Testing

Testing standards specify what types of tests should be performed and who should participate in the various types of testing. The organization should provide guidelines that describe the types of test cases required at a minimum, how much regression testing to perform, and under what circumstances to regression test. A brief description of a test plan, perhaps even a template, as well as instructions for how to organize and manage the various testing activities should be included.

Reconciliation

The BI decision-support environment will have multiple target databases and multiple BI applications. Since BI applications are not stand-alone systems, their development must be coordinated and reconciled to guarantee consistency across the BI decision-support environment. That includes having one (logical) central staging area with reconciliation programming for every input-process-output module regardless of whether the module is written in native code or produced by an ETL tool.

Security

BI data is derived from operational data. Therefore, security guidelines that apply to the operational data also apply to the BI data. However, if data is summarized and the ability to drill down to the details is not enabled, some of the security features can be relaxed. But rather than allowing the members of each project team to make up the rules as they please, the data owners should establish security standards to guide the project teams on what types of security measures are mandatory for what types of data exposure. These standards should include guidelines for categorizing security risks. Security risks should be considered for data sensitivity, application security, network security, and security against intrusions, hacks, viruses, and other nuisances on the Web.

Service-Level Agreements

Organizations function according to explicit or implicit business principles. Business principles are *explicit* if stated in mission or vision statements, *implicit* if they are just "understood" by the staff. For example, if an organization rewards project managers for meeting deadlines even though their applications are full of errors while it punishes project managers for missing deadlines even though their applications are flawless, the implicit business principle is "speed before quality." Service-level agreements (SLAs) ordinarily support the explicit as well as the implicit business principles. Therefore, SLA standards should state the business principles and outline the minimum acceptable SLA measures to support those principles. For example, "All projects must meet a 98 percent data quality threshold for financial data." SLA measures can also apply to query response time, timeliness, availability, and level of ongoing support.

Policies and Procedures

Standards and guidelines should also cover the policies and procedures of an organization, such as operating procedures, project change-control procedures, issues management procedures, and dispute resolution procedures. Additional topics (e.g., communication processes, estimating guidelines, roles and responsibilities, standard document format) should also be part of the policies and procedures. The purpose of having policies and procedures, along with standards and guidelines, is to help streamline and standardize the BI decision-support environment. In other words, policies, procedures, standards, and guidelines must add value for the organization as a whole—or they should not exist.

NONTECHNICAL INFRASTRUCTURE EVALUATION ACTIVITIES

The nontechnical infrastructure activities need to be performed linearly, as indicated in Figure 2.11. The list below briefly describes the activities associated with Step 2, Section B, Nontechnical Infrastructure Evaluation.

Figure 2.11: Nontechnical Infrastructure Evaluation Activities

1. **Assess the effectiveness of existing nontechnical infrastructure components.** The policies, procedures, guidelines, and standards, which are all part of the nontechnical infrastructure, exist to assist in the coordination and management of the BI decision-support environment. They should not hinder the project teams or slow them down unnecessarily. Therefore, review the appropriateness and effectiveness of all nontechnical infrastructure components at the beginning of each BI project. Expand, reduce, or revise any inadequate components as necessary.
   - Eliminate unnecessary activities or tasks from the development methodology or add missing activities or tasks.

- Ensure that naming standards and abbreviations make sense and are comfortable to the business community.
- Review the logical data modeling and meta data strategies, and ensure that the data administration and meta data administration groups are adequately staffed.
- Refine the organization's data quality initiative.
- Examine the testing standards, and ensure that a sufficient amount of reconciliation is being performed.
- Review the guidelines for SLAs and security.

Tasks within this activity can be performed concurrently.

2. **Write the nontechnical infrastructure assessment report.**
Once you have assessed all the components of the existing nontechnical infrastructure, prepare a report that outlines your findings and gives recommendations for improvement. If there are missing nontechnical infrastructure components, prioritize which ones to include in the next BI project and which ones to defer.

3. **Improve the nontechnical infrastructure.**
In the project plan, give time estimates for modifying or improving nontechnical infrastructure components as well as for establishing new components. If the improvements must be completed prior to starting the BI project, create a separate infrastructure project with a separate team and a separate project plan.

DELIVERABLE RESULTING FROM THESE ACTIVITIES

1. **Nontechnical infrastructure assessment report**
This report should document the deficiencies of the existing nontechnical infrastructure and should cover the following items:
   – Standards
   – Use of a development methodology
   – Estimating guidelines
   – Scope management procedure
   – Issues management procedure
   – Roles and responsibilities
   – Security process
   – Meta data capture and delivery

   – Process for merging project-specific logical data models into the enterprise logical data model
   – Data quality measures and triage process
   – Testing process
   – SLAs
   – Support function
   – Dispute resolution procedure
   – Communication process

Include a section for proposed improvements for those selected nontechnical infrastructure components that will be included in the BI project.

ROLES INVOLVED IN THESE ACTIVITIES

◆ **BI infrastructure architect**
In some organizations, the BI infrastructure architect may have responsibility over the nontechnical architectural components of the BI decision-support environment. In other organizations, he or she works closely with the data administrator, meta data administrator, and data quality analyst. Occasionally the BI infrastructure architect oversees the activities of the data administrator, meta data administrator, and data quality analyst. It is up to the organization to select the enterprise architecture reporting structure that is most appropriate for its organizational culture.

◆ **Data administrator**
In many organizations, data administration has the responsibility for most of the nontechnical infrastructure components, in particular logical data modeling, data quality, naming standards, and meta data. However, since the area of nontechnical infrastructure involves so many disciplines, the traditional data administration responsibilities should be divided among the data administrator, the meta data administrator, the data quality analyst, and sometimes even the BI infrastructure architect. All of these roles are usually staffed by members of the enterprise architecture group.

◆ **Data quality analyst**
The data quality analyst takes charge of finding and analyzing dirty data in the source files. Since it is impossible to cleanse all the dirty data, the organization must establish triaging procedures and prioritization guidelines. The data quality analyst is the steward of those data quality standards.

◆ **Meta data administrator**
The meta data administrator is responsible for the meta data repository. He or she must create it (or buy and install it), maintain it, and populate it. During the BI project, the data administrator will provide the business meta data, and the database administrator and data quality analyst (with the help of the ETL and application lead developers) will provide the technical meta data. The meta data administrator must then merge all the meta data into the meta data repository and make it available to IT staff and to the business people. The meta data administrator should therefore establish the standards related to the meta data repository activities.

RISKS OF NOT PERFORMING STEP 2, SECTION B

Business intelligence is all about creating an enterprise architecture solution to the decision-support chaos that exists today. It is a cross-organizational initiative. Therefore, cross-organizational activities are of critical importance. The absence of those activities will lead to stovepipe development and will add to the "spaghetti chart" more data marts and more stand-alone BI applications that are neither integrated nor reconciled. As a result, the organization would continue to lose the opportunity to enhance its business decisions and competitive advantages.

BIBLIOGRAPHY AND ADDITIONAL READING

Technical Infrastructure Evaluation

Bischoff, Joyce, and Ted Alexander. *Data Warehouse: Practical Advice from the Experts.* Upper Saddle River, NJ: Prentice Hall, 1997.

Devlin, Barry. *Data Warehouse: From Architecture to Implementation.* Reading, MA: Addison-Wesley, 1997.

Inmon, William H. *Building the Data Warehouse.* New York: John Wiley & Sons, 1996.

Inmon, William H., Claudia Imhoff, and Greg Battas. *Building the Operational Data Store.* New York: John Wiley & Sons, 1996.

Jarke, Matthias, Maurizio Lenzerini, Yannis Vassiliou, and Panos Vassiliadis. *Fundamentals of Data Warehouses.* New York: Springer, 2000.

Kelly, Sean. *Data Warehousing: The Route to Mass Customization.* New York: John Wiley & Sons, 1996.

Kimball, Ralph, and Richard Merz. *The Data Webhouse Toolkit: Building the Web-Enabled Data Warehouse.* New York: John Wiley & Sons, 2000.

Linthicum, David S. *Enterprise Application Integration.* Boston, MA: Addison-Wesley, 2000.

Moeller, R. A. *Distributed Data Warehousing Using Web Technology: How to Build a More Cost-effective and Flexible Warehouse.* New York: AMACOM American Management Association, 2001.

Nontechnical Infrastructure Evaluation

Adelman, Sid, and Larissa Terpeluk Moss. *Data Warehouse Project Management.* Boston, MA: Addison-Wesley, 2000.

Brackett, Michael H. *Data Resource Quality: Turning Bad Habits into Good Practices.* Boston, MA: Addison-Wesley, 2000.

———. *The Data Warehouse Challenge: Taming Data Chaos.* New York: John Wiley & Sons, 1996.

Bruce, Thomas A. *Designing Quality Databases with IDEF1X Information Models.* New York: Dorset House, 1992.

English, Larry P. *Improving Data Warehouse and Business Information Quality: Methods for Reducing Costs and Increasing Profits.* New York: John Wiley & Sons, 1999.

Hoberman, Steve. *Data Modeler's Workbench: Tools and Techniques for Analysis and Design.* New York: John Wiley & Sons, 2001.

Inmon, William H. *Building the Data Warehouse.* New York: John Wiley & Sons, 1996.

Inmon, William H., Claudia Imhoff, and Greg Battas. *Building the Operational Data Store.* New York: John Wiley & Sons, 1996.

Inmon, William H., Claudia Imhoff, and Ryan Sousa. *Corporate Information Factory.* New York: John Wiley & Sons, 1997.

Inmon, William H., John A. Zachman, and Jonathon G. Geiger. *Data Stores, Data Warehousing and the Zachman Framework: Managing Enterprise Knowledge.* New York: McGraw-Hill, 1997.

Kuan-Tsae, Huang, Yang W. Lee, and Richard Y. Wang. *Quality Information and Knowledge Management.* Upper Saddle River, NJ: Prentice Hall, 1998.

Reingruber, Michael C., and William W. Gregory. *The Data Modeling Handbook: A Best-Practice Approach to Building Quality Data Models.* New York: John Wiley & Sons, 1994.

Ross, Ronald G. *Business Rule Concepts.* Houston, TX: Business Rule Solutions, 1998.

Simsion, Graeme. *Data Modeling Essentials: Analysis, Design, and Innovation.* Boston, MA: International Thomson Computer Press, 1994.

Zachman, John. *The Zachman Framework: A Primer for Enterprise Engineering and Manufacturing.* La Canada, CA: Zachman International, 2002.

Zachman Institute for Framework Advancement: *http://www.zifa.com*

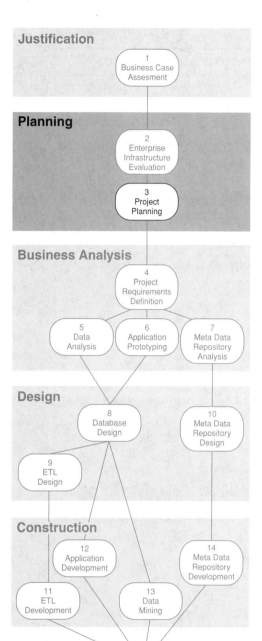

Justification
1 Business Case Assesment

Planning
2 Enterprise Infrastructure Evaluation
3 Project Planning

Business Analysis
4 Project Requirements Definition
5 Data Analysis
6 Application Prototyping
7 Meta Data Repository Analysis

Design
8 Database Design
9 ETL Design
10 Meta Data Repository Design

Construction
12 Application Development
14 Meta Data Repository Development
11 ETL Development
13 Data Mining

Deployment
15 Implementation
16 Release Evaluation

CHAPTER THREE

Step 3: Project Planning

CHAPTER OVERVIEW

This chapter covers the following topics:

- Things to consider about project planning

- Managing the BI project and planning for setbacks

- Items to address when creating a project charter, such as goals and objectives, scope issues, project risks, constraints, assumptions, change control, and issues management

- Aspects of project planning, with a focus on activities and tasks, estimating techniques, resource assignment, task and resource dependencies, critical path determination, and creation of the final project schedule

- Brief descriptions of the project planning activities, the deliverables resulting from those activities, and the roles involved

- The risks of not performing Step 3

THINGS TO CONSIDER

Business Involvement

✓ Do we have a strong business sponsor? Do we have a backup business sponsor?
✓ Do we have stakeholders with whom we need to communicate regularly?
✓ How much time is the business representative committing to this project? Is he or she assigned to this project full-time, or will he or she be available on request only?

Project Scope and Deliverables

✓ Did we receive a formal request for a BI project?
✓ How detailed are the requirements?
✓ What are the requested deliverables?
✓ Can we implement the requested scope given the schedule and the available resources?

Cost-Benefit Analysis

✓ Have we already performed a cost-benefit analysis?
✓ What is the expected return on investment (ROI)?
✓ How soon do we expect the ROI to materialize?

Infrastructure

✓ Did we review our technical and nontechnical infrastructure components?
✓ Does our infrastructure have any gaps?
✓ Which infrastructure components will we need to work on and deliver as part of the BI project?
  –Which technical infrastructure components?
  –Which nontechnical infrastructure components?

Staffing and Skills

✓ Have we already identified the team members?
✓ Do all team members have the skills needed to perform the responsibilities of their assigned roles?
✓ Should we schedule any training before the project kickoff?
✓ Is the project manager assigned to this project full-time? Or does he or she have other administrative responsibilities? If the latter, who will take over those other responsibilities for the duration of this project?

BI projects are not like other projects with a finite and static set of requirements from one business person or one department. Instead, the purpose of an integrated BI decision-support environment is to provide cross-organizational business analysis capabilities to all business people and all departments in the organization. That involves a variety of new tasks, shifted roles and responsibilities, and a more *hands-on* project management approach.

MANAGING THE BI PROJECT

Project management in most organizations is treated as an administrative reporting function. Detailed project planning and hands-on daily project control are often minimized, if not ignored, especially when organizations try to get several BI applications up and running very quickly. In their shortsightedness, organizations forget that extended planning activities often lead to shorter testing and implementation cycles and thus a shorter delivery time—exactly what the business community wants.

No BI project gets off the ground without a few "kinks and bends"; delays are common. For example, some products may not have enough capacity; others may not work well in a distributed environment. Switching vendors and products can prove costly in terms of time and money. Vendors often cannot offer the comprehensive solutions that businesses expect because the vendors are still struggling to integrate all the pieces of their BI products. This leaves integration up to the organizations' information technology (IT) staffs.

Many organizations do not adequately plan for these types of delays and setbacks, nor do they test their BI concepts and strategies adequately. Setbacks are inevitable on a project as resource intensive as a BI application—even under the best of circumstances. Planning for setbacks will help management set realistic rollout dates for the project.

Describing project management activities in the most simplistic terms, the goal is to answer four basic questions.

1. What will be delivered?
2. When will it be done?
3. How much will it cost?
4. Who will do it?

Figure 3.1: Project Constraints

These questions translate, respectively, into the four major project constraints of scope, effort (time), budget, and resources (Figure 3.1). Before the project manager can create a project plan to address these constraints, he or she must spend some time defining the project to clearly understand the related requirements, risks, constraints, and assumptions.

DEFINING THE BI PROJECT

Project planning includes creating a project charter, which defines the project in terms of:

- Goals and objectives
- Scope (the expected project deliverable)
- Risks
- Constraints
- Assumptions
- Change-control procedures
- Issues management procedures

The project charter is the agreement made between the business sponsor and the IT staff for developing the BI application. If any component of the project charter changes, the entire project has to be reevaluated and all project constraints have to be renegotiated.

Project Goals and Objectives

When defining a BI project, first address the goals and objectives. What is the reason for building this BI application? How much business pain (in hard currency) does that business problem, which the BI application is supposed to solve, currently cause? What are the strategic business drivers? Do the BI project objectives fall in line with the strategic business objectives, or is this someone's pet project?

Project objectives should be measurable statements, such as, "In order to increase market share by 10 percent next year, the sales department must have access to month-end sales data as well as pipeline data merged with prospect data within five business days after the close of the weekly accounting cycle." Project objectives must tie in with the expected ROI. The business representative will have to measure the effectiveness of the delivered BI application and report to the business sponsor whether the project was successful or not.

Project Scope

It is impossible to create valid estimates for a project without a solid understanding of the scope. Traditionally, scope has been measured by the number of functions the system will perform (function point analysis). On BI projects that is a sure way to underestimate effort, budget, and resources. BI applications are data-intensive, not function-intensive. Therefore, scope must be measured by the number of *data elements* that have to be extracted from the source systems, transformed and cleansed, and loaded into the BI target databases.

The main reason for concentrating on data rather than functions is that analyzing and preparing source data takes much longer than providing data access and enabling data analysis through reports and queries. The typical 80/20 rule usually applies: 80 percent effort for data and 20 percent effort for functionality.

Project Risks

Every project is subject to some risks—risks are unavoidable. Such risks could severely affect the project schedule as well as the project deliverables, depending on the likelihood that the risks will materialize and on the impact they would have on the project. Therefore, the risk assessment performed during Step 1, Business Case Assessment, must be reviewed and expanded if necessary. The project manager must identify triggers for each risk and incorporate a mitigation plan as well as a contingency plan into the project plan.

- *Triggers* are situations that signal a potential, perhaps imminent materialization of a risk. For example, if management is reviewing the budget for the project for no apparent reason, this indicates a possible trigger for the risk of losing management support for your BI project.

- The *mitigation plan* specifies what actions the project team can take to prevent the risk from materializing. Continuing with the example above, you could solicit support from your business sponsor and promote the BI initiative to other key executives in your organization to keep management's interest in the BI project. Should the project run into trouble, the risk of having it cancelled is mitigated or prevented.

- The *contingency plan* specifies alternatives in case the risk does materialize. For example, if you lose management support for the BI project due to a long project schedule, plan to shorten the release cycles by delivering a smaller scope sooner. If you lose management support due to the business sponsor's departure from the organization, have an alternate sponsor ready to become the champion for the BI project.

Some common project risks include the following:

- Lack of management commitment
- Lost sponsor
- Lack of business participation
- Imposed, unrealistic schedule
- Unrealistic scope for the schedule
- Unrealistic expectations
- Unrealistic budget
- Untrained or unavailable staff
- Constantly changing business priorities
- Ineffective project management
- Limited scalability

Project Constraints

All projects are subject to the same project constraints mentioned earlier: scope, effort (time), budget, and resources (capable and available people). In reality, there is a fifth constraint: quality. Although quality is a measure of how well the deliverables meet the requirements, it can also be considered a constraint that must be balanced with the other four constraints.

While everyone on the business side and in the IT department wants quality, rarely is the extra time given or taken to achieve it because quality and effort are polarized constraints. Higher quality requires more effort and thus more time to deliver. Since time factors drive most organizations, effort is their number one constraint (highest priority), followed by scope, budget, and resources (usually in that order); and quality gets pushed to the bottom of the heap (lowest priority), as illustrated in Table 3.1. BI project constraints should *never* be in this order.

Fortunately, organizations have full control over changing the priority of project constraints. To insist that time and scope be the top two constraints is acceptable only on projects that have requirements connected to government-imposed regulations. But in most of those cases, the operational systems (and operational reports) are the ones affected by government-imposed deadlines, rarely the downstream strategic decision-support applications. We strongly advise you to get quality out from the bottom of the heap and put scope there because scope can and will continually be expanded through future BI application releases. Table 3.2 shows our recommended order of project constraints.

Assumptions

An assumption is anything taken for granted; it is a supposition or a presumption. It is important to document assumptions because a wrong assumption could very quickly turn into a risk. Here is an example of how two assumptions on a project backfired.

Table 3.1: Typical Order of Project Constraints

| Constraint | Priority (Highest to Lowest) | | | | |
	1	2	3	4	5
Effort (time)	✓				
Scope		✓			
Budget			✓		
Resources				✓	
Quality					✓

Table 3.2: Recommended Order of Project Constraints

Constraint	Priority (Highest to Lowest)				
	1	2	3	4	5
Quality	✓				
Budget		✓			
Resources			✓		
Effort (time)				✓	
Scope					✓

- Assumption 1: "The vendor promises to deliver a new database server in May, and by the end of June the IT staff will install and test a new database management system (DBMS) product on that server. This allows plenty of time before the project deadline, which is September 30, the fiscal year-end."

- Assumption 2: "Joe Bamberg will be the database administrator on the project because he is the only person in our organization who has that particular DBMS skill, which is needed for the project. He has already joined the project team."

- Problems: On June 20 (one month late) the new server finally arrives, and on July 1 Joe Bamberg quits the organization. The new DBMS product does not get installed and tested on the new server until the end of September.

- Impact: The project is delayed by three months at a budget overrun of $60,000 (much of it paid as consulting fees for the high-priced consultant who had to fill in for Joe Bamberg).

Important assumptions should have counterpart risks, in case the assumptions either turn out to be false or do not materialize, as in the example above. For each counterpart risk, identify triggers, a mitigation plan, and a contingency plan.

Change-Control Procedures

Traditional waterfall methodologies became so popular in part because the signed-off, phased development approach attempted to curb scope creep. The mental model was "Change is bad—business people must be held to their decisions." Since BI applications are supposed to be catalysts for improved decision making, the mental model must change to "Change is good—business people should refine and improve their decisions." However, uncontrolled change can still kill a project.

The solution is to manage the changes. Many organizations track their change requests by logging the date of the change request, the name of the requestor, the desired change, to whom it was assigned, and when it was implemented. That is a good practice, but *tracking* changes is not the same thing as *managing* them.

To manage a change, you need to start with a baseline—the agreement between the business sponsor and the IT staff, as documented in the project charter. Every change request, once logged, undergoes an impact analysis and a cost-benefit analysis to determine the effects of the change on the project. Changes, unless they are minute, always impact the three constraints of effort (time), scope, and quality. Some changes also impact the other two constraints (budget and resources). When one constraint changes, the remaining constraints will have to be renegotiated. Unfortunately, business managers and IT managers frequently put the project teams under unwarranted pressure to incorporate scope changes without slipping the schedule.

 It is not rational to request a significant scope change to a carefully deliberated and agreed-upon project plan without adjusting any of the other constraints.

It is not rational because the business representative, the project manager, and the core team members who developed the plan together believed they could complete the project under the agreed-upon constraints. When the scope constraint changes, the plan is no longer doable without changes to some of the other constraints, namely effort (time), budget, resources, and quality, to absorb the impact of the scope change. Therefore, depending on how critical the change request is, the business representative has to decide whether to:

- Cut back from the current scope by eliminating some of the originally requested data and functionality
- Extend the deadline
- Declare the requested change unfeasible at this time and postpone it
- Incorporate the requested change in the next release
- Eliminate complicated transformations, edit checking, and testing, which will impact the quality of the deliverable

Issues Management Procedures

Issues, whether related to business or technical concerns, always come up during projects. Similar to change requests, issues must be not only tracked but also managed. Every issue must be assigned to a person who has the responsibility for its resolution. Any activity regarding the issue must be dated and described on the issues log. At the end of the project, all issues must have a resolution, even if that resolution is a deferral of the issue to a future BI release. Table 3.3 shows an example of an issues log.

Some issues are minor and can be resolved without impact on the project. Other issues can turn into risks or change requests and have to be dealt with accordingly. Therefore, managing issues includes impact analysis and change control.

PLANNING THE BI PROJECT

Project planning is not a one-time activity. Since a project plan is based on estimates, which are frequently no more than best guesses, project plans must be adjusted constantly. The number one telltale sign that a project is not being managed is a static project plan on which estimates and milestones have never changed from the day they were first developed.

Here is the sequence of activities for preparing a project plan.

1. Create a work breakdown structure listing activities, tasks, and subtasks.
2. Estimate the effort hours for these activities, tasks, and subtasks.
3. Assign resources to the activities, tasks, and subtasks.
4. Determine the task dependencies.
5. Determine the resource dependencies.
6. Determine the critical path based on the dependencies.
7. Create the detailed project plan.

Activities and Tasks

BI projects are composed of many activities, each with a long checklist of tasks. Regardless of how experienced the project manager is, it is impossible for any person to remember all the tasks that need to be performed on a BI project. At a

Table 3.3: Issues Log

Issue No.	Issue Date	Issue Description	Assigned To	Action Taken	Action Date	Resolution	Closed Date
001	7/23/ 2003	Delay of server installation expected. Problem with supplier. Impact on project deadline could be one month or more.	Bill	Met with Ron Leard from tech. support to discuss alternatives. He may be able to switch to another supplier. Follow-up in one week.	7/24/ 2003	Switched suppliers. Delay to the project schedule: only three weeks. Delay accepted by Robert Black (sponsor).	8/21/ 2003
				Received call from Ron Leard. He will be able to get a server from another supplier. Delivery date is in one week.	7/31/ 2003		
				Called Ron Leard. Server is installed and being tested. Expected to be available next week.	8/14/ 2003		
				Received call from Ron Leard. Server is available.	8/21/ 2003		

minimum, the project manager must rely on some existing comprehensive list of the most necessary activities. Naturally, not all activities have to be performed on every project. Not even every step has to be performed on every project. The project manager selects the minimum number of steps and activities needed to produce an acceptable deliverable under the imposed constraints.

The development approach in *Business Intelligence Roadmap* is neither as linear nor as rigorous as that followed in traditional methodologies. It is a much more dynamic approach to application development. When using our development approach, it may often look and feel like you are working on a prototype— but it is *not* a prototype. The same discipline applied under a traditional methodology must be applied to BI projects in terms of controlling scope, mitigating risks, and time-boxing weekly activities. (*Time-boxing* refers to planning, assigning, and managing activities on a detailed level in weekly increments.) Despite the discipline, you must expect constant rework during the development cycle and build time for it into the project plan. For example, analysis activities can show up on your project plan as early as Step 3, Project Planning, and as late as Step 12, Application Development. Or you may want to plan another short iteration through database design activities during Step 11: Extract/Transform/Load Development.

The project plan must reflect this dynamic nature of application development. Since changes and setbacks are to be expected, certain "completed activities" will have to be revisited and reworked. The project plan should anticipate that and reflect it on the schedule. The easiest way to plan for these internal iterations is to use the concept of "looping" or "refactoring" by dividing the project into multiple small subprojects, each with a deliverable, albeit not completed. Then revisit and revise each deliverable, adding more data and more functionality until the entire BI application is completed with the desired deliverable. This iterative refinement approach gives the project development effort the feeling of prototyping.

Estimating Techniques

Once you have selected the activities and tasks for the project and organized the project into subprojects, you can derive the base estimates by using one of three methods:

1. *Historical,* based on learned patterns (how long it took on the last project)

2. *Intuitive,* based on intuition and experience ("gut" estimating)

3. *Formulaic,* based on the average of possibilities (Figure 3.2)

$$\frac{\text{Best Estimate} + (4 \times \text{Average Estimate}) + \text{Worst Estimate}}{6}$$

Figure 3.2: Formula-Based Estimating

Estimating BI project activities is much more difficult than estimating traditional projects because no two BI projects are alike. For example, you may use a new tool, work with new team members, or have no experience with a new design method. All three estimating techniques listed above expect you to relate to some prior project experience.

- The historical estimating technique expects you to have statistics on how long similar projects took in the past—but you may not have had a similar project before.

- The intuitive estimating technique expects you to predict, or guess, based on prior experience how long it will take to complete a similar activity—but you may have never performed a similar activity.

- The formula-based estimating technique expects you to know the longest time it may take to complete an activity, the shortest time, and the most probable time—but you would not know what the longest, shortest, and most probable times for an activity could be if you had never performed that activity before.

In all those cases, it is best to consult with other people (in-house staff or outside consultants) who have already developed a similar BI application because your own uneducated guesses may be gross underestimates. This also demonstrates how important it is to track actual time on BI projects. You will need that information for estimating your next BI project.

Resource Assignment

Effort estimates cannot be completed until the activities and tasks are assigned because the estimates must take into consideration each team member's skills and subject matter expertise as well as the environmental factors that affect him or her.

- *Skills*—the ability to perform specific tasks. Has the team member done this type of work before?

Table 3.4: Environmental Factors That Can Affect Team Members' Availability

Administrative Factors	*Non-Work-Related Factors*
Lack of computer access	Vacation
Time required to troubleshoot other systems	Illness
	Jury duty
Meetings	Personal time off
E-mails and in-baskets	Medical appointments
Training seminars	Religious holidays

- *Subject matter expertise*—the possession of facts or concepts about a specific subject matter. Is the team member an expert in this business area?
- *Environmental factors*—administrative and non-work-related activities. Table 3.4 lists some examples.

Task Dependencies

Not all activities and tasks have to be performed serially—many can be performed in parallel as long as there is sufficient staff. The first step in determining which tasks can be performed in parallel is to identify task dependencies and develop the critical path. Most project-planning tools support the four types of task dependencies (Figure 3.3). *Finish to Start* and *Start to Start* are the most common task dependencies; *Start to Finish* is the most infrequent.

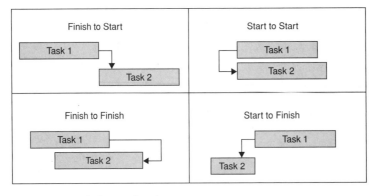

Figure 3.3: Task Dependencies

1. *Finish to Start* indicates that Task 2 cannot start until Task 1 finishes.
2. *Start to Start* indicates that Task 2 can start at the same time as Task 1.
3. *Finish to Finish* indicates that Task 2 cannot finish until Task 1 finishes.
4. *Start to Finish* indicates that Task 2 cannot finish until Task 1 starts.

The more tasks that can be performed simultaneously, the faster the project will get done. To take advantage of task dependencies, you need the right number of resources with the right skills at the right time.

Resource Dependencies

A shortage of staff can quickly reverse the benefits of having few task dependencies. For example, tasks that could have been performed in parallel but cannot be assigned to multiple staff members because of a staff shortage must revert to being executed in sequence. Figure 3.4 shows how four tasks can be accomplished in 10 days with adequate staffing; Figure 3.5 shows that it will take 14 days to complete the same tasks if only one person is available to work on them. (Note that in Figure 3.5 the time required to compile the findings is reduced by one day because there is no longer a need for two analysts to collaborate.)

Critical Path Method

Once you have identified the task dependencies and leveled the resources (that is, assigned the tasks and adjusted the dependencies for the available resources), use

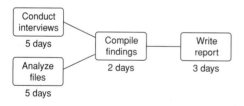

Figure 3.4: Elapsed Days When Two People Can Work on the Tasks

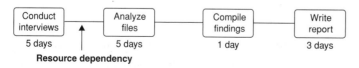

Figure 3.5: Elapsed Days When Only One Person Is Available

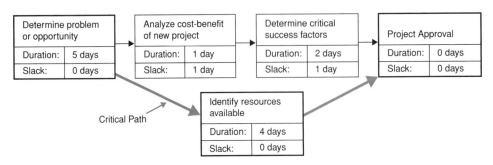

Figure 3.6: Critical Path Method

the critical path method (CPM) to outline task duration, indicating any lag time for tasks not on the critical path (Figure 3.6). This provides the visibility needed to reassign resources or to renegotiate project constraints.

In this example, the task "Identify resources available" can be performed in parallel with the tasks "Analyze cost-benefit of new project" and "Determine critical success factors." Since the task "Identify resources available" is estimated to take 4 days, and the other two tasks combined are estimated to take only 3 days, the task "Identify resources available" is on the critical path. If this task were to take 5 days to complete instead of 4, it would delay the milestone "Project approval" by one day. However, if either of the other two tasks were delayed by one day, it would not affect the milestone "Project approval."

Project Schedules

Once you have determined all the tasks, resources, dependencies, and estimates, you can schedule the project on the calendar. The most common and most familiar representation of a project schedule is a Gantt chart. Figure 3.7 shows an example.

Creating a useful project plan requires some effort, but maintaining the project plan (adjusting it) is not as labor intensive as it used to be prior to the availability of project management tools. Becoming proficient on a sophisticated project management tool takes some time and requires a solid understanding of project management principles.

Once you key into the tool all the planning components (e.g., tasks, estimates, resources, dependencies), any adjustments you subsequently make to the components automatically cascade through the entire project plan, updating all

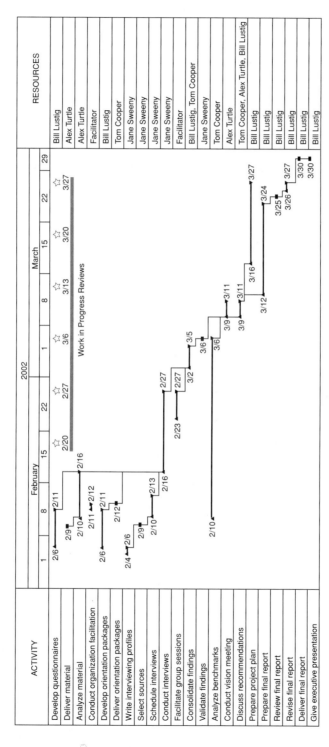

Figure 3.7: Example of a Gantt Chart

charts and reports. Although the results must still be reviewed and validated, an experienced project manager who is skilled on the project management tool does not need to become a slave to the tool or to the project planning activities.

PROJECT PLANNING ACTIVITIES

The project planning activities do not need to be performed linearly. Figure 3.8 indicates which activities can be performed concurrently. The list below briefly describes the activities associated with Step 3, Project Planning.

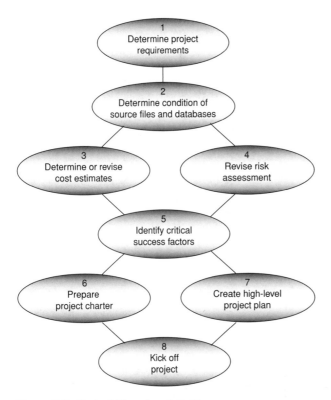

Figure 3.8: Project Planning Activities

1. Determine the project requirements.

You may have already prepared the objectives for the project and some high-level requirements for the proposed scope during Step 1, Business Case Assessment. However, most likely they are not of sufficient detail to start the planning process. As part of the scope definition, review and revise the following requirements: data, functionality (reports and queries), and infrastructure (technical and nontechnical).

2. **Determine the condition of the source files and databases.**

   You can neither complete the project schedule nor commit to a delivery date without a good understanding of the condition of the source files and databases. Take some time to review the data content of these operational files and databases. Although you will perform detailed source data analysis during Step 5, Data Analysis, right now you need to glean just enough information to make an educated guess about the effort needed for data cleansing.

3. **Determine or revise the cost estimates.**

   Detailed cost estimates must include hardware and network costs as well as purchase prices and annual maintenance fees for tools. In addition, you must ascertain the costs for contractors, consultants, and training. A more indirect cost is associated with the learning curve for the business and IT staff members. Remember to factor that into the cost estimates as well as the time estimates.

4. **Revise the risk assessment.**

   Review and revise the risk assessment performed during Step 1, Business Case Assessment (or perform a risk assessment now if you skipped that step). Rank each risk on a scale of 1 to 5 according to the severity of its impact on the BI project, with 1 indicating low impact and 5 indicating high impact. Similarly, rank the likelihood of each risk materializing, with 1 being "probably won't happen" and 5 being "we can almost count on it."

5. **Identify critical success factors.**

   A critical success factor is a condition that must exist for the project to have a high chance for success. Some common critical success factors are a proactive and very supportive business sponsor, full-time involvement of a business representative, realistic budgets and schedules, realistic expectations, and a core team with the right skill set.

6. **Prepare the project charter.**

   The project charter is similar to a scope agreement, a document of understanding, or a statement of work. However, the project charter is much more detailed than the usual 3- to 4-page general overview of the project that contains only a brief description of resources, costs, and schedule. The project charter is a 20- to 30-page document developed by the core team, which includes the business representative. Present the project charter and the project plan to the business sponsor for approval.

7. **Create a high-level project plan.**
   Project plans are usually presented in the form of a Gantt chart that shows activities, tasks, resources, dependencies, and effort mapped out on a calendar (Figure 3.7). Some project managers also create Pert charts, which show the graphic representation of the CPM on the calendar.

8. **Kick off the project.**
   Once you have planned the project, assigned the resources, and scheduled the training, you are ready to kick off the project. This is usually accomplished with an orientation meeting for the entire team (the core team members as well as the extended team members). Project kickoff should also include setting up communication channels (e.g., newsletters, e-mails, Web pages) with the rest of the organization to keep stakeholders and interested parties up-to-date on the project's progress.

DELIVERABLES RESULTING FROM THESE ACTIVITIES

1. **Project charter**
   This document represents the agreement between the IT staff and the business sponsor about the definition, scope, constraints, and schedule of the BI project. It also serves as the baseline for all change requests. A project charter contains the following sections:
   - Goals and objectives (both strategic goals for the organization and specific objectives for the BI project)
   - Statement of the business problem
   - Proposed BI solution
   - Results from the cost-benefit analysis
   - Results from the infrastructure gap analysis (technical and nontechnical)
   - Functional project deliverables (reports, queries, Web portal)
   - Historical requirements (how many years of history to store)
   - Subject area to be delivered
   - Entities (objects), significant attributes, relationships (high-level logical data model)
   - Items not within the project scope (originally requested but subsequently excluded from the scope)
   - Condition of source files and databases
   - Availability and security requirements
   - Access tool requirements

- Roles and responsibilities
- Team structure for core team and extended team members
- Communication plan
- Assumptions
- Constraints
- Risk assessment
- Critical success factors

2. **Project plan**

A project plan may contain multiple graphs (such as a CPM chart, a Pert chart, or a Gantt chart) detailing task estimates, task dependencies, and resource dependencies. Most project-planning tools can also produce additional tabular reports on resources and schedule.

Roles Involved in These Activities

◆ **Application lead developer**

The application lead developer works closely with the data administrator and the database administrator to understand the data access, data analysis, and general data requirements as well as the tool capabilities. He or she must estimate the effort for application prototyping and development, which the project manager will include in the project plan.

◆ **Business representative**

Although the business representative does not actively produce estimates for the work to be performed by the technicians, he or she must be involved in the entire planning process in order to negotiate the project constraints. The business representative must also understand how much of his or her time will be required on the BI project and what is expected of him or her.

◆ **Data administrator**

The data administrator needs to participate in the requirements discussions in order to determine the data scope of the BI project. The data administrator will provide any data models that exist for the objects and data elements in the requested subject area. If no data models exist, the data administrator can draw a straw-man model (that is, a first-cut draft of a logical data model) and use it to validate the understanding of the requirements and the scope. The data administrator works with the data quality analyst to assess the condition of the source files and databases.

◆ **Data quality analyst**

The main responsibility of the data quality analyst is to assess the condition of the source files and databases and to estimate the data-cleansing effort based on that assessment. To assess the quality of the source data quickly, the data quality analyst can use the functions of a data-cleansing tool, or he or she can write customized domain analysis reports.

◆ **Database administrator**

The database administrator needs to understand the scope and schedule of the project from the DBMS perspective so that he or she can be available for database design and application design activities, as well as ongoing project reviews.

◆ **ETL lead developer**

The ETL lead developer works with the data administrator and the data quality analyst to understand what types of data transformations and data cleansing the BI application will require. Based on the condition of the source files and databases, he or she will give ETL estimates to the project manager for the project plan.

◆ **Meta data administrator**

The meta data administrator is responsible for defining the tasks and estimates for the meta data repository track. Working closely with the data administrator, the meta data administrator has to start exploring what the meta data requirements for this BI project are and whether they can be met with the current meta data repository (if one exists). He or she has to determine the meta data repository effort for the project plan.

◆ **Project manager**

BI projects are not for rookie project managers. The project manager must have successfully managed several large projects before. The project manager must also be familiar with a project management tool to minimize the time required for preparing charts and reports.

◆ **Subject matter expert**

The subject matter expert will assist the other team members in preparing the project plan and the project charter. Either the subject matter expert or the business representative must be an active, full-time participant in this step.

RISKS OF NOT PERFORMING STEP 3

It is impossible to build a BI application ad hoc without a plan. You may as well take a dart, throw it at a calendar, and commit to the date the dart hits. In other words, the project will veer out of control if it is not planned well. You may miss deadlines, have runaway expenses without accountability, implement the wrong solution—or you may never get to the implementation. A BI decision-support environment is very complicated, and BI projects are very costly. The risks of undertaking such projects without adequate planning and control are unacceptable.

BIBLIOGRAPHY AND ADDITIONAL READING

Adelman, Sid, and Larissa Terpeluk Moss. *Data Warehouse Project Management.* Boston, MA: Addison-Wesley, 2000.

Adelman, Sid, et al. *Impossible Data Warehouse Situations: Solutions from the Experts.* Boston, MA: Addison-Wesley, 2003.

Brooks, Frederick P., Sr. *The Mythical Man-Month: Essays on Software Engineering, Second Edition.* Reading, MA: Addison-Wesley, 1995.

Charvat, Jason. *Project Management Nation: Tools, Techniques, and Goals for the New and Practicing IT Project Manager.* New York: John Wiley & Sons, 2001.

DeMarco, Tom. *Slack: Getting Past Burnout, Busywork, and the Myth of Total Efficiency.* New York: Broadway Books, 2001.

Humphrey, Watts S. *Winning with Software: An Executive Strategy.* Boston, MA: Addison-Wesley, 2002.

Jarke, Matthias, Maurizio Lenzerini, Yannis Vassiliou, and Panos Vassiliadis. *Fundamentals of Data Warehouses.* New York: Springer, 2000.

Lewis, James P. *The Project Manager's Desk Reference, Second Edition.* McGraw-Hill Trade, 1999.

Marmel, Elaine. *Microsoft Project 2000 Bible.* New York: John Wiley & Sons, 2000.

Moeller, R. A. *Distributed Data Warehousing Using Web Technology: How to Build a More Cost-Effective and Flexible Warehouse.* New York: AMACOM American Management Association, 2001.

Yourdon, Edward. *Death March.* Upper Saddle River, NJ: Prentice Hall, 1997.

Project Management Institute: *http://www.pmi.org* .

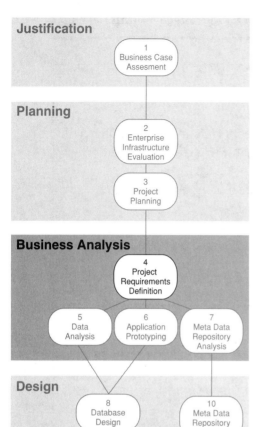

Justification

1
Business Case
Assesment

Planning

2
Enterprise
Infrastructure
Evaluation

3
Project
Planning

Business Analysis

4
Project
Requirements
Definition

5
Data
Analysis

6
Application
Prototyping

7
Meta Data
Repository
Analysis

Design

8
Database
Design

10
Meta Data
Repository
Design

9
ETL
Design

Construction

12
Application
Development

14
Meta Data
Repository
Development

11
ETL
Development

13
Data
Mining

Deployment

15
Implementation

16
Release
Evaluation

CHAPTER FOUR

Step 4: Project Requirements Definition

CHAPTER OVERVIEW

This chapter covers the following topics:

- Things to consider when defining requirements

- The differences between general business requirements and project-specific requirements

- The appropriate people to interview to determine general business requirements

- The sections to complete in a business requirements report

- The appropriate people to interview when gathering project-specific requirements for a BI application

- The sections to include in an application requirements document

- Interviewing considerations and interviewing tips

- Brief descriptions of the activities involved in requirements definition, the deliverables resulting from those activities, and the roles involved

- The risks of not performing Step 4

THINGS TO CONSIDER

Functional Requirements

✓ What types of information do the business people in our organization need? What types of business questions are they unable to answer today and why?

✓ What reports do they want?

✓ Which reports are most important? Which are least important? Which reports can be replaced with "canned" queries?

✓ What types of queries will the business analysts run?

✓ Who will administer the query libraries and set up the universes, for example, data views in online analytical processing (OLAP) tools?

✓ Are the business analysts and knowledge workers planning to write many ad hoc queries? Can we get some samples of old queries from them?

Data Requirements

✓ What data do the business people need? Where do they get that data today?

✓ How clean is the data today? How clean does it have to be?

✓ What data is considered most critical to the business?

✓ Can the data be summarized? If yes, by what dimensions?

✓ Will the business analysts want the capability to drill down to the detail? How granular does the detail have to be?

✓ Do other business people need the same data? Do we know who they are? Will they be available to validate the meta data?

✓ What are the expectations for the timeliness of the data and the availability of the data?

Historical Requirements

✓ How many years of history do we need to keep?

✓ Can we start collecting history from this point forward or do we have to load data from old archived files?

Security Requirements

✓ How secure does the data have to be? What type of security exists on the operational source data?

✓ Are the security requirements homogeneous (should all the data have the same level of security)?

✓ Who should have access to the data?

> **Performance Requirements**
>
> ✓ What is the slowest response time the business people will accept for a query?
> ✓ Can reports be run overnight rather than during the day in order to avoid resource contention with interactive usage of the BI target databases?
> ✓ How often and for how long will knowledge workers and business analysts access the BI target databases during the day for ad hoc reporting and data analysis?

Requirements come in two flavors: (1) general high-level business requirements for the BI decision-support environment, which are identified at the onset of a BI initiative and are periodically reviewed, and (2) project-specific requirements, which concentrate on the detailed deliverables expected from each BI application release. Table 4.1 lists the differences between the two types of requirements.

Table 4.1: General Business Requirements versus Project-Specific Requirements

	General Business Requirements	*Project-Specific Requirements*
Purpose	• Determine the general business needs of the organization for a BI decision-support environment	• Define the specific functions and data to be delivered at the end of a BI project
Interviewees	• Business executives • Information technology (IT) managers • IT staff • Line-of-business managers • Subject matter experts	• Business sponsor • Business representative • "Power users" • Stakeholders (knowledge workers, business analysts, data owners) • Subject matter experts
Deliverable	• Business requirements report	• Application requirements document
Content of deliverable	• Findings • Issues • Opportunities • Recommendations • Next steps	• Functional requirements • Data requirements • Data-cleansing requirements • Security requirements • Performance requirements • Availability requirements

GENERAL BUSINESS REQUIREMENTS

Marketing strategies often propel the BI decision-support initiatives at organizations because of the constant challenge to keep up with the competition and to retain market share. To a large degree, it is the marketing focus that drives the impetus for more knowledge about the business, in particular about its customers. Marketing strategies have had an impact on the evolution of decision-support systems since the early days of IT. Figure 4.1 shows the effect this evolution has had on increasing the decision-support value of customer-centric applications.

- **Traditional decision-support systems** focused on product-related operational processes of the organization. Decision-support capabilities were limited, and marketing efforts revolved around products, not customers.

- **Customer information files** were the first attempt to aggregate all customer-related data from dozens, if not hundreds, of disparate operational systems into one central file. Decision-support focus started to shift from products to customers.

- **House-holding databases** contained customer hierarchies in order to help business managers understand customer-to-customer relationships. These databases also contained organizational hierarchies in order to help business executives understand organizational and regional profitability. House-holding was the rudimentary precursor of customer relationship management (CRM).

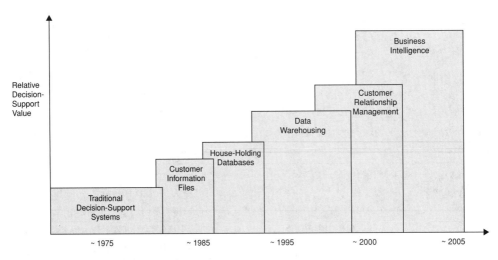

Figure 4.1: Increasing Decision-Support Value

- **Data warehousing** was the first ambitious undertaking of cross-organizational integration of data for decision-support purposes, such as sales reporting, key performance indicators, performance trend analysis, and so on. Due to the enormous effort involved, a wave of new tools started to flood the market, with extract/transform/load (ETL) and OLAP tools leading the pack.

- **Customer relationship management** focuses on customer-product (sales) relationships, as well as on customer service, customer buying behavior, and other knowledge about customers. The goal is to improve customer sales and services through personalization and mass customization.

- **Business intelligence** is a more holistic and sophisticated approach to cross-organizational decision-support needs. It uses data mining to gain hidden (nonexplicit) knowledge about customers, general market conditions, and competitive products. The goal is to "predict" the future by analyzing the present, thereby gaining a competitive edge.

Besides marketing, other departments in the organization are also keen to take advantage of today's technologies to solve their business needs. Such departments include finance, product management, portfolio management, customer service, engineering, and inventory management, to name a few.

Interviewees for General Business Requirements

Determining the general business needs of the organization requires interviewing individuals at every level of the organizational hierarchy, both on the business side and on the IT side.

- **Business executives** are the visionaries. They know which direction the organization should move and how to achieve new goals. They also know what the organization's business pains are. The business executives' requirements will be focused around strategic information from the BI decision-support environment.

- **IT managers** support the operational systems of the business areas. They know the deficiencies of these systems very well, and they are aware of the backlog for decision-support requirements. Their input can be helpful in identifying unfulfilled decision-support requirements and in determining how the BI application can improve the workload for IT.

- **IT staff** work directly with the business staff. The IT staff have firsthand knowledge of the unfulfilled requirements. They also know the technical skills of the business people with whom they work. This information will become valuable input for access and analysis tool selection.

- **Line-of-business managers** are responsible for the smooth operations of the organization. They focus on tactical decisions on a daily basis. Their requirements frequently include a mixture of strategic information and operational information.

- **Subject matter experts** are the senior business analysts with the 10,000-foot view of a department or a division. Sometimes they are the "power users"; other times they act as internal business consultants. In addition to having an overall business view, subject matter experts are usually very familiar with detailed operational data and can give a lot of insights into current data quality problems.

Data Quality Requirements

Data quality must be discussed with all interviewees. Questions to ask fall into three categories: existing data quality, desired data quality, and prioritization for data cleansing.

1. **Existing data quality:** Different interviewees might have a different perspective of what is clean and what is not. They will also have a different perspective of what should be cleansed and what can remain "dirty."

2. **Desired data quality:** Knowledge workers "in the trenches" typically have a higher tolerance for dirty data than business executives do, mainly because the knowledge workers have learned over the years how to decipher and interpret their bad data.

3. **Prioritization for data cleansing:** Critical and important data must be sorted out from insignificant data. Business executives and line-of-business managers should make that decision.

Data quality affects business people in all critical business areas of an organization, especially strategic decision-makers, business operations staff, customer support staff, and marketing staff.

- **Strategic decision-makers:** Probably more than anyone else, strategic decision-makers (the business executives of the organizations) are affected by poor-quality data. The decisions they make have an effect on the organizational lifeline.

- **Business operations staff:** Line-of-business managers and their staff could be much more efficient if they did not have to constantly resolve errors and waste time on rework.

- **Customer support staff:** The customer representatives and the sales force have direct contact with the organizations' customers. Poor-quality data puts a tremendous burden on this group to keep the customers satisfied and to prevent them from leaving.

- **Marketing staff:** Managers and knowledge workers in the marketing department do not want to waste millions of dollars by soliciting customers who are not worth soliciting, by sending marketing materials to customers who have moved, or by pursuing dissatisfied customers who have defected to the competition.

Business Requirements Report

The deliverable from a high-level business requirements activity is a report on the findings, issues, opportunities, recommendations, and next steps, as shown in Figure 4.2.

Findings, Issues, Opportunities   Recommendations   Next Steps

Figure 4.2: Business Requirements Report Content

- **Findings:** The compilation of all requirements from the interviewees should be sorted by topic. Each finding should be associated with the interviewees and the interview dates.

- **Issues:** A separate list should highlight critical business issues, so that these issues can be addressed immediately. Not all business issues require a BI solution.

- **Opportunities:** Obvious business opportunities should also be extracted and highlighted from the findings. Again, not all business opportunities will translate into BI requirements.

- **Recommendations:** After analyzing the findings, issues, and opportunities, a list of recommendations should be added. These can be recommendations for correcting a problem on the existing systems or for building a new BI solution.

• **Next steps:** Certain recommended actions are more critical than others, and some recommended actions may depend on the completion of others. This section of the report should list the prioritized sequence of actions to be taken toward implementing a BI solution.

This report is not listed as a deliverable for a BI project because it occurs outside of an already approved BI project. It may be used in lieu of a business case assessment report, if the business case assessment is high-level and not specific to a BI application.

PROJECT-SPECIFIC REQUIREMENTS

Requirements gathering for a specific project deliverable focuses on defining the explicit business needs of the business sponsor for whom the BI application is being developed. The project requirements should be stated in business terms and should describe the business problem to be solved as well as the acceptance criteria for the BI solution. Figure 4.3 shows an example of a requirements statement.

 A precompiled wish list of data elements and a stack of mock reports do not constitute a requirements definition.

"It currently takes us 3 weeks to compile sales data from all regions and another 3 weeks to analyze it and make an investment correction. Every week of delay is costing us an estimated $50,000. Our expectation is to reduce the delay to 1 week. If we could have the data integrated and available within 3 days after close of business, and if we could have the following query capabilities . . . , we could complete our analysis in 2 days. In order to do that we require the following data. . . ."

Figure 4.3: Requirements Definition Statement

The application requirements document must clearly state the BI project objectives and expected deliverables in terms of:

- Nature of the existing business problem
- Damage (lost business opportunity, exceeded operating costs) caused to the organization by the existing business problem
- Why the problems cannot be solved without a BI solution
- How the BI application will solve the problem
- Detailed requirements for reports and canned queries on the desired subject areas
- Requirements for graphical representation tools, such as OLAP
- Prioritized, detailed data requirements for:
  - All data required for the BI target database(s) as well as for reports and queries
  - All potential data source files and source databases

 Source data requirements should be defined in as much detail as possible and as early as possible to enable rigorous source data analysis in the next step. Waiting until the design stage to determine how to source the BI target databases is too late.

- Prioritized, detailed functional requirements for the data-cleansing transformations
- Requirements for historical data (how many years of history)
- Required security features
- Requested service-level agreements (SLAs) for query response time, data cleanliness, hours and days of the BI application's availability, and tool functionality

 Defining requirements is a different activity than designing a solution. Exercise caution—do not jump into designing the BI application at this time, as many technicians tend to do.

Interviewees for Project-Specific Requirements

The interviews for project-specific requirements are limited to those individuals who are directly involved with the BI project and those who are directly impacted by the BI application.

- The **business representative** should provide the details about the work he or she is performing. It is important to understand the business workflow and where the bottlenecks are since they point to potential challenges with the data or the functionality. Overlooking these challenges could possibly lead to underestimating the project effort.

- The **business sponsor** sets the objectives for the BI application and states the business need as well as the expectations for the return on investment. He or she should prioritize the requested deliverables if the scope is too large given the project constraints of effort (time), budget, resources, and quality.

- **"Power users"** often perform the analysis functions, which the BI application is supposed to replace. They have a wealth of information about the detailed requirements for solving the stated business problem.

- **Stakeholders** could be other knowledge workers, business analysts, or business managers who are performing similar functions and who will use the data in the BI target databases for their own decision-support needs. The BI project team should identify these stakeholders early to determine potential overlapping needs. Stakeholders could also be the data owners. The data owners should always be included in the interviewing process because it is their responsibility to verify that their data is being used and interpreted correctly.

- **Subject matter experts** could be the same people as the "power users" or could be senior business analysts. They, along with the business representative, are the prime interviewees for project-specific requirements.

Application Requirements Document

The deliverable from a project-specific requirements definition activity is a requirements document itemizing the detailed functional requirements, the detailed data requirements, and the potential sources of data. This document should also detail the requirements for data cleansing, performance, data security, and availability, as shown in Figure 4.4.

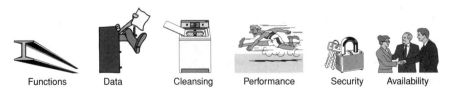

Functions   Data   Cleansing   Performance   Security   Availability

Figure 4.4: Application Requirements Document Content

- **Functions:** All functional requirements for reporting and for data access and analysis should be listed and prioritized. This includes contents and algorithms for reports and queries, ad hoc capabilities, Web displays, and other graphical representations. Summarization and aggregation requests as well as drill-down capabilities must be described as well.

- **Data:** The desired subject areas (e.g., product, customer, orders, campaign) should be confirmed, and the required data elements should be defined. Be judicious about the data scope because going after too much data "just in case they'll need it some day" leads to more complex data models and more time and money spent for data extraction, cleansing, and maintenance.

 IT technicians can help identify which source data may *not* have to be included in the BI target databases based on current low usage of data. However, the final decision on whether or not to include rarely used source data must be made by a business person, not by IT.

In addition, all previously identified potential source files and source databases should be reviewed. If storing history is a requirement, the archived source files must also be identified and reviewed. Additional data-specific requirements should be defined, such as data load frequency (e.g., daily, weekly, monthly) and data security.

- **Data cleansing:** The list of requested data elements must be prioritized into critical, important, and insignificant categories. The tolerance level for dirty data must be defined for each data element in the critical category, for example, "Monthly Sales Total: dirty data threshold = 2 percent; Daily Average Portfolio Amount: dirty data threshold = 0.05 percent." Next, the dirty data tolerance level must be defined for each data element in the important category. Insignificant data elements are often passed across without cleansing, mainly due to time constraints.

- **Performance:** Most knowledge workers of operational systems are accustomed to subsecond response times. Expectations must be set and managed in this respect. Techniques and technologies can improve report and query response times, but rarely—if ever—will the response times be as low as subseconds. The question to ask is not what the *desired* response time is but what an *acceptable* response time is, followed by the question of how much business management is willing to pay in order to get a better response time.

- **Security:** Since the data in the BI target databases is the same data as in the operational systems, it should be given similar security considerations. Some exceptions may apply if the data is highly summarized and no drill down to the detail is allowed or even available.

- **Availability:** Requests for 24/7 availability are rarely valid since a BI decision-support environment primarily supports strategic decision making. The requirement for 24/7 availability is typically an operational requirement. However, it could be valid under some circumstances, such as for international companies that have offices around the globe and that will access a centralized database. In addition to determining hours and days of availability, the percentage of availability during scheduled hours should also be specified, for example, "97 percent availability Monday through Saturday between 5 A.M. and 11 P.M. EST and 90 percent availability Sunday between 5 A.M. and 3 P.M. EST."

THE INTERVIEWING PROCESS

The more detailed the requirements document, the more the scope can be solidified and the more the estimates for the effort can be validated. To accumulate the necessary details in order to understand the business process, the interview team must spend some time interviewing all the stakeholders of the application and studying their environment. When documenting the project requirements, use graphic techniques whenever possible, such as bubble charts, cause-and-effect diagrams, entity-relationship diagrams, star schema models, and even functional decomposition diagrams and data flow diagrams where appropriate. Diagrams make excellent communication tools. Through visualization, the interviewee can better verify the interviewer's understanding of the requirements.

Interviewing Considerations

Before scheduling the interviews, some preparation is required. Figure 4.5 lists items that need to be considered for the interviewing process.

Interview Team   Interviewees   Research   Questionnaire   Schedule

Figure 4.5: Items to Consider for the Interviewing Process

- **Interview team:** Preferably, the interviewer should not conduct the interview and take notes at the same time. He or she should team up with a "scribe" who can take notes during the interviews. It is difficult to keep the momentum of the meeting going if you have to ask the questions, write down the answers, and think of the next question to ask all at the same time.

- **Interviewees:** Interviews can be conducted with individuals or groups of individuals. Group interviews work well among peers from the same work area if they share similar responsibilities. What one person says often triggers a thought in another person. This synergy can be very productive. The drawback of group interviewing is that some interviewees may not be as honest or forthcoming in their responses. The most effective approach to interviewing is often a balance between individual interviews and group interviews.

- **Research:** Before scheduling the interviews, the interviewer should spend some time researching existing documents, reports, and Web sites, including competitors' Web sites. It helps to have as much understanding as possible of the industry, the business processes, and the organization's terminology and acronyms.

- **Questionnaire:** A questionnaire for the major topics should be prepared and mailed to the interviewees before the scheduled interviews. That gives the interviewees a chance to prepare and to bring supporting documentation to the interview.

- **Interview schedule:** Do not schedule more than four one-hour interviews per day because it will take at least one hour after each interview to review, fill in, or clarify the interview notes. It is imperative to complete or rewrite the notes taken during an interview on the same day of that interview, so that no ambiguity or incompleteness remains.

Interviewing Tips

The following interviewing practices can make the process run smoothly and effectively:

- The initial interview should focus on the basic requirements necessary to solve a specific business problem. Do not dwell on any of the mechanical and logistical aspects, and do not promise anything hastily. There will be time to get into detailed analysis later.

- Frequently, interviewees will be quite comfortable telling you what they currently have, but they can provide only minimal insight into what they want but do not have. Be prepared to guide them with leading questions.

- Be prepared to hear and resolve conflicting views and priorities. This is especially true when speaking with knowledge workers, business analysts, and business managers from different departments and from different levels of the organizational hierarchy.

- Taking notes usually involves a fair amount of scribbling (or, if using a laptop, a fair amount of abbreviating). While the discussions are still fresh in the minds of the interviewer and the scribe, they should review the notes immediately after each interview and expand on the scribbles and abbreviations. By the end of the day, the notes must be in such condition that they can be understood several days or weeks later.

- Tape recording interviews can be very helpful when the interview team consists of only one person. Making a tape allows the interviewer to concentrate on the questioning rather than on note taking. It is imperative to ask the interviewees for their permission to record the interview session. Many interviewees do not like to be recorded, and other interviewees may not be as forthcoming and honest when they know they are being recorded.

- As soon as time permits after each interview, transcribe the interview notes into a clean interview notes document and send it to all interviewees who participated in that interview for their approval. Ask the interviewees to change any misinterpretations and add anything they forgot to mention during the interview.

PROJECT REQUIREMENTS DEFINITION ACTIVITIES

The activities for defining project requirements do not need to be performed linearly. Figure 4.6 indicates which activities can be performed concurrently. The list below briefly describes the activities associated with Step 4, Project Requirements Definition.

1. **Define the requirements for technical infrastructure enhancements.**
   You should have already reviewed the technical infrastructure components to determine whether they can support the BI application or whether changes are required. Requirements for technical infrastructure components could include one or more of the following:
   – New or additional hardware
   – New database management system (DBMS) or upgrades to the existing DBMS
   – New development tools

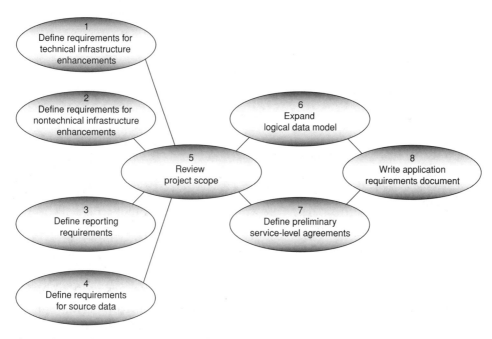

Figure 4.6: Project Requirements Definition Activities

  − New data access or reporting tools
  − New data mining tool
  − New meta data repository or enhancements to it
  − New network requirements

2. **Define the requirements for nontechnical infrastructure enhancements.**
   You should have also reviewed and evaluated the nontechnical infrastructure
   components. If changes are required, define these requirements now. Non-
   technical infrastructure components to be added or revised could include:
   − Estimating guidelines
   − Roles and responsibilities
   − Standards
   − Procedures for:
     » Use of a methodology
     » Scope management (change control)
     » Issues management
     » Security process
     » SLAs

» Prioritization
» Testing process
» Support functions
» Dispute resolution
» Meta data capture and meta data delivery
» Data quality measures and triage process
» Communication

3. **Define the reporting requirements.**

    During the interview process, collect or create sample report layouts and queries. Define and document business rules for deriving data and for creating aggregations and summaries. It is advisable to determine who will be the stewards of the query libraries and universes (data views in OLAP tools).

4. **Define the requirements for source data.**

    Define the detailed data requirements and select the most appropriate source files and source databases from the potential list of sources created during prior steps. Spend some time on defining the data-cleansing requirements and the critical business rules for the data. Perform some cursory data analysis on suspected poor-quality data so that the scope and the effort estimates created during Step 3, Project Planning, can be validated.

5. **Review the project scope.**

    Compare the detailed requirements to the high-level scope in the project charter. Determine whether the scope is still doable and whether the estimates are still realistic. If you have learned something that puts the commitment in the project charter in question, it is time to renegotiate.

6. **Expand the logical data model.**

    A high-level logical data model was probably produced during earlier steps (Step 1, Business Case Assessment, or Step 3, Project Planning). Using the information from the interview sessions, expand the logical data model with newly discovered entities, relationships, and attributes. If a logical data model was not produced during prior steps, create a high-level logical data model for the data requirements in preparation for the data analysis activities.

7. **Define preliminary service-level agreements.**

    Although many technicians may argue that it is much too early to commit to SLAs, most business people will ask for them because they constitute the acceptance criteria. It is best to find the outermost acceptable limits for each of the following SLAs and refine them as the project progresses:

– Availability
– Security
– Response time
– Data cleanliness
– Ongoing support

8. **Write the application requirements document.**

In the application requirements document, itemize the requirements for functions, data, cleansing, performance, security, and availability. In addition, list the requirements for enhancing technical and nontechnical infrastructure components during the BI project. Include the high-level logical data model in this document.

DELIVERABLE RESULTING FROM THESE ACTIVITIES

1. **Application requirements document**

This document should contain the following sections:
– Technical infrastructure requirements
– Nontechnical infrastructure requirements
– Reporting requirements
– Ad hoc and canned query requirements
– Requirements for source data, including history
– High-level logical data model
– Data-cleansing requirements
– Security requirements
– Preliminary SLAs

Include a list of conducted interviews in date order, a list of the interviewees, and a summary of the interview notes.

ROLES INVOLVED IN THESE ACTIVITIES

◆ **Application lead developer**

The application lead developer should add application-specific data access and data analysis questions to the interview questionnaire and should lead that portion of the interviews. He or she should not conduct separate interviews but should participate with the data quality analyst and data administrator in the same interviews. Business people get very annoyed when different IT people ask them the same questions in different interviews.

◆ **Business representative**
In addition to sharing the same responsibilities as the subject matter expert, the business representative should be prepared to demonstrate his or her daily work routine to the data quality analyst, data administrator, and application lead developer either before or after the interview sessions.

◆ **Data administrator**
The data administrator can be of great help to the data quality analyst by participating with follow-up questions and scribing the answers. In addition, the data administrator will get a jump start on his or her logical data modeling activities by hearing the interview discussions firsthand. Such participation in the interviews also eliminates the need for the data administrator to revisit some topics with the interviewees where he or she might have had questions.

◆ **Data quality analyst**
The data quality analyst, the data administrator, and the application lead developer should develop an approach for conducting the interviews. They need to decide when and how they will take turns being the interviewer, the scribe, and the observer. Most likely, the data quality analyst will be the principal interviewer.

◆ **Meta data administrator**
The meta data administrator may join the interview team either as a participant or as an observer, depending on the scope of the proposed meta data repository solution. The meta data administrator should add his or her own set of meta data requirements questions to the questionnaire and should lead that portion of the interviews.

◆ **Subject matter expert**
The subject matter expert together with the business representative must be prepared to address the topics on the questionnaire. He or she should also bring to the interview sessions any reports, forms, screen layouts, code manuals, and other documents that support or explain the project requirements.

RISKS OF NOT PERFORMING STEP 4

Some organizations combine requirements definition activities with data analysis or with application prototyping activities. While that can be an effective approach, the danger lies in losing sight of the big picture, that is, the objectives and scope of the project. When data modelers dig into the data details too soon, analysis paralysis often results. When the application developers start prototyping too soon, scope creep often occurs. Other potential risks are that functionality or data are missed, security issues are ignored, requirements are not prioritized, and business objectives are not targeted. For all these reasons it is advisable to separate requirements gathering from data analysis and prototyping.

BIBLIOGRAPHY AND ADDITIONAL READING

Adelman, Sid, and Larissa Terpeluk Moss. *Data Warehouse Project Management.* Boston, MA: Addison-Wesley, 2000.

Cockburn, Alistair. *Writing Effective Use Cases.* Boston, MA: Addison-Wesley, 2000.

Dyché, Jill. *e-Data: Turning Data into Information with Data Warehousing.* Boston, MA: Addison-Wesley, 2000.

English, Larry P. *Improving Data Warehouse and Business Information Quality: Methods for Reducing Costs and Increasing Profits.* New York: John Wiley & Sons, 1999.

Hoberman, Steve. *Data Modeler's Workbench: Tools and Techniques for Analysis and Design.* New York: John Wiley & Sons, 2001.

Imhoff, Claudia, Lisa Loftis, and Jonathan G. Geiger. *Building the Customer-Centric Enterprise: Data Warehousing Techniques for Supporting Customer Relationship Management.* New York: John Wiley & Sons, 2001.

Inmon, William H., Claudia Imhoff, and Ryan Sousa. *Corporate Information Factory.* New York: John Wiley & Sons, 1997.

Jackson, Michael. *Software Requirements and Specifications: A Lexicon of Practice, Principles, and Prejudices.* Reading, MA: Addison-Wesley, 1995.

Jarke, Matthias, Maurizio Lenzerini, Yannis Vassiliou, and Panos Vassiliadis. *Fundamentals of Data Warehouses.* New York: Springer, 2000.

Kimball, Ralph, Laura Reeves, Margy Ross, and Warren Thornthwaite. *The Data Warehouse Lifecycle Toolkit: Expert Methods for Designing, Developing, and Deploying Data Warehouses.* New York: John Wiley & Sons, 1998.

Kovitz, Benjamin L. *Practical Software Requirements: A Manual of Content and Style.* Greenwich, CT: Manning Publications Company, 1998.

Moeller, R. A. *Distributed Data Warehousing Using Web Technology: How to Build a More Cost-Effective and Flexible Warehouse.* New York: AMACOM American Management Association, 2001.

Ross, Ronald G. *The Business Rule Concepts.* Houston, TX: Business Rule Solutions, Inc., 1998.

Von Halle, Barbara. *Business Rules Applied: Building Better Systems Using the Business Rules Approach.* New York: John Wiley & Sons, 2001.

Wiegers, Karl E. *Software Requirements.* Redmond, WA: Microsoft Press, 1999.

Wood, Jane, and Denise Silver. *Joint Application Development.* New York: John Wiley & Sons, 1995.

Yourdon, Edward. *Death March.* Upper Saddle River, NJ: Prentice Hall, 1997.

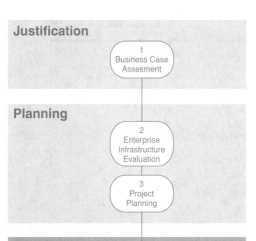

Justification

Planning

Business Analysis

Design

Construction

Deployment

1 Business Case Assesment

2 Enterprise Infrastructure Evaluation

3 Project Planning

4 Project Requirements Definition

5 Data Analysis

6 Application Prototyping

7 Meta Data Repository Analysis

8 Database Design

9 ETL Design

10 Meta Data Repository Design

12 Application Development

14 Meta Data Repository Development

11 ETL Development

13 Data Mining

15 Implementation

16 Release Evaluation

CHAPTER FIVE

Step 5: Data Analysis

CHAPTER OVERVIEW

This chapter covers the following topics:

- Things to consider when analyzing source data for BI applications

- The difference between the systems analysis phase of a traditional methodology and the business-focused data analysis performed during this step

- Top-down logical data modeling, including project-specific logical data models, integrated enterprise logical data models, and data-specific business meta data components gathered during the logical data modeling process

- Bottom-up source data analysis, including how to apply three sets of transformation rules to the source data: technical data conversion rules, business data domain rules, and business data integrity rules

- The responsibilities for data archeology, data cleansing, and data quality enforcement, plus the need to triage (prioritize) data-cleansing activities

- Brief descriptions of the activities involved in data analysis, the deliverables resulting from those activities, and the roles involved

- The risks of not performing Step 5

THINGS TO CONSIDER

Source Data

✓ Do we know where the source data resides? In what systems? In what files? In what databases?

✓ Are there multiple potential sources for the same data?

✓ Has the requested source data already been modeled?

✓ How current is the business meta data on those models?

✓ Have the data owners ratified the business meta data?

✓ Do we know who the data owners are? Who has authority over the source data?

✓ Is there any other type of documentation available for the requested source data? Is it current and complete?

✓ Where is that documentation? In a meta data repository? In programs? In manuals?

Data Quality

✓ Do we know how clean the source data is?

✓ How clean does the data have to be according to our business representative?

✓ Will that be clean enough for *other* knowledge workers, business analysts, and business managers who will use the same data?

✓ Do we know who they are?

✓ Where do we get the business rules for the data? From the data owners? From the business representative on the project?

Data Cleansing

✓ Have data errors already been documented by other project teams? If so, where is that documentation?

✓ Who would know what the known data errors are?

✓ Are codes being translated inside operational programs? If so, in which programs?

✓ Does a code translation book exist for encoded fields?

✓ Do we already know which data is critical, which is important, and which is insignificant (for data-cleansing triage purposes)?

Operational systems are developed as stovepipe automation solutions for individual business units and not as support for the executive decision-making process. Therefore, operational systems are not designed to integrate or reconcile with each other in order to provide a consistent cross-organizational view. BI applications, on the other hand, are designed to do just that—provide integrated and reconciled business data to the business community.

BUSINESS-FOCUSED DATA ANALYSIS

For many organizations, the BI decision-support initiative is the first attempt to bring business data together from multiple sources in order to make it available across different departments. Organizations that use a traditional systems development methodology on their BI projects usually run into severe source data problems when they try to implement their extract/transform/load (ETL) processes because traditional development methodologies do not have steps for analyzing data domains *early* in the development process. They have, at best, a systems analysis phase for the application functions but no business-focused data analysis phase for the underlying data.

 The business-focused data analysis step is the most critical cross-organizational step described in *Business Intelligence Roadmap.*

Step 5, Data Analysis, is different from a systems analysis phase in a traditional methodology. The activities traditionally performed during systems analysis are geared toward producing a design decision for the system to be built. The activities performed during data analysis are geared toward understanding and correcting the existing discrepancies in the business data, irrespective of any system design or implementation method. Data analysis is therefore a *business-focused* activity, not a system-focused activity.

Figure 5.1 points out that two complementary methods are required to perform rigorous data analysis:

1. Top-down logical data modeling for integration and consistency
2. Bottom-up source data analysis for standardization and quality

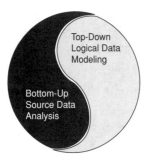

Figure 5.1: Complementary Data Analysis Techniques

TOP-DOWN LOGICAL DATA MODELING

The most effective technique for discovering and documenting the single cross-organizationally integrated and reconciled view of business data is entity-relationship (E-R) modeling, also known as logical data modeling. A popular approach to E-R modeling in the early 1980s was to model all the data for the entire organization all at once. While this approach was a worthwhile architectural endeavor, it did not yield better systems because the process was not integrated with the systems development lifecycle. A more effective approach is to incorporate E-R modeling into every project and then merge the project-specific logical data models into one consolidated enterprise data model over time.

Project-Specific Logical Data Model

E-R modeling is based on normalization rules, which are applied during top-down data modeling as well as during bottom-up source data analysis. Using normalization rules along with other data administration principles assures that each data element within the scope of the BI project is uniquely identified, correctly named, and properly defined and that its domain is validated for *all* business people who will be accessing the data. Thus, the normalized project-specific logical data model yields a formal representation of the data exactly as it exists in the real world, without redundancy and without ambiguity.

This formal representation of data follows another normalization rule: process independence. Therefore, by definition, a logical data model, which is based on normalization rules, is also process independent. Process independence means that the structure and content of the logical data model are not influenced

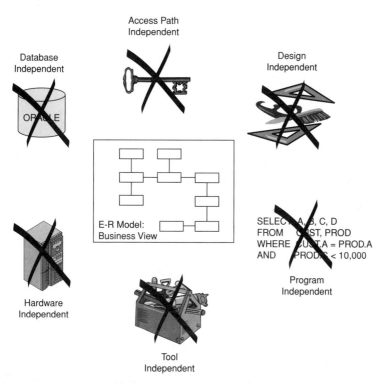

Figure 5.2: Process Independence of Logical Data Models

by any type of database, access path, design, program, tool, or hardware, as shown by the **X** markings in Figure 5.2.

Because of its process independence, a logical data model is a business view, not a database view and not an application view. Therefore, a unique piece of data, which exists only once in the real business world, also exists only once in a logical data model even though it may be physically stored in multiple source files or multiple BI target databases.

Enterprise Logical Data Model

It is the responsibility of an enterprise architecture group, or of data administration if the organization does not have an enterprise architecture group, to merge the project-specific logical data models into an integrated and standardized enterprise logical data model, as illustrated in Figure 5.3.

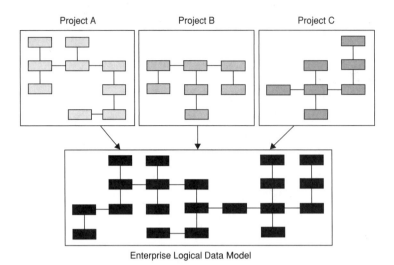

Figure 5.3: Creating an Enterprise Logical Data Model

This enterprise logical data model, also known as the enterprise information architecture, is not constructed all at once, nor is it a prerequisite for BI projects to have a completed one. Instead, the enterprise logical data model evolves over time and may never be completed. It does not need to be completed because the objective of this process is not to produce a finished model but to discover and resolve data discrepancies among different views and implementations of the same data.

These data discrepancies exist en masse among stovepipe operational systems and are the root causes of an organization's inability to provide integrated and consistent cross-organizational information to its business people. The discovery of these discrepancies should be embraced and celebrated by the BI project team, and especially by the business people, because poor-quality data is finally being addressed and resolved. Gaining control over the existing data chaos is, after all, one major function of any BI decision-support initiative.

 If organizations would follow business analysis best practices by developing logical data models for all their operational applications and merging them (over time) into an enterprise logical data model, the BI decision-support development effort could be significantly reduced. This would enable BI project teams to increase the speed of delivering *reliable* decision-support information to the business people. In other words, the BI project teams could deliver the "quick hits" that everyone wants—and deliver them with quality.

Logical Data Modeling Participants

Logical data modeling sessions are typically facilitated and led by a data administrator who has a solid business background. If the data administrator does not have a good understanding of the business, a subject matter expert must assist him or her in this task.

The business representative and the subject matter expert assigned to the BI project are active participants during the modeling sessions. If the data is being extracted from several different operational systems, multiple data owners may have to participate on the BI project because each operational system may be under the governance of a different owner. Data owners are those business individuals who have authority to establish business rules and set business policies for those pieces of data originated by their departments. When data discrepancies are discovered, it is the data owners' responsibility to sort out the various business views and to approve the legitimate usage of their data. This data reconciliation process is and should be a business function, not an information technology (IT) function, although the data administrators, who usually work for IT, facilitate the discovery process.

Systems analysts, developers, and database administrators should also be available to participate in some of the modeling sessions on an as-needed basis. These IT technicians maintain the organization's applications and data structures, and they often know more than anyone else about the data—how and where it is stored, how it is processed, and ultimately how it is used by the business people. In addition, these technicians often have in-depth knowledge of the accuracy of the data, how it relates to other data, the history of its use, and how the content and meaning of the data have changed over time. It is important to obtain a commitment to the BI project from these IT resources since they are often busy "fighting fires" and working on enhancements to the operational systems.

Standardized Business Meta Data

A logical data model, representing a single cross-organizational business view of the data, is composed of an E-R diagram and supporting business meta data. Business meta data includes information about business data objects, their data elements, and the relationships among them. Business meta data as well as technical meta data, which is added during the design and construction stages, ensure data consistency and enhance the understanding and interpretation of the data in the BI decision-support environment. A common subset of business meta data components as they apply to data (as opposed to processes) appears in Figure 5.4.

Figure 5.4: Data-Specific Business Meta Data Components

- A **data name**, an official label developed from a formal data-naming taxonomy, should be composed of a prime word, a class word, and qualifiers. Each data name uniquely identifies one piece of data within the logical data model. No synonyms and no homonyms should exist.

- A **data definition** is a one- or two-sentence description of a data object or a data element, similar to a definition in a language dictionary. If a data object has many subtypes, each subtype should have its own unique data definition. A data definition explains the meaning of the data object or data element. It does *not* include who created the object, when it was last updated, what system originates it, what values it contains, and so on. That information is stored in other meta data components (e.g., data ownership, data content).

- A **data relationship** is a business association among data occurrences in a business activity. Every data relationship is based on business rules and business policies for the associated data occurrences under each business activity.

- A **data identifier** uniquely identifies an occurrence of a data object. A data identifier should be known to the business people. It should also be "minimal," which means it should be as short as possible (composed of just enough data elements to make it unique). In addition, a data identifier should be nonintelligent, with no embedded logic. For example, account numbers 0765587654 and 0765563927, where 0765 is an embedded branch number, would be poor data identifiers.

 A logical data identifier is not the same thing as a primary key in a database. Although a data identifier can be used as a primary key, it is often replaced by a surrogate ("made-up") key during database design.

- **Data type** describes the structure of a data element, categorizing the type of values (character, number, decimal, date) allowed to be stored in it.
- **Data length** specifies the size of a data element for its particular data type. For example, a decimal data element can be an amount field with two digits after the decimal point or a rate field with three digits after the decimal point.
- **Data content** (domain) identifies the actual allowable values for a data element specific to its data type and data length. A domain may be expressed as a range of values, a list of allowable values, a generic business rule, or a dependency rule between two or more data elements.
- A **data rule** is a constraint on a data object or a data element. A data constraint can also apply to a data relationship. A data constraint can be in the form of a business rule or a dependency rule between data objects or data elements, for example, "The ceiling interest rate must be higher than the floor interest rate."
- **Data policy** governs the content and behavior of a data object or a data element. It is usually expressed as an organizational policy or a government regulation. For example, "Patients on Medicare must be at least 65 years old."
- **Data ownership** identifies the persons who have the authority to establish and approve the business meta data for the data objects and data elements under their control.

Although logical data models are extremely stable, some of these business meta data components (such as data content, data rules, data policy, data ownership) occasionally change for legitimate reasons. It is important to track these changes in the meta data repository.

BOTTOM-UP SOURCE DATA ANALYSIS

Data analysis cannot stop after top-down logical data modeling because the source data often does not follow the business rules and policies captured during the modeling sessions. If bottom-up source data analysis were not performed, the data problems and business rule violations would not be discovered until the ETL process was being implemented. Some data quality problems would not be discovered at all until after implementation, and then only if somebody complained about them. As Figure 5.5 shows, source data mapping must adhere not only to the usual technical data conversion rules but also to the business data domain rules and to the business data integrity rules.

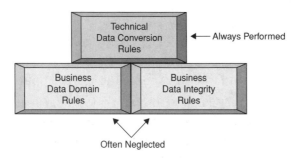

Figure 5.5: Source Data-Mapping Rules

Technical Data Conversion Rules

Any time data is mapped from one system to another, whether for traditional systems conversion or for source-to-target mapping in BI applications, the following technical rules must be observed.

1. The data types of the source data elements must match the data types of the target data elements.

2. The data lengths must be adequate to allow the source data elements to be moved, expanded, or truncated into the target data elements.

3. The logic of the programs manipulating the source data elements must be compatible with and applicable to the content of the source data elements. Otherwise the results will be unpredictable.

Business Data Domain Rules

A much larger effort of source data analysis revolves around business data domain rules. These rules are more important to the business people than the technical data conversion rules. A source data element can meet all three technical data conversion rules but still have incorrect values. Business data domain rules are rules about the semantics (meaning and interpretation) of data content. They are used to identify and correct data violations like those listed in Table 5.1.

Business Data Integrity Rules

Similar to business data domain rules, business data integrity rules are much more important to improving information quality than are the technical data conversion rules. The business data integrity rules govern the semantic content among dependent or related data elements, as well as constraints imposed by business rules and business policy. Table 5.2 lists examples of violations to business data integrity rules.

Table 5.1: Data Domain Violations

1. Missing data values (a big issue on BI projects)
2. Default values; for example, "0", "999", "FF", *blank*
3. Intelligent "dummy" values, which are specific default (or dummy) values that actually have a meaning; for example, using a value of "888-88-8888" for the social security number to indicate that the person is a nonresident alien
4. Logic embedded in a data value, such as an implied business rule; for example, using lower-valued ZIP codes (postal codes) to indicate a state on the east coast, such as 07456 in New Jersey, and higher-valued ZIP codes to indicate a state on the west coast, such as 91024 in California
5. Cryptic and overused data content; for example, using the values "A, B, C, D" of a data element to define type of customer, while the values "E, F, G, H" of the same data element define type of promotion, and the values "I, J, K, L" define type of location
6. Multipurpose data elements, that is, programmatically and purposely redefined data content; for example, the `redefines` clause in COBOL statements
7. Multiple data elements embedded in, concatenated across, or wrapped around free-form text fields; for example, Address lines 1 through 5 containing name and address data elements: Address line 1: `Brokovicz, Meyers, and Co`   Address line 2: `hen, Attorneys at Law`   Address line 3: `200 E. Washington Bouleva`   Address line 4: `rd,`   Address line 5: `Huntsville OR 97589`

Table 5.2: Data Integrity Violations

1. Contradicting data content between two or more data elements; for example, "Boston, CA" (instead of MA)
2. Business rule violation; for example, for the same person, "Date of Birth = 05/02/1985" and "Date of Death = 11/09/1971"
3. Reused primary key (same key value used for multiple object instances); for example, two employees with the same employee number (when one employee left the company, his or her employee number was reassigned to a new employee)
4. No unique primary key (multiple key values for the same object instance); for example, one customer with multiple customer numbers
5. Objects without their dependent parent object; for example, job assignment points to employee 3321, but the employee database contains no employee 3321
6. A real-world relationship between two data objects, or between two occurrences of the same data object, that cannot be built because it is not tracked by the operational systems; for example, a customer refinances a mortgage loan but the operational system does not track the relationship between the old paid-off loan and the new refinanced loan

Every critical and important data element must be examined for these defects, and a decision must be made whether and how to correct them. The information consumers (business people who will be using those data elements to make business decisions) and data owners should make that decision after discussing the impact of the cleansing effort with the business sponsor, the project manager, and the core team.

DATA CLEANSING

One of the goals stated most frequently for BI applications is to deliver clean, integrated, and reconciled data to the business community. Unless all three sets of data-mapping rules are addressed, this goal cannot be achieved. Many organizations will find a much higher percentage of dirty data in their source systems than they expected, and their challenge will be to decide how much of it to cleanse.

Data Quality Responsibility

Data archeology (the process of finding bad data), data cleansing (the process of correcting bad data), and data quality enforcement (the process of preventing data defects at the source) are all business responsibilities—not IT responsibilities. That means that business people (information consumers as well as data owners) must be involved with the data analysis activities and be familiar with the source data-mapping rules.

Since data owners originate the data and establish business rules and policies over the data, they are directly responsible to the downstream information consumers (knowledge workers, business analysts, business managers) who need to use that data. If downstream information consumers base their business decisions on poor-quality data and suffer financial losses because of it, the data owners must be held accountable. In the past, this accountability has been absent from stovepipe systems. Data quality accountability is neither temporary nor BI-specific, and the business people must make the commitment to accept these responsibilities permanently. This is part of the required culture change, discussion of which is outside the scope of this book.

The challenge for IT and for the business sponsor on a BI project is to enforce the inescapable tasks of data archeology and data cleansing to meet the quality goals of the BI decision-support environment.

 Step 5, Data Analysis, may be time intensive since many battles may rage among the business people as to the valid meaning and domain of data.

Although data-cleansing tools can assist in the data archeology process, developing data-cleansing specifications is mainly a manual process. IT managers, business managers, and data owners who have never been through a data quality assessment and data-cleansing initiative often underestimate the time and effort required of their staff by a factor of four or more.

Source Data Selection Process

Poor-quality data is such an overwhelming problem that most organizations will not be able to correct all the discrepancies. When selecting the data for the BI application, consider the five general steps shown in Figure 5.6.

Figure 5.6: Source Data Selection Process

1. *Identify the required data.*
   Identify the data of interest and the significance of this data. Data cleansing is a collaborative effort between business analysts who are familiar with the semantics of the data and data quality analysts who know the program-specific meanings of the data (e.g., the use and meaning of a "flag" value or redefined record layouts).

2. *Analyze the data content.*
   Analyze the data for content, meaning, and importance. Many organizations have accumulated massive amounts of data in files and databases. This data constitutes a prospective gold mine of valuable business knowledge and is potentially a good source for data mining. However, the quality of the data content must be assessed first, since mining dirty data is of little value.

3. *Select the data for BI.*
   Determine which data to include in the BI application. Select only the data that will meet core business requirements. Even with automated tools, the cost of assuring data quality for an all-inclusive BI decision-support environment becomes prohibitive for most organizations. Some questions to consider when selecting data appear below.
   – Is this data clean enough for decision-support usage?
   – If not, can this data be cleansed, at least partially? Do we know how?
   – Is the dirty data the reason for building this BI application? Is cleansing this data therefore mandatory?
   – How much effort will it take to figure out how to cleanse the data?
   – How much will the data-cleansing effort cost?
   – What is the benefit of cleansing the data as opposed to moving it into the BI application at the current level of dirtiness?
   – What are the data quality expectations from the information consumers and from business management in general?

4. *Prepare the data-cleansing specifications.*

   The IT staff, working with the business representative, will get to know the business rules needed to write the data-cleansing specifications. In essence, this is a source data reengineering process.

5. *Select the tools.*

   Select the ETL and cleansing tools. Determine whether it is appropriate and cost-effective to acquire an ETL tool, a cleansing tool, or both. Examine the suitability and effectiveness of those tools. Some data-cleansing specifications can be very complicated. Be sure the tools are capable of handling them.

 Automated tools do not eliminate the manual labor of source data analysis; they only reduce it.

Key Points of Data Selection

When identifying and selecting the operational data to be used to populate the BI target databases, some key points should be considered. Applying the source data selection criteria shown in Figure 5.7 minimizes the need for and effort of data cleansing.

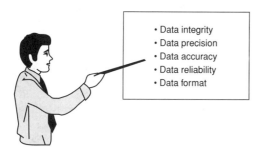

- Data integrity
- Data precision
- Data accuracy
- Data reliability
- Data format

Figure 5.7: Source Data Selection Criteria

- **Data integrity:** How internally consistent is the data? This is the most important criterion.
  - The greater the proportion of manually entered data (data keyed in with few or no data controls, edits, and validations), the lower the integrity.
  - Programming errors also contaminate great masses of data—and do so automatically.
  - The lower the integrity, the greater the cleansing requirement.

- **Data precision:** How precise is the data? This is the next important criterion.
  - How is the data represented internally?
  - For numeric data, what is the scale and precision of the data?
  - For date data, how is it formatted?
- **Data accuracy:** How correct is the data?
  - Are there edit checks in the data entry program?
  - Are dependent values cross-checked? For example, does the data entry program forbid an expiration date to precede an effective date?
  - Is there an operational process in place for correcting data?
  - Are calculated values stored? What, if any, mechanisms are in place to keep these values accurate?
- **Data reliability:** How old is the data?
  - What generation is the data (month-end, weekly, daily)?
  - Was the data obtained from direct sources or from downloads?
  - Is the source of the data known?
  - Is the data a duplicate of data in another data store? If so, is the data current?
- **Data format:** The closer the data is to the destination data format, the fewer the conversion requirements will be. From highest to lowest, the format priorities are:
  - Data from a relational database (e.g., DB2, Oracle)
  - Data from a nonrelational database (e.g., IMS, CA-IDMS)
  - Flat files (e.g., VSAM, ISAM)

 Source data quality will be only as good as the enforcement of quality processes in the operational systems. Mandatory quality processes should include data entry rules and edit checks in programs. If those processes are not enforced or do not exist, data usually gets corrupted, regardless of whether the data is in a relational database or in an old VSAM file.

To Cleanse or Not to Cleanse

Many organizations struggle with this question. Data-cleansing research indicates that some organizations downplay data cleansing to achieve short-term goals. The consequences of not addressing poor-quality data usually hit home when their business ventures fail or encounter adverse effects because of inaccurate data.

It is important to recognize that data cleansing is a labor-intensive, time-consuming, and expensive process. Cleansing all the data is usually neither cost-justified nor practical, but cleansing none of the data is equally unacceptable. It is therefore important to analyze the source data carefully and to classify the data elements as critical, important, or insignificant to the business. Concentrate on cleansing all the critical data elements, keeping in mind that not all data is equally critical to all business people. Then, cleanse as many of the important data elements as time allows, and move the insignificant data elements into the BI target databases without cleansing them. In other words, you do not need to cleanse all the data, and you do not need to do it all at once.

Cleansing Operational Systems

When the selected data is cleansed, standardized, and moved into the BI target databases, a question to consider is whether the source files and source databases should also be cleansed. Management may ask, why not spend a little extra money and time to cleanse the source files and databases so that the data is consistent in the source as well as in the target? This is a valid question, and this option should definitely be pursued if the corrective action on the source system is as simple as adding an edit check to the data entry program.

If the corrective action requires changing the file structure, which means modifying (if not rewriting) most of the programs that access that file, the cost for such an invasive corrective action on the operational system is probably not justifiable—especially if the bad data is not interfering with the operational needs of that system. Remember that many companies did not even want to make such drastic changes for the now infamous Y2K problem; they made those changes only when it was clear that their survival was at stake. Certainly, a misused code field does not put an organization's survival at stake. Hence, the chances that operational systems will be fixed are bleak.

DATA ANALYSIS ACTIVITIES

The activities for data analysis do not need to be performed linearly. Figure 5.8 indicates which activities can be performed concurrently. The list below briefly describes the activities associated with Step 5, Data Analysis.

1. **Analyze the external data sources.**
   In addition to requiring internal operational source data, many BI applications need data from external sources. Merging external data with internal data presents its own set of challenges. External data is often dirty and incomplete,

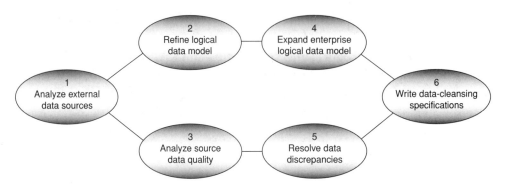

Figure 5.8: Data Analysis Activities

and it usually does not follow the same format or key structure as internal data. Identify and resolve these differences during this step.

2. **Refine the logical data model.**
   A high-level, project-specific logical data model should have been created during one of the previous steps. In addition, some or all of the internal and external data may have been modeled on other projects and may already be part of the enterprise logical data model. In that case, extract the representative portion of the enterprise logical data model and expand it with the new data objects, new data relationships, and new data elements. If the required data has not been previously modeled, create a new logical data model for the scope of this BI project. It should include all internal as well as external data elements.

3. **Analyze the source data quality.**
   At the same time that the logical data model is created or expanded, the quality of the internal and external source files and source databases must be analyzed in detail. It is quite common that existing operational data does not conform to the stated business rules and business policies. Many data elements are used for multiple purposes or are simply left blank. Identify all these discrepancies and incorporate them into the logical data model.

4. **Expand the enterprise logical data model.**
   Once the project-specific logical data model is relatively stable, merge it back into the enterprise logical data model. During this merge process additional data discrepancies or inconsistencies may be identified. Those will be sent back to the BI project for resolution.

5. **Resolve data discrepancies.**

Occasionally data discrepancies discovered during data analysis involve other business representatives from other projects. In that case, summon the other business representatives as well as the data owners to work out their differences. Either they will discover a new legitimate subtype of a data object or a new data element, which must be modeled as such, or they will have to resolve and standardize the inconsistencies.

6. **Write the data-cleansing specifications.**

Once all data problems are identified and modeled, write the specifications for how to cleanse the data. These specifications should be in plain English so they can be validated by the data owner and by business people who will use the data.

DELIVERABLES RESULTING FROM THESE ACTIVITIES

1. **Normalized and fully attributed logical data model**

This project-specific logical data model is a fully normalized entity-relationship diagram showing kernel entities, associative entities, characteristic entities, cardinality, optionality, unique identifiers, and all attributes.

2. **Business meta data**

The business entities and attributes from the logical data model must be described with meta data. Data-specific business meta data components include data names, data definitions, data relationships, unique identifiers, data types, data lengths, domains, business rules, policies, and data ownership. These are usually captured in the tool repository of the computer-aided software engineering (CASE) tool.

3. **Data-cleansing specifications**

This document describes the cleansing logic that must be applied to the source data in order to bring it into compliance with the technical data conversion rules, the business data domain rules, and the business data integrity rules. This document will be used to create the transformation specifications on the source-to-target mapping document in Step 9, ETL Design.

4. **Expanded enterprise logical data model**

This deliverable is produced behind the scenes by data administration or the enterprise architecture group when it merges the project-specific logical data model into the enterprise logical data model. Any rejected entities or attributes and any discrepancies between the models will be presented to the BI project team for resolution.

ROLES INVOLVED IN THESE ACTIVITIES

◆ **Business representative**

The business representative assigned to the BI project is a major contributor during the top-down logical data modeling activities as well as the bottom-up source data analysis activities. He or she provides the business meta data to the data administrator and assists the data quality analyst in analyzing the source files.

◆ **Data administrator**

The data administrator is trained in logical data modeling, business meta data, normalization techniques, business data domain rules, business data integrity rules, and standardization methods. The job description of a data administrator matches the activities of the Data Analysis step. The data administrator will be the lead person during this step and will facilitate all of the data modeling sessions. He or she also has the responsibility of documenting the logical data model and the supporting business meta data in the CASE tool.

◆ **Data quality analyst**

The data quality analyst is a systems analyst, trained in using the technical data conversion rules, in reading as well as writing programs, and in extracting data from all types of source files and source databases. Finding the data violations in the source files and source databases is the prime responsibility of the data quality analyst. He or she works closely with the data administrator to model data anomalies and to correct the data violations with help from the business representative and the data owners.

◆ **ETL lead developer**

The ETL lead developer must be involved in the modeling reviews and must be aware of the magnitude of data quality problems found in the source files and source databases. He or she needs to understand the complexity of cleansing the data because the cleansing algorithms must be incorporated into the ETL process. In some cases, the ETL tool will not be able to support some cleansing algorithms, and custom code may have to be written.

◆ **Meta data administrator**

As the custodian of meta data and the administrator of the meta data repository, the meta data administrator needs to know what business meta data components are being collected and how. Some meta data components may be entered into a CASE tool, while other components may be captured in word processing documents or in spreadsheets. The meta data administrator will have to extract the meta data components from the various files and tools and merge them into the meta data repository.

◆ **Stakeholders (including data owners)**

The business people using the BI applications are usually downstream information consumers and not the data owners. During this step, both information consumers and data owners have the responsibility to standardize the business data and to set rules and policies for the data. Continuing disagreements over data between data owners and information consumers must be pushed up to business executives for resolution.

◆ **Subject matter expert**

The subject matter expert assists the data administrator and data quality analyst by interpreting the business data, explaining the business rules and policies for the data, and determining the domain (valid values) of the data. In addition, the subject matter expert is responsible for finding data problems in the source data files and source databases and for suggesting how to correct them.

RISKS OF NOT PERFORMING STEP 5

Business managers, IT managers, and IT technicians often do not want to take the time to perform rigorous data analysis, which involves logical data modeling, source data archeology, and data cleansing. They see those activities as a waste of time. They judge the success of a BI project by the speed with which it gets delivered, rather than by the quality of its deliverable. As a result, organizations often create stovepipe data marts and populate them "suck and plunk" style with the same data they have on the source files and source databases, thereby copying all the existing data impairments to the new BI decision-support environment. Instead of eliminating their existing data problems, they just compounded them—now there are additional redundant and inconsistent BI target databases and applications to maintain.

Of all the 16 steps presented in *Business Intelligence Roadmap*, Step 5, Data Analysis, is the most critical cross-organizational step. This step is a major differentiator between a traditional systems development approach and a cross-organizational development approach. The activities of business-focused data analysis force the information consumers and the data owners to reconstruct a cross-organizational view and to clean up their expensive data chaos, not only in the BI decision-support environment but in their operational systems as well. These are all prerequisites for improving the business executives' abilities to make decisions. Without this step, you are just building another traditional stovepipe decision-support system, not a BI solution.

BIBLIOGRAPHY AND ADDITIONAL READING

Adelman, Sid, and Larissa Terpeluk Moss. *Data Warehouse Project Management.* Boston, MA: Addison-Wesley, 2000.

Aiken, Peter H. *Data Reverse Engineering: Slaying the Legacy Dragon.* New York: McGraw-Hill, 1995.

Atre, Shaku. *Data Base: Structured Techniques for Design, Performance, and Management, Second Edition.* New York: John Wiley & Sons, 1988.

Bischoff, Joyce, and Ted Alexander. *Data Warehouse: Practical Advice from the Experts.* Upper Saddle River, NJ: Prentice Hall, 1997.

Brackett, Michael H. *Data Resource Quality: Turning Bad Habits into Good Practices.* Boston, MA: Addison-Wesley, 2000.

———. *The Data Warehouse Challenge: Taming Data Chaos.* New York: John Wiley & Sons, 1996.

Downes, P. M. *Practical Data Analysis.* Pinner, Middlesex, UK: Blenheim Online Publications, 1989.

English, Larry P. *Improving Data Warehouse and Business Information Quality: Methods for Reducing Costs and Increasing Profits.* New York: John Wiley & Sons, 1999.

Hoberman, Steve. *Data Modeler's Workbench: Tools and Techniques for Analysis and Design.* New York: John Wiley & Sons, 2001.

Inmon, William H., John A. Zachman, and Jonathon G. Geiger. *Data Stores, Data Warehousing and the Zachman Framework: Managing Enterprise Knowledge.* New York: McGraw-Hill, 1997.

Jarke, Matthias, Maurizio Lenzerini, Yannis Vassiliou, and Panos Vassiliadis. *Fundamentals of Data Warehouses.* New York: Springer, 2000.

Kuan-Tsae, Huang, Yang W. Lee, and Richard Y. Wang. *Quality Information and Knowledge Management.* Upper Saddle River, NJ: Prentice Hall, 1998.

Reingruber, Michael C., and William W. Gregory. *The Data Modeling Handbook: A Best-Practice Approach to Building Quality Data Models.* New York: John Wiley & Sons, 1994.

Ross, Ronald G. *The Business Rule Concepts.* Houston, TX: Business Rule Solutions, Inc., 1998.

Simsion, Graeme. *Data Modeling Essentials: Analysis, Design, and Innovation.* Boston, MA: International Thomson Computer Press, 1994.

Von Halle, Barbara. *Business Rules Applied: Building Better Systems Using the Business Rules Approach.* New York: John Wiley & Sons, 2001.

Zachman, John. *The Zachman Framework: A Primer for Enterprise Engineering and Manufacturing.* La Canada, CA: Zachman International, 2002.

Information Impact International, Inc.: *http://www.infoimpact.com*

Zachman Institute for Framework Advancement: *http://www.zifa.com*

CHAPTER SIX

Step 6: Application Prototyping

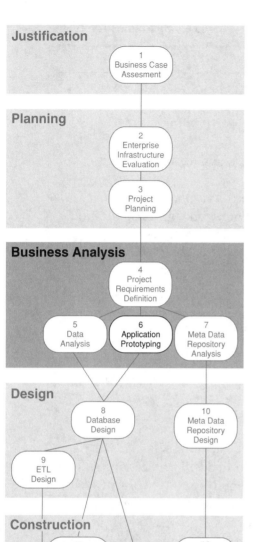

Justification
1 Business Case Assesment

Planning
2 Enterprise Infrastructure Evaluation
3 Project Planning

Business Analysis
4 Project Requirements Definition
5 Data Analysis
6 Application Prototyping
7 Meta Data Repository Analysis

Design
8 Database Design
9 ETL Design
10 Meta Data Repository Design

Construction
12 Application Development
11 ETL Development
13 Data Mining
14 Meta Data Repository Development

Deployment
15 Implementation
16 Release Evaluation

CHAPTER OVERVIEW

This chapter covers the following topics:

- Things to consider about prototyping

- How prototyping can provide an effective way to validate application requirements

- The concept of "time-boxing" prototyping activities

- Best practices for prototyping

- Prototyping considerations such as proper team structure, deadline management, scope and deliverables, and business participation

- The purposes and implications of the six different types of prototypes: show-and-tell, mock-up, proof-of-concept, visual-design, demo, and operational

- Guidelines for prototyping

- An example of a skill survey used to determine the skill sets of the business people who will participate in the prototype and will later use the BI application

- Brief descriptions of the activities involved in application prototyping, the deliverables resulting from those activities, and the roles involved

- The risks of not performing Step 6

THINGS TO CONSIDER

Objectives

✓ Are the objectives for this prototype clear?

✓ Do we know what kind of prototype we want to build?

✓ Have we developed a prototype in the past?

✓ If we have, what was our experience? What lessons did we learn?

✓ How will the business people benefit from prototyping this BI application?

✓ How will the organization benefit?

Scope and Schedule

✓ What is the scope of the prototype?

✓ How will we manage scope changes?

✓ How much time do we have for this prototype?

✓ How many versions (iterations) of the prototype are we planning to create before starting real development work?

✓ How will we time-box prototype activities? By version? By activity? By deliverable?

Deliverables

✓ Are the requirements clear about the prototype deliverables?

✓ What reports do the business people expect from the BI application? Will we prototype all of those reports? If not, which ones?

✓ What queries will the business analysts write against the BI target databases? Which of these queries should we prototype?

✓ Are any business analysts currently using spreadsheets to satisfy their query needs? Will the prototype include reports to replace all those spreadsheets?

✓ What data do we need for the prototype database?

✓ Will a BI application interface be required? If so, are we prototyping it? For how many business people? What do they have now?

✓ Are we going to include a Web front end in the prototype?

Business Participation

✓ Who will use the BI application? How many of those business people will be involved with the prototype?

✓ Where are the business people located? How will they connect to the BI application? By local area network (LAN)? By wide area network (WAN)? Through the intranet?

✓ Have we worked with these business people in the past?

✓ What types of technical skills do they have? What technical skills are needed to participate in the prototype?

✓ How much will they participate in this prototype? Hands-on, full-time involvement? Occasional demo reviews only?

Tools and Methods

✓ What tools will we use to develop the prototype?

✓ Will we use the same tools to develop the final BI application?

✓ How will lessons learned be communicated to the extract/transform/load (ETL) team?

There is nothing business people like more than to see their requirements turn into a tangible deliverable they can "touch and feel" very quickly. A prototype accomplishes that goal.

PURPOSES OF PROTOTYPING

Prototyping can be an effective method for validating the project requirements and finding missing pieces and discrepancies in the requirements. Business people seldom think of all the details when they state their requirements. They often forget to include dependent processes or related data. A prototype can also help them focus on their access path requirements because they will see the capabilities of the BI technology and the access and analysis portion of their BI application.

If time and budget permit, building a prototype for the original requirements allows the business community to test, extend, or change those requirements at an early stage when the impact on the project schedule is not yet high. The costs of experimenting with different database designs, different visualization methods, different development tools, or different application programming techniques are much less during prototyping than during development because they do not affect a full-scale application.

Another purpose for prototyping is to verify that the design as well as the selected tools, database management system (DBMS), and other technology components will be appropriate for the BI decision-support environment. If the functions of all technology components perform as expected during the prototype development, then the chances of having a successful BI implementation are increased. Therefore, testing the technology features is a valuable benefit of prototyping, regardless of whether you are using existing technology components or buying new ones.

 Testing the technology for *performance*, however, is usually not a valid purpose for a prototype. A prototype is not a stress-test environment. It is usually loaded with only small sets of data, and its main purpose is to try out visual interfaces and functionality.

Time-Boxing

Everyone likes prototyping. It is fun and creative, dynamic and exciting—and it is meant to be short. Thus, a word of caution: It is tempting to endlessly expand the scope of the prototype. Prolonging the prototyping effort beyond its original purpose reduces the cost-effectiveness of the prototype and produces diminishing returns, as shown in Figure 6.1. It also reduces control over the project as the prototype starts to feel like a runaway train.

Each prototype iteration should be limited in duration to just a few weeks, and the activities within each prototype iteration should be time-boxed for every week, as illustrated in Figure 6.2. Prototyping activities are carefully planned and monitored. Each participant must know which tasks to perform and which task deliverables to produce by the end of every week.

As unexpected discoveries arise (one main reason for prototyping is to find out what does not work), the plan should be revised for every team member who is affected by that discovery. The plan and schedule for the prototype can be extended or shortened. A plan does not dictate what *must* be done; it is only a proposal for activities that make the most sense at the time. If something does not make sense anymore, change it.

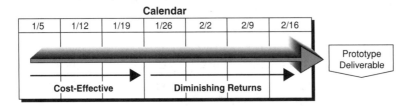

Figure 6.1: Uncontrolled Prototyping Activity

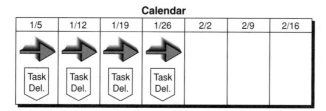

Figure 6.2: Controlled (Time-Boxed) Prototyping Activity

BEST PRACTICES FOR PROTOTYPING

A few lessons learned regarding prototyping appear below.

- **Limit the scope:** Limit the functional scope as well as the data scope of each prototype iteration to a specific subset of the application. This helps to focus the business people on one small piece of their overall requirements. They can learn about the capabilities and limitations of the new environment without getting bogged down with the complexities of the whole development effort. It is also a good general training indoctrination in how to use the new technology and the new application.

- **Understand database requirements early:** The prototype will help the database administrator understand the access path requirements to the BI target databases, the reporting dimensions needed for application development with online analytical processing (OLAP) tools, the levels of aggregation and summarization needed, and what type of data is usually accessed together. The database administrator will be able to start making some database design decisions, such as how to cluster tables and where to place the data sets. The database administrator will also get a sense of the performance expectations and the anticipated size of the databases.

- **Choose the right data:** Carefully select sample data for the prototype. The sample data set should be a meaningful representation of the source data so that all functions and features of the prototype can be tested. Keep the sample data set small so as not to spend too much time on loading and testing. Try to select clean data for the prototype. You do not want to have your prototype results tarnished because of dirty data. You also do not want to take the time to cleanse data while creating the prototype unless the purpose of the prototype is to test your transformation logic or the transformation functionality of an ETL tool or a data-cleansing tool.

- **Test tool usability:** Test the usability of the access and analysis tools. Make sure the query tools are easy to use and do not intimidate the business people who need to use them. Test the features of the report writer on one of the more complicated reports. Give the business people hands-on experience with the OLAP tool. Although multidimensional analysis is relatively intuitive for most business people, the capability of dynamically drilling down and rolling up with a tool is still a new experience for many.

- **Involve the business people:** Test the prototype with more than one business person. Try it with a single business person first, then add more business people from different business units or departments. Be sure to measure the performance of the prototype as you add more people. Observe the business people while they use the prototype. You will be able to see how they react to the prototype when you test it with them. Address any difficulties or misgivings immediately so that the problems do not become roadblocks during application development.

Considerations for Prototyping

To build a successful prototype and to produce the optimal physical database design, the prototyping team must first understand how the business people will retrieve the data and what they will do with it. The team members should ask such questions as the following:

- Are there frequently asked business questions?
- What dimensions of the data are prevalent on reports?
- Are there reporting patterns among departments?

Prototyping is a useful technique to ensure that the business people and the prototyping team understand and agree on the functional business requirements. A prototype could also ensure that everyone agrees on what is expected from the final BI application. Important considerations about developing a prototype are briefly described below.

- **Prototyping team:** The prototyping team should be small. One of the many reasons why some software companies have become successful is that their project teams are very small. They do not staff their projects with more than seven or eight people.

- **Deadline management:** When project teams routinely miss deadlines, shrink the size of the team. This is exactly the opposite of what many organizations do. Most organizations put more people on the team, which usually backfires because more people require more time for communication, and that slows down the project even more. By shrinking the size of the team, the people remaining on the team may have more work to do, but they will get things done faster.

- **Scope:** Try to build "slimware," that is, deliverables with the barest number of features possible to satisfy the purpose of the prototype. This can head off "code bloat" down the road when the application code needs to be written.

- **Deliverables:** Each prototype should have a well-defined deliverable. Plan to use an iterative process for prototyping, and try to control the activities on each prototype iteration in weekly increments with weekly deliverables.

- **Delivery methods:** Test the graphical user interfaces (GUIs), Web-enabled interfaces, and other delivery methods.

- **Data integration:** Try to have only a few data integration requirements in your prototype scope. Prototyping should *not* be used to address all project requirements but only to get a basic understanding of the major deliverables.

- **Business participation:** The prototype should include at the most five to eight business people. Consider the politics involved in selecting the right blend of business people for the prototyping activities.

- **Success criteria:** Encourage business participation in the prototyping process from the beginning, especially during the activities of needs assessment and GUI construction. Be sure to include the business representative and the business sponsor when establishing the success criteria for the prototype. Remember, *their* definition of success or failure is the one that counts. You may also consider building a coalition comprised of the business representative and the business sponsor, IT managers, and other senior business managers who will support the BI project beyond the prototype.

Before starting the prototype, review the Things to Consider section at the beginning of this chapter to determine the overall scope of the prototype, the prototype's purpose, how many business people will participate, and the level of complexity. Use this information to carve out and focus on one or two essential functions that have the highest payback.

TYPES OF PROTOTYPES

Prototyping is a visual communication technique used to help the BI project team understand and refine the scope of the project requirements. There are different types of prototypes, each with a different purpose and life expectancy. These prototypes are discussed below in the order of least to most functionality, sophistication, and reusability.

Show-and-Tell Prototype

A show-and-tell prototype serves as a demo for management and business people, as described in Table 6.1. It could also be used to obtain budget approval or to get a business sponsor for the BI application during Step 1, Business Case Assessment.

Table 6.1: Show-and-Tell Prototype

Purposes	*Implications*
• Avoid costly coding by only demonstrating "look and feel." • Gain buy-in from business people. • Gain business support for the BI application. • Secure funding for the BI application.	• Business people may mistake the prototype for a functioning system. Be sure to explain that there is no functionality at all—it is only for visual communication. • Concentrate on displaying the most important screens to get business buy-in.

Mock-Up Prototype

The purpose of a mock-up prototype is to understand the access and analysis requirements and the business activities behind them. Therefore, mock-up prototypes are completed in a very short time, as mentioned in Table 6.2. Since the mock-up prototype is just a front for a BI application, it is usually a throwaway.

Table 6.2: Mock-Up Prototype

Purposes	*Implications*
• Understand the application requirements. • Understand the business activities. • Initiate system functions. • Speed is of the essence.	• Pay attention to interfaces: building interfaces gives the impression of working code. • Use a less sophisticated programming language to build the prototype faster. For example, you may want to use Visual Basic for the prototype and write the final access and analysis application in C++.

Proof-of-Concept Prototype

The purpose of a proof-of-concept prototype is to explore implementation uncertainties. This method allows the identification of risks and unknowns, thereby enabling the decision whether or not to proceed with the project, as indicated in Table 6.3.

Table 6.3: Proof-of-Concept Prototype

Purpose	*Implications*
• Explore implementation risks and unknowns to decide whether or not to proceed.	• Stay narrow in scope. • Do not build any application interfaces. • Build only enough functionality to make a go/no-go decision.

Visual-Design Prototype

A visual-design prototype is a step up from a mock-up. It is ideal for developing interface specifications for the access and analysis portion of the BI application. Good interface specifications are mandatory, as listed in Table 6.4. Visually, it is important for business people to have as much information as possible on the same screen to avoid toggling between screens. Once the code is generated, this type of prototype may survive and be incorporated into the final BI application.

Therefore, unless you are certain that this prototype is a throwaway, stay away from "quick and dirty" code. There is no such thing as a one-time-use-only program. Once a program works, even if it does not work well, it is liable to be used forever.

Table 6.4: Visual-Design Prototype

Purposes	*Implications*
• Understand the design of visual interfaces. • Develop specifications for visual interfaces and displays.	• If the intent is to use the prototype like a mock-up only, write it in a language different from the delivery language so you can complete it faster. • If the intent is to potentially use the prototype for the final BI application, write it in the delivery language from the start so you can reuse it for the real BI application. Allocate additional time for writing quality code.

Demo Prototype

A demo prototype is used to convey vision and partial functionality to business people, business managers, potential customers, or other external groups, as indicated in Table 6.5. It is not fully functioning, but it is more sophisticated than code stubs.

Table 6.5: Demo Prototype

Purposes	*Implications*
• Convey the vision of the BI application to the business people or to external groups. • Test the market for the viability of a full-scale BI application. • Test or demonstrate the usability of the proposed access and analysis portion of the BI application.	• On the initial screen, graphically convey what percentage of the application is represented by the prototype so you set realistic expectations. Otherwise, the business people may mistake this prototype for a functioning application.

Operational Prototype

An operational prototype is the most involved, most extensive, and most time-consuming of all prototypes. As a result, it is also the most expensive, most complete, most functional, and most likely to survive and evolve into the real access and analysis portion of the BI application. The purpose of this prototype is to obtain feedback from the business people who participate in the prototyping activities through the actual use of the application's functionality. This is accomplished by designing the entire access and analysis application up front but using only a basic part of the code to generate the prototype. It can be considered a bare-bones application, with just enough functionality to evoke feedback, as mentioned in Table 6.6. This type of prototype is also excellent for hands-on training.

Table 6.6: Operational Prototype

Purposes	*Implications*
• Create an almost fully functioning pilot for alpha or beta use of the access and analysis portion of the BI application. • Obtain feedback through real hands-on trials of the bare-bones application.	• On the initial screen, graphically convey what percentage of the application is represented by the prototype so you can set realistic expectations. • This prototype has a high potential for evolving into the final access and analysis portion of the BI application. • Write the prototype in the delivery language. Allocate additional time for writing quality code.

BUILDING SUCCESSFUL PROTOTYPES

Building a successful prototype starts with defining its purpose and setting its scope. The purpose and scope of a prototype can never be the implementation of a full-scale BI application, which is comprised of an ETL process, an access and analysis application, and a meta data repository. There are two main reasons why a prototype can never produce a complete BI application.

1. While portions of the ETL process and some functionality of the ETL tool can be tested in a prototype, the entire ETL process is too complicated and would take too long to be an appropriate scope for prototyping.

2. Similarly, the design and some functionality of the meta data repository can be tested in prototyping, but developing a robust, production-worthy, enterprise-wide meta data repository is outside the scope of prototyping.

Therefore, the most appropriate and the most common purpose and scope for prototyping is to demonstrate the overall usefulness of the access and analysis portion of a BI application by using a small subset of functionality and data. Consequently, prototyping is the best way for the project team members of the Application track to perform "systems analysis," which is systems-focused analysis of functional requirements that leads to application design. To take it a step further, if the BI project team chooses to build an operational prototype, it is conceivable that after several prototyping iterations the operational prototype can evolve into the final access and analysis application.

Once the prototyping activities are in progress, it is quite common to make new discoveries that lead to new requirements, which can affect not only the scope of the prototype but also the scope of the source data analysis activity, the ETL process, and the meta data repository. Be sure to review and renegotiate the project constraints when the scope changes, and be sure to communicate daily with the project team members of the ETL track and the Meta Data Repository track.

Prototype Charter

Prepare a prototype charter, which is similar to a project charter but much smaller and less formal. A prototype charter is an agreement between the business sponsor and the IT staff for developing a prototype. It should include the following sections:

- **The primary purpose of the prototype,** for example, whether the focus is on testing queries for marketing analysis, demonstrating executive information, running a financial analysis report, or fulfilling another specific purpose.
- **The prototype objectives,** including a statement of what type of prototype will be built. Each type of prototype takes a different amount of effort and produces different results. It must be clear to the business people what the limitations of the prototype will be.
- **A list of business people** who will:
  - Participate in building the prototype
  - Sign off on the prototype
  - Use (test) the prototype
- **The data,** including information on the type of data, the amount of data, and the consolidation level of data that will initially be brought into the prototype

- **The hardware and software platforms** on which the prototype will be constructed and the language in which it will be written.
- **The measures of success** should be itemized for the prototype. How will you know whether it was worthwhile to prototype portions of your BI application?
- **An application interface agreement** is also important to cover the following:
  - Compliance with standards (or development of standards if none exist)
  - Necessary level of understanding and skills required
  - Ease of use ("user-friendliness")

Regardless of how much we use the term "*user*-friendly system," it is still an oxymoron, like a "*simple* programming change." In most cases, we seem to be looking for "*system*-friendly users" instead of developing "*user*-friendly systems."

Express the goals for ease of use in terms of quantifiable criteria for:

- The minimum time it takes to learn the new application.
- The speed of task accomplishment (e.g., time to analyze a market condition).
- The retention rate of queries over a period of time.
- Subjective satisfaction; business people like applications that are intuitive and forgiving.
- The effectiveness of the help function (if included in the prototype). Is the help function really helping people resolve problems? Are the business people making use of the help function frequently? What is their feedback about the content of the help function?

Guidelines for Prototyping

Create prototyping guidelines and communicate them to all prototype participants. Table 6.7 lists some sample guidelines.

Additional considerations appear below.

- With each prototype iteration, plan to expand the number of data types, and plan to increase the functionality and the volume of data.
- Keep the type and placement of GUI components consistent among prototypes. If you are choosing a pull-down menu for certain types of displays, do not switch to radio buttons on another prototype. The business people may need to reach consensus on some basic standardization for the BI decision-support environment.

Table 6.7: Prototyping Guidelines

1. Do not deviate from the basic purpose for which the prototype is being developed.

2. Develop a working prototype quickly; therefore, keep the scope small.

3. Acknowledge that the first iteration will have problems.

4. Frequently demonstrate the prototype to stakeholders.

5. Solicit and document top-down as well as bottom-up feedback on the prototype.

6. Ask for ongoing validation of the prototype results.

7. Continue to cycle between demonstrating and revising the prototype until its functionality is satisfactory to all parties.

8. Review your prototyping approach and modify it if necessary before proceeding with the next prototype iteration.

Skills Survey

The business people who will participate in the prototype and will later use the BI application should be evaluated to determine their skill sets. What level of business knowledge do they have about the business functions addressed by the BI application? Are they experts in using computers but do not know much about the business functions? Or are they experts in the business functions but have not used a computer extensively before?

You may want to use a skills matrix, similar to Table 6.8, to assess the skill sets of the business people in order to determine how simple or how sophisticated the prototype and the final BI application need to be.

If the survey shows an overwhelming number of people with XX skill sets (expert in computer skills and expert in application knowledge), build as many shortcuts as possible. If the survey shows an overwhelming number of people

Table 6.8: Skills Matrix

	Computer Skill		
Business Functions Knowledge	*Beginning (B)*	*Advanced (A)*	*Expert (X)*
Beginning (B)	BB	BA	BX
Advanced (A)	AB	AA	AX
Expert (X)	XB	XA	XX

with BB skill sets (beginner in computer skills and beginner in application knowledge), provide as much guidance and help functionality as possible. If the survey shows an overwhelming number of people with any other skill set combination, you need to take a hard look at your proposed solution and decide whether only one solution will be sufficient. If the BI application is designed for only one level of skills but has to satisfy everybody using the application, either it will be perfect for beginners but the experts will be bored and frustrated, or it will be perfect for experts but the beginners will be lost and frustrated.

APPLICATION PROTOTYPING ACTIVITIES

The activities for application prototyping do not need to be performed linearly. Figure 6.3 indicates which activities can be performed concurrently. The list below briefly describes the activities associated with Step 6, Application Prototyping.

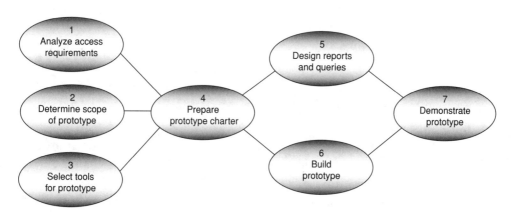

Figure 6.3: Application Prototyping Activities

1. **Analyze the access requirements.**
   Based on the business needs, determine the access requirements for reports and queries. Most access requirements will probably be multidimensional, which makes them perfect candidates for prototyping. Also, assess the skill sets of the business people participating in the prototype activities.

2. **Determine the scope of the prototype.**
   The business representative and the project manager should determine the scope of the prototype. The scope should be small enough that the prototype can be built and tested in a matter of days or weeks. It should contain only a

subset of data, just enough to support the functionality chosen for the prototype. Prototyping by definition is iterative, which allows functionality and data to be added with each prototype iteration.

3. **Select tools for the prototype.**

   You may want to evaluate the existing suite of tools at your organization available for building the prototype. People are already trained on those tools and feel comfortable using them. The comfort factor is a big enabler. If you decide to select new tools, determine how much training is required, and schedule the training sessions as soon as possible.

4. **Prepare the prototype charter.**

   Put together a short and informal prototype charter that outlines the main purpose for the prototype, the scope of the prototype, what platform it will be built on, how many iterations you are planning, the time frame for completing the prototype, and who will participate.

5. **Design the reports and queries.**

   Based on the access requirements, design the prototype database and the reports and queries. If a Web front end is part of the prototype, design the Web pages as well. Select the relevant data for the prototype, and map the data from the source files and source databases to the prototype database. Be sure to consult with the data quality analyst to learn about source data problems. It is best to leave out poor-quality data rather than contaminate the prototype with it.

6. **Build the prototype.**

   Build the prototype based on the initial database design, report and query designs, and Web page designs. Expect that the design will change several times. Use this opportunity to test various database and application tuning techniques. The database structures as well as the reports and queries developed during the prototype could be used as a yardstick to validate the time and cost estimates for the final BI application.

7. **Demonstrate the prototype.**

   Prepare demonstrations with as much functionality as the type of prototype you have chosen allows. A show-and-tell prototype will have much less functionality than an operational prototype. Run the demonstrations for a short time and solicit approval for the BI project and additional support for the BI initiative as a whole. The demonstrations should be considered a BI marketing activity in addition to being a vehicle for validating the requirements and functionality of the BI application.

Repeat the process outlined above for additional prototype iterations.

DELIVERABLES RESULTING FROM THESE ACTIVITIES

1. **Prototype charter**
   This document is similar to a project charter because it represents an agreement between the business sponsor and the IT staff regarding the prototyping activities for the BI project. It contains the following sections:
   – Primary purpose for the prototype
   – Prototype objectives
   – Prototype participants
   – Data to be used for the prototype
   – Hardware and software platforms to be used
   – Measures of success
   – Application interface agreement

2. **Completed prototype**
   The main deliverable from this step is a completed prototype. This can be a demo, a few mocked-up screens, or a partially functioning BI application.

3. **Revised application requirements document**
   During prototyping, you may discover new requirements or decide to change or drop some of the original ones. Reflect these changes in the application requirements document.

4. **Skills survey matrix**
   This matrix indicates the skill sets of the business people. It should state whether a business person has beginning, advanced, or expert skills in computer usage as well as knowledge about the business functions pertaining to the BI application.

5. **Issues log**
   Document any issues that came up during prototyping (whether they were resolved or not) in an issues log, indicating status or final resolution, impact on the real BI application, action items to pursue, and to whom the action items were assigned.

ROLES INVOLVED IN THESE ACTIVITIES

◆ **Application lead developer**
   The application lead developer should review the application requirements document with the business representative, and together they should prepare a short and informal prototype charter. The application lead developer should also review the existing or mock-up report and query layouts, which will form

the basis for the prototype design. He or she also has to make plans for scheduling the prototype demonstrations.

◆ **Business representative**
The primary responsibility of a business representative is to use the prototype to learn about the feasibility and the look and feel of the BI application. The business representative should assist the application lead developer in creating the prototype charter. The business representative also needs to review the overall BI project requirements and revise them if necessary. This can be accomplished only if the business representative participates in the design and the review of the prototype and is actively involved in the demonstrations.

◆ **Database administrator**
The database administrator is responsible for designing and loading the prototype database with sample source data or sample test data. He or she should also review all database access calls (Structured Query Language [SQL] statements).

◆ **Stakeholders**
The stakeholders do not directly participate in the BI project activities, but they have a vested interest in the project. They should take part in the prototype demonstrations and provide input regarding any additional common access requirements for reports, queries, and ad hoc usage.

◆ **Subject matter expert**
The subject matter expert has to analyze and discuss the access and analysis requirements for reports and queries with the prototyping team. He or she should work with the business representative and project manager to determine the purpose, goals, and primary use of the prototype.

◆ **Web master**
The Web master has to review the existing tools slated for use with Web access to the BI application. The Web master also has to evaluate the usability of the prototype design with regard to Web access and has to determine the necessary interfaces.

RISKS OF NOT PERFORMING STEP 6

The main purpose of prototyping is to make sure that the design of the database, the design of the access and analysis application, and the BI technologies selected will be able to meet the business requirements when the BI application is implemented as intended. By building a successful prototype, you can also validate the accuracy of your cost and time estimates for the full-scale final BI application. The risk of not performing this step is that you may build a BI solution that will cost much more and take much longer than you expected—and that you will not realize it until it is too late.

BIBLIOGRAPHY AND ADDITIONAL READING

Bajaj, Chandrajit. *Trends in Software: Data Visualization Techniques.* New York: John Wiley & Sons, 1999.

Beck, Kent. *Extreme Programming Explained: Embrace Change.* Boston, MA: Addison-Wesley, 2000.

Cockburn, Alistair. *Agile Software Development.* Boston, MA: Addison-Wesley, 2002.

Devlin, Barry. *Data Warehouse: From Architecture to Implementation.* Reading, MA: Addison-Wesley, 1997.

Humphrey, Watts S. *Winning with Software: An Executive Strategy.* Boston, MA: Addison-Wesley, 2002.

Kimball, Ralph, Laura Reeves, Margy Ross, and Warren Thornthwaite. *The Data Warehouse Lifecycle Toolkit: Expert Methods for Designing, Developing, and Deploying Data Warehouses.* New York: John Wiley & Sons, 1998.

Shneiderman, Ben. *Designing the User Interface: Strategies for Effective Human-Computer Interaction.* Boston, MA: Addison-Wesley, 1998.

Turkle, Sherry. *Life on the Screen: Identity in the Age of the Interface.* New York: Simon & Schuster, 1997.

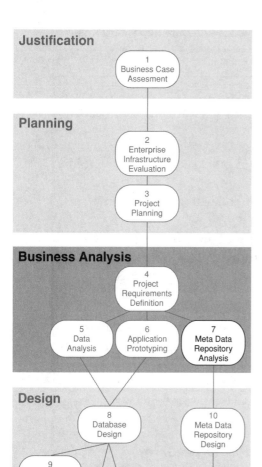

1
Business Case
Assesment

Planning

2
Enterprise
Infrastructure
Evaluation

3
Project
Planning

Business Analysis

4
Project
Requirements
Definition

5
Data
Analysis

6
Application
Prototyping

7
Meta Data
Repository
Analysis

Design

8
Database
Design

10
Meta Data
Repository
Design

9
ETL
Design

Construction

12
Application
Development

14
Meta Data
Repository
Development

11
ETL
Development

13
Data
Mining

Deployment

15
Implementation

16
Release
Evaluation

CHAPTER SEVEN

Step 7: Meta Data Repository Analysis

CHAPTER OVERVIEW

This chapter covers the following topics:

- Things to consider when analyzing whether to license (buy) or build a meta data repository

- Why it is important to deliver meta data with every BI project

- The differences between the two categories of meta data: business meta data and technical meta data

- How a meta data repository can help business people find and use their business data after the data has been standardized for the BI decision-support environment

- The four groupings of meta data components: ownership, descriptive characteristics, rules and policies, and physical characteristics

- How to prioritize meta data for implementation purposes

- Five common difficulties encountered with meta data repository initiatives: technical, staffing, budget, usability, and political challenges

- The entity-relationship (E-R) meta model used to document the meta data requirements

- A definition and examples of meta-meta data

- Brief descriptions of the activities involved in meta data repository analysis, the deliverables resulting from those activities, and the roles involved

- The risks of not performing Step 7

THINGS TO CONSIDER

Meta Data Repository Usage

✓ Who will be using the meta data in the meta data repository?

✓ What standards do we have in place for its use? What standards do we need to develop?

✓ Do we already have a meta data repository? If not, will we license (buy) one or build one?

✓ Will this meta data repository support only the BI decision-support environment, or will it be used for all systems throughout the organization?

✓ How will we know if we are using the meta data repository effectively?

Meta Model Requirements

✓ Do we need to create a meta model for the meta data repository, or do we already have one?

✓ If we have one, what meta data objects do we need to add to it?

✓ Which meta data repository products support our meta model?

✓ Are these meta data repository products extendable?

Meta Data Repository Security

✓ What type of security will we need for the meta data repository?

✓ Who will be authorized to enter and maintain the meta data?

✓ Will everyone be authorized to access any meta data at any time?

Meta Data Capture

✓ What types of business meta data do we need to capture?

✓ Will we be using a computer-aided software engineering (CASE) tool to capture the business meta data?

✓ What type of technical meta data do we need to capture?

✓ Will we be capturing technical meta data in the extract/transform/load (ETL), online analytical processing (OLAP), and other access and analysis tools?

✓ How will we extract the meta data from these tools and migrate it to the meta data repository? Who is responsible for migrating it?

✓ Who will connect the business meta data from the CASE tool to the technical meta data from the ETL, OLAP, and other tools?

> **Meta Data Delivery**
>
> ✓ How will meta data be displayed? How will it be accessed? Will we have a Web interface to the meta data repository?
> ✓ Will we need to produce meta data reports? What types of reports?
> ✓ How will these reports be distributed?
> ✓ Will there be a help function (online tutorial)? Will the help function be context sensitive?
>
> **Staffing**
>
> ✓ Do we already have a meta data administrator? If not, do we have a data administrator with technical skills who can perform the functions of a meta data administrator?
> ✓ Will we have to hire more meta data administrators?
> ✓ How will meta data responsibilities be divided among data administrators and meta data administrators?

A meta data repository is a database. But unlike ordinary databases, a meta data repository is not designed to store business data for a business application. Instead, it is designed to store *contextual information* about the business data. Examples of contextual information about business data include the following:

- Meaning and content of the business data
- Policies that govern the business data
- Technical attributes of the business data
- Specifications that transform the business data
- Programs that manipulate the business data

Contextual information about business data inherently exists in every organization, whether it is documented or not. When contextual information is documented, it is known as *meta data*. When the information is not documented, it is usually not known to everyone in the organization. As a result, business people often invent their own business rules and create their own redundant data along with redundant processes, not realizing (or sometimes not caring) that what they need may already exist. Forty years of such practices have now brought most organizations to the brink of drowning in data and dehydrating from lack of information.

THE IMPORTANCE OF META DATA

Meta data describes an organization in terms of its business activities and the business objects on which the business activities are performed. Consider, for example, a *sale* of a *product* to a *customer* by an *employee*. The *sale* is a business activity and the *product, customer,* and *employee* are the business objects on which the sale activity is performed. Business activities and business objects, whether manual or automated, behave according to a set of relationships and rules, which are defined by the business. These activities and objects, and the relationships and rules that govern them, provide the context in which the business people use the business data every day.

Meta data is so important for the BI decision-support environment because it helps metamorphose business data into information. The difference between data and information is that information is raw data within a business context. Meta data provides that business context; that is, meta data ensures the correct interpretation (based on activities, objects, relationships, and rules) of what the business data actually means.

For example, what is *profit*? Is it the amount of money remaining after a product has been sold and everybody who was involved in that product has been paid? Or is it a more complicated calculation, such as "total annual revenue minus sum of average base cost per product minus actual staff overhead minus accumulated annual production bonuses minus wholesale discounts minus coupons divided by twelve?" Does every business person have the same understanding of profit? Is there one and only one calculation for profit? If there are different interpretations of profit, are all interpretations legitimate? If there are multiple legitimate versions for profit calculations, then multiple data elements must be created, each with its own unique name, definition, content, rules, relationships, and so on. All of this contextual information about profit is meta data.

Since meta data provides the business context in which business data is used, meta data can be viewed as a semantic (interpretive) layer of the BI decision-support environment. This semantic layer helps the business people navigate through the BI target databases, where the business data resides. It also helps the technicians manage the BI target databases as well as the BI applications.

Some important characteristics of meta data and meta data repositories are listed below.

- A meta data repository is populated with meta data from many different tools, such as CASE tools, ETL tools, OLAP tools, and data mining tools.

- Meta data documents the transformation and cleansing of source data and provides an audit trail of the periodic data loads.
- Meta data helps track BI security requirements, data quality measures, and growth metrics (for data volume, hardware, and so on).
- Meta data provides an inventory of all the source data that populates the BI applications.
- Meta data can be centrally managed, or it can be distributed. Either way, each instance of a meta data component should be unique, regardless of its physical location.

Meta Data Categories

There are two categories of meta data: business meta data and technical meta data.

1. **Business meta data** provides business people with a roadmap for accessing the business data in the BI decision-support environment. Since many business people are relatively nontechnical, they should have access to meta data, which defines the BI decision-support environment in business terms they understand.

2. **Technical meta data** supports the technicians and "power users" by providing them with information about their applications and databases, which they need in order to maintain the BI applications.

Table 7.1 highlights some differences between business meta data and technical meta data.

Table 7.1: Business Meta Data versus Technical Meta Data

Business Meta Data	*Technical Meta Data*
• Provided by business people	• Provided by technicians or tools
• Documented in business terms on data models and in data dictionaries	• Documented in technical terms in databases, files, programs, and tools
• Used by business people	• Used by technicians, "power users," databases, programs, and tools (e.g., ETL, OLAP)
• Names fully spelled out in business language	• Abbreviated names with special characters, such as "_" (underscore) or "–" (dash), used in databases, files, and programs

META DATA REPOSITORY AS NAVIGATION TOOL

Meta data is not new; it has always been part of operational systems. It can be found in systems documentation, record layouts, database catalogs, and data declaration sections in programs. The role of meta data in an operational environment was always viewed as *systems documentation*, which was mainly used by the technicians who maintained the operational systems. When some of the systems documentation (meta data) became outdated, the technical staff had enough skills to read through the actual programming code to extract the information they were looking for, such as the meaning and content of a data element. Thus, more often than not, meta data was treated as an afterthought.

In a BI decision-support environment, meta data takes on a new level of importance. A new audience has to be serviced, namely, the business people. Meta data helps them locate, manage, understand, and use the data in the BI target databases. Meta data has a new role: *navigation*, not just documentation. Business people ordinarily do not have the technical skills, nor the time or desire, to decipher programming code. They also do not want to stay dependent on the IT department to interpret the meaning and content of the data after it has been manipulated by the programs. Rather than calling a programmer, a business person should be able to access the meta data, which would then help him or her effectively navigate through the BI decision-support environment and interpret the BI data. As illustrated in Figure 7.1, meta data describes what data is available

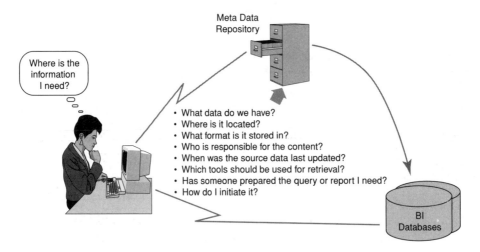

Figure 7.1: Using a Meta Data Repository as a Navigation Tool

in which BI target database, where the data came from, how to access it, how to drill down to the detailed data for closer examination, and how to use it.

Data Standardization

If business data had been stored and used in a consistent, approved manner all along, the data redundancy and inconsistency problems that currently plague many operational systems would not exist to the extent they do today. Unfortunately, bad habits die hard. Developers and business people still explicitly or implicitly reuse the business data in operational systems for different purposes. For example, developers still explicitly redefine data elements in their programs, and business people still implicitly redefine (invent new codes for) existing data elements to capture unrelated information. Documentation of these redefinitions also remains poor or nonexistent. If any documentation exists, it is rarely distributed to everyone in the organization who needs it, and it is very seldom kept up-to-date. Therefore, business people continue to invent their own business rules and create their own redundant data along with redundant processes.

Every BI project team must address this existing data chaos and must make every attempt to promote the standardization of data. While standardizing the business data for the BI decision-support environment, the BI project team should document all changes made to the data so that everyone can be aware of them. This documentation takes the form of meta data in the meta data repository. For example, a source data element could be renamed to conform to new naming standards, or data values could be filtered, added, or transformed to enforce a business rule. In both cases, the BI data in the BI target database would no longer match the source data in the source file or source database. The meta data would provide the navigation between the two.

Using BI applications without knowing that the business data was changed and how it was changed can be a frustrating experience that can eventually end with the business people no longer wanting to use the BI applications at all. That would be devastating since one of the most important aspects of a BI decision-support initiative is to provide an easy-to-use, intuitive way for the business people to access and query the data. An easy-to-use application means the business people:

- Have no need to be relational technology experts
- Have no need to know Structured Query Language (SQL)
- Have no need to know the physical structure of the databases
- Have no need to know the location of their data

- Have no need to guess the meaning of the data
- Have no need to search for the required information

META DATA CLASSIFICATIONS

Since BI projects can generate a great number of meta data components, it is useful to classify these components and to prioritize them for incremental implementation.

Groupings of Meta Data Components

Meta data components can be sorted into four meta data groupings or classifications: ownership, descriptive characteristics, rules and policies, and physical characteristics (Figure 7.2). The meta data repository should be able to store the meta data components of all four classifications, as listed below.

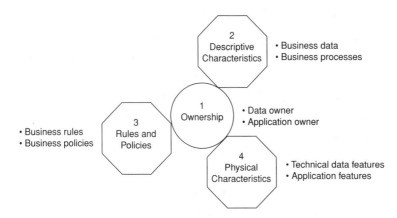

Figure 7.2: Meta Data Classifications

Ownership

- **Data owner:** Data is owned by the organization. However, since the organization is a legal entity and not a person, someone in the organization must take on the authority and responsibility to set policy, determine rules, and establish standards for the organizational data. This authority and responsibility can be distributed among line-of-business managers or assigned to a data ownership committee (whose members will most likely be some or all of the line-of-business managers). An example of distributed data ownership is a manager of the human resource department who has the authority and responsibility to establish policies, rules, and standards for payroll data but not for product data. With data ownership by committee, the committee establishes policies, rules, and standards for *all* data by consensus, by delegation to a committee member, or by some other committee rule.

- **Application owner:** Traditionally, ownership has been assigned to a system as a whole. Since a system is usually composed of an application and its data, "system ownership" implies that the same person has authority to set policy, determine rules, and establish standards for both data and functionality (the application). That may be a valid condition for operational systems where data is originated, but it is not valid for BI applications because most business people using the BI applications are not the same individuals who originate the operational data. Therefore, BI information consumers may own the BI application, but most of them will not own the data.

Descriptive Characteristics

- **Name:** Every data object, data element, and business process should have a unique name.
- **Definition:** Every data object, data element, and business process should have a brief definition explaining what it is.
- **Type and length:** Every data element should have an official type and length declared for it, even if the data elements in the source systems or the columns or cells on the target databases may deviate from it. That deviation would also be defined as meta data under the data element, the column, or the cell where it occurred.
- **Domain:** Every data element should have a declared set of allowable values, even if the set is all-inclusive, such as "any character, number, or sign."
- **Notes:** Additional facts of interest about data or processes should be included. This is a catchall for free-form comments, such as "Dispute between engineering and marketing regarding the meaning of Product Subcomponent Type Code was turned over to the BI steering committee for resolution."

Rules and Policies

- **Relationships:** Data objects are related to each other through business activities. The meta data repository should be able to store information about these relationships.

- **Business rules and business policies:** These components can apply to data as well as to processes. They can be technical data conversion rules, business data domain rules, business data integrity rules, or processing rules.

- **Security:** Requirements for security can apply to data, meta data, processes, databases, applications (programs and screens), tools, and Web sites.

- **Cleanliness:** Metrics about the ETL reconciliation totals and about the quality of the BI data should be stored. The metrics can be expressed as reliability percentages of a data load (e.g., 89 percent of the customer type code is valid) or as record counts stating the number of records filtered (rejected) and the number of records passed through during the ETL process.

- **Applicability:** Data does not live forever. Occasionally, new data is invented and captured, and old data is retired and no longer used. Since the BI target databases store many years of history, some columns or cells will not have values for all time periods because the data was not applicable or did not exist during certain time periods. If spikes appear on trend analysis graphs, the meta data repository should be consulted to determine the applicability of that particular piece of data.

- **Timeliness:** Business people will want to know when the source data was last updated and which of the versions of the operational systems were used for the update. Not all operational systems run daily or on the same day of the month. One operational system may run on the last calendar day of the month while another may run on the last business day of the month. Some operational systems do not "close out the month" until they complete an adjustment run four to ten days after the last calendar day of the month.

Physical Characteristics

- **Origin (source):** Since BI target databases only store existing operational data (internally generated and externally purchased), the origin or source for each data element should be documented. One column in the BI target database can be populated with data elements from multiple sources. For example, the column Account Balance in the Account table could be populated from the data element Demand Deposit Account Balance in the Checking Account source database and from the data element Time Deposit Account Daily Balance in the Savings Account Transaction file. Conversely, one source data element can feed multiple columns in the BI target database. For example, the data element Type Code may be used for two purposes in the operational system.

The data values "A", "B", and "C" of Type Code may be used to populate the column Customer Type Code in the Customer table, and the data values "N", "O", and "P" of the same Type Code may be used to populate the column Product Type Code in the Product table.

- **Physical location:** Several meta data components (e.g., tables, columns, dataset names) should describe where the data resides in the BI decision-support environment.

- **Transformation:** Very few data elements can be moved from source to target without any type of transformation. At a minimum, the data type and length may have to change, or single-character codes may have to be translated into multi-character mnemonics. In the worst case, lengthy business rules may require more complicated transformations involving editing, filtering, combining, separating, or translating data values.

- **Derivation:** This component stores the calculation for derived columns. While derived columns are customarily not stored in operational systems, it is the norm to store them in BI target databases.

- **Aggregation and summarization:** Similar to derivation, aggregation and summarization rules should be stored as meta data.

- **Volume and growth:** The size and growth of BI target databases are often enormous. Therefore, projected as well as actual volumes should be documented as meta data in terms of the number of rows and the percentage of expected growth.

Business people most frequently access the meta data components in the *descriptive characteristics* classification as well as the *rules and policies* classification (Figure 7.3). Technicians typically access the meta data components in the *physical characteristics* classification (Figure 7.4).

Prioritization of Meta Data Components

Capturing all meta data components may not be necessary or practical for all BI projects. However, capturing none is unacceptable. As a rule, meta data should be a deliverable with every BI project. It will serve the business people to recognize their old data, trace what happened to it (transformation), locate it in the new BI target databases, and determine how to use it properly. In other words, the business people will greatly benefit from having meta data available to help them navigate through the BI decision-support environment.

Figure 7.3: Meta Data Usage by Business People

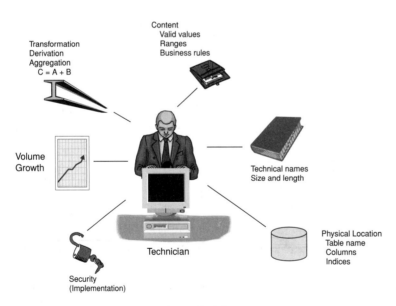

Figure 7.4: Meta Data Usage by Technicians

Not all meta data components have the same value to all business people or all BI applications. It might be useful to prioritize the meta data components into three groups: mandatory, important (beneficial but not mandatory), and optional. Table 7.2 shows a recommended prioritization scheme for capturing meta data components in a meta data repository.

Table 7.2: Prioritization of Meta Data Components

Meta Data	*Mandatory*	*Important*	*Optional*
Owner		✓	
Business data name		✓	
Technical data name	✓		
Definition	✓		
Type and length	✓		
Content (domain)		✓	
Relationships		✓	
Business rules and policies		✓	
Security			✓
Cleanliness		✓	
Applicability		✓	
Timeliness			✓
Origin (source)	✓		
Physical location (BI databases)	✓		
Transformation	✓		
Derivation		✓	
Aggregation		✓	
Summarization		✓	
Volume and growth			✓
Notes			✓

All *mandatory* meta data components, and as many *important* meta data components as possible, should be captured and stored in the meta data repository. *Optional* meta data components could be postponed to future BI application releases.

META DATA REPOSITORY CHALLENGES

Good ideas are often hard to implement. Providing a meta data repository is a good idea but also quite a challenging one, regardless of whether the decision is made to license (buy) a commercially available product or to build a repository from scratch. This section briefly describes the challenges faced when implementing a meta data repository (Figure 7.5).

Figure 7.5: Meta Data Repository Challenges

Technical Challenges

Building a meta data repository is not a trivial task. It is a project in itself, with its own project plan, its own development steps, and its own staff. All the technology challenges that apply to databases and applications can surface on meta data repository projects.

Licensing a meta data repository product is an alternative to building one, but the "plain vanilla" versions of commercially available meta data repository products often do not meet all the meta data requirements of a BI decision-support environment. Therefore, licensing a meta data repository product still necessitates extensive analysis of the requirements in order to select the right product, as well as a considerable implementation effort to enhance it.

Enhancing licensed software comes with its own challenges. The source code for the product may not be available. The vendor may insist on incorporating the requested enhancements for a price and at his or her own speed. The time and effort required for product maintenance increase because the enhancements must be reapplied to the new releases and versions of the licensed meta data repository product.

Staffing Challenges

Meta data should be "living" documentation stored in a database, that is, in the meta data repository. Storing meta data as paper documents is guaranteed to turn it into "shelfware" within months, if not weeks. This means that, at a minimum, one meta data administrator must be dedicated full-time to managing the meta data repository content and the software. If a meta data repository is being built as part of the BI project, a staff of one person will not be enough. The meta data repository effort will require an analyst, a data modeler, a database designer, and one or more developers.

Budget Challenges

Although many BI experts think of meta data as the "glue" of the BI decision-support environment, most organizations allocate little or no money for creating and maintaining a meta data repository. They still regard meta data as systems documentation for technicians, rather than a navigation tool for business people. The pain of access frustration and data confusion must often reach an intolerable level before organizations include meta data as a mandatory and standard deliverable of their BI projects.

 Lack of meta data has frequently been cited as one of the reasons for BI application failure.

Usability Challenges

Using a meta data repository should be completely intuitive. Business people should be able to click on an icon and immediately get the requested information about a table or column, a chart or report, or even a business query. More complex inquiries against the meta data repository should be handled with built-in or customized macros. However, the most polished way to present meta data is to include it in BI queries, as shown in Figure 7.6.

Monthy Sales Report				
Month	Produce	US Sales ($)	Canada Sales ($)	Total Sales ($)
January	Apples	22,000	8,000	30,000
	Bananas	11,900	6,000	17,900
	Coconuts	2,000	800	2,800
February	Apples	22,500	8,500	31,000
	Bananas	10,000	5,800	15,800
	Coconuts	2,200	350	2,550
March	Apples	23,700	9,300	33,000
	Bananas	9,900	7,000	16,900
	Coconuts	2,400	750	3,150

Meta Data ⟶
Data Quality Load Statistics:
51% of $ values not loaded
10% of source records not loaded

Figure 7.6: Example of Meta Data in a BI Query

Unfortunately, many meta data repository products are still designed by technicians for technicians rather than for business people. Some of these products still have a cryptic meta data language, lack sophisticated reporting capabilities, are not context sensitive, and require an understanding of the meta model that describes the meta data objects and their relationships.

Political Challenges

Building an enterprise-wide meta data solution is difficult because departmental differences must be reconciled and cross-departmental politics must be resolved. These disputes, although totally predictable, are rarely taken into account when the project plan is created. As a result, projects are delayed while these issues are addressed or pushed up to business executives and steering committees. This gives the impression that BI projects are difficult, controversial, tiresome, draining, slow, and generally undesirable work.

 Despite all these challenges, a meta data repository is a mandatory component of every BI decision-support environment.

THE LOGICAL META MODEL

Regardless of whether the meta data repository is licensed or built, and regardless of the implementation method (centralized, decentralized, or distributed, as discussed in Step 10, Meta Data Repository Design), the meta data repository should support a logical meta model, which reflects the meta data requirements. As with business data, each component of meta data is unique by nature. It is important to define these unique meta data objects, their contents, their interrelationships, and their interdependencies, *independent* of how they will be stored or accessed. The technique for this activity is logical data modeling, only in this case it will produce a logical meta model.

A logical meta model is a data model that indicates objects, the relationships between the objects, and the cardinality and optionality of the relationships. The difference between a logical meta model for a meta data repository and a logical data model for a business application lies in the nature of the objects. Objects in a logical meta model represent *meta data*, such as entity, attribute, definition, domain, table, column, and index. Objects in a logical data model represent *business data*, such as customer, product, employee, account, and location.

The Entity-Relationship Meta Model

A logical meta model is created during the first meta data initiative and is expanded with each subsequent initiative. The logical representation of meta data objects should be captured as an E-R diagram because of its explicit definitions of the meta data objects, the relationships among them, and the contents of the objects. Figure 7.7 shows an example of an E-R meta model.

An E-R meta model primarily helps people understand, communicate, and validate the meta data requirements. Therefore, an E-R meta model should be viewed as a *requirements* model to be used for evaluating meta data repository

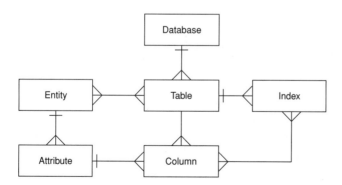

Figure 7.7: Entity-Relationship Meta Model. (Short vertical lines indicate "one," and the crow's feet indicate "many.")

products and for setting a baseline when designing a customized meta data repository, even if its physical meta model (database design) ends up being object-oriented (OO).

Meta-Meta Data

Since meta data is the contextual information about business data, *meta-meta data* is the contextual information about meta data. Many components of meta-meta data are similar to those of meta data. For example, every meta data object should have components that cover name, definition, size and length, content, ownership, relationship, business rules, security, cleanliness, physical location, applicability, timeliness, volume, and notes. The meta-meta data for a meta data object might look like this:

- Name: Entity
- Relationship: related to one or many tables
- Security: read by all, updated by the data administrator
- Ownership: the data administrator
- Origin: ERWIN CASE tool
- Physical location: MDRSYSENT table
- Cleanliness: 2 percent missing data
- Timeliness: last updated on November 1, 2002
- Volume and growth: 2,391 rows, growth rate 1 percent annually

META DATA REPOSITORY ANALYSIS ACTIVITIES

The activities for meta data repository analysis do not need to be performed linearly. Figure 7.8 indicates which activities can be performed concurrently. The list below briefly describes the activities associated with Step 7, Meta Data Repository Analysis.

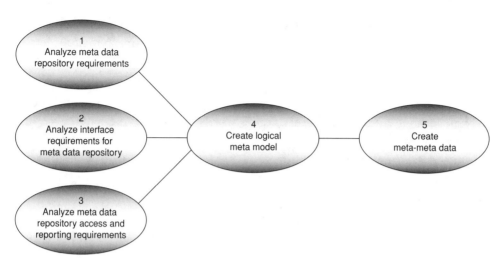

Figure 7.8: Meta Data Repository Analysis Activities

1. **Analyze the meta data repository requirements.**
   Work with the business representative to determine and prioritize the meta data requirements for your specific BI project. Indicate which of the meta data components are mandatory, important, and optional. If a meta data repository already exists, determine which meta data components need to be added, if any. Update the latest version of the application requirements document (revised during or after prototyping).

2. **Analyze the interface requirements for the meta data repository.**
   Whether a meta data repository is licensed or built, it must accept meta data from different sources. Business meta data will have to be extracted from CASE tools, word processing documents, or spreadsheets. Technical meta data will have to be extracted and merged from database management system (DBMS) dictionaries, ETL tools, data-cleansing tools, OLAP tools, report writers, and data mining tools.

3. **Analyze the meta data repository access and reporting requirements.**
   Populating a database is meaningless unless the content can be accessed, queried, and reported. This is as true for meta data as it is for business data. Identify the meta data access requirements, security requirements, and help function requirements. Evaluate alternative display modes, such as Portable Document Format (PDF), Hypertext Markup Language (HTML), SQL,

canned queries, or proprietary meta data repository reporting software. A context-sensitive help tutorial would be a beneficial feature to include.

4. Create the logical meta model.

Draw the logical meta model as an E-R model to explicitly show the relationships between meta data objects, even if you plan to implement the meta data repository as an OO database. In other words, the logical meta model should always be an E-R model, while the physical meta model (the meta data repository database design created in Step 10, Meta Data Repository Design) can be either an E-R model or an OO model.

5. Create the meta-meta data.

While the logical meta model shows the meta data repository requirements at a glance, the meta-meta data describes the required meta data components in detail.

DELIVERABLES RESULTING FROM THESE ACTIVITIES

1. Logical meta model

This data model is a fully normalized E-R diagram showing kernel entities, associative entities, characteristic entities, relationships, cardinality, optionality, unique identifiers, and all attributes for meta data repository objects.

2. Meta-meta data

The meta data entities and attributes from the logical meta model must be described with meta data. Meta data–specific meta data components (meta-meta data) are meta data names, meta data definitions, meta data relationships, unique identifiers, types, lengths, domains, business rules, policies, and meta data ownership.

ROLES INVOLVED IN THESE ACTIVITIES

◆ Data administrator

The data administrator gathers the business meta data in a CASE tool during the logical data modeling activities. This meta data will be one of the sources for the meta data repository. The data administrator, in collaboration with the meta data administrator, writes and publishes the data standards. He or she may also assist with creating the meta model and the meta-meta data.

◆ **Meta data administrator**

The meta data administrator has primary responsibilities for storing and providing access to the meta data and for maintaining the meta data repository. He or she must analyze the meta data requirements, identify the meta data components, and produce or enhance the logical meta model and the meta-meta data.

◆ **Subject matter expert**

The subject matter expert participates in this step by representing the business people and their meta data requirements. The subject matter expert identifies security requirements and data ownership and works with the data administrator, the meta data administrator, the data owners, and other business people to standardize names, definitions, content, and business rules.

RISKS OF NOT PERFORMING STEP 7

Since one of the BI decision-support objectives is to eliminate inconsistencies, the source data must be standardized. Standardization invariably results in changing much of the source data. Changes may include renaming the data, splitting one source data element into multiple target columns, or populating one target column from multiple source data elements. It can also mean translating codes into mnemonics, standardizing (changing) data values, and filtering out inappropriate or invalid data. In the end, business people will not be able to reconcile their operational source data to the BI target data unless they have a trace of these changes. This trace is called meta data, and business people need it to navigate effectively through the BI decision-support environment.

Without meta data, the business people would have a difficult time understanding and using the transformed data in the BI target databases. It would be as frustrating as aimlessly driving a car for weeks or months without a map, guessing your way to your destination. Once the business people perceive the BI application as difficult to use or they think the BI data is unreliable because it no longer matches the source data in the operational systems, they could label the BI decision-support initiative a failure.

BIBLIOGRAPHY AND ADDITIONAL READING

Adelman, Sid, and Larissa Terpeluk Moss. *Data Warehouse Project Management.* Boston, MA: Addison-Wesley, 2000.

Brackett, Michael H. *Data Resource Quality: Turning Bad Habits into Good Practices.* Boston, MA: Addison-Wesley, 2000.

———. *The Data Warehouse Challenge: Taming Data Chaos.* New York: John Wiley & Sons, 1996.

Devlin, Barry. *Data Warehouse: From Architecture to Implementation.* Reading, MA: Addison-Wesley, 1997.

Hackney, Douglas. *Understanding and Implementing Successful Data Marts.* Reading, MA: Addison-Wesley, 1997.

Inmon, William H., J. D. Welch, and Katherine L. Glassey. *Managing the Data Warehouse: Practical Techniques for Monitoring Operations and Performance, Administering Data and Tools and Managing Change and Growth.* New York: John Wiley & Sons, 1996.

Marco, David. *Building and Managing the Meta Data Repository: A Full Lifecycle Guide.* New York: John Wiley & Sons, 2000.

Reingruber, Michael C., and William W. Gregory. *The Data Modeling Handbook: A Best-Practice Approach to Building Quality Data Models.* New York: John Wiley & Sons, 1994.

Ross, Ronald G. *The Business Rule Concepts.* Houston, TX: Business Rule Solutions, Inc., 1998.

Simsion, Graeme. *Data Modeling Essentials: Analysis, Design, and Innovation.* Boston, MA: International Thomson Computer Press, 1994.

Sperley, Eric. *The Enterprise Data Warehouse: Planning, Building, and Implementation.* Upper Saddle River, NJ: Prentice Hall, 1999.

Tannenbaum, Adrienne. *Metadata Solutions: Using Metamodels, Repositories, XML, and Enterprise Portals to Generate Information on Demand.* Boston, MA: Addison-Wesley, 2002.

Data Management Association (DAMA): *http://www.dama.org*

DM Review magazine: *http://www.dmreview.com*

Enterprise Warehousing Solutions, Inc.: *http://www.EWSolutions.com*

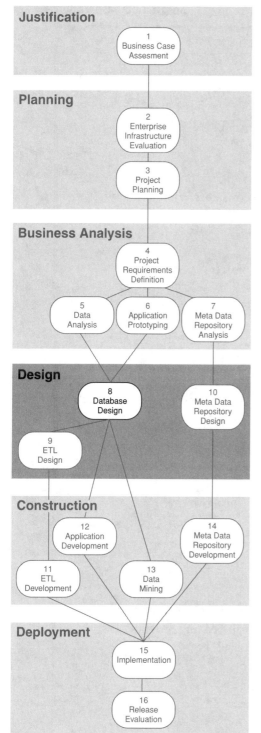

CHAPTER EIGHT

Step 8: Database Design

CHAPTER OVERVIEW

This chapter covers the following topics:

■ Things to consider about database design

■ The differences in database design philosophies and in best design practices for operational databases and for BI target databases

■ The multidimensional design premise of aggregation and summarization

■ Basic explanations of a star schema and a snowflake schema

■ Aspects of physical database design, including implementation options (such as free space and buffer space), physical dataset placement, partitioning, clustering, indexing, reorganizations, backup and recovery, and parallel query execution

■ Brief descriptions of the activities involved in database design, the deliverables resulting from those activities, and the roles involved

■ The risks of not performing Step 8

THINGS TO CONSIDER

Reports and Queries

✓ What common reporting patterns exist across departments?

✓ What level of detailed data will the business people require for drill-down queries?

✓ How much ad hoc querying against detail data do we project will occur?

✓ How many reporting dimensions should we consider? What are they?

✓ How many new dimensions may have to be added in the future?

Design Considerations

✓ Should we store aggregated and summarized data?

✓ How much concurrent usage of the data should we expect?

✓ How big will the BI target databases be? What are the projected data volumes and growth factors?

✓ How much historical data will we keep?

✓ What will be the frequency of loads?

✓ Will the databases need to be distributed?

✓ What are the availability requirements?

Performance Considerations

✓ What are the performance requirements?

✓ How will we cluster the tables? By the date column or by other columns?

✓ What tables should be co-located?

✓ How will we partition the tables? Will we partition by date?

✓ What types of indexing algorithms should we use (B-tree, hash, inverted file, sparse, binary)?

✓ Can we run multiple operations (queries, loads) in parallel?

Selection of Database Management System

✓ Which database management system (DBMS) are we using for our existing applications? Will we use the same DBMS for the BI target databases?

✓ Will our current DBMS scale to the expected size?

✓ Are we satisfied with the current DBMS? If not, what are we doing about it?

✓ Will we need to license (buy) another DBMS?

Staffing

✓ What skills do we have available to design the BI target databases?

✓ Do we have enough database administrators?

✓ Can one database administrator be dedicated to this project full-time?

✓ Does he or she have multidimensional design skills? If not, how soon can he or she receive training?

✓ Will we need to hire a consultant to mentor the database administrator and the team?

BI decision-support requirements for aggregated and summarized data have introduced a new type of database design and a new way of storing data. This new multidimensional database design schema, coupled with new BI technology, supports the ability to "slice and dice" information in myriad ways for reporting and analysis purposes. In order to implement the capabilities of slicing and dicing, database administrators and developers must learn new design techniques and must acquire a new way of working with the databases. They must begin by understanding the ways in which the data will be accessed. Data can be accessed either in a conventional way (usually detailed records retrieved with Structured Query Language [SQL] queries) or in a multidimensional way (usually summarized records retrieved with an online analytical processing [OLAP] tool). Multidimensional data storage and data access techniques, which support slicing and dicing, allow information to be viewed from a variety of perspectives, such as Products by Factory by Market Segment and Market Segments by Product by Factory.

DIFFERENCES IN DATABASE DESIGN PHILOSOPHIES

There is a completely different design philosophy behind BI target databases as compared with operational databases. Table 8.1 summarizes the differences between these two types of databases.

Operational Databases

The intent of operational database design is to prevent the storage of the same data attributes in multiple places and thus to avoid the update anomalies caused by redundancy. In other words, from an operational perspective you want to

Table 8.1: Operational Databases versus BI Target Databases

Operational Databases	*BI Target Databases*
• Geared toward eliminating redundancy, coordinating updates, and repeating the same types of operations many times a day, every day (for example, airline reservations, deposits and withdrawals from bank accounts, hotel room reservations).	• Geared toward supporting a wide range of queries and reports. Queries and reports may vary from one business analyst to another or from one department to another. All of the queries and reports may not run on the same day and may not run every day (for example, quarterly trend analysis reports on regional sales, monthly order fulfillment report).
• Most of the transactional systems require subsecond response time.	• Although response time is important, subseconds *cannot* be expected. Typical response times are seconds, minutes, or hours.
• Highly normalized to support consistent updates and maintenance of referential integrity.	• Highly denormalized to provide quick retrieval of a wide range and a large amount of data. Data that belongs together from an analytical reporting perspective is usually stored together.
• Store very little derived data. Data is usually derived dynamically when needed.	• Store large amounts of derived data. This saves time for the queries and reports.
• Do not store historical data. Historical records are archived.	• Store large amounts of historical data, often at some level of summarization, but just as often at a detailed level.
• Lightly summarized, mostly for reporting purposes.	• Many levels of precalculated, summarized data, from lightly summarized to highly summarized.

avoid storing the same data in multiple columns in multiple tables so they do not get out of synch. Designing normalized database structures is key for developing relational databases in support of that intent. Normalization ensures that the data is created, stored, and modified in a consistent, nonredundant way.

Most operational systems are designed with a *data-in* philosophy (data entry), not a *data-out* philosophy (reporting and querying). The objective of a data-in philosophy is to make data entry as efficient as possible, running hundreds of thousands of transactions per day, while eliminating or minimizing redundancies in the data. Data redundancy leads to inconsistencies, and inconsistencies are often the reason for poor-quality data. Therefore, in trying to solve the enormous data quality and data redundancy problems in operational systems, the goal is to *avoid redundancy* (except for key redundancy, which is unavoidable). This goal is achieved through normalization.

While normalization works well for operational systems, the requirements for reporting are different from the requirements for data entry. Reporting uses data that has already been created, which means update anomalies cannot occur. While it is of great benefit that the data is consistent and nonredundant as a result of a normalized database design, that same design makes reporting difficult. For example, to create strategic trend analysis reports, many tables have to be accessed, and every row in those tables has to be read. This is not only complex but also extremely inefficient when run against a normalized database design because it requires scanning tables and performing large multi-table JOINs. For that reason, most BI target databases are based on a multidimensional design, in which the data for the strategic trend analysis reports is stored in a precalculated and presummarized way.

Figure 8.1 illustrates the general difference between an operational normalized design and a BI multidimensional design.

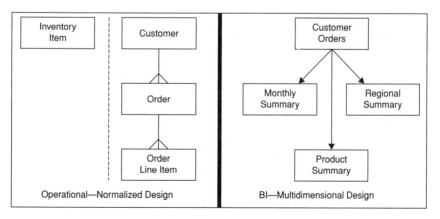

Figure 8.1: Operational normalized versus BI Multidimensional Designs

In this example, the operational database design shows an Order database where customers are associated with orders, and each order is composed of many line items. With each placed order, the line items have to be subtracted from a separate Inventory database. The BI target database design shows a database with summaries that are used to identify trends over time. In this design, the same data about orders, line items, and inventory may exist in multiple tables (Monthly Summary, Regional Summary, Product Summary), albeit summarized by different dimensions. While operational databases generally store granular (atomic) data, BI target databases, for the most part, store summarized data.

BI Target Databases

Contrary to the *data-in* philosophy (data entry) of operational systems, the *data-out* philosophy (reporting and querying) of BI applications includes the following design considerations.

- BI target databases are designed for simplified, high-performance data retrieval, not for efficiency of data storage and maintenance (which are important design considerations for operational databases).

- Eliminating or minimizing data redundancy is not a goal in designing BI target databases. If a choice must be made, data redundancy is favored over complexity, but the redundancy must be controlled. Redundant data must be consistent and reconcilable.

- Basic assumptions for designing BI target databases are listed below.
  - Data is stored in such a manner that it is readily accessible in ways that are of interest to the business people.
  - The design is driven by access and usage.
  - A normalized design is not necessarily intuitive for a business person and could therefore become quite complex.
  - No BI data can be invented! All data in the BI target databases must exist in or be derivable from current internal or external operational data sources.

A key decision for all BI applications is whether or not, and at what level, to store summarized data in the BI target databases. The database administrator and the lead developer may decide to store both detailed data and summarized data, either together in the same BI target database or in different BI target databases. This database design decision must be based on access and usage requirements.

LOGICAL DATABASE DESIGN

Because of the differences in intent and purpose between operational systems and BI applications, different database design techniques have been devised for BI target databases. These highly denormalized designs store aggregated and summarized data in a multidimensional fashion. Logical database designs are documented as physical data models with technical meta data.

Aggregation and summarization are probably the most significant contributors to good BI application performance. If most business analysts need to see their data summarized, these totals should be precalculated and stored for quick retrieval. It is important to discuss the level of granularity with the business representative, as well as with other business analysts who will be using the BI target databases, since they will expect the database design to allow them to drill down to a certain level of detail.

Multidimensional database designs support the quick retrieval of a wide range of data. Two popular multidimensional design techniques are the star schema and the snowflake schema, both described below.

The Star Schema

In a star schema, data is represented as an array of precalculated values, called *facts*, around which analysis is performed. These precalculated facts represent atomic operational data values that have been presummarized by certain dimensions, such as customer, product, and time. A *dimension* in a star schema is similar to an entity in a logical data model: it is a business object about which data is collected for business purposes.

The star schema mirrors the view of a business query. As the name implies, the star schema has a single object in the middle, called the *fact table*, which is connected in a radial fashion to a number of objects, called *dimension tables*. Figure 8.2 presents an example of a star schema.

A star schema has two, and only two, levels: the fact table and a series of single-level dimension tables. Fact tables have the following characteristics:

- A fact table represents a critical business event (a business activity or transaction, such as a sale or a claim).
- The facts are the quantifiable aspects of the business event; that is, they are columns in the fact table.

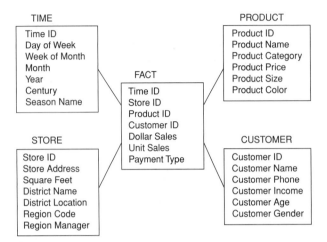

Figure 8.2: Star Schema

- A fact table links to its related dimension tables (business objects, such as customer or product).
- A fact table has a long composite key comprised of the primary keys of the related dimension tables (which are foreign keys in the fact table).
- A number of highly redundant fact tables may exist for a given subject area. Each fact table could contain a different aggregation level of the same data. For example:
  - Sales facts by store by region by date
  - Sales facts by product by store by date
  - Sales facts by customer by region by date
- Fact tables are long and narrow: the tables have an immense number of rows (long), but there are relatively few columns in the tables (narrow).

Dimension tables have very different characteristics.

- Dimension tables are business objects, which represent the different perspectives from which the facts in a fact table can be viewed and analyzed.
- Dimension tables usually have a one-attribute primary key.
- Dimension tables are denormalized, which means that data belonging together from a specific business perspective, such as a roll-up hierarchy, is grouped together into one table. This produces some redundant data values, which is acceptable in this design schema.

- Dimension tables are short and wide: the tables have relatively few rows (short), but there are many columns in the tables (wide).

- Whenever possible, dimension tables should be shared by the fact tables (conformed dimensions).

- One dimension is always a time dimension with attributes describing the timestamp, such as calendar year, quarter, season, fiscal period, or accounting period. Some other examples of common dimension tables are customer, product, policy, sales representative, region, and store.

Most multidimensional DBMSs effectively deal with the optimization of large multi-table JOINs. One method for determining whether the DBMS is resolving the query efficiently is to look at the optimized plan for the query. For example:

- If the fact table is the last table JOINed, this is an indicator of optimization. If the fact table appears to be somewhere in the middle, or even somewhere toward the beginning, the DBMS may not be resolving the JOIN optimally, unless it uses more sophisticated JOIN algorithms.

- If the DBMS does not use Cartesian product JOINs, the DBMS may take the qualifying row keys and apply them against a composite fact table index, or it may apply them via an index intersection against multiple fact table single-column indices.

In either case, verify that your DBMS is executing multidimensional queries in the most efficient manner since your performance depends on it.

The star schema is the most popular database design schema for BI applications for a variety of reasons.

- It yields the best performance for trend analysis queries and reports that include years of historical data.

- It provides maximum flexibility for multidimensional data analysis.

- It is supported by most of the relational DBMS vendors with modifications to their DBMS optimizer.

- Its simplicity makes complex data analysis much less difficult than with a standard normalized design. It is much easier to ask questions such as the following:
  - Which insurance broker is giving us the most or the least lucrative business?
  - What are the most frequently occurring types of claims from this insurance broker?
  - When are these claims occurring?

The preceding questions are typical drill-down questions (asking for more detailed data) and typical roll-up questions (asking for more summarized data).

The Snowflake Schema

A snowflake schema is a variation of a star schema, except in a snowflake the points of the star radiate into more points, as shown in Figure 8.3.

In snowflake schemas, the levels of the hierarchies in the dimension tables are normalized, thereby increasing the number of tables. Table 8.2 lists the advantages and disadvantages of snowflake schemas.

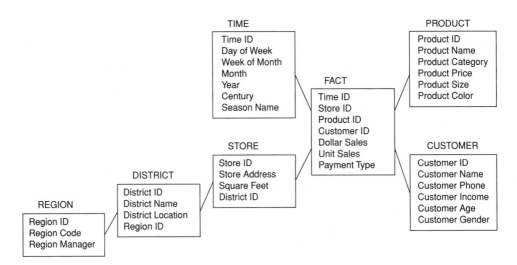

Figure 8.3: Snowflake Schema

Table 8.2: Advantages and Disadvantages of Snowflake Schemas

Advantages	*Disadvantages*
• The size of the dimension tables is reduced and data value redundancy is avoided because parent-child hierarchies are no longer collapsed.	• The increased number of tables may adversely affect query performance because of the necessary additional JOINs.
• Application flexibility is increased.	• Database maintenance effort is increased because there are more tables to maintain.

PHYSICAL DATABASE DESIGN

Because BI applications usually require operational detailed data as well as summarized data, and because they often need to store some or all of that data redundantly, the size of some BI target databases can be enormous. Databases approaching or exceeding one terabyte of data are called *very large databases* (VLDBs). Designing VLDBs is a big challenge, and the day-to-day chores of maintaining these VLDBs are demanding. Many difficult physical design decisions need to be made, and some highly effective performance enhancements need to be used. The following sections present some suggested guidelines.

Implementation Options

Almost every DBMS lets the database administrator choose from a number of implementation options. Give considerable attention to selecting the right options when implementing a BI target database. It takes experience to know which combination of options will meet the desired performance level. Implementation decisions include the following:

- How much free space to choose
- How much buffer space to declare
- How large to set the blocksize
- Whether to use any compaction technique

Physical Dataset Placement

Another basic issue that affects performance is the placement of the datasets. Methods for achieving fast response include combinations of:

- Storing frequently referenced data on fast devices.
- Storing different aggregation levels on different platforms. For performance reasons, it may be necessary to store aggregate data on distributed midrange servers while keeping detail data on the mainframe.
- Striping disks in an interleaved fashion to optimize input/output (I/O) controller usage. Using lots of small disks instead of a few large disks, separating those disks onto separate controllers, and writing the data across devices increases I/O throughput.
- Placing datasets in a way that lengthy seeks are avoided when possible.

- Selecting address and search schemes that require few seeks, preferably only one per retrieval.
- Running multiple operations in parallel.

Also consider whether to separate indices from data and put them on separate disks.

Partitioning

Ensure that tables are partitioned effectively across multiple disks. This is particularly important for VLDBs where fact tables can reach several hundred gigabytes. Partitioning allows the data of one "logical" table to be spread across multiple physical datasets. The physical data distribution is based on a partitioning column, which is most commonly *date*. Since a partitioning column must be part of the table's primary key, the partitioning column cannot be a derived column, and it cannot contain NULL values. Partitioning enables you to back up and restore a portion of a table without impacting the availability of other portions of the same table that are not being backed up or restored.

Clustering

Define cluster table requirements, and physically co-locate related tables on the disk drive. Clustering is a very useful technique for sequential access of large amounts of data. Clustering is accomplished through clustering indices that determine in which sequential order the rows in the tables are physically stored in the datasets. Ideally, you want to cluster the primary key of each table to avoid page splits, that is, to make sure that new rows inserted into the tables will be stored sequentially on the disk according to the columns in their clustering index. Using this technique can dramatically improve performance because sequential access of data is the norm in BI applications. When the rows of a table are no longer stored in the same order as its clustering index (data fragmentation), performance will suffer and the table has to be reorganized.

Indexing

There are two extreme indexing strategies, neither of which is advisable: one strategy is to index everything, and the other is to index nothing. Instead of veering to these extremes, index those columns that are frequently searched and that have a high distribution in values, such as Account Open Date. Do not index columns that have a low distribution in values, such as Gender Code.

Once you have decided which columns to index, determine the index strategy to use. Most DBMSs provide several access methods to choose from, either sequential access or direct access using any of the following well-known indexing algorithms:

- B-tree
- Hash
- Inverted file
- Sparse
- Binary

Consult with your DBMS vendor to choose the most optimum access method (indexing algorithm) for the DBMS product you are using.

Reorganizations

Occasionally you will need to reorganize the databases because incremental loads will fragment the datasets over time, and inserted rows will no longer be stored in a logical sequence. This fragmentation may result in long data retrieval chains, and performance can drop off significantly. Most DBMSs provide reorganization routines to rearrange the fragmented database in order to reclaim space occupied by deleted data or to move records from overflow areas into free space in prime data areas.

The basic activities involved in reorganizing a database are to copy the old database onto another device, reblock the rows, and reload them. This is not a trivial effort for BI target databases. The good news is that all DBMSs can perform a partial reorganization routine on database partitions, which is another reason for the database administrator to partition the BI target databases.

Backup and Recovery

Since software and hardware may fail, it is necessary to establish backup and recovery procedures. DBMSs provide utilities to take full backups as well as incremental backups. Many organizations are under the misguided impression that the BI target databases can always be recreated from the original source data. They neglect to realize that it may take a very long time to recreate the BI target databases if they have to rerun all the initial and historical extract/transform/load (ETL) programs—assuming the original source files are still available.

Disaster recovery is also an issue for BI applications. If the backup tapes or cartridges are destroyed during a disaster, it could be difficult to recreate your BI target databases, and it could take a very long time (if recovery is possible at all). For this reason, many companies choose to store their database backups in remote locations.

Parallel Query Execution

To improve the performance of a query, break down a single query into components to be run concurrently. Some DBMS products offer transparent parallel execution, which means you do not need to know how to break down a query into components because the DBMS does it for you. Performance is greatly increased when multiple portions of one query run in parallel on multiple processors. Other applications of parallel query execution are loading tablespace partitions, building indices, and scanning or sorting tables. Parallel processing is a very important concept for BI applications and should be considered whenever possible.

DATABASE DESIGN ACTIVITIES

The activities for database design do not need to be performed linearly. Figure 8.4 indicates which activities can be performed concurrently. The list below briefly describes the activities associated with Step 8, Database Design.

1. **Review the data access requirements.**
   The database administrator must review the data access and analysis requirements (reports, queries), which were analyzed and finalized during Step 6, Application Prototyping. He or she also has to review the prototyping results with the application lead developer to help determine the most appropriate design schema for the BI target databases.

2. **Determine the aggregation and summarization requirements.**
   Before committing to the final design schema for the BI target databases, the database administrator needs to finalize the data aggregation and summarization requirements with the business representative and the application lead developer. Pay close attention to aggregation and summarization explosion and to data explosion in general. Business people often ask for data "just in case" they will need it some day, and then they rarely use it, if ever.

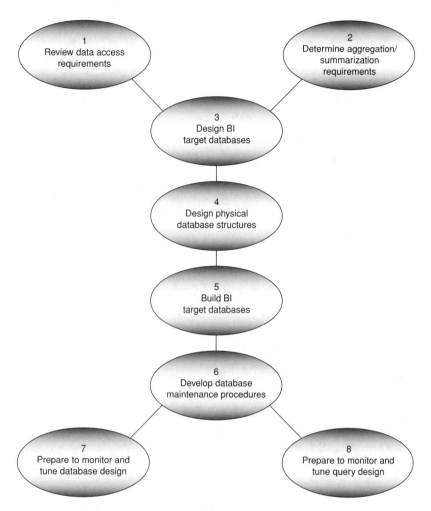

Figure 8.4: Database Design Activities

3. Design the BI target databases.

The widespread claims that all BI applications are only about multidimensional analysis and multidimensional reporting are not true! For example, some financial analysts (statisticians) reporting to the CFO or the CEO will emphatically state their requirements similar to this: "I need to be able to ask any question of any detailed data in any way. Don't try to box me into any predetermined reporting patterns. I have none!" These analysts need total ad hoc flexibility against historical detailed data and are always willing to give up performance, even if it means that their queries will run for hours or overnight. Although these types of analysts are definitely in the minority, they do exist, and you must take their data access requirements into consideration. Therefore, while the designs of most of your BI target databases will be based on a multidimensional schema, some will be based on an entity-relationship schema. Database designs are documented as physical data models.

The data access requirements and the data aggregation and summarization requirements will determine the most appropriate database design. If there are obvious reporting patterns or if the requirements ask for slice and dice analysis capabilities, then the most appropriate database design is a multidimensional one. If there are no reporting requirements and if the business analysts insist that they need ad hoc access to their detail data, then the most appropriate design is the entity-relationship design, which is more normalized with few or no aggregations or summaries.

These are not the only two design schemas applicable for BI target databases. For some types of access and analysis requirements, a hybrid design may be the most appropriate.

4. **Design the physical database structures.**
   Clustering, partitioning, indexing, and appropriately placing the datasets are the four most important characteristics of physical database design. The database administrator should cluster the most frequently used tables in order to reduce the disk arm movement. He or she must also determine where to place the datasets and how to partition tables across multiple disks. Finally, he or she has to select an index strategy.

5. **Build the BI target databases.**
   The physical databases are built when the data definition language (DDL) is run against the DBMS. The database administrator uses the DDL to describe the database structures (e.g., storage groups, database partitions) to the DBMS.

   Database security is established when the data control language (DCL) is run against the DBMS. In standard relational databases, security is imposed at the table or view level. Because of the dimensional nature of BI target databases, the capability to drill down into detail data, sometimes across databases, presents an often-overlooked security risk.

   Grant database authority either to individuals or to groups into which individuals have been assigned. Managing security on an individual level can quickly become a maintenance nightmare, which is why most organizations prefer to set up group identifiers (group IDs). Each group ID is granted some form of create, read, update, delete (CRUD) access to the tables. An audit trail can then show which specific "user ID" under which group ID accessed the database. If there is a breach of security, the "infiltrator" can often be located through this audit trail.

6. **Develop database maintenance procedures.**
Once the database goes into production, it will be important to set aside time for taking database backups or reorganizing fragmented tables. Therefore, establish procedures to address database maintenance functions.

7. **Prepare to monitor and tune the database designs.**
Once the BI application is implemented, the BI target databases have to be monitored and tuned. The best database design does not guarantee continued good performance, partly because tables become fragmented and partly because actual usage of the BI target databases changes over time. Monitor performance of queries at runtime with a performance-monitoring utility that has diagnostic capabilities. It does not help to know that performance has degraded without knowing the causes. Diagnosing performance problems is usually much harder than discovering them.

8. **Prepare to monitor and tune the query designs.**
Since performance is such a challenge on BI applications, you must explore all tricks of the trade to address this problem. Parallel query execution is one of those tricks that could boost query performance.

DELIVERABLES RESULTING FROM THESE ACTIVITIES

1. **Physical data model**
The physical data model, also known as the logical database design, is a diagram of the physical database structures that will contain the BI data. Depending on the selected database design schema, this diagram can be an entity-relationship diagram, a star schema diagram, or a snowflake diagram. It shows tables, columns, primary keys, foreign keys, cardinality, referential integrity rules, and indices.

2. **Physical design of the BI target databases**
The physical database design components include dataset placement, index placement, partitioning, clustering, and indexing. These physical database components must be defined to the DBMS when the BI target databases are created.

3. **Data definition language**

   The DDL is a set of SQL instructions that tells the DBMS what types of physical database structures to create, such as databases, tablespaces, tables, columns, and indices.

4. **Data control language**

   The DCL is a set of SQL instructions that tells the DBMS what types of CRUD access to grant to people, groups, programs, and tools.

5. **Physical BI target databases**

   Running (executing) the DDL and DCL statements builds the actual BI target databases.

6. **Database maintenance procedures**

   These procedures describe the time and frequency allocated for performing ongoing database maintenance activities, such as database backups, recovery (including disaster recovery), and database reorganizations. The procedures should also specify the process for and the frequency of performance-monitoring activities.

ROLES INVOLVED IN THESE ACTIVITIES

◆ **Application lead developer**

   The application lead developer and the database administrator should review all lessons learned during the prototyping activities. The application lead developer should help the database administrator determine which queries and reports can be executed in parallel and what type of security is needed.

◆ **Data administrator**

   The data administrator should provide the logical data model and the meta data to the database administrator. The logical data model and the meta data will be helpful to the database administrator when he or she designs the BI target databases. This is true even if a multidimensional database design schema was chosen because the entities and relationships on the logical data model are the perfect starting point for designing conformed dimensions and normalized snowflake dimensions.

◆ **Database administrator**

   The database administrator has the primary responsibility for database design. He or she needs to know the access paths, weigh the projected data volumes and growth factors, and understand the platform limitations. He or she must create and run the DDL and DCL to build the physical databases. In addition, he or she is responsible for choosing the most appropriate implementation options.

 Database administrators, not programmers, should design databases. Database design usually is—and should be—part of the job description for database administrators because it requires special product-specific training on the DBMS optimizer.

◆ **ETL lead developer**
The ETL process is dependent on the database design. The ETL lead developer should be involved in the database design activities in order to stay informed about any database design changes that will affect the ETL process or the ETL programming specifications.

RISKS OF NOT PERFORMING STEP 8

Tables are not flat files in a database, and they are not just a different way to casually store some data. Relational DBMS engines are based on intricate internal sets of rules. These rules must be understood and followed. Organizations hire database administrators to do just that. However, too often programmers who are not intimately familiar with the internal workings of their DBMS engines are allowed to design the BI target databases, and they design them poorly. This could have a catastrophic effect on performance. In fact, it could kill the BI application, if not the entire BI decision-support initiative.

BIBLIOGRAPHY AND ADDITIONAL READING

Atre, Shaku. *Distributed Databases, Cooperative Processing and Networking.* New York: McGraw-Hill, 1992.

————. *Data Base: Structured Techniques for Design, Performance, and Management, Second Edition.* New York: John Wiley & Sons, 1988.

Bischoff, Joyce, and Ted Alexander. *Data Warehouse: Practical Advice from the Experts.* Upper Saddle River, NJ: Prentice Hall, 1997.

Bontempo, Charles J., and Cynthia Maro Saracco. *Database Management: Principles and Products.* Upper Saddle River, NJ: Prentice Hall, 1996.

Bruce, Thomas A. *Designing Quality Databases with IDEF1X Information Models.* New York: Dorset House, 1992.

Corey, Michael J., and Michael Abbey. *Oracle Data Warehousing: A Practical Guide to Successful Data Warehouse Analysis, Build, and Roll-out.* Berkeley, CA: Osborne McGraw-Hill, 1996.

Hackney, Douglas. *Understanding and Implementing Successful Data Marts.* Reading, MA: Addison-Wesley, 1997.

Hoberman, Steve. *Data Modeler's Workbench: Tools and Techniques for Analysis and Design.* New York: John Wiley & Sons, 2001.

Inmon, William H. *Building the Data Warehouse.* New York: John Wiley & Sons, 1996.

Inmon, William H., Claudia Imhoff, and Greg Battas. *Building the Operational Data Store.* New York: John Wiley & Sons, 1996.

Kimball, Ralph, and Richard Merz. *The Data Webhouse Toolkit: Building the Web-Enabled Data Warehouse.* New York: John Wiley & Sons, 2000.

Kimball, Ralph, Laura Reeves, Margy Ross, and Warren Thornthwaite. *The Data Warehouse Lifecycle Toolkit: Expert Methods for Designing, Developing, and Deploying Data Warehouses.* New York: John Wiley & Sons, 1998.

DBMS-specific optimization rules obtainable from the DBMS vendors:
IBM: *http://www.ibm.com/support/us*
Oracle: *http://www.oracle.com*
NCR Teradata: *http://www.teradata.com/library/default.asp*
Microsoft SQL Server: *http://www.microsoft.com/sql/default.asp*

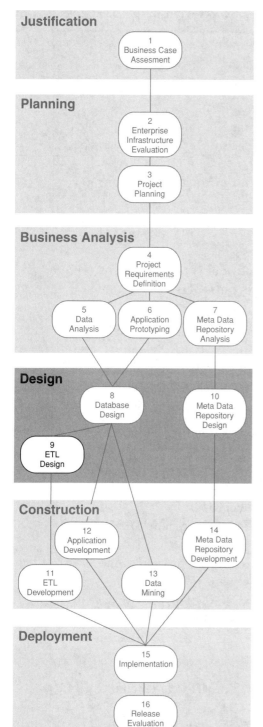

CHAPTER NINE

Step 9: Extract/ Transform/ Load Design

CHAPTER OVERVIEW

This chapter covers the following topics:

- Things to consider about extract/transform/load (ETL) design

- Common BI implementation strategies, such as data marts, operational data stores, enterprise data warehouses, and Web warehouses

- How to reformat, reconcile, and cleanse the source data for three different sets of ETL programs: initial load, historical load, and incremental load

- Various approaches for extracting data from the operational source files and source databases

- Typical source data problems encountered during transformation, such as duplicate primary keys, inconsistent data values, different data formats, and embedded process logic

- Load considerations, such as referential integrity and indexing

- The source-to-target mapping document, the process flow diagram, and the staging area

- Eight steps to follow when evaluating ETL products and vendors

- Brief descriptions of the activities involved in ETL design, the deliverables resulting from those activities, and the roles involved

- The risks of not performing Step 9

211

THINGS TO CONSIDER

Tools

✓ Have we selected an ETL tool, or are we writing the ETL programs from scratch?
✓ Will the ETL tool run on the platform where the source files are? On a separate server?
✓ Do we have a separate data-cleansing tool? Will we run it before or during the ETL process?
✓ Do we have an efficient sort utility?

ETL Staging

✓ How big is our ETL staging window? How many hours per night? Per week? Do we have a smaller window at month-end because of other month-end processes? How much smaller?
✓ Can we fit our ETL process into those windows or will we have to run over several days or nights?
✓ How many source data elements do we have to extract? And how many source files and source databases do we have to access?

ETL Process Flow

✓ How many programs can we run in parallel to shorten the ETL runtime?
✓ How long will the initial load take? Have we prototyped it?
✓ How long will it take to load the historical data? How many years of history do we need to load?
✓ Do we know how long the incremental loads will run?
✓ Should we insert rows or use the database management system (DBMS) load utility?
✓ Should we use a third-party load utility to speed up the process? Do we already have a third-party load utility, or do we need to buy one?
✓ When and how will the data be archived? On disk? On tape? Do we have to write archival programs at this time or can we postpone that additional programming effort to a future release?

Performance Considerations

✓ How would ETL load performance be affected if we left referential integrity (RI) turned on?
✓ How high would the risk of data corruption be if we turned RI off?
✓ How much RI checking do we want to perform in the ETL programs?

Reconciliation

✓ At how many points in the ETL process do we need to count input and output records?

✓ Are the record layouts and database structures different on the old historical files and databases than they are on the current files and databases? How do we reconcile them?

✓ Do we need to reconcile changed codes? Reused and redefined fields?

✓ How many data elements do we have to reconcile? How many codes? How many amounts?

✓ Will dirty data be rejected? How will that be reflected in the reconciliation totals?

✓ Will the load counts and reconciliation totals be stored as meta data?

Quality Metrics

✓ How will data quality errors be counted? What data quality metrics do we need to compile in the programs?

✓ Will we store those metrics as meta data in the meta data repository or print them in a report?

Source data for the BI applications will come from a variety of platforms, which are managed by a variety of operating systems and applications. The purpose of the ETL process is to merge data from these heterogeneous platforms into a standard format for the BI target databases in the BI decision-support environment, as shown in Figure 9.1.

IMPLEMENTATION STRATEGIES

There are several types of BI decision-support implementation strategies with every conceivable combination of BI target databases (e.g., operational data store and enterprise data warehouse; Web warehouse and data marts; exploration warehouses and data mining databases; data marts and operational marts [oper marts]). By far the most popular implementation strategy is a data mart environment.

Regardless of which implementation strategy is selected, there is a right way and a wrong way to implement it. The wrong way is to build a collection of stand-alone BI target databases, each with its own independent ETL process. This

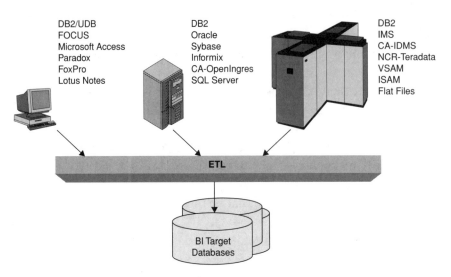

Figure 9.1: Heterogeneous Data Sources

approach will not produce an integrated and reconciled BI decision-support environment because creating separate ETL processes is no different than developing traditional stovepipe decision-support systems.

The right way to implement a chosen strategy is to build a BI decision-support environment in which all BI target databases are integrated and reconciled. When building this environment, it is critical to perform the common data transformations for all BI target databases only once and to reconcile these data transformations back to the operational source files and source databases. This will demonstrate the validity of the data in the various BI target databases. It is also important to reconcile all the data across the different BI target databases in order to demonstrate the data consistency among the various BI target databases. Both reconciliation processes are best accomplished with a coordinated ETL effort for all BI target databases, as illustrated in Figure 9.2.

 The most important ETL rule for an integrated BI implementation strategy is to *share one coordinated ETL process*. This is what differentiates BI from a traditional decision-support approach.

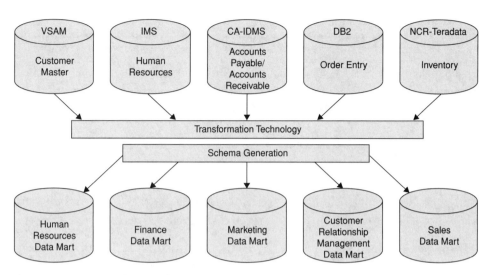

Figure 9.2: Integrated BI Implementation Strategy

PREPARING FOR THE ETL PROCESS

The ETL process begins with preparations for reformatting, reconciling, and cleansing the source data.

- **Reformatting:** The source data residing in various different source files and source databases, each with its own format, will have to be unified into a common format during the ETL process.

- **Reconciling:** The tremendous amount of data in organizations points to staggering redundancy, which invariably results in staggering inconsistencies. These have to be found and reconciled during the ETL process.

- **Cleansing:** Dirty data found during data analysis and prototyping will have to be cleansed during this process.

Before designing the ETL process, it is necessary to review the following:

- Record layouts of the current as well as the historical source files

- Data description blocks for the current as well as the historical source databases

- Data-cleansing specifications for the source data elements

Most source data for the ETL process is current operational data from the operational systems, but some of the source data may be archived historical data.

Table 9.1: Sets of ETL Programs

Initial Load	*Historical Load*	*Incremental Load*
Initial population of BI target databases with current operational data	Initial population of BI target databases with archived historical data	Ongoing population of BI target databases with current operational data
1	*2*	*3*

If the data requirements include a few years of history to be backfilled from the start, three sets of ETL programs must be designed and developed, as listed in Table 9.1.

If the decision is made to write the ETL programs in a procedural language (e.g., C++ or COBOL), the transformation specifications for the three sets of programs must be prepared and given to the ETL developers. If an ETL tool will be used, ETL instructions (technical meta data) must be created for the three sets of load processes. The ETL technical meta data will reflect the same logic that would have been written in custom programs if no ETL tool had been available. The technical meta data should be stored in a meta data repository.

The Initial Load

The process of preparing the initial load programs is very similar to a system conversion process, such as the one many organizations perform when they move their old operational systems to an enterprise resource planning (ERP) product. In general, the first task of a system conversion process is to map selected data elements from the source files or source databases to the most appropriate data elements in the target files or target databases. A "most appropriate data element" in a target file or target database is one that is the most similar in name, definition, size, length, and functionality as the source data element. The second task of a system conversion process is to write the conversion (transformation) programs to transform the source data. These conversion programs must also resolve duplicate records, match the primary keys, and truncate or enlarge the size of the data elements.

Usually missing from conversion programs, and unfortunately also missing from most ETL processes, are data cleansing and reconciliation. Organizations repeatedly miss prime opportunities to bring order to their data chaos when they continue to "suck and plunk" the data from source to target as is. Their only concern is that the receiving database structure does not reject the source data for *technical* reasons, such as duplicate keys, or data type and length violations. That is not good enough for BI applications because business people expect data quality and data consistency for *business* reasons. Thus, when designing the load processes, data cleansing and reconciliation must become part of the ETL process flow.

The Historical Load

The historical load process could be viewed as an extension of the initial load process, but this type of conversion is slightly different because historical data is *static* data. In contrast to *live* operational data, static data has served its operational purpose and has been archived to offline storage devices. The implication is that, as some old data expires and some new data is added over the years, the record layouts of archived files are usually not in synch with the record layouts of the current operational files. Therefore, the conversion programs written for the current operational files usually cannot be applied to archived historical files without some changes. For example, in a frequently changing operational system, it is not unusual for five years of archived historical files to have five (or more) slightly different record layouts. Even though the differences in the record layouts may not be drastic, they still have to be reconciled. In addition, the cleanliness of the data may not be the same across all archived files. What was once valid in a historical file may no longer be valid. The data transformation specifications have to address these differences and reconcile them. All these factors contribute to the reasons why the ETL process can get very lengthy and very complicated.

The Incremental Load

Once the processes for populating the BI target databases with initial and historical data have been devised, another process must be designed for the ongoing incremental load (monthly, weekly, or daily). Incremental loads can be accomplished in two ways, extract all records or deltas only, as shown in Table 9.2. The design of the ETL extract process will differ depending on which option is selected.

Table 9.2: Incremental Load Options

Extract All Records	*Extract Deltas Only*
Extract source data from all operational records, regardless of whether any data values have changed since the last ETL load or not.	Extract source data only from those operational records in which some data values have changed since the last ETL load ("net change").

Extracting all records is often not a viable option because of the huge data volumes involved. Therefore, many organizations opt for delta extracts (extracting only records that changed). Designing ETL programs for delta extraction is much easier when the source data resides on relational databases and the timestamp can be used for determining the deltas. But when the data is stored in flat files without a timestamp, the extract process can be significantly more complex. You may have to resort to reading the operational audit trails to determine which records have changed.

An alternative may be to extract a complete copy of the source file for every load, then compare the new extract to the previous extract to find the records that changed and create your own delta file. Another alternative is to ask the operational systems staff to add a system timestamp to their operational files. Occasionally they may agree to do that if the change to their operational systems is trivial and does not affect many programs. However, in most cases operations managers will not agree to that because any changes to their file structures would also require changes to their data entry and update programs. Additional code would have to be written for those programs to capture the system timestamp. It would not be cost-effective for them to change their mission-critical operational systems and spend a lot of time on regression testing—just for the benefit of a BI application.

Processing Deleted Records

Another aspect that needs to be carefully considered for incremental loads is that of deleted operational source records. When certain records are *logically* deleted from the source files and source databases (flagged as deleted but not physically removed), the corresponding rows cannot automatically be deleted from the BI target databases. After all, one of the main requirements of BI target databases is to store historical data.

The ETL process must follow a set of business rules, which should define when an operational deletion should propagate into the BI target databases and when it should not. For example, perhaps an operational record is being deleted because it was previously created in error, or because the record is being archived, or because the operational system stores only "open" transactions and deletes the "closed" ones. Most likely, the business rules would state that you should delete the related row from the BI target database only in the case where the record was created in error. Since your BI target database stores historical data, the business rules would probably not allow you to delete the related row in the other two instances.

When records are *physically* deleted from the source files or source databases, you would never know it if you are extracting only deltas. Delta extract programs are designed to extract only those existing records in which one of the data values changed; they cannot extract records that do not exist. One way to find the physically deleted records is to read the operational audit trails. Another option is to extract a complete copy of the source file, compare the new extract to the previous extract to find the records that were deleted, and then create your own delta files. In either case, once the deleted records are identified, the ETL process has to follow a set of business rules to decide whether or not to physically remove the related rows from the BI target databases.

DESIGNING THE EXTRACT PROGRAMS

From an operational systems perspective, the most favored way to create extracts might be to just duplicate the entire contents of the operational source files and source databases and to give the duplicates to the BI project team. However, the ETL developers would have the burden of working with huge files when they only need a subset of the source data.

From the BI project perspective, the most favored way to create extracts might be to sort, filter, cleanse, and aggregate all the required data in one step if possible and to do it right at the source. However, in some organizations that would impact the operational systems to such a degree that operational business functions would have to be suspended for several hours.

The solution is usually a compromise: the extract programs are designed for the most efficient ETL processing, but always with a focus on getting the required source data as quickly as possible. The goal is to get out of the way of operational systems so that the daily business functions are not affected. This is easier said than done, for a number of reasons.

Selecting and merging data from source files and source databases can be challenging because of the high data redundancy in operational systems. The extract programs must know which of the redundant source files or source databases are the *systems of record*. For example, the same source data element (e.g., Customer Name) can exist in dozens of source files and source databases. These redundant occurrences have to be sorted out and consolidated, which involves a number of sort and merge steps, driven by a number of lookup tables cross-referencing specific keys and data values.

Another way to produce small and relatively clean extract files is to extract only those source data elements that are needed for the BI application and to resolve only those source data quality problems that pertain to the business data domain rules, without attempting to sort out and consolidate redundant occurrences of data. However, even that compromise will not work in many large organizations because the data-cleansing process would slow down the extract process, which in turn would tie up the operational systems longer than is acceptable.

In many large organizations, the BI project team is lucky to get three to four hours of processing time against the operational systems before those operational systems have to "go live" for the operational functions of the next business day. This is the main reason why populating the BI target databases is split into three separate processes: extract, transform, and load (Figure 9.3).

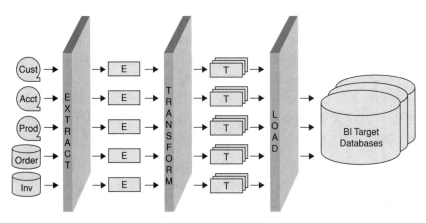

Figure 9.3: ETL Processes

DESIGNING THE TRANSFORMATION PROGRAMS

Using the 80/20 rule, 80 percent of ETL work occurs in the "T" (transform) portion when extensive data integration and data cleansing are required, while extracting and loading represent only 20 percent of the ETL process.

Source Data Problems

The design of the transformation programs can become very complicated when the data is extracted from a heterogeneous operational environment. Some of the typical source data problems are described below.

- **Inconsistent primary keys:** The primary keys of the source data records do not always match the new primary key in the BI tables. For example, there could be five customer files, each one with a different customer key. These different customer keys would be consolidated or transformed into one standardized BI customer key. The BI customer key would probably be a new surrogate ("made-up") key and would not match any of the operational keys, as illustrated in Figure 9.4.

- **Inconsistent data values:** Many organizations duplicate a lot of their data. The term *duplicate* normally means the data element is an exact copy of the original. However, over time, these duplicates end up with completely different

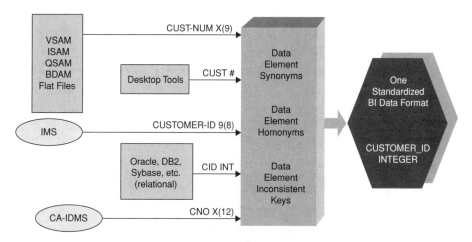

Figure 9.4: Resolution of Inconsistent Primary Keys

data values because of update anomalies (inconsistent updates applied to the duplicates), which have to be reconciled in the ETL process.

- **Different data formats:** Data elements such as dates and currencies may be stored in a completely different format in the source files than they will be stored in the BI target databases. If date and currency conversion modules already exist, they need to be identified; otherwise, logic for this transformation has to be developed.

- **Inaccurate data values:** Cleansing logic has to be defined to correct inaccurate data values. Some of the data-cleansing logic can get extremely complicated and lengthy. The correction of one data violation can take several pages of cleansing instructions. Data cleansing is not done only once—it is an ongoing process. Because new data is loaded into the BI target databases with every load cycle, the ETL data-cleansing algorithms have to be run every time data is loaded. Therefore, the transformation programs cannot be written "quick and dirty." Instead, they must be designed in a well-considered and well-structured manner.

- **Synonyms and homonyms:** Redundant data is not always easy to recognize because the same data element may have different names. Operational systems are also notorious for using the same name for different data elements. Since synonyms and homonyms should not exist in a BI decision-support environment, renaming data elements for the BI target databases is a common occurrence.

- **Embedded process logic:** Some operational systems are extremely old. They run, but often no one knows how! They frequently contain undocumented and archaic relationships among some source data elements. There is also a very good chance that some codes in the operational systems are used as cryptic switches. For example, the value "00" in the data element Alter-Flag could mean that the shipment was returned, and the value "FF" in the same data element could mean it was the month-end run. The transformation specifications would have to reflect this logic.

Data Transformations

Besides transforming source data for reasons of incompatible data type and length or inconsistent and inaccurate data, a large portion of the transformation logic will involve precalculating data for multidimensional storage. Therefore, it should not be surprising that the data in the BI target databases will look quite different than the data in the operational systems. Some specific examples appear below.

- Some of the data will be renamed following the BI naming standards (synonyms and homonyms should not be propagated into the BI decision-support environment). For example, the data element Account Flag may now be called Product_Type_Code.

- Some data elements from different operational systems will be combined (merged) into one column in a BI table because they represent the same logical data element. For example, Cust-Name from the CMAST file, Customer_Nm from the CRM_CUST table, and Cust_Acct_Nm from the CACCT table may now be merged into the column Customer_Name in the BI_CUSTOMER table.

- Some data elements will be split across different columns in the BI target database because they are being used for multiple purposes by the operational systems. For example, the values "A", "B", "C", "L", "M", "N", "X", "Y", and "Z" of the source data element Prod-Code may be used as follows by the operational system: "A," "B," and "C" describe customers; "L," "M," and "N" describe suppliers; and "X," "Y," and "Z" describe regional constraints. As a result, Prod-Code may now be split into three columns:
  - Customer_Type_Code in the BI_CUSTOMER table
  - Supplier_Type_Code in the BI_SUPPLIER table
  - Regional_Constraint_Code in the BI_ORG_UNIT table

- Some code data elements will be translated into mnemonics or will be spelled out. For example:
  - "A" may be translated to "Corporation"
  - "B" may be translated to "Partnership"
  - "C" may be translated to "Individual"

- In addition, most of the data will be aggregated and summarized based on required reporting patterns and based on the selected multidimensional database structure (star schema, snowflake). For example, at the end of the month, the source data elements Mortgage-Loan-Balance, Construction-Loan-Balance, and Consumer-Loan-Amount may be added up (aggregated) and summarized by region into the column Monthly_Regional_Portfolio_Amount in the BI_PORTFOLIO fact table.

DESIGNING THE LOAD PROGRAMS

The final step in the ETL process is loading the BI target databases, which can be accomplished in either of two ways: (1) by inserting the new rows into the tables or (2) by using the DBMS load utility to perform a bulk load. It is much more efficient to use the load utility of the DBMS, and most organizations choose that approach.

Once the extract and transformation steps are accomplished, it should not be too complicated to complete the ETL process with the load step. However, it is still necessary to make design decisions about referential integrity and indexing.

Referential Integrity

Because of the huge volumes of data, many organizations prefer to turn off RI to speed up the load process. However, in that case the ETL programs must perform the necessary RI checks; otherwise, the BI target databases can become corrupt within a few months or even weeks. Acting on the idea that RI checking is not needed for BI applications (because no new data relationships are created and only existing operational data is loaded) does not prevent database corruption! Corruption of BI target databases often *does* occur, mainly because operational data is often not properly related in the first place, especially when the operational data is not in a relational database. Even if the operational data comes from a relational database, there is no guarantee of properly enforced RI because too many relational database designs are no more than unrelated flat files in tables.

 When RI is turned off during the ETL load process (as it should be, for performance reasons), it is recommended to turn it back on again after the load process has completed in order to let the DBMS determine any RI violations between dependent tables.

Indexing

Poorly performing databases are often the result of poorly performing indexing schemes. It is necessary to have efficiently performing indices, and to have many of them, because of the high volume of data in the BI target databases. However, building index entries while loading the BI tables slows down the ETL load process. Thus, it is advisable to drop all indices before the ETL load process, load the BI target databases, and then recreate the indices after completing the ETL load process and checking RI.

DESIGNING THE ETL PROCESS FLOW

The Source-to-Target Mapping Document

Before the ETL process flow can be designed (or enhanced), the detailed ETL transformation specifications for data extraction, transformation, and reconciliation have to be developed, given that they will dictate the process flow. A common way to document the ETL transformation specifications is in a source-to-target mapping document, which can be a matrix or a spreadsheet (Table 9.3).

The source-to-target mapping document should list all BI tables and columns and their data types and lengths. It should map the applicable source data elements to the columns, along with their data types and lengths, and it should show the source files and source databases from which the source data elements are being extracted. Finally, and most importantly, the document should specify the transformation logic for each column.

This document can then be used to create the actual programming specifications for the ETL developers or to create instructions (technical meta data) for the ETL tool.

The ETL Process Flow Diagram

Once the source-to-target mapping document has been completed, the ETL lead developer, with the help of the database administrator and the data quality analyst, must design the ETL process flow, as illustrated by the example in Figure 9.5.

The purpose for the ETL process flow diagram is to show the process dependencies between all extracts, sorting and merging utilities, transformations, temporary work files or tables, error-handling processes, reconciliation activities, and the load sequence. The ETL programs, or ETL tool modules, will have to run in this sequence.

- **Extracts:** There may be operational interdependencies among several source files and source databases from which data is being extracted. These interdependencies have to be understood because they may affect the timing and the sequence of running the ETL extract programs.
- **Sorting and merging utilities:** Almost every step requires the extracted data to be sorted in a particular fashion so that it can be merged before further processing can occur. Sorting can also greatly improve load performance.

Table 9.3: Example of a Source-to-Target Mapping Document

Table	Column	Type/ Length	Data Element	Type/ Length	Source File/ Database	Transformation Specifications
CUSTOMER	CUSTOMER_ID	INTEGER	CUST-NUM	X(9)	Cust-Master	If ABC-Code = "R" then
			CID	INT	CUSTOMER	Assign new customer number to record with CUST-NUM
			CNO	X(12)	CUST	Else
						If ABC-Code = "S"
						Assign new customer number to record with CID
						Else
						Assign new customer number to record with CNO

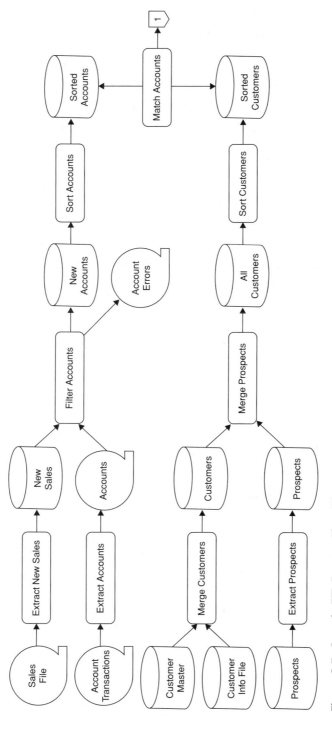

Figure 9.5: Sample ETL Process Flow Diagram

- **Transformations:** Most of the data has to be transformed for a variety of reasons. It is important to examine the most opportune times to perform the transformations. Remember that there is only one coordinated ETL process for the BI decision-support environment. Therefore, transformations applicable to all source data, such as data type and code conversions or data domain enforcements, should be performed early in the ETL process flow. Transformations specific to a target database, such as aggregation and summarization for a specific data mart, should occur toward the end of the ETL process flow.

- **Temporary work files or tables:** Sorting, merging, and transforming require a lot of temporary storage space to hold the interim results. These temporary work files and tables can be as large or larger than the original extracts. Furthermore, these temporary work files and tables are not really "temporary." Plan to have that space available for your staging area permanently.

- **Error-handling processes:** During the ETL process many errors are detected as the data-cleansing specifications are applied to the source data. If error reports are created or erroneous records are rejected into a suspense file, they should be shown on the ETL process flow diagram.

- **Reconciliation activities:** Every program module that manipulates data should produce reconciliation totals. This can be in the form of input and output record counts, specific domain counts, or amount counts. Record counts are sufficient for extract, sort, and merge modules. Domain counts are appropriate for more complicated transformation specifications, such as separating data values from one source data element into multiple target columns. Amount counts are usually performed on all amount data elements, whether they are moved as is, transformed into a new format, or used in a calculation. (ETL reconciliation will be described in more detail in Step 11, ETL Development.)

- **Load sequence:** It is necessary to determine the sequence in which the tables have to be loaded because of their potential interdependencies and because of a possible recursive relationship on one table. For example, the Product dimension table may have to be loaded before the Sales table is loaded, if RI is turned on and if the sales data references products. Other tables may be loaded simultaneously, which can greatly improve the speed of the load process.

The Staging Area

A staging area is the place where the ETL process runs. It refers to dedicated disk space, ETL program libraries, temporary and permanent work files and tables—even a dedicated server. The staging area can be centralized or decentralized. For example, it can be a central mainframe staging area if most of the source data is in flat files on a mainframe. It can also be on a dedicated server onto which the source data is loaded. Many times the staging area is decentralized. For example, a convoluted mainframe file with many `redefines` and `occurs` clauses may have to be flattened out with a COBOL program in a staging area on the mainframe before it is downloaded to a staging area on a UNIX box for further processing by an ETL tool.

The ETL process is by far the most complicated process to be designed and developed in any BI project. Since there is only one (logical) coordinated ETL process for the BI decision-support environment, expanding the ETL programs with each new BI application becomes very complicated, and regression testing requires more and more time. For these reasons, most organizations prefer to use an ETL tool for all or some of the ETL process, especially for the extract and transformation processes, as shown in Figure 9.6.

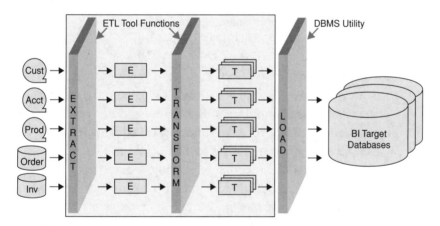

Figure 9.6: Common Use of ETL Tools in the ETL Process

EVALUATING ETL TOOLS

When using an ETL tool, the transformation specifications get translated into instructions for the ETL tool. These instructions can then be stored as technical meta data in the meta data repository. Expanding the ETL process and running regression tests are made easier with the tool because there is less human intervention and therefore fewer chances to introduce errors.

When evaluating ETL products, follow these steps.

1. *Perform a cost-benefit analysis* to compare licensing (buying) an ETL product with building the ETL process in-house. Although both options can be expensive for different reasons (licensing a very sophisticated ETL tool is expensive, but so is maintaining custom-built software), your first choice should be licensing an ETL tool. If the ETL tool cannot handle all of the required transformations, supplement the licensed product with your own specialized code for those transformations. If your transformation requirements are simple and you have a small budget, you may want to buy a less sophisticated ETL tool or consider building your own ETL process.

2. *Compile a list of ETL products and vendors* that are likely to meet your requirements. Attend trade shows to learn more about the products and vendors. *Caveat emptor*—be a cautious and skeptical buyer.

 Let your transformation and cleansing *requirements*—not vendor hype—drive your product evaluation and selection process.

3. *Compare the ETL products and vendors* to your weighted data transformation requirements. Include the business rules for data cleansing as part of your ETL tool selection criteria. For example, some ETL tools cannot read flat files and cannot perform some of the very complicated transformations. If you need those capabilities, you must be aware of ETL tool limitations because you may need to license an additional data-cleansing tool to perform those processes, or augment the ETL tool functionality with custom-written code.

4. *Evaluate each ETL product objectively* and prepare a scorecard that compares the product features and their effectiveness. The reputation and responsiveness of a vendor are equally as important as the features of the products. Therefore, prepare another scorecard comparing the vendors.

5. *Check the vendors' client references* by talking with people at organizations that already use the tools you are considering. This is the most cost-effective and informative way to evaluate the tools.

6. *Narrow the list of ETL products and vendors* to a short list of two or three candidates. Otherwise, you will waste too much time comparing all the products,

and it may take "forever" to make the final decision. You might then select an inferior tool just to end the frustration and delay.

7. *Arrange for product demos* since "seeing is believing." Spend some time preparing the test cases so that all vendors on the short list get to demonstrate the performance and effectiveness of their products using the same test cases.

8. *Test the vendor products* even though it takes away time from your project schedule. Testing is the best way to discover any glitches that may happen before using a vendor product in production. Try to negotiate a 30-day trial period.

(The process of evaluating and selecting products and vendors is described in more detail in Step 10, Meta Data Repository Design.)

ETL DESIGN ACTIVITIES

The activities for ETL design do not need to be performed linearly. Figure 9.7 indicates which activities can be performed concurrently. The list below briefly describes the activities associated with Step 9, ETL Design.

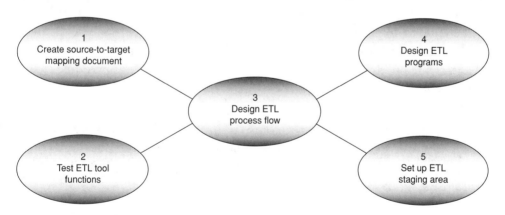

Figure 9.7: ETL Design Activities

1. Create the source-to-target mapping document.
Use the source data analysis results and the business rules from the previous steps and incorporate them into the transformation specifications. Docu-

ment the transformation specifications in a source-to-target mapping matrix or spreadsheet.

2. **Test the ETL tool functions.**

   It is very important to test the ETL tool functions before designing the ETL process flow and before deciding how to set up the staging area. For example, it would be worthless to install a currently popular ETL tool that cannot read flat files on a mainframe if 90 percent of your source data is in flat files on your mainframe. Therefore, test the ETL tool functions and determine whether supplemental code must be written to perform some complicated and lengthy transformations that the tool cannot handle.

3. **Design the ETL process flow.**

   The most challenging aspect of ETL design is creating an efficient ETL process flow. Because most data staging windows are very small—only a few hours per night—the ETL process must be streamlined as much as possible. That means breaking the ETL process into small program components so that as many as possible can be run in parallel.

4. **Design the ETL programs.**

   Since most organizations require several years of historical data to be loaded with the first BI application release, there are three sets of ETL programs to consider: the initial load, the historical load, and the incremental load. The incremental load will probably be a delta load and will therefore be the most complicated to design. Modularize the ETL programs as much as possible, and create programming specifications for each ETL program module.

5. **Set up the ETL staging area.**

   Determine whether you need a centralized staging area on a dedicated server or whether it would make more sense to implement a decentralized staging area in your environment. Deciding factors are the type and location of source files and source databases, as well as the functions, capabilities, and licensing terms of the ETL tool.

 Do not create a separate staging area for each data mart. A decentralized, coordinated staging area is not the same thing as separate, uncoordinated staging areas for different BI target databases and different BI applications.

DELIVERABLES RESULTING FROM THESE ACTIVITIES

1. **Source-to-target mapping document**
   This document contains the transformation specifications for each BI column, including instructions for data cleansing, RI checking, reconciliation, and error handling, as well as algorithms for aggregations and summarizations.

2. **ETL process flow diagram**
   The ETL process flow diagram shows the process sequence and the process dependencies among all ETL process components, such as program modules, temporary and permanent work files and tables, and sort, merge, and load utilities.

3. **ETL program design document**
   This document is created from the source-to-target mapping document after the ETL process flow has been determined. It contains the actual programming specifications for every ETL program module for the initial load, historical load, and incremental load. Portions of this document will be given to different ETL developers to code the program modules.

4. **Staging area**
   The staging area should contain program libraries with version control as well as dedicated space for temporary and permanent work files and tables.

ROLES INVOLVED IN THESE ACTIVITIES

◆ **Data quality analyst**
   Working with the ETL lead developer, the data quality analyst must transfer his or her knowledge about the condition of the source files and source databases discovered during Step 5, Data Analysis. Since the data quality analyst usually has a systems analysis background, he or she can assist in or even take over creating the source-to-target mapping document.

◆ **Database administrator**
   The database administrator must be involved in the design of the ETL process because of its database aspects (RI, indexing, clustering, and the use of the DBMS load utility). The database administrator can provide valuable input to the ETL process flow and can sometimes reduce the ETL staging window by several hours.

◆ **ETL lead developer**

The ETL lead developer is responsible for the entire ETL process. With the help of the database administrator, the data quality analyst, and the subject matter expert, the ETL lead developer designs the ETL process flow and creates the ETL program design document with the actual programming specifications for the ETL developers (or instructions for the ETL tool).

◆ **Subject matter expert**

The subject matter expert plays an advisory role during this step. Since the subject matter expert was involved in identifying the source data and finding the data quality problems, he or she should participate in creating the source-to-target mapping document. The subject matter expert will also be the liaison to the business representative who must validate the business rules used in the ETL process.

RISKS OF NOT PERFORMING STEP 9

This is not an optional step—not even if you plan to use an ETL tool. Every BI project team must evaluate the source data and figure out how to improve it, change it, standardize it, and make it more useful before moving it into the BI target databases. A BI project is not like a systems conversion project, where you simply try to move from one technology platform to another while transferring the data as is. A BI project is more like a system redesign or a business process improvement project, where you want to *change* the data. You cannot afford to move data as is from source to target and then wait for the database to reject a data element for technical reasons. You must plan and design the required changes for business reasons.

BIBLIOGRAPHY AND ADDITIONAL READING

Adelman, Sid, and Larissa Terpeluk Moss. *Data Warehouse Project Management.* Boston, MA: Addison-Wesley, 2000.

Aiken, Peter H. *Data Reverse Engineering: Slaying the Legacy Dragon.* New York: McGraw-Hill, 1995.

Brackett, Michael H. *Data Resource Quality: Turning Bad Habits into Good Practices.* Boston, MA: Addison-Wesley, 2000.

————. *The Data Warehouse Challenge: Taming Data Chaos.* New York: John Wiley & Sons, 1996.

Hackney, Douglas. *Understanding and Implementing Successful Data Marts.* Reading, MA: Addison-Wesley, 1997.

Imhoff, Claudia, Lisa Loftis, and Jonathan G. Geiger. *Building the Customer-Centric Enterprise: Data Warehousing Techniques for Supporting Customer Relationship Management.* New York: John Wiley & Sons, 2001.

Kimball, Ralph, and Richard Merz. *The Data Webhouse Toolkit: Building the Web-Enabled Data Warehouse.* New York: John Wiley & Sons, 2000.

Kimball, Ralph, Laura Reeves, Margy Ross, and Warren Thornthwaite. *The Data Warehouse Lifecycle Toolkit: Expert Methods for Designing, Developing, and Deploying Data Warehouses.* New York: John Wiley & Sons, 1998.

Ponniah, Paulraj. *Data Warehousing Fundamentals: A Comprehensive Guide for IT Professionals.* New York: John Wiley & Sons, 2001.

Sperley, Eric. *The Enterprise Data Warehouse: Planning, Building, and Implementation.* Upper Saddle River, NJ: Prentice Hall, 1999.

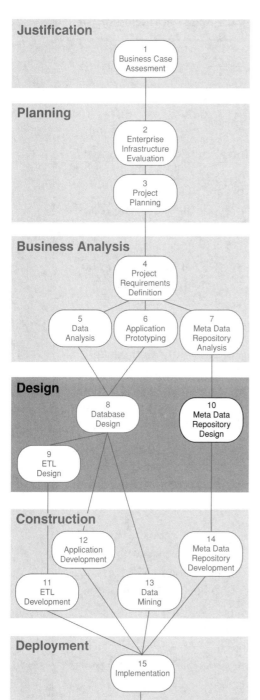

Justification

1
Business Case
Assesment

Planning

2
Enterprise
Infrastructure
Evaluation

3
Project
Planning

Business Analysis

4
Project
Requirements
Definition

5
Data
Analysis

6
Application
Prototyping

7
Meta Data
Repository
Analysis

Design

8
Database
Design

10
Meta Data
Repository
Design

9
ETL
Design

Construction

12
Application
Development

14
Meta Data
Repository
Development

11
ETL
Development

13
Data
Mining

Deployment

15
Implementation

16
Release
Evaluation

CHAPTER TEN

Step 10: Meta Data Repository Design

CHAPTER OVERVIEW

This chapter covers the following topics:

■ Things to consider when designing a meta data repository or when evaluating meta data repository vendor products

■ How the shortcomings of early meta data initiatives contributed to failures to effectively manage meta data

■ The multitude of meta data sources we now have to manage in a BI decision-support environment

■ The advantages and disadvantages of three different types of implementation strategies: a centralized meta data repository, either built or licensed (bought); a decentralized meta data repository; and a distributed meta data solution enabled through the use of Extensible Markup Language (XML) tags

■ The advantages and disadvantages of two different types of meta data repository designs: an entity-relationship (E-R) design and an object-oriented (OO) design

■ Detailed examples of the product and vendor evaluation process

■ Brief descriptions of the activities involved in meta data repository design, the deliverables resulting from those activities, and the roles involved

■ The risks of not performing Step 10

THINGS TO CONSIDER

Existing Meta Data Repository

✓ Do we already have a meta data repository?

✓ Do we have to expand it? Do we have to add more meta data components? Or expand the functionality?

✓ Who is keeping the meta data repository up-to-date?

✓ Who is using it? How are they using it? What parts of the meta data repository are they using?

✓ Do they like it? Are there any complaints?

✓ If we do not have a meta data repository, how are we coping without one?

✓ Why do we not have one? Lack of budget? Lack of resources? Lack of understanding?

Meta Data Repository Products

✓ Are there meta data repository products that will satisfy our meta data requirements? Or do we have to build a meta data repository from scratch?

✓ How many of our meta data requirements cannot be satisfied by the meta data repository products on the market? How important are those meta data requirements?

✓ Can the meta data repository products be enhanced to meet those specific meta data requirements?

✓ Which meta data repository products have import and export capabilities?

Interfaces

✓ How will we automate the interfaces from the meta data repository to other tools that have their own meta data dictionaries, for example, computer-aided software engineering (CASE), extract/transform/load (ETL), and online analytical processing (OLAP) tools? Will we have to buy additional middleware?

✓ Do the other tools from which we have to extract meta data have import and export capabilities? Are those tools XML-enabled?

✓ How will we deliver the meta data to the business people? Through reports? Through a help function? Through a Web interface?

✓ Will it be hard for the business people to learn how to use the meta data repository interfaces? What training do we have to develop?

> **Staffing**
>
> ✓ Will we need more staff to install, enhance, and maintain a licensed meta data repository product?
> ✓ Will we need more staff to design, build, and maintain our own custom-built meta data repository?

The term *meta data* is not new, and efforts to manage meta data are not new either. What *is* new is the increased awareness that meta data is an important extension to business information and that managing meta data is therefore mandatory. Another important recognition is that new tools and techniques for managing meta data are needed—and are becoming available.

META DATA SILOS

Data administrators have tried to inventory, define, and organize meta data since the early 1980s. Most data administrators used generic data dictionary products (meta data repositories used to be called *data dictionaries*); only few tried to design and build their own. Some of the generic data dictionary products were rather sophisticated and expandable, and they could store most of the required meta data components. However, there were multitudes of problems associated with these early efforts.

- *Populating* these early data dictionaries required a manual effort, which was time consuming and tedious, as all manual efforts are.

- The *lack of technical skills* on the part of most data administrators prevented them from expanding the data dictionary products with custom features to make them more useful.

- The *reporting capabilities* of the early data dictionary products were less than desirable. Some products did not even have application programming interface (API) capabilities that would allow data administrators to generate customized reports.

- The *immature technologies* used in most early data dictionaries (which were mainframe products) did not provide automated interfaces, easy-to-use graphical user interface (GUI) displays, or context-sensitive help functions.

- The *lack of standards* (or the lack of enforcement of standards) created an insurmountable burden for the data administrators who had to resolve conflicting and inconsistent data names, data definitions, and data domains.

- *No management appreciation* for the value of meta data made meta data a low priority in most organizations. Business managers and business executives, as well as some information technology (IT) managers, viewed meta data as systems documentation, which they considered important but could live without.

- *No cross-organizational initiatives* existed in organizations, except departmental initiatives usually spearheaded by data administrators in IT. Therefore, many business managers and business executives did not understand the value of the effort and did not buy into it. The popularity of data warehouse initiatives in the 1990s helped raise the understanding of the value of cross-organizational initiatives.

Because of these problems, data administration efforts to manage meta data were only marginally successful in the past. On many projects, these efforts were even considered project obstructions because of the extra time it took to define and capture the meta data when the technicians were eager to rush into coding. IT managers and business managers often asked, "Why aren't we coding yet?"— obviously, they perceived writing programs as the only productive project development activity.

Sources of Meta Data

It was not until the advent of cross-organizational BI initiatives and the associated plethora of BI tools that meta data started to receive its proper recognition. People began to realize that these BI tools, with their own sets of meta data in their own proprietary dictionary databases, were creating the all-too-familiar problems of redundancy and inconsistency, only this time with meta data. Knowledge workers, business analysts, managers, and technicians were getting very frustrated with the tangled web of meta data silos (Figure 10.1).

Meta data cannot be avoided, especially technical meta data, because database management systems (DBMSs) and most tools do not function without it. It is their "language." For example, meta data instructs the DBMS what type of database structures to create, tells the ETL tool what data to transform, and lets the OLAP tool know how to aggregate and summarize the data. Different meta data components are stored in different tools, and none of the tools (except a meta data repository) is designed to store all the other meta data components from all the other tools. For example:

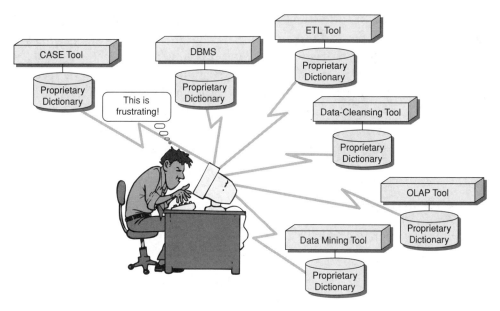

Figure 10.1: Meta Data Silos

- *CASE tools* store the business meta data for the logical data model components and the technical meta data for the physical data model (logical database design) components.

- *DBMS dictionaries* store the technical meta data for the database structure, such as databases, tables, columns, indices, and so on.

- *ETL tools* store the technical meta data about source-to-target data mappings and the transformation specifications, which are used by these tools to perform their ETL processes.

- *Data-cleansing tools* store the business meta data for data domains and for business rules that allow these tools to identify data quality problems. They also store the cleansing specifications, which are used by these tools to perform their data-cleansing functions.

- *OLAP tools* store the technical meta data of the tables and columns in the BI target databases, the report definitions, and the algorithms for deriving, aggregating, summarizing, and in other ways manipulating BI data.

- *Data mining tools* store the technical meta data about the various analytical models and the algorithms for the data mining operations.

As with vendors of other relatively new software and middleware product lines, the vendors of meta data repository products are competing for dominance, which slows down standardization of the product line. As a result, organizations end up with a tangled web of disparate and distributed meta data scattered across the proprietary dictionaries of their tools. To manage this situation, they now have to extract, merge, and accurately integrate meta data from these tool dictionaries, which can be as much of a challenge as extracting, merging, and accurately integrating business data from the operational systems.

META DATA REPOSITORY SOLUTIONS

The solution to meta data silos is clearly an enterprise-wide meta data repository approach. This can be accomplished in one of three ways:

1. One centralized meta data repository database solution

2. A decentralized meta data solution that uses one integrated meta model but physically distributes the meta data across multiple databases

3. A distributed XML-enabled solution in which the meta data is XML-tagged and stored (kept) in the different types of proprietary tool dictionaries on different platforms

 Regardless of which meta data repository solution is chosen, meta data repository projects and subprojects are large and costly. Therefore, any meta data repository solution should be built in iterations.

Centralized Meta Data Repository

A centralized meta data repository is the most popular solution and the easiest to implement because there is only one database, either relational or object-oriented, and only one application to maintain (Figure 10.2).

Updating the meta data repository does not have to be coordinated across databases, and retrieving the meta data from the repository can easily be accomplished with a simple GUI front end or Web application. A centralized meta data repository solution can either be custom built or licensed from a vendor.

- **Custom-built repository:** Designing and building a customized centralized meta data repository is an alternative that should be considered. Since the meta data repository solution should be enterprise-wide, the meta models (both logical and physical) will be generalized and not application-specific.

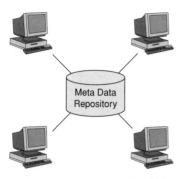

Figure 10.2: Centralized Meta Data Repository

This means that there will not be a meta data repository for a marketing application and another one for a sales application; instead, there will be one centralized meta data repository for all applications. The advantages and disadvantages of building a customized centralized meta data repository are similar to those of building a customized business application (Table 10.1).

Table 10.1: Advantages and Disadvantages of a Custom-Built Centralized Meta Data Repository

Advantages	*Disadvantages*
• A customized database design incorporates all meta data requirements.	• Full-time staff is needed to maintain the meta data repository database and the meta data reports.
• The front end for access and the interfaces to tools (ETL, OLAP, and so on) are custom designed to meet all requirements.	• The front end for access and the interfaces to tools must be programmed and maintained, both of which are time-consuming processes.
• Reports as well as help functions are designed exactly as desired.	• The meta data repository would have to be enhanced periodically (sometimes redesigned) because it cannot be built with all functionality from the start.
• Technicians have full control over the design and functionality of the meta data repository.	• Content may become out of synch with the proprietary dictionaries of the tools and the DBMS.

- **Licensed repository:** Licensing (buying) a centralized meta data repository product is an attractive alternative to building one. Losing some of the benefits inherent in a customized solution is offset by gaining the advantages that come with licensing a vendor product (Table 10.2).

Table 10.2: Advantages and Disadvantages of a Licensed Centralized Meta Data Repository

Advantages	*Disadvantages*
• Time is saved by not having to design and build a meta data repository database, interfaces, front end, and reports.	• The "plain vanilla" version of the licensed product will probably not satisfy all meta data requirements. Therefore, a full-time administrator is needed to maintain and enhance the licensed product.
• Most licensed meta data repository products come with interfaces, and most come with a full set of APIs.	• There will be a learning curve to become familiar with the product's architecture, interfaces, and APIs.
• If the meta data repository product is certified for the tools where the meta data resides, it will provide the tool interfaces.	• The more sophisticated the meta data repository product is, the more expensive it is, and the more skills the technicians need to maintain it.

Decentralized Meta Data Repository

As the term implies, a decentralized meta data repository solution stores the meta data in multiple databases in multiple locations (Figure 10.3).

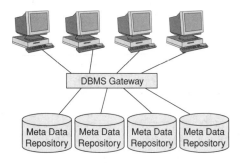

Figure 10.3: Decentralized Meta Data Repository

Commonly accessed meta data components could be replicated across multiple databases, but great care must be taken to keep those components consistent. A gateway directs the meta data access calls to the appropriate database to retrieve the desired meta data. There are some distinct advantages and disadvantages to this solution, whether it is built in-house or licensed from a vendor (Table 10.3).

Table 10.3: Advantages and Disadvantages of a Decentralized Meta Data Repository

Advantages	*Disadvantages*
• Various owners can maintain and manage their own sets of meta data separately.	• Controlling redundancy across multiple meta data repositories and keeping the meta data consistent is difficult.
• Meta data repository databases are smaller and easier to use because each database contains only those meta data components that are of interest to a specific group of business people.	• It will take longer to maintain and manage multiple databases on multiple platforms. There could also be synchronization problems with new DBMS releases.
• Each meta data repository can have its own meta model, that is, its own customized design.	• Communication among the custodians of the various meta data repositories will have to increase. Plus, it will require maintaining a meta-meta model, which is an integrated (merged) overall architecture of multiple meta models.
• Reports can be customized for each individual meta data repository.	• Relating meta data across various databases may be difficult. For example, business meta data is not automatically linked to technical meta data if they reside on different databases.
• A gateway makes the name and location of the meta data repository transparent to the person accessing it.	• The architecture of this solution is more complicated and the learning curve to use multiple databases with potentially different designs may be high.

Distributed XML-Enabled Meta Data Solution

Although the most promising meta data repository answer is a distributed XML-enabled meta data solution, it is also the most difficult to implement because it

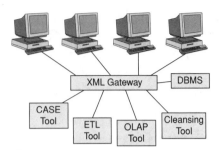

Figure 10.4: Distributed XML-Enabled Meta Data Solution

takes the concept of a decentralized meta data repository to the next level. Rather than storing meta data across multiple databases, in an XML-enabled solution the meta data remains at its originating location, that is, in the various tool dictionaries (Figure 10.4).

A gateway acts as a directory to the various locations where the meta data components are stored (e.g., the DBMS system catalog tables or the ETL tool dictionary). Vendors are vigorously exploring this "bleeding-edge" solution because it reduces the necessity for double maintenance of the meta data. *Double maintenance* refers to maintaining the meta data in the originating sources (DBMS and tool dictionaries) as well as maintaining it in the separate meta data repository database. Table 10.4 lists the advantages and disadvantages of this solution.

Table 10.4: Advantages and Disadvantages of a Distributed XML-Enabled Meta Data Solution

Advantages	*Disadvantages*
• XML tags enable access of meta data across any type of data storage through standardized categorization and tagging of meta data components.	• The initial tagging of all meta data with XML tags is a manual and laborious process. Plus, XML tagging cannot be used for all meta data.
• Meta data never has to be duplicated or moved from its original source (except for reporting purposes).	• XML tags add to the storage requirements for the dictionary databases that store meta data (DBMS and tool dictionaries).

(Continued)

Table 10.4: *(Continued)*

Advantages	*Disadvantages*
• A gateway makes the location of the meta data transparent to the person accessing it.	• A meta-meta model has to be created as a map of all the various types of meta data storage, each of which is designed according to its own unique meta model.
• Standard Web search engines should be able to locate any meta data anywhere.	• DBMS and tool vendors must follow industry standards* for meta data XML tags in order to enable seamless meta data access across all products. Multiple standards need to be supported.
• Meta data and business data can be coupled and transmitted simultaneously.	• Not all DBMSs and tools are XML-enabled. This is a bleeding-edge and unproven technology.

* Meta data standards are being developed by two competing groups: the Meta Data Coalition (MDC, influenced by Microsoft) and the Object Management Group (OMG, influenced by Oracle). The jury is still out on which meta data standards will be adopted as the industry standards.

DESIGNING A META DATA REPOSITORY

If the decision is made to custom build a meta data repository in-house, you have to choose between an E-R design and an OO design.

Entity-Relationship Design

Because an E-R design represents the meta data objects and their relationships explicitly, and because E-R designs are intuitive and easy to understand, many organizations choose this type of database design for their meta data repositories. To illustrate the intuitiveness of an E-R design, assume that the physical meta model contains four objects (Database, Table, Column, and Attribute) and that these objects are related in a one-to-many cardinality, as shown in Figure 10.5.

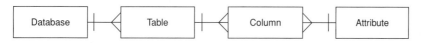

Figure 10.5: Example of Entity-Relationship Design. (Short vertical lines indicate "one," and the crow's feet indicate "many.")

This type of database structure is easy enough to understand that technology-savvy business people could write their own ad hoc Structured Query Language (SQL) queries against it. However, if these ad hoc queries are executed against a large centralized meta data repository, performance could be a problem. It is relatively easy to write poorly performing SQL queries. In addition, since each meta data object is implemented as a separate table, there will be dozens of tables, and some queries will contain very complicated JOINs across many of these tables. This could also affect performance.

Table 10.5 lists the advantages and disadvantages of E-R designs.

Table 10.5: Advantages and Disadvantages of Entity-Relationship Designs

Advantages	*Disadvantages*
• E-R designs are easy to read and easy to understand.	• Changes and enhancements may require a database redesign, as well as unloading and reloading the meta data repository.
• Because of the intuitive and explicit nature of the design, queries can be written with relatively simple SQL statements.	• The physical meta model is fairly large, with many objects and many relationships, which makes the architecture somewhat complex.
• E-R designs are easy to implement as relational database structures.	• Meta data objects and their relationships must be very well defined and understood for the physical meta model to be accurate.

Object-Oriented Design

As popular as E-R designs may be for meta data repository databases, OO designs are more efficient. Since they are more abstract, they result in fewer tables, run queries more efficiently, and are much easier to expand. Using the same example as above, the OO model would contain only three objects, but these objects would be more generic, as shown in Figure 10.6.

This type of database structure is not easy to understand, and business people will probably not be able to write their own ad hoc SQL queries against it. It is

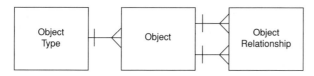

Figure 10.6: Example of Object-Oriented Design. (Short vertical lines indicate "one," and the crow's feet indicate "many.")

not intuitively obvious that the object named Object contains the instances (rows) for all meta data objects, such as database instances, table instances, column instances, attribute instances, and so on. It is also not obvious that the object named Object Type differentiates the various meta data object instances by assigning the appropriate label of Database, Table, Column, Attribute, and so on. And the untrained eye would have an even more difficult time discerning that all relationships between these object instances are reflected in the third object named Object Relationship. However, it is easy to see that expanding this type of generic design is as simple as adding new instances (rows) to these three objects (tables).

Table 10.6 lists the advantages and disadvantages of OO designs.

Table 10.6: Advantages and Disadvantages of Object-Oriented Designs

Advantages	*Disadvantages*
• OO designs are extremely flexible; they will not need any database redesigns when changes are necessary.	• Since the object named Object contains all instances (rows) of meta data, this table will become very large. This may affect access performance.
• OO designs are simplistic and therefore easy to maintain and to enhance.	• Queries are much more difficult to write and will require many recursive JOINs. Advanced SQL knowledge is required.
• OO designs are easy to implement as object-oriented database structures.	• OO designs require a high learning curve. The very abstract physical data model is difficult to comprehend, and the extensive rules take time to understand.

Designing and building your own meta data repository may not be within the scope of your BI project. There may be no budget and no staff for a separate meta data repository project. Maybe your organization would prefer to license (buy) a meta data repository product. As with all off-the-shelf products, a licensed meta data repository product will probably not be the perfect solution, but it may be the most cost-effective one. It would certainly be better than ignoring meta data altogether.

LICENSING (BUYING) A META DATA REPOSITORY

When selecting a meta data repository product (or any type of product), you should never start with the question, "What is the best product of this type on the market?" Instead, always start with the following questions:

- What are our requirements?
- Which requirements are:
  - Mandatory (must have)
  - Important (beneficial to have)
  - Optional (nice to have)
- Which products address our mandatory requirements?
- Which products address our important requirements?

Compare each vendor's logical meta model (if one exists) or their physical meta model (product design) with your logical meta model, and determine whether the vendor's model covers all the meta data requirements reflected in your "requirements meta model." At a minimum, the vendor's model must support all your *mandatory* meta data requirements. If it does, find out if the vendor's meta model and software can be expanded so that you can add your own features to support your *important* meta data requirements. Expansion capabilities of meta data repository products should include the following:

- Adding meta data objects
- Adding relationships
- Changing inappropriate relationships
- Adding meta-meta data attributes to the meta data objects
- Changing the size and length of meta-meta data components
- Customizing vendor-provided reports

- Creating and storing code for additional reports
- Importing meta data from other tools
- Exporting meta data to other tools

Product Evaluation

Use standard evaluation techniques to select a meta data repository product. For example, prepare a list of product evaluation criteria for your meta data requirements and assign a weighting factor from 1 to 10 to each criterion (1 being least important and 10 being most important), like the sample criteria list shown in Table 10.7.

 Notice that "Product can satisfy our *mandatory* meta data requirements" is not a weighted criterion. If the product cannot support the mandatory requirements, do not even consider it.

Rate each product on all product evaluation criteria by assigning a rating on a scale of 0 to 10 (0 means the product does not have that feature, 10 means that the product feature is outstanding), as illustrated in the example in Table 10.8.

Multiply the product ratings by the criteria weighting factors to obtain final scores for each product. Add up all the scores and list the products in the order of highest total score down to lowest total score, as shown in Table 10.9.

Table 10.7: Example of Product Evaluation Criteria with Weights

Criterion #	Product Evaluation Criteria	Weight
1	Product closely matches our logical meta model	10
2	Product can satisfy our important meta data requirements	6
3	Product can satisfy our optional meta data requirements	1
4	Product can be expanded	8
5	Product has interfaces	9
6	Product has a Web front end	4
7	Product has APIs	9

Table 10.8: Example of Product Ratings

Product*	Criterion #						
	1	2	3	4	5	6	7
Autumn Dictionary	3	7	6	0	9	9	10
Helixor	9	0	2	8	6	0	5
Leeches Repository	6	6	1	6	4	0	7
Springrep	8	2	0	10	10	2	10
Tamroller MDR	7	5	5	0	6	2	7

* The product names presented in this table are fictitious.

Table 10.9: Example of Weighted Product Ratings

Product*	Criterion #							Total Score
	1	2	3	4	5	6	7	
Springrep	80	12	0	80	90	8	90	360
Autumn Dictionary	30	42	6	0	81	36	90	285
Helixor	90	0	2	64	54	0	45	255
Leeches Repository	60	36	1	48	36	0	63	244
Tamroller MDR	70	30	5	0	54	8	63	230

* The product names presented in this table are fictitious.

Vendor Evaluation

Most organizations do not spend enough time, if any, evaluating the vendors in addition to evaluating the products. It is important to understand each vendor's company stability, its commitment to the product, and its level of support. Create a list of vendor evaluation criteria and assign a weighting factor to each criterion on a scale from 1 to 10 (1 being least important and 10 being most important), similar to the sample criteria shown in Table 10.10. Other criteria to consider are reputation for support, vendor integrity, and prior experience with the vendor.

Table 10.10: Example of Vendor Evaluation Criteria with Weights

Criterion #	Vendor Evaluation Criteria	Weight
1	Vendor has been in business for at least five years	8
2	Vendor has at least five Fortune 1000 clients	6
3	Vendor company is publicly traded and stock is healthy	8
4	Vendor has 24/7 telephone support	10
5	Vendor has an 800 hotline telephone number	9
6	Vendor has at least 50 employees	4
7	Vendor includes at least two weeks of free training	1

Rate each vendor on all vendor evaluation criteria by assigning a rating on a scale of 0 to 10 (0 means the vendor cannot meet that criterion, 10 means the vendor excels in that criterion), as illustrated in Table 10.11.

Multiply the vendor ratings by the criteria weighting factors to get final scores for each vendor. Add up all the scores and list the vendors in the order of highest total score down to lowest total score, as shown in Table 10.12.

Finally, compare the lists for product and vendor ratings and select the top two products. Check the vendors' references, schedule product demos, and arrange for a 30-day trial installation before making your final product selection.

Table 10.11: Example of Vendor Ratings

Vendor*	Criterion #						
	1	2	3	4	5	6	7
Autumn, Ltd.	9	7	4	9	10	9	5
Helix Corporation	5	3	0	8	0	1	0
Leeches, LLC	2	2	0	5	0	5	10
Springer, Inc.	10	9	7	10	10	10	10
Tamroller AG	10	10	8	5	0	10	1

* The vendor names presented in this table are fictitious.

Table 10.12: Example of Weighted Vendor Ratings

Vendor*	Criterion #							Total Score
	1	2	3	4	5	6	7	
Springer, Inc.	80	54	56	100	90	40	10	430
Autumn, Ltd.	72	42	32	90	90	36	5	367
Tamroller AG	80	60	64	50	0	40	1	295
Helix Corporation	40	18	0	80	0	4	0	142
Leeches, LLC	16	12	0	50	0	20	10	108

* The vendor names presented in this table are fictitious.

META DATA REPOSITORY DESIGN ACTIVITIES

The activities for meta data repository design do not need to be performed linearly. Figure 10.7 indicates which activities can be performed concurrently. The list below briefly describes the activities associated with Step 10, Meta Data Repository Design.

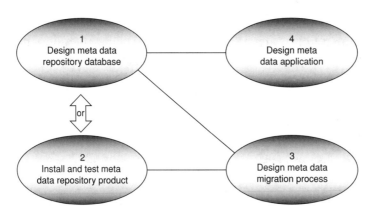

Figure 10.7: Meta Data Repository Design Activities

1. **Design the meta data repository database.**
   If the decision is made to build a meta data repository rather than to license (buy) one, design the meta data repository database. Choose between an E-R design and an OO design, and create (or enhance) the physical meta model

(database design). Generate the DDL for the database structures. Develop the meta data repository database maintenance procedures, such as backup and recovery, and create plans for versioning and archiving.

2. **Install and test the meta data repository product.**
   If the decision is made to license a meta data repository rather than to build one, evaluate the meta data repository products as well as their vendors. Products and vendors with the highest scorecard ratings should go on the short list (top two choices) from which the final product will be selected. Install and test the meta data repository product.

3. **Design the meta data migration process.**
   Identify all tools and DBMSs from which business meta data and technical meta data will have to be extracted. Determine the import, export, and API capabilities of those tools and DBMSs as well as of your meta data repository product if you licensed one. Design the meta data migration programs, including the tool interfaces, and write the programming specifications.

4. **Design the meta data application.**
   Unless you licensed a meta data repository product, design the meta data application, which includes access interfaces, Web features, reports, and an online help function. Once the reporting medium (e.g., Portable Document Format [PDF], Hypertext Markup Language [HTML]) has been selected, prepare the programming specifications for the various types of application programs.

DELIVERABLES RESULTING FROM THESE ACTIVITIES

If you are licensing a meta data repository product, your deliverable is an installed and tested product. If you are designing your own meta data repository, you should produce the following design deliverables:

1. **Physical meta model**
   The physical meta model is a diagram of the physical database structures for the meta data repository. Depending on the selected database design schema, this diagram can be an E-R model or an OO model. It shows tables, columns, primary keys, foreign keys, cardinality, and referential integrity rules.

2. **Data definition language for the meta data repository**
   The data definition language (DDL) is a set of SQL instructions that tells the DBMS what types of physical database structures to create for the meta data repository, such as databases, table spaces, tables, columns, and indices.

3. **Data control language for the meta data repository**

   The data control language (DCL) is a set of SQL instructions that tells the DBMS what type of read/write access to the meta data repository to grant. Access can be granted to a person, a group of persons, a program, or a tool.

4. **Meta data repository programming specifications**

   For the meta data migration process, these programming specifications should define the programming logic for meta data extract, transformation, and load programs, as well as tool interfaces. For the meta data application, these program specifications should define the programming logic for meta data reports and queries, access interfaces, and an online help function.

ROLES INVOLVED IN THESE ACTIVITIES

◆ **BI infrastructure architect**

   Since the BI infrastructure architect has the ultimate architectural responsibility over the BI decision-support environment as a whole, he or she needs to review all design activities. If a meta data repository is licensed, the BI infrastructure architect may participate in preparing the evaluation criteria and in deciding the weighting factors for the criteria. He or she will also be involved in the final product selection.

◆ **Data administrator**

   The data administrator will collaborate with the meta data administrator on the meta data requirements and help the meta data administrator with the data-modeling activities. The data administrator can also be an effective liaison between the meta data administrator, the subject matter expert, and the business representative when meta data requirements need to be verified or design decisions need to be reviewed or communicated.

◆ **Meta data administrator**

   The meta data administrator holds the primary responsibility over the meta data and the meta data repository. If the meta data repository is built in-house, he or she is responsible for designing and developing it. If a meta data repository is licensed, he or she is responsible for installing, testing, enhancing, and maintaining it. The meta data administrator is also responsible for designing the access interfaces as well as the migration programs to the DBMS, CASE tool, ETL tool, OLAP tool, and other tools.

RISKS OF NOT PERFORMING STEP 10

Providing a meta data repository solution is not a casual undertaking. The same disciplines and rigor that apply to building a BI application also apply to developing a meta data repository. "Whipping out" a database and a few canned SQL queries does not equate to a sustainable meta data repository solution. Like every other system, it must be designed with a lot of thought and foresight to assure the desired level of functionality, performance, scalability, and maintainability over time. If the decision is to license a meta data repository product, you must give the same care to the evaluation process as you would give to the purchase of a critical operational systems package. If you do not take the time to design a robust and sustainable meta data repository solution, you will have to redo your solution or end up with an inferior BI decision-support environment. As the saying goes: "Pay me now or pay me later, but you *will* pay."

BIBLIOGRAPHY AND ADDITIONAL READING

Devlin, Barry. *Data Warehouse: From Architecture to Implementation.* Reading, MA: Addison-Wesley, 1997.

Dick, Kevin. *XML: A Manager's Guide.* Boston, MA: Addison-Wesley, 2000.

Marco, David. *Building and Managing the Meta Data Repository: A Full Lifecycle Guide.* New York: John Wiley & Sons, 2000.

Sperley, Eric. *The Enterprise Data Warehouse: Planning, Building, and Implementation.* Upper Saddle River, NJ: Prentice Hall, 1999.

Tannenbaum, Adrienne. *Metadata Solutions: Using Metamodels, Repositories, XML, and Enterprise Portals to Generate Information on Demand.* Boston, MA: Addison-Wesley, 2002.

Data Management Association: *http://www.dama.org*

Enterprise Warehouse Solutions: *http://www.EWSolutions.com*

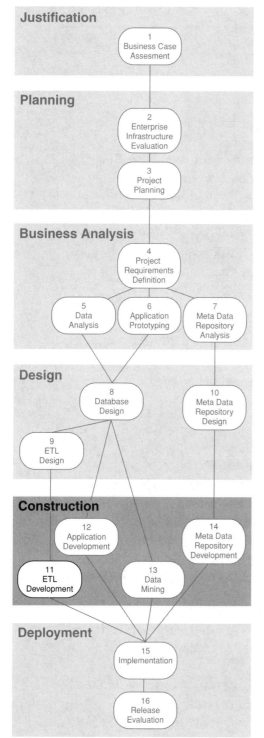

CHAPTER ELEVEN

Step 11: Extract/ Transform/Load Development

CHAPTER OVERVIEW

This chapter covers the following topics:

- Things to consider about extract/transform/load (ETL) development

- Common data transformation activities and the chronic underestimating of data transformation efforts

- Three types of reconciliation totals that should be produced by the ETL process: record counts, domain counts, and amount counts

- Peer reviews

- Six applicable ETL testing procedures: unit testing, integration testing, regression testing, performance testing, quality assurance (QA) testing, and acceptance testing

- How to create a formal test plan

- Brief descriptions of the activities involved in ETL development, the deliverables resulting from those activities, and the roles involved

- The risks of not performing Step 11

THINGS TO CONSIDER

Source Data Extracts

✓ Who will write the ETL programs? Have those developers written ETL programs before? Do they understand the ETL process?

✓ Do ETL programs already exist from a previous release or another BI application? How many of them have to be expanded?

✓ Can we ask the programmers of the operational systems to give us the extract files, or do we have to get the source data ourselves?

✓ What do we need to know about the operational systems before we can get the data? What operational programs have to finish running before we can extract the data from the source files and source databases?

ETL Tool

✓ Have we worked with this ETL tool before, or is it new to us?

✓ Has the ETL team been sufficiently trained on the ETL tool?

✓ Can the ETL tool perform all the required transformations, or will we have to write some custom code? In what language (C++, COBOL)?

ETL Process Dependencies

✓ What are the dependencies among program modules? In what sequence do we have to run our ETL programs (or the ETL tool modules)?

✓ How many program modules can we run in parallel?

✓ What are the dependencies among the tables? Do some tables have to be loaded before others?

✓ How many tables can we load in parallel?

Testing

✓ Will we conduct peer reviews? Are we using extreme programming (XP) techniques?

✓ How many testers will we have on the project?

✓ Will the subject matter expert and business representative participate in testing?

✓ Who will be the testing coordinator? Who will log the test results and maintain the test log?

✓ What type of testing do we need to perform? Integration or regression testing? Performance testing? QA testing? Acceptance testing?

✓ Which business people will participate in acceptance testing? Only the business representative? The subject matter expert? Other business people?

Technical Considerations

✓ What technical platform issues do we have to take into consideration?

✓ How is the staging area set up? On a dedicated server?

✓ Will the ETL process be split between the mainframe and one or more servers?

✓ What environments does the ETL tool run in?

✓ What type of middleware do we need?

The use of ETL tools has become very widespread, but organizations that use them discover very quickly that these tools have their limitations. Depending on the complexity of the required source data transformations and on the age and condition of the source files, custom code often has to be written to augment the ETL tool functionality.

SOURCE DATA TRANSFORMATION

The technical rules and the business rules for the required source data transformations were accumulated and defined throughout the steps of project planning, project requirements definition, data analysis, application prototyping, and meta data repository analysis. During those steps, the rules were probably extracted from old manuals, old memos, e-mails, programs (operational and decision support), and computer-aided software engineering (CASE) tools and provided by people who remember when and why a business rule was created. These rules are now reflected as data transformation activities in the ETL process.

Data Transformation Activities

BI projects present the best opportunity to eliminate dead and useless data because it allows the business people to see their information requirements in a different light. When properly implemented, the data transformation activities of cleansing, summarization, derivation, aggregation, and integration will produce data that is clean, condensed, new, complete, and standardized, respectively (Figure 11.1).

Figure 11.1: Data Transformation Activities

- **Cleansing:** By definition, cleansing is a BI transformation process in which source data that violates the business rules is changed to conform to those rules. Cleansing is usually accomplished through edits in the ETL programs, which use table lookups and program logic to determine or derive the correct data values and then write those data values into the load files used to populate the BI target databases.

- **Summarization:** Numeric values are summarized to obtain total figures (amounts or counts), which can then be stored as business facts in multidimensional fact tables. Summary totals can be calculated and stored at multiple levels (e.g., departmental summary of sales, regional summary of sales, and total sales by country).

- **Derivation:** During this process, new data is created from existing atomic (detailed) source data. Derivation is typically accomplished by calculations, table lookups, or program logic. Examples include the following:
  - Generating a new code for classifying customers based on a certain combination of existing data values
  - Calculating profit from income and expense items
  - Appending the last four digits of a ZIP code based on the address in a postal lookup table
  - Calculating a customer's age based on his or her date of birth and the current year

- **Aggregation:** All the data about a business object is brought together. For example, data elements for a customer may be aggregated from multiple source files and source databases, such as a Customer Master file, a Prospect file, a Sales file, and demographic data purchased from a vendor. (In multidimensional database design jargon, the term *aggregation* also refers to the roll-up of data values.)

- **Integration:** Data integration based on normalization rules forces the need to reconcile different data names and different data values for the same data element. The desired result is to have each unique data element known by one standard name, with one standard definition and an approved domain. Each data element should also be associated with its sources files and source databases as well as its BI target databases. Standardizing the data should be a business objective.

Underestimating Data Transformation Efforts

Source data transformation is similar to opening a Russian doll—you open one and there is another inside. It could be an endless process. That is why the time required for the ETL process is chronically underestimated. The original estimates are usually based on the amount of technical data conversions required to transform data types and lengths, and they often do not take into account the overwhelming amount of transformations required to enforce business data domain rules and business data integrity rules.

The transformation specifications given to the ETL developer should never be limited to just technical data conversion rules. For some large organizations with many old file structures, the ratio of a particular data transformation effort could be as high as 80 percent effort toward enforcing business data domain rules and business data integrity rules and only 20 percent effort toward enforcing technical data conversion rules. Therefore, expect to multiply your original estimates for your ETL data transformation effort by four. Even if you think you have a very realistic timetable for the ETL process, do not be surprised if you still miss deadlines due to dirty data. If you do not miss deadlines, do not be surprised to discover you have not cleansed enough of the data sufficiently.

Insist on full-time involvement from the business representative, and insist on getting the *right* business representative—someone who is knowledgeable about the business and who has authority to make decisions about the business rules. These stipulations are essential for speeding up the ETL process. Furthermore, urge the business sponsor and the business representative to launch a data quality initiative in the organization, or at least in the departments under their control or influence. When business people drive a data quality initiative, they are more likely to assist with the ETL transformation process. Remind them that while IT technicians may know the process semantics, the business people know the data contents and business semantics. They understand what the data *really* means.

RECONCILIATION

One of the most common complaints about BI applications is that the data in the BI target databases does not match the data in the source systems. As a result, business people often do not trust the BI data. Ironically, most of the time the data in the BI target databases is more accurate than the data in the operational source files or source databases because the data has been reformatted, standardized, and cleansed. However, without proof this trust cannot be restored. Reconciliation totals provide that proof and must be available as meta data in the meta data repository.

ETL reconciliation totals are ETL process control totals, not operational reconciliation totals back to the organization's financial statement or general ledger. The purpose for ETL reconciliation totals is to ensure that all the data values going into the ETL process can be reconciled with all the data values coming out of the ETL process.

Storing ETL reconciliation totals, as well as data quality and load statistics, as meta data highlights the importance of providing a meta data repository. This meta data is crucial information for the business people who want to see which data was loaded, which data was rejected and for what reasons, and what the data reliability (cleanliness) factor is for the BI data after each load cycle. For example, source data from multiple source files and source databases may not have been properly synchronized (a timeliness error), which may have caused inconsistencies in analysis results. With load statistics available as meta data, the business analysts can quickly recognize and reconcile the problem.

Calculating Reconciliation Totals

Far too many BI projects do not employ the good IT practices commonly enforced in operational systems. Believing the notion that BI applications are "just" for decision support and are therefore less critical than operational systems is a grave mistake. BI applications are as critical as operational systems because the decisions that are made based on the data in the BI decision-support environment can affect an organization's strategic direction and vitality.

One time-proven discipline when manipulating data, whether changing the data in some way or copying it or moving it from one place to another, is to reconcile every new output to its old input. Every program or program module that reads data and then writes it to a new file, even if only into a temporary file, must produce reconciliation totals.

There are three types of reconciliation totals: record counts, domain counts, and amount counts.

Record Counts

One of the most fundamental reconciliation totals is a simple count of records read and records written. If records are rejected because they fail an edit check in the ETL process, the number of records rejected must also be counted. The total count of records written and records rejected must equal the count of records read (Figure 11.2).

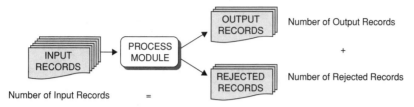

Figure 11.2: Record Counts

Domain Counts

Domain counts involve counting the number of records for each unique domain (data value) of an input field and counting the number of records for the same unique domain on the output file. The complication with domain counts enters when an "overloaded" source data element must be split into multiple columns. An overloaded source data element is a data element used for multiple purposes, as many of the one-byte and two-byte code fields are in operational systems. The domain of an overloaded data element describes not *one* business object but *many* business objects and must therefore be separated into different columns for different tables. (Business objects are usually implemented as dimension tables.) In that case, the total of the multiple domain counts on the output side must equal the one domain count on the input side. If data values were rejected because they did not pass the data quality edits, there would be an additional count of all the rejected records. Thus, the total of the multiple output domain counts and the rejected data values count must equal the input domain count (Figure 11.3).

Amount Counts

Even more important than domain counts are amount counts. They are the primary mechanism for reconciling source files and source databases to the BI target databases. Reconciling amounts happens in two ways. One is to summarize every amount field in every input file and every corresponding amount field in every output file. If records were rejected, there would be a third summary for the total amount figure rejected. The combined total of the output amount total and the rejected amount total must equal the input amount total.

A more complicated amount reconciliation algorithm must be developed if the incoming amount field is an overloaded source data element that has to be

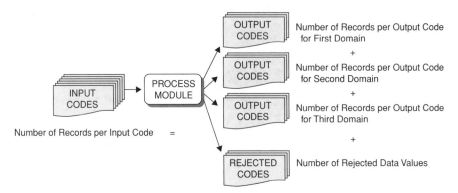

Figure 11.3: Domain Counts

separated into several different amount columns for the BI target databases. In that case, the selection and edit criteria in the transformation specifications must be used to create multiple output amount totals. In addition, the same selection and edit criteria must be run against the input file to produce the same multiple amount totals for verification (Figure 11.4).

Storing Reconciliation Statistics

Because of the extensive amount of transformation and cleansing that typically occurs in the ETL process, the business people should expect the data to be different on the BI target databases than in the original source files and source databases. Their desire or need to reconcile the data between source and target is valid. However, it must be accomplished through using reconciliation totals, not by comparing source data elements to target columns dollar for dollar.

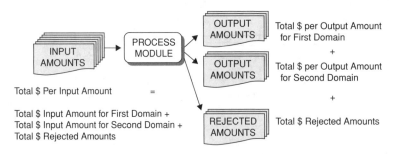

Figure 11.4: Amount Counts

Therefore, all reconciliation totals produced by every program module for each BI application load cycle must be stored as meta data in the meta data repository. If possible, additional categorization of rejected records should be considered with short descriptions for the rejection reason. These descriptions can be composed based on the ETL edit criteria.

PEER REVIEWS

Peer reviews are similar to the "pair programming" concept of extreme programming (XP), except that the coding itself does not occur in pairs, the meetings often involve more than two people, and the reviews apply to all types of task deliverables besides programs. Peer reviews are informal meetings that combine reviewing, testing, and a limited amount of brainstorming about a project task deliverable. The purpose of peer reviews is to allow the developer of a given piece of project work to present a task deliverable to his or her peers for validation or discussion. This is best accomplished in a core team setting, but a peer review can also involve team members from the extended team who have a vested interest in that project task.

At the completion of a project task, the developer of the work (or any other core team member) may decide to ask for a peer review to solicit input to a complex problem, get feedback to a creative solution, or ask for opinions on an item that is uncertain or poorly defined. He or she then determines which team members should participate in the peer review, schedules the informal peer review meeting, and distributes copies of documents (e.g., specifications, programs, data models, reports) to the invited peers before the meeting.

The developer of the work leads the meeting. The project manager, who should always participate in peer reviews, ensures that the meeting does not bog down in disagreements nor stray from the issues at hand. Each attendee should have reviewed the distributed documents and should be prepared to comment and to brainstorm on the issues. Together, the participants are responsible for uncovering errors or misconceptions in the task deliverable. Discussions are initiated to help the developer understand the problems uncovered or to allow the developer to justify his or her work to the satisfaction of all in attendance.

Brainstorming is usually limited to finding the errors or misconceptions; it does not extend to solving them unless a solution is obvious and can be presented or discussed within a few minutes. At the conclusion of a peer review the uncovered errors or misconceptions should be documented, and the developer of the deliverable is tasked with correcting them or with creating a new solution to the project task.

Peer reviews sound more formal than they really are. They can be best compared to high-powered, structured brainstorming sessions. Peer review meetings should be limited to about one hour.

ETL TESTING

Unfortunately, testing, like reconciliation, is often done very poorly on BI projects, if at all. That is not acceptable—and neither is the excuse that "it can be fixed in the next release." The next release will be even larger and more complicated, and it will require more time to test. In other words, if it takes too long to test now, it will take even longer to test later, which usually means that adequate testing is never done. Rushing into deployment at the expense of testing is inexcusable, especially if it is done to meet some artificial deadline.

The same types of testing that apply to operational systems also apply to BI applications (Figure 11.5). The following sections briefly describe each type.

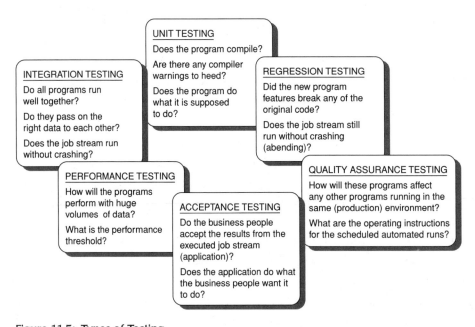

Figure 11.5: Types of Testing

Unit Testing

Unit testing refers to the testing of discrete program modules and scripts, not to testing the flow or the links between the programs. Every developer must test his or her program modules and scripts individually (if XP techniques are utilized, this is done in pairs). There are three components to unit testing: compilation, functionality, and edits.

- **Compilation:** Obviously, each program module must compile successfully or it cannot be implemented. There are many testing tools on the market for every conceivable programming language. These tools allow the developer to trace every step of the code as it is being executed, displaying the before and after images of the data for each line of code.

- **Functionality:** Each program module must perform the functions for which it was designed and must produce the expected test results. Therefore, each developer must create a small test file with valid as well as invalid data to test every function of his or her program modules. He or she must know in advance what the program modules should do with the valid and the invalid test data (expected test results). Unit testing is not completed until all program modules produce all of the expected results.

- **Edits:** Each program module must catch errors and, depending on the severity of the error, either produce an error message or gracefully end the program. No program should ever stop abruptly ("crash" or abend) with a cryptic system error message. With the high degree of poor-quality data in the source files, it is quite common that more lines of code are written for edits than for functionality.

 Consider allowing someone other than the developer to test any given piece of code. This along with peer reviews should snare most errors that may not be caught because of pride of ownership and being too close to one's own code.

If an ETL tool is used, unit testing still applies to the individual ETL tool modules. In that case, you are testing the validity of your ETL instructions, that is, the ETL technical meta data. It is important to note that if an ETL tool does not meet the standards of your organization, you will have to supplement the tool with your own custom-written code. In that case, unit testing will be a combination of testing the ETL technical meta data, testing the custom-written code, and testing the "handshake" between them.

Integration Testing

Integration testing, also known as system testing, is the first complete ETL process run. This includes all three sets of ETL processes: the initial load, the historical load, and the incremental load. Just because all program modules pass their individual unit tests, it cannot be assumed that the entire ETL process will run smoothly. The interactions and flow of all programs, as specified in the ETL process flow diagram, must be observed and validated.

- **Interactions:** Program modules receive data, manipulate it, and hand it off to other program modules. This interaction between the modules must be tested. The test data used for integration testing is different from that used for unit testing. A copy of a relatively large subset of representative operational source data is used for integration testing.

- **Flow:** The ETL process flow diagram should indicate which programs must run in which sequence, which programs can run in parallel, and where sort and merge utilities are interjected. This flow must be tested for functionality and efficiency. Testing for functionality ensures that the right process is performed on the right data at the right time, that is, that the programs run in the correct sequence. Testing for efficiency ensures that the entire ETL process can complete within the expected time frame. If it cannot, the flow must be redesigned, and the entire ETL process must be retested.

If an ETL tool is used, the entire ETL process must still be tested from beginning to end, except that you are running the ETL tool processes instead of custom-written programs.

The business representative and the subject matter expert should be involved in integration testing. They are the first to know whether a particular run was successful or not. This is also an excellent opportunity for some advanced training for them, and it will go a long way toward allaying any future suspicions about the accuracy and quality of the data in the BI target databases.

Integration testing, like unit testing, requires many test runs to remove all the defects and to tune the flow. Every time the actual test results do not equal the expected test results, the program producing the error must be corrected, and *all* programs must be rerun. But unlike unit testing, integration testing is far too complicated to be performed without a formal test plan, which should include a description of the test cases and the sequence in which the programs should be executed.

Regression Testing

The most complicated and most time-consuming of all types of testing is regression testing. It is similar to integration testing, but this time the programs that are being tested are not new. Since the BI decision-support environment is evolving and new BI applications are added to the ETL process continuously, the project team will have to perform extensive regression testing on all releases except the first one. With every new BI release the ETL process has to be modified (enhanced) to extract more data from the operational systems for the new BI application. The new BI application may have a separate set of data access and analysis programs, but the ETL process is shared.

The main goal of regression testing is to make sure that the modifications to existing ETL programs did not inadvertently produce some errors that did not exist before. If new programs were added to the ETL process flow, the new interactions between programs must be tested, and any affected subsequent old programs must be retested. If the ETL process flow had to be enhanced or redesigned to increase efficiency, the entire ETL process has to be retested.

 To develop a new test plan for every regression test would be much too time-consuming. Thus, it is advisable to save the original test plan and the original test data created for integration testing of the first release. Then enhance the original test plan for subsequent regression tests with new programs, new data, and new test cases.

Performance Testing

Performance testing, also known as stress testing, is performed to predict system behavior and performance. This is very similar to traditional performance testing on operational systems, but BI performance testing is more complicated because of the enormous volumes of data in the BI target databases. Since most organizations do not have more than three to four hours left in their nightly batch windows, the goal is to find out how much data can be processed during that time and how many nights it will take to complete the entire ETL process.

Unlike integration testing or regression testing, performance testing does not have to be performed on every program module. Performance testing could be limited to only the most critical program modules with the highest volumes of data and the longest runtimes. In addition to running physical tests, you can use stress test simulation tools. These simulation tools allow you to describe the production platform, including other programs running on the same server and sharing the same space. Based on your input, the tools calculate and project estimated performance numbers. It is highly recommended to run a simulation prior to actual performance testing with real data.

Quality Assurance Testing

Most large organizations have strict procedures for moving an application into production. These procedures usually include QA testing, and in most cases a separate QA environment is established for such testing. Operations staff direct the developers in moving databases and programs into the QA environment. Then all operating instructions and scheduled jobs have to be turned over to the operations staff for testing. They will go through a simulated production run before allowing the application components to transfer to the production environment.

Acceptance Testing

Acceptance testing can be performed in one of two ways, depending on how testing as a whole is set up. Ideally, there should be a separate acceptance test environment, which could also be used for regression testing of future releases. With a separate acceptance test environment, QA testing and acceptance testing could be done at the same time. However, it may not be feasible or justifiable to maintain a separate acceptance test environment. A simpler alternative is to perform acceptance testing after QA testing in the same QA environment.

If the business representative actively participated during integration testing or regression testing, there should be very few surprises during acceptance testing. In fact, if the business representative is comfortable with the integration or regression test results, and barring any unforeseen problems detected during QA testing, separate acceptance testing may not be necessary at all. However, if a traditional approach was followed in which the business representative was not involved in any design or testing activities except for occasional reviews, acceptance testing is the most important test of all.

Some project teams limit acceptance testing to the access and analysis portion of the BI application and exclude the business representative from ETL testing. That is a big mistake. When business analysts and business managers complain about incorrect data in the BI target databases, the reason may not be that the report programs do not work properly but that the ETL process is faulty. Therefore, testing how to get the data into the BI target databases correctly is more important than testing how to get it out correctly because an error in a report program is a lot easier to find and correct than an error in the ETL process. Moreover, since the business representative is involved in source data analysis and in providing the business rules for data cleansing, it is only logical that he or she should test the ETL process that implements those rules. The business representative should ask some of the following questions.

- Is the appropriate data being extracted?
- If the source data element is split into multiple columns, is it done correctly during the transformation process?
- If some data elements are merged together, did any integrity problems result from this transformation process?
- Is the data loaded correctly into the appropriate BI target databases and the appropriate BI tables?
- Can the data in the BI target databases be reconciled with the source files and source databases? Where are the reconciliation totals stored?
- Are data values correctly transformed and cleansed? Is bad data slipping through without notice?
- Is the load performance adequate? And is the BI data available to the business people when they expect it?

FORMAL TEST PLAN

With the possible exceptions of unit testing and performance testing, ETL testing sessions are organized events that are guided and controlled by an agenda called a test plan. Each test plan should specify the information illustrated in Figure 11.6.

Test Plan

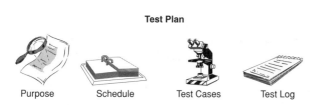

Purpose　　　Schedule　　　Test Cases　　　Test Log

Figure 11.6: Test Plan Components

- **Purpose:** Describe in general terms what is being tested. For example:

  "Data is extracted from the Customer Master file, Account Tran file, Sales History database, and Product Master database. The extracted data from Customer Master, Account Tran, and Sales History must be merged under Customer Number, and the extracted data from Product Master and Sales History must be merged under Product Number. The ETL programming specifications include 28 transformations and 46 cleansing algorithms. We will run 20 test cases to test the transformations and 42 test cases to test the cleansing algorithms."

- **Schedule:** After reviewing the ETL process flow diagram and determining which programs have to run in which sequence and which ones can run in parallel, every program in the job stream must be scheduled to run in exactly that sequence on certain dates at certain times.

- **Test cases:** The bulk of the test plan will be the list of test cases. It is important to have the business representative participate in writing the test cases. Each test case specifies the input criteria and the expected output results for each run. It also describes the program logic to be performed and how the resulting data should look. For example:

  "Submit module ETL3.3 using the T11Customer temporary VSAM file and the T11Product temporary VSAM file. Both temporary files are sorted in descending order. Module ETL3.3 merges the two files and rejects records that do not match on Sale-Tran-Cd and Cust-Num. All rejected records must trigger the error message: 'ETL3.3.e7 No match found on <*print out* Cust-Num> and <*print out* Prd-Nbr> <*print out* system date-time stamp>.'"

- **Test log:** A detailed audit trail must be kept of all test runs, itemizing the date and time the programs ran, the program or program module numbers, who validated them, the expected test results, the actual test results, whether the test was accepted or not, and any additional comments. Table 11.1 shows a sample test log.

 Remember that *all* programs in the ETL process are tested and retested until the complete ETL process runs from beginning to end as expected.

Table 11.1: Example of a Test Log

Date	Time	Program Number	Tester	Expected Test Results	Actual Test Results	Accepted (Yes/No)	Comments
8/25/2003	8:45 A.M.	ETL1.1v1	BLB	232,489 sold loans 983,731 purchased	230,876 sold loans 983,689 purchased	Yes	There were 1,655 rejected loans. Rejections are valid and expected.
8/25/2003	8:45 A.M.	ETL3.1v1	JAL	$30,555,791.32 daily loan balance	$33,498,231.11 daily loan balance	No	Double-counting occurs on ARM IV loans funded after 10/01/2003.
8/25/2003	9:10 A.M.	ETL1.2v1	BLB	SRP-Code totals: A 398,220 B 121,209 C 228,734	SRP-Code totals: A 398,208 B 120,871 C 228,118	No	966 codes have invalid characters like @ : ^ -.

ETL DEVELOPMENT ACTIVITIES

The activities for ETL development do not need to be performed linearly. Figure 11.7 indicates which activities can be performed concurrently. The list below briefly describes the activities associated with Step 11, ETL Development.

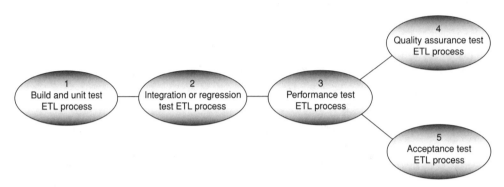

Figure 11.7: ETL Development Activities

1. **Build and unit test the ETL process.**

   Under the direction of the ETL lead developer, the ETL programs must be developed for the three sets of load processes: initial load, historical load, and incremental load. If you plan to use a database management system (DBMS) load utility to populate the BI target databases, then only the extract and transformation programs need to be written, including the programs that create the final load files. If you plan to use an ETL tool, the instructions (technical meta data) for the ETL tool must be created. All custom-written ETL programs and all ETL tool modules must be unit tested for compilation, functionality, and edits.

2. **Integration or regression test the ETL process.**

   Once you have unit tested all the individual ETL programs or program modules, the entire ETL process flow must be tested. This is accomplished with integration testing on the first release and with regression testing on subsequent releases. Both types of testing must be performed under a formal test plan with test cases, expected test results, actual test results, and a log of test runs.

3. **Performance test the ETL process.**

   Since many BI target databases are very large databases (VLDBs), it is important to stress test selected programs or ETL tool modules. Perform stress testing with full volume data on those programs or ETL tool modules that read or write to high-volume tables and that perform complicated operations, especially when running in parallel against high-volume tables. Performance tests can also be simulated with stress test simulation tools.

4. **Quality assurance test the ETL process.**
   Most organizations do not allow programs to be moved into production until they have passed through a QA test process. This test is usually run under the supervision of the operations staff in a separate QA environment.

5. **Acceptance test the ETL process.**
   If the business representative and the subject matter expert have been actively involved in integration or regression testing activities, then acceptance testing should be little more than a final, formal certification from the business representative. If they have not been involved, all functions of the ETL process must be validated to be complete and correct, especially the reconciliation process.

DELIVERABLES RESULTING FROM THESE ACTIVITIES

1. **ETL test plan**
   The test plan should state the purpose for each test and show a schedule for running the tests in a predefined sequence. It should also describe the test cases, including input criteria and expected output results. A test log should accompany the test plan, documenting when the tests were run, who ran the tests, and what the test results were.

2. **ETL programs**
   All extract, transformation, and load programs and scripts for the entire ETL process should be coded and tested. If an ETL tool is being used, instructions for the ETL tool modules should be written and the ETL tool modules should be tested.

3. **ETL program library**
   All ETL programs, scripts, and ETL tool modules should reside in a version-controlled ETL program library or ETL tool library. These ETL programs, scripts, and ETL tool modules should have been integration or regression tested, performance tested, QA tested, and acceptance tested for the entire ETL process.

ROLES INVOLVED IN THESE ACTIVITIES

◆ **Business representative**
  The business representative should be involved in integration or regression testing and in acceptance testing. With the help of the ETL lead developer, he or she and the subject matter expert write the test cases.

◆ **Database administrator**
  The database administrator can be very instrumental during the ETL development process. The database administrator assists the ETL lead developer with the ETL process flow and also reviews all database calls written by the ETL developers. On more than one occasion a database administrator has been able to streamline the ETL process by invoking little-known DBMS utilities at the appropriate point in the ETL process flow.

◆ **ETL developers**
  One of the main tasks assigned to ETL developers is to code or enhance the ETL programs and to unit test them. If the organization is using an ETL tool, the ETL developers must write the ETL instructions (technical meta data) for the ETL tool processes.

◆ **ETL lead developer**
  The ETL lead developer manages the entire ETL process. He or she reviews the ETL process flow diagram and the ETL program design document with the other ETL developers and assigns the programming modules to them. He or she creates the test plan and works with the business representative and the subject matter expert on creating the test cases. He or she is also responsible for coordinating the test runs and keeping the test log current.

◆ **Subject matter expert**
  The subject matter expert, either alone or with the business representative, writes or enhances the test cases for the test plan. He or she also suggests what reconciliation totals have to be produced. The subject matter expert should participate as a tester during integration or regression testing and during acceptance testing.

◆ **Testers**
  Testers can be developers, systems analysts, "power users," subject matter experts, and anyone else who has some technical skills and is available to participate in testing. Developers should not test their own code, but they can test the code written by other developers. Testing is an activity that can easily be modularized.

It is advisable to get as many testers involved as possible to accelerate the testing process.

RISKS OF NOT PERFORMING STEP 11

A well-designed and well-tested ETL process is the backbone of a BI decision-support environment. This step is a very time-consuming step, but without it, you do not have a BI application. End of story.

BIBLIOGRAPHY AND ADDITIONAL READING

Aiken, Peter H. *Data Reverse Engineering: Slaying the Legacy Dragon.* New York: McGraw-Hill, 1995.

Beck, Kent. *Extreme Programming Explained: Embrace Change.* Boston, MA: Addison-Wesley, 2000.

Cockburn, Alistair. *Agile Software Development.* Boston, MA: Addison-Wesley, 2002.

Devlin, Barry, *Data Warehouse: From Architecture to Implementation.* Reading, MA: Addison-Wesley, 1997.

Hackney, Douglas. *Understanding and Implementing Successful Data Marts.* Reading, MA: Addison-Wesley, 1997.

Hetzel, William. *The Complete Guide to Software Testing, Second Edition.* New York: John Wiley & Sons, 1993.

Humphrey, Watts S. *Winning with Software: An Executive Strategy.* Boston, MA: Addison-Wesley, 2002.

Imhoff, Claudia, Lisa Loftis, and Jonathan G. Geiger. *Building the Customer-Centric Enterprise: Data Warehousing Techniques for Supporting Customer Relationship Management.* New York: John Wiley & Sons, 2001.

Kimball, Ralph, and Richard Merz. *The Data Webhouse Toolkit: Building the Web-Enabled Data Warehouse.* New York: John Wiley & Sons, 2000.

Kimball, Ralph, Laura Reeves, Margy Ross, and Warren Thornthwaite. *The Data Warehouse Lifecycle Toolkit: Expert Methods for Designing, Developing, and Deploying Data Warehouses.* New York: John Wiley & Sons, 1998.

Ponniah, Paulraj. *Data Warehousing Fundamentals: A Comprehensive Guide for IT Professionals.* New York: John Wiley & Sons, 2001.

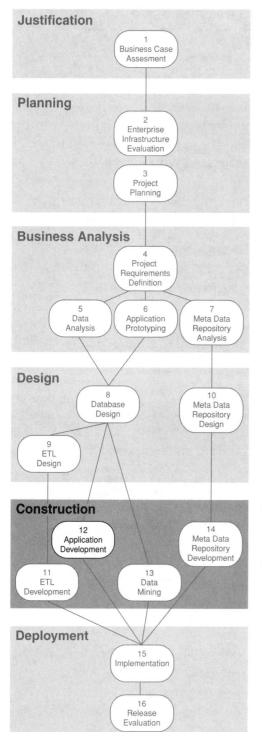

CHAPTER TWELVE

Step 12: Application Development

CHAPTER OVERVIEW

This chapter covers the following topics:

■ Things to consider about access and analysis tools

■ The advantages of using online analytical processing (OLAP) tools and some of their popular features

■ Multidimensional analysis factors, with emphasis on multivariate analysis using both object dimensions and variable dimensions

■ Three OLAP architectural layers: presentation services, OLAP services, and database services

■ Four common application development environments: prototyping, development, quality assurance (QA), and production

■ A short discussion of the Web environment

■ Brief descriptions of the activities involved in application development, the deliverables resulting from those activities, and the roles involved

■ The risks of not performing Step 12

THINGS TO CONSIDER

Prototyping Results

✓ Did we prototype the access and analysis components of the BI application? If so, what did we learn from the prototype?

✓ What portions of the application prototype can we save? What portions have to be redesigned?

✓ Did we decide to develop the access and analysis components using the *operational* prototype as a rapid and iterative development method? Will this be the final iteration?

Access and Analysis Tools

✓ What access and analysis tools do we already have in place? Are we happy with them?

✓ Will the business people use an OLAP tool for multidimensional analysis?

✓ In what other ways will they analyze the data? Do we need to acquire another query or reporting tool?

Skills and Training

✓ What skill sets (beginning, advanced, expert) do the business people have? What type of additional training do they need?

✓ How many business people have already been trained on the access and analysis tools? How many more need training?

✓ Are they familiar with OLAP and multidimensional reporting concepts?

✓ Do we need to implement a context-sensitive online help function for the access and analysis components of the BI application?

Scope and Project Requirements

✓ Are our project requirements still the same? Or has the scope changed?

✓ How many reports and canned queries do we need to develop? Which ones?

✓ Have we validated the necessary number of dimensions needed for those reports and queries?

✓ Do we know how the knowledge workers, business analysts, and business managers want to drill down and roll up when working with the data? Are their requirements similar or different?

Web Considerations

✓ Do we have to include a Web portal with this BI application?
✓ Have we developed Web portals before? Have we prototyped one?
✓ What are the additional security requirements for the Web? Do we have the necessary firewalls and security packages installed?

Technical Considerations

✓ Are the development and production environments configured the same or are they different?
✓ What are the differences? A different database management system (DBMS)? A different operating system? Different hardware?

The main reason for a BI decision-support initiative is to provide fast and easy access to data for business analysis. A high percentage of that access will be by predefined patterns. A predefined pattern means that data has been precalculated (derived, aggregated, summarized) and stored in that fashion for faster access. This is the reason for the high popularity of multidimensional OLAP tools, and it is the hallmark of BI decision-support applications.

ONLINE ANALYTICAL PROCESSING TOOLS

Multidimensional OLAP tools are a major component of the BI decision-support tool suite. Terms such as *OLAP*, *relational OLAP* (ROLAP), *multidimensional OLAP* (MOLAP), *decision support*, *multidimensional analysis*, and *executive information system* (EIS) are all used to describe the explosive growth in the field of data access and data analysis tools. These terms are frequently associated with expectations of built-in functionality and ease of use. While much of the literature uses *OLAP* to represent all of these terms, each OLAP tool vendor seems to have its own definition of OLAP. Hence, OLAP tools support only the definitions of their vendors—most of the time.

A widely accepted definition of OLAP is the following: *OLAP* refers to online analytical processing technology that creates new business information through a robust set of business transformations and calculations executed upon existing data.

Advantages of OLAP Tools

Although BI decision-support applications use conventional reporting and querying tools as much as multidimensional OLAP tools, the majority of business people seem to favor OLAP tools because of their additional functionalities. There are two distinct advantages for business people who use OLAP tools.

1. The focus in analytical processing is on the data, specifically the multidimensional aspects of the data that are supported by OLAP tools. Business objects are represented as dimensions (e.g., product, customer, department), which are naturally interrelated through functional subject areas (e.g., sales) and are often hierarchical (e.g., products roll up into product categories, departments roll up into divisions).

2. Business analysts navigate through these dimensions by drilling down, rolling up, or drilling across. They can drill down to access the detailed level of data, and they can roll up to see the summarized data. They can roll up through the hierarchy levels of dimensions or to specific characteristics or data elements (columns) of the dimensions. They can also drill across dimensions to access the data of interrelated dimensions. In addition, powerful computational services provide functions such as ranks, averages, return on investment (ROI), and currency conversions.

The OLAP category of software tools makes many business analysts self-sufficient by giving them easy and intuitive access to their data for analysis—and getting developers out of the report-writing business. This is accomplished through the following tool characteristics:

- OLAP tools allow business analysts to combine their data in any order they desire, at any level of summarization, and over several time periods. Business analysts can design their queries by clicking on the dimensions and by selecting the desired data elements for the analysis they need to perform.
- Different OLAP tools support a variety of access and analysis needs. They provide multiple views for data access, from the senior executive's desire to browse through summarized data to the business analyst's need to perform complex detailed analysis.

OLAP tools are a very important component of application development in a BI decision-support environment. While conventional query and reporting tools are used to describe *what* is in a database, multidimensional OLAP tools are used to answer *why* certain business events are true. For example, an OLAP tool could be used to prove or disprove a hypothesis that a business analyst has formulated about a correlation among certain data values. Let us assume that a business analyst makes the observation that customers with low income and high debt often default on their loans. The business analyst then concludes that this group of customers should be considered bad credit risks. In order to verify this conclusion, the business analyst prepares a query against the BI target databases, for example: "Compare write-off amounts for products by product type, by territory, by customer, by month, where the customer income level is below a certain amount to those where the customer income level is above a certain amount." This type of analysis query would run against a multidimensional database in which summarized data is stored as precalculated measures (facts), with one such measure being "write-off amount."

OLAP Tool Features

OLAP tools are popular not only because they make the business analysts more self-sufficient but also because the tools provide innovative ways to analyze data.

- **Tools present a multidimensional view** of the data, which is intuitive and familiar to the business people. For example, organizations always like to set their strategies for increasing revenue by:
  - Introducing new products
  - Exploring new markets
  - Increasing price

  These three characteristics are based on increases or decreases in revenue that can be tracked more easily through a multidimensional view of the sales data (by product, by region, by customer).

- **Tools provide summarizations and aggregations** of the data at every dimensional intersection. The terms *summarization* and *aggregation* are commonly used interchangeably. Even though both terms refer to "adding up" atomic data values and both are used in creating measures or facts, their precise definitions are not the same.
  - *Summarization* refers to totaling or summing one atomic data value (vertically) to produce a total or sum of that value, for example, adding up the annual salaries of all employees to produce the value Total Annual Salary Amount. (In popular multidimensional database design jargon, *summarization* is referred to as *aggregation*.)

- *Aggregation* refers to derived data, which is produced from gathering or adding multiple atomic values (horizontally) to create a new aggregated value, for example, adding the annual salary, the bonuses, and the dollar value of an employee's benefits package (health care plan, retirement plan) to produce the value Employee Compensation Plan Amount.

- **Tools provide interactive querying and analysis capabilities** of the data. Business analysts can perform "what if" analysis with the help of OLAP tools, for example, "What if we lowered the price of the product by $5? How much would our sales volume increase in the state of Alaska?" Business analysts like to run queries interactively and act upon the query results by changing the values of some variables and rerunning the query to produce a new result.

- **Tools support business analysts** in designing their own analysis queries, in creating their own custom members within dimensions, and in creating custom measures.
  - One of the main goals of a BI decision-support environment is to make the business analysts as self-sufficient as possible. This can be done with parameterized queries, where business analysts can change their assumptions (parameters) and rerun the same queries with new parameters. A prerequisite for effective use of parameterized queries is a well-documented query library.
  - OLAP tools can also give business analysts the ability to create custom members (also called *aggregates*) within a dimension (e.g., Hot-Car, which would be defined as any red convertible) that can SUM, AVG, MAX, and MIN a group of member values.
  - OLAP tools can also provide the ability to create custom measures or facts (e.g., Percent Female, which would be defined by a formula provided by a business analyst). These custom measures can then be picked as a new measure from a drop-down menu for a fact table.

- **Tools support drill-down, roll-up, and drill-across features** of multidimensional analysis. For example, a business analyst who wants to find a way to lower the cost of manufactured goods could drill down into the actual detailed costs of purchased raw materials. He or she could also summarize these costs by rolling up the raw materials into predefined categories. Then he or she could drill across to another table to include the production costs of the manufactured goods.

- **Tools offer analytical modeling capabilities** useful to business people. To expand on the previous example, lowering the cost of manufactured goods could also be accomplished by reducing the working capital so that the borrowing costs are lower. Analytical modeling techniques provided by the OLAP tools could be used to find the optimum amount of working capital.

- **Tools support functional models for trend analysis** and forecasting. OLAP trend analysis functionality could be used to analyze past data and make predictions about the future.

- **Tools display data in charts and graphs** that offer quick visual summaries. The saying "A picture is worth a thousand words" has never been so true as when analyzing vast amounts of data from BI target databases. Visually appealing, understandable, and useful charts and graphs are important components of every OLAP tool.

There is a diversity of OLAP tools based on different architectures and features. It is important to know the access and analysis requirements of BI applications in order to make an informed decision about purchasing the right OLAP tools.

MULTIDIMENSIONAL ANALYSIS FACTORS

One of the distinguishing factors of multidimensional OLAP tools, as opposed to conventional querying tools, is the way they present the information. Measures or facts are usually presented in a multidimensional format, such as columns in a fact table or cells in a cube. These columns and cells contain precalculated numeric data about a functional subject area and are related to business objects (dimension tables) associated with the subject area. For example, Sales Amount, Net Profit Amount, Product Cost, and Monthly Account Fee are numeric data (facts) precalculated by account, by purchase, by customer, and by geography, which are the associated business objects (dimensions). In contrast, a conventional relational table would be a flat matrix of rows and columns, containing numeric data about one and only one business object (dimension). For example, Opening Account Balance, Daily Account Balance, and Account Interest Rate are numeric data of only one business object, namely account.

Figure 12.1 illustrates multidimensionality through a four-dimensional cube with the dimensions customer, account, purchase, and geography. The two examples of geography in this figure are the regions northeast USA and southeast USA.

Customer profiling and customer profitability are popular multidimensional BI applications. The dimensions of a customer profitability example are listed in Figure 12.2.

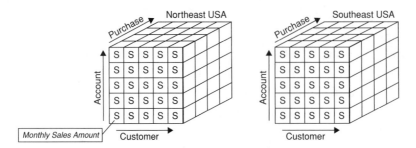

Figure 12.1: Four-Dimensional Data Representation

Figure 12.2: Multidimensional Customer Profitability

The eight dimensions of customer type, buying behavior, credit rating, region, demographics, psychographics, purchasing history, and product category can be used to analyze the various perspectives of customer profitability.

Some additional examples of complex multidimensional analysis commonly performed in the BI decision-support environment include those listed below.

- *Customer information:* Buying patterns by product, geography, time, age, gender, number of children, types of cars owned, education level, or income level
- *Financial planning:* Business analysis on profit margins, costs of goods sold, tax codes, or currency exchange rates
- *Marketing:* Impact of promotions and marketing programs, pricing, competitors' initiatives, and market trends

Multivariate Analysis

Another term for multidimensional analysis is *multivariate analysis*. This term is derived from a specific aspect of this type of analysis, namely, to analyze measures (facts) from the perspective of multiple variables or characteristics. These variables (characteristics) usually describe business objects or dimensions. For example, Product Type describes product and Customer Age describes customer, with product and customer being the business objects or dimensions. Occasionally, the variables can become dimensions in their own right. For example, the variables Product Type and Customer Age can be treated as dimensions. In other words, a dimension can be built for a business object or for a variable of that business object.

These two types of dimensions (the object dimension and the variable dimension) can be illustrated by a simplified example of earthquake analysis. Earthquakes are typically reported by their epicenter, such as the intersection of latitude and longitude coordinates of a location, and by their intensity, such as 7.5 on the Richter scale. Location is normally a business object; thus epicenter can be used as an object dimension, which may be described by variables such as Location Name, Location Address, and Population Size. Intensity, on the other hand, is normally not a business object but a variable that describes the business object earthquake. In this example, however, intensity is treated as an object in its own right and is therefore used as a variable dimension. Another example of a variable dimension might be Shock Type (foreshock, aftershock), which is normally also a variable of the business object earthquake.

Variable dimensions are often "degenerate" dimensions, which means that even though they are being treated as dimensions when precalculating or analyzing the facts, they are not implemented as physical dimension tables. The main reason is that variable dimensions usually do not have other variables describing them—or they would not be variable dimensions in the first place. For example, intensity is simply a set of numerical values (numbers on a Richter scale), and there are no other descriptive characteristics about it.

ONLINE ANALYTICAL PROCESSING ARCHITECTURE

Conceptually, OLAP architecture consists of three functional components: presentation services, OLAP services, and database services (Figure 12.3).

Information Display	Querying, Reporting, Analyzing	Relational, Multidimensional
Presentation Services	**OLAP Services**	**Database Services**

Figure 12.3: Functional Components of OLAP Architecture

Presentation Services

OLAP is supposed to provide the link everyone has been looking for between data and the business. Yet most organizations still seem to be data rich and information poor because the real world of business exists in bits and pieces, not in bits and bytes. Information is data that can be analyzed, synthesized, and used in a valid business context. The people who need this data are knowledge workers, business analysts, business managers, and business executives, not technicians. Therefore, the data needs to be presented in a format that enables the business people to develop proposals, decide how many widgets to buy, define investment levels, and set hiring targets.

Presentation services have to be easy to use, and ease of use has to be determined by the *business people*, not by the information technology (IT) staff. For example, business people want an intuitive graphical user interface (GUI) and the ability to work with familiar business terms. Therefore, an easy-to-use OLAP tool should hide the underlying structure of the data and hide the processes that run behind the scenes. Furthermore, ease of use should be expressed in quantifiable terms.

- How much time is needed to learn the OLAP tool?
- How fast can a person perform his or her analysis tasks?
- Do business people like using the OLAP tool?
- Does the OLAP tool have all of the required functionality?
- Can the OLAP tool integrate with other desktop tools, such as Microsoft Excel?

Presentation services have to be flexible and adaptable because different business people have different preferences and different skill sets. For example, some business people like tabular reports; others like graphs and charts. Some business people have no computer skills at all, some are more advanced, and some are experts. The menus, icons, and functions should be configured depending on the skill set profile, and they may have to be reconfigured over time. When the beginners start to become experts, they no longer like the cute messages that were originally provided to them for encouragement. Experts expect better performance and faster responses, and in order to provide that, there should be less clutter on their screens. An ideal OLAP tool should be able to adjust to all these different levels of preferences and skill sets and should be able to provide different levels of presentation.

OLAP Services

An OLAP tool should provide a wide range of services. It should be able to support simple querying with just a few dimensions, and at the same time, it should be able to support powerful querying with many dimensions. In addition, an OLAP tool should be able to integrate all the analytical processing requirements of "What happened?" with those of "Why did this happen?" Querying capabilities (from very simple to complex), reporting capabilities (from very basic to sophisticated), and multidimensional analysis and presentation of the results are some of the OLAP services that help turn data into useful information.

Querying, reporting, and analyzing are interrelated, interactive, and iterative. For example, the results of a query might appear in the form of a table, chart, or graph, presented in several dimensions. While studying these query results, a business analyst may think of a new question, which may lead to a new query. He or she may then want to have the results of the new query printed out as a report. Therefore, OLAP tools should have integrated querying, reporting, and analyzing services. A person should not have to log off the querying tool to get into a different reporting tool and then log off the reporting tool to get into an analysis tool. Querying, reporting, and analyzing should be a seamless transition performed by the tool, not by the person.

In order to leverage these OLAP services, we need to change the way we develop applications and the way we present information. BI applications, which emphasize quick delivery of functionality, ease of use, and affordable desktop hardware and software, should be the vehicles for IT to provide OLAP capabilities to more business people in the organization.

Database Services

OLAP architecture supports two types of databases, conventional relational databases (e.g., DB2, Oracle), which are accessible with ROLAP tools, and proprietary multidimensional databases, which are supplied with MOLAP tools.

- **ROLAP tools** can access any of the major relational DBMSs as long as the underlying application database design is multidimensional, such as star schemas (facts and denormalized dimensions), snowflake schemas (facts and normalized dimensions), and hybrid schemas (combination of normalized and denormalized dimensions). Depending on the DBMS, the database designer would use common physical design techniques such as:
  - Selecting the most efficient indexing schema for the underlying DBMS product in order to improve performance
  - Partitioning the database into smaller, manageable partitions to improve performance and to facilitate database maintenance activities
  - Clustering the data and physically co-locating related tables
  - Determining the most appropriate data and index placements
- **MOLAP tools** are designed to access their own proprietary databases, which are special data structures (e.g., Essbase), and to perform their OLAP operations on these data structures. MOLAP tools implement their functionality in a variety of different ways.
  - Some products store data in arrays or cubes and therefore have different data preparation requirements.
  - Some products require prebuilding dimensions in the staging area before loading them; others build the dimensions from the data at load time.
  - Some products provide an application programming interface (API); others do not.
  - Some products offer "turnkey" applications with multidimensional servers and substantial OLAP functionality.
  - Most products have their own proprietary access methods and front ends.

DEVELOPMENT ENVIRONMENTS

The development of vital business applications does not happen ad hoc on someone's personal computer. Most organizations require some kind of formal or structured approach for developing these applications, testing them, and delivering them. Some organizations (and some projects) require more structure than others. Also, on BI applications, some application components need more structure than others.

For example, an informal and dynamic development approach for building the front-end access and analysis components is quite appropriate. Front-end applications are usually built with flexible tools that lend themselves quite well to rapid and iterative development cycles. It is quite common for the application track to go through several stages of prototyping, especially multiple iterations of operational prototyping, while performing analysis, design, coding, and testing activities almost all at the same time. However, developing the back-end ETL process in such an informal and dynamic way is not appropriate. ETL development requires a more formalized or structured approach because of its size and complexity. Even when ETL tools are used, the activities of the ETL development track are much more similar to a large operational systems development project than to the dynamic prototyping activities of the application development track.

To support these different types of activities, organizations usually set up different development environments for different purposes. While smaller organizations may have only two environments (development and production), large organizations usually have at least four different environments:

1. The *prototyping environment,* where the testing of the technology and the solidifying of the project requirements occur

2. The *development environment,* where the programs and scripts are written and tested by the developers

3. The *QA environment,* where the operations staff tests the final programs and scripts before allowing them to be moved into the production environment

4. The *production environment,* where the programs and scripts run after being rolled out

Depending on the overall setup of the environments, early prototyping activities (such as creating show-and-tell, mock-up, proof-of-concept, visual-design, and demo prototypes) typically take place in a special-purpose prototyping environment, while development activities (including operational prototyping) are performed in the development environment. However, it is just as common to perform all prototyping and development activities in the same development environment. In either case, the entire BI application should be moved to the QA environment for final QA and acceptance testing before being implemented in the production environment.

If the different development environments are configured differently, moving your application from one environment to another could have major implications for your BI project.

The prototyping and development environments are usually configured similarly, as are the QA and production environments. The configuration differences are typically between the development and production environments. Key considerations appear below.

- If the application works well in the development environment, there is no guarantee that the application will run equally well in the production environment.
- It is conceivable that the migration costs from one environment to another could be substantial.
- New or different tools may be required for differently configured environments.

The Web Environment

Another environment that is becoming more and more popular for BI applications is the Web. Since most OLAP tools are Web-enabled, the data from the BI target databases can be and often is published company-wide through the intranet. A subset of that data can also be made available through a separate portal to business partners via the extranet or to customers via the Internet. Special security and authentication measures must be taken in the Web environment. Only qualified persons should be able to access authorized databases, and all access requests must pass through a firewall.

In addition to being a data delivery platform, the Web environment can also be a source for BI data. Capturing Web logs is a standard practice on Web sites, and the ability to extract, filter, summarize, and report the log data for click-stream analysis is a popular type of BI application (Web warehouse). Click-stream analysis can help identify customer interest (number of hits), gauge the effectiveness of Internet advertisements, and track the results of promotions. Table 12.1 shows a list of commonly available Web log data.

Table 12.1: Common Web Log Data

Click-Stream Data
Client IP address
User ID
Date and time of server response
Request (GET, POST)
Status from server to browser
Number of bytes sent
Prior site information (URL, path, documents, and so on)
Browser name
Cookie information

APPLICATION DEVELOPMENT ACTIVITIES

The activities for application development do not need to be performed linearly. Figure 12.4 indicates which activities can be performed concurrently. The list below briefly describes the activities associated with Step 12, Application Development.

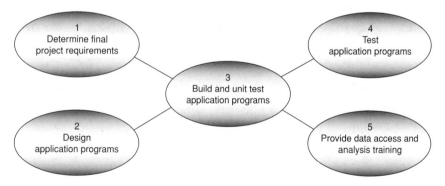

Figure 12.4: Application Development Activities

1. Determine the final project requirements.

If you built a prototype, review the prototype results and determine what changes were requested and what issues were logged during that activity. This will give you an understanding of the stability of the requirements. In addition, adjust your design or renegotiate the requirements based on what worked and what did not work during the prototype.

2. **Design the application programs.**

   While reviewing the prototype results and the required query and report mock-ups, design the access and analysis components of the BI application, including the final reports, queries, front-end interface (GUI, Web), and online help function. Develop a test plan with detailed test cases.

3. **Build and unit test the application programs.**

   Create test data and write the programs and scripts for the reports, queries, front-end interface, and online help function. Be sure to unit test the programs and scripts not only to prove that they compile without errors but also to verify that they perform their functions correctly, trap all potential errors, and produce the right results.

4. **Test the application programs.**

   Perform integration or regression testing on all programs and scripts in the sequence in which they will run in the production environment. Load the development databases with sample "live" data, and test the programs and scripts against them. Check the actual test results against the expected test results, then revise and retest the programs and scripts until they perform as expected.

   Be sure to performance test some of the more complicated programs that have many JOINs and that read high-volume tables. A performance test will indicate how the BI application will perform when fully loaded in the production environment. The easiest way to run a performance test is through a stress test simulation tool.

   The final tests should be the QA test with the operations staff and the acceptance test with the subject matter expert and the business representative. Besides determining whether the access and analysis programs function correctly, acceptance testing should determine the overall usability of the BI application and the interfaces to the BI application, especially for Web-based development.

5. **Provide data access and analysis training.**

   Identify the training needs of the help desk staff, "power users," knowledge workers, business analysts, and business managers. Schedule the training sessions, either in-house or with a vendor. If the training is provided internally, create the training materials and conduct the training sessions. Be sure to measure the effectiveness of the training, including the effectiveness of the style in which the training is delivered, the content of the material, the pace with which the material is covered, and the quality of the workbooks (e.g., too much text or not enough explanations).

DELIVERABLES RESULTING FROM THESE ACTIVITIES

1. **Application design document**
   This document contains the formal design specifications for the access and analysis components of the BI application. It contains report layouts, screen designs, interface designs, calculations for reports and queries, and the design of the online help function. In addition, it contains the programming specifications for every access and analysis component. Portions of this document will be given to different application developers to code the program modules and query scripts.

2. **Application test plan**
   The application test plan should include the purpose for each test, a schedule for running the tests, and the test cases, including input criteria and expected output results. A test log should accompany the test plan, documenting when the tests were run, who ran the tests, and what the test results were.

3. **Application programs**
   All access and analysis programs and scripts for the BI application should be coded and tested. If an OLAP tool is being used, all of the OLAP functions should be developed and tested.

4. **Application program library**
   All access and analysis programs and scripts should reside in the application program library or OLAP tool library. All access and analysis programs and scripts should have been integration tested or regression tested, performance tested, QA tested, and acceptance tested.

5. **Training materials**
   Training materials include presentation slides, instructor notes, student workbooks, and exercises and their solutions, as well as any additional pertinent handouts.

ROLES INVOLVED IN THESE ACTIVITIES

◆ **Application developers**

The application developers have to code and unit test the access and analysis programs and scripts. They have to be proficient in the OLAP tool, Structured Query Language (SQL), and the programming languages used to develop the BI application.

◆ **Application lead developer**

The application lead developer should be the "guru" and mentor to the other application developers. He or she will work closely with the ETL lead developer and the database administrator on any design and implementation issues. If internal training is provided, he or she will develop the training materials and schedule the training sessions (assisted by the training staff if the organization has a training department).

◆ **Business representative**

The business representative must actively participate in integration or regression testing, as well as acceptance testing. He or she should assist the subject matter expert in writing the test cases and in validating the test results. In addition, the business representative must attend the scheduled training sessions.

◆ **Database administrator**

The database administrator, who designs and builds the BI target databases, will assist with accessing these databases. The database administrator should review all database calls from programs and OLAP tools and write pass-through queries where required.

◆ **Subject matter expert**

The subject matter expert is a key participant during development and testing because he or she is probably the person most familiar with the access and analysis requirements the BI application is meant to satisfy. The subject matter expert must provide input and guidance during report and query design. He or she should write (or assist in writing) the test cases and participate in integration or regression testing as well as acceptance testing. In addition, he or she should assist in preparing and scheduling the training sessions.

◆ **Testers**

There can never be enough testers. It usually takes three times longer to test an application than it does to develop it. The business representative and the subject matter expert make excellent testers. As an additional benefit, they will learn the BI application while they are testing it.

◆ **Web developers**

Web developers are responsible for designing and building the Web site as well as designing and developing the reports and queries using Web-enabled OLAP tools. They have to be proficient in Web development tools, SQL, and languages such as Java or Perl.

◆ **Web master**

The Web master is responsible for the administration of the Web environment, such as the Web server, the firewall, the Web site, and so on. He or she should be the "guru" and mentor to the Web developers and may also be the main designer of the Web site. He or she should be able to interface between the Web and the OLAP tools and be able to troubleshoot any problem.

RISKS OF NOT PERFORMING STEP 12

The capabilities of a BI application are notably enhanced with OLAP technology. Besides enabling multidimensional analysis, OLAP tools provide additional functionality, such as screen painting, "what if" analysis, conversion of data to graphs and charts, and Web displays of query results. By excluding this step, the business community would be missing an important value-added aspect of the BI experience for better decision making.

BIBLIOGRAPHY AND ADDITIONAL READING

Beck, Kent. *Extreme Programming Explained: Embrace Change.* Boston, MA: Addison-Wesley, 2000.

Berson, Alex, and Stephen J. Smith. *Data Warehousing, Data Mining, and OLAP.* New York: McGraw-Hill, 1997.

Bischoff, Joyce, and Ted Alexander. *Data Warehouse: Practical Advice from the Experts.* Upper Saddle River, NJ: Prentice Hall, 1997.

Cockburn, Alistair. *Agile Software Development.* Boston, MA: Addison-Wesley, 2002.

Corey, Michael J., and Michael Abbey. *Oracle Data Warehousing: A Practical Guide to Successful Data Warehouse Analysis, Build, and Roll-out.* Berkeley, CA: Osborne McGraw-Hill, 1996.

Dick, Kevin. *XML: A Manager's Guide.* Boston, MA: Addison-Wesley, 2000.

Dyché, Jill. *e-Data: Turning Data into Information with Data Warehousing.* Boston, MA: Addison-Wesley, 2000.

Gill, Harjinder S., and Prakash C. Rao. *The Official Client/Server Guide to Data Warehousing.* Indianapolis, IN: Que Corporation, 1996.

Hackney, Douglas. *Understanding and Implementing Successful Data Marts.* Reading, MA: Addison-Wesley, 1997.

Humphrey, Watts S. *Winning with Software: An Executive Strategy.* Boston, MA: Addison-Wesley, 2002.

Inmon, William H., J. D. Welch, and Katherine L. Glassey. *Managing the Data Warehouse: Practical Techniques for Monitoring Operations and Performance, Administering Data and Tools and Managing Change and Growth.* New York: John Wiley & Sons, 1997.

Kimball, Ralph, and Richard Merz. *The Data Webhouse Toolkit: Building the Web-Enabled Data Warehouse.* New York: John Wiley & Sons, 2000.

Kimball, Ralph, Laura Reeves, Margy Ross, and Warren Thornthwaite. *The Data Warehouse Lifecycle Toolkit: Expert Methods for Designing, Developing, and Deploying Data Warehouses.* New York: John Wiley & Sons, 1998.

Shneiderman, Ben. *Designing the User Interface: Strategies for Effective Human-Computer Interaction.* Boston, MA: Addison-Wesley, 1998.

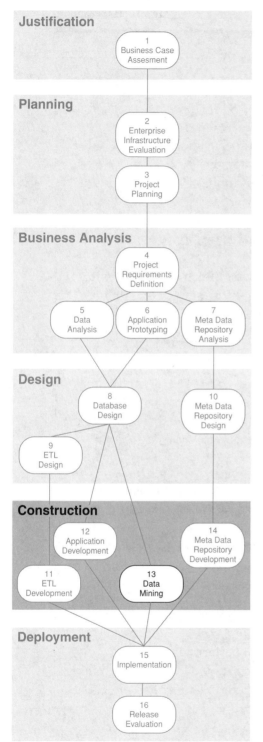

Justification

1
Business Case
Assesment

Planning

2
Enterprise
Infrastructure
Evaluation

3
Project
Planning

Business Analysis

4
Project
Requirements
Definition

5
Data
Analysis

6
Application
Prototyping

7
Meta Data
Repository
Analysis

Design

8
Database
Design

10
Meta Data
Repository
Design

9
ETL
Design

Construction

12
Application
Development

14
Meta Data
Repository
Development

11
ETL
Development

13
Data
Mining

Deployment

15
Implementation

16
Release
Evaluation

CHAPTER THIRTEEN

Step 13: Data Mining

CHAPTER OVERVIEW

This chapter covers the following topics:

- Things to consider about data mining

- Traditional analysis techniques versus data mining

- The importance of data mining

- Data sources for data mining

- The five most common data mining techniques: associations discovery, sequential pattern discovery, classification, clustering, and forecasting

- Data mining operations such as predictive and classification modeling, link analysis, database segmentation, and deviation detection

- Applications of data mining in the areas of market management, fraud detection, risk management, financial services, and distribution

- Brief descriptions of the activities involved in data mining, the deliverables resulting from those activities, and the roles involved

- The risks of not performing Step 13

THINGS TO CONSIDER

Marketing Questions

✓ Do we know what general classes of customers we have?

✓ Are there subclasses of customers with similar behavioral patterns? Can we use targeted marketing messages for these customers?

✓ Do we know what our best customers have in common? Is there a pattern that will verify our hunch that if we offer new products or services "just in time" to our best customers, they will buy them?

✓ Do we know how to retain our best customers? How can we predict which customers are more likely to leave us?

✓ How can we sell more to our existing customers? Which of our customers are more likely to buy more products or services from us?

✓ Do we have customers who are costing us money?

✓ Do we suspect fraudulent activities that need to be discovered?

Data

✓ Is our data clean enough for data mining?

✓ Is the data understood? Will it be used and interpreted correctly?

✓ Is it coded properly for data mining?

✓ Is the data organized correctly for data mining?

Data Mining Tool

✓ What type of data mining tool is appropriate for our organization?

✓ What type of criteria should we consider when we evaluate data mining tools?

✓ How will we determine the return on investment (ROI) for a data mining initiative and a data mining tool?

Staffing

✓ Do we have statisticians or skilled analysts who can interpret the data mining results?

✓ Will we need to hire additional statisticians to perform data mining?

✓ Will a database administrator be available to create and load the data mining databases? Will we need a database administrator full-time? Part-time?

Many organizations have accumulated massive amounts of data in their operational systems. This data constitutes a potential source of valuable business information that can be mined. Analytical models can be generated to find patterns in the data and to allow the information to be used for competitive advantage. This gives the business managers and executives the information they need in order to take action, enabling them to increase profits, reduce costs, create innovative product strategies, and expand market share.

DEFINING DATA MINING

Data mining capability is not something you can buy off the shelf. Data mining requires building a BI decision-support application, specifically a data mining application, using a data mining tool. The data mining application can then use a sophisticated blend of classical and advanced components like artificial intelligence, pattern recognition, databases, traditional statistics, and graphics to present hidden relationships and patterns found in the organization's data pool.

Data mining is the analysis of data with the intent to discover gems of hidden information in the vast quantity of data that has been captured in the normal course of running the business. Data mining is different from conventional statistical analysis, as indicated in Table 13.1. They both have strengths and weaknesses.

Table 13.1: Statistical Analysis versus Data Mining

Statistical Analysis	*Data Mining*
• Statisticians usually start with a hypothesis.	• Data mining does not require a hypothesis.
• Statisticians have to develop their own equations to match their hypothesis.	• Data mining algorithms can automatically develop the equations.
• Statistical analysis uses only numerical data.	• Data mining can use different types of data (e.g., text, voice), not just numerical data.
• Statisticians can find and filter dirty data during their analysis.	• Data mining depends on clean, well-documented data.

(Continued)

Table 13.1: *(Continued)*

Statistical Analysis	*Data Mining*
• Statisticians interpret their own results and convey these results to the business managers and business executives.	• Data mining results are not easy to interpret. A statistician must still be involved in analyzing the data mining results and conveying the findings to the business managers and business executives.

Tables 13.2 and 13.3 use specific examples (insurance fraud and market segmentation, respectively) to illustrate the differences between traditional analysis techniques and discovery-driven data mining.

Table 13.2: Example of Insurance Fraud Analysis

Traditional Analysis Technique	*Discovery-Driven Data Mining*
• An analyst notices a pattern of behavior that might indicate insurance fraud. Based on this hypothesis, the analyst creates a set of queries to determine whether this observed behavior actually constitutes fraud. If the results are not conclusive, the analyst starts over with a modified or new hypothesis and more queries. Not only is this process time-consuming, but it also depends on the analyst's subjective interpretation of the results. More importantly, this process will not find any patterns of fraud that the analyst does not already suspect.	• An analyst sets up the data mining application, then "trains" it to find all unusual patterns, trends, or deviations from the norm that might constitute insurance fraud. The data mining results unearth various situations that the analyst can investigate further. For the follow-up investigation, the analyst can then use verification-driven queries. Together, these efforts can help the analyst build a model predicting which customers or potential customers might commit fraud.

Table 13.3: Example of Market Segmentation Analysis

Traditional Analysis Technique	*Discovery-Driven Data Mining*
• An analyst wants to study the buying behaviors of known classes of customers (e.g., retired school teachers, young urban professionals) in order to design targeted marketing programs. First, the analyst uses known characteristics about those classes of customers and tries to sort them into groups. Second, he or she studies the buying behaviors common to each group. The analyst repeats this process until he or she is satisfied with the final customer groupings.	• The data mining tool "studies" the database using the clustering technique to identify all groups of customers with distinct buying patterns. After the data is mined and the groupings are presented, the analyst can use various query, reporting, and multidimensional analysis tools to analyze the results.

The Importance of Data Mining

Discovery-driven data mining finds answers to questions that decision-makers do not know to ask. Because of this powerful capability, data mining is an important component of business intelligence. One may even say that data mining, also called *knowledge discovery*, is a breakthrough in providing business intelligence to strategic decision-makers. At first glance, this claim may seem excessive. After all, many current decision-support applications provide business intelligence and insights.

- Executive information systems (EISs) enable senior managers to monitor, examine, and change many aspects of their business operations.

- Query and reporting tools give business analysts the ability to investigate company performance and customer behavior.

- Statistical tools enable statisticians to perform sophisticated studies of the behavior of a business.

- New multidimensional online analytical processing (OLAP) tools deliver the ability to perform "what if" analysis and to look at a large number of interdependent factors involved in a business problem.

Many of these tools work with BI applications and can sift through vast amounts of data. Given this abundance of tools, what is so different about discovery-driven data mining? The big difference is that traditional analysis techniques, even sophisticated ones, rely on the analyst to know what to look for in the data. The analyst creates and runs queries based on some hypotheses and guesses about possible relationships, trends, and correlations thought to be present in the data. Similarly, the executive relies on the business views built into the EIS tool, which can examine only the factors the tool is programmed to review. As problems become more complex and involve more variables to analyze, these traditional analysis techniques can fall short. In contrast, discovery-driven data mining supports very subtle and complex investigations.

Data Sources for Data Mining

BI target databases are popular sources for data mining applications. They contain a wealth of internal data that was gathered and consolidated across business boundaries, validated, and cleansed in the extract/transform/load (ETL) process. BI target databases may also contain valuable external data, such as regulations, demographics, or geographic information. Combining external data with internal organizational data offers a splendid foundation for data mining.

The drawback of multidimensional BI target databases is that since the data has been summarized, hidden data patterns, data relationships, and data associations are often no longer discernable from that data pool. For example, the data mining tool may not be able to perform the common data mining task of market basket analysis (also called *associations discovery*, described in the next section) based on summarized sales data because some detailed data pattern about each sale may have gotten lost in the summarization. Therefore, operational files and databases are also popular sources for data mining applications, especially because they contain transaction-level detailed data with a myriad of hidden data patterns, data relationships, and data associations.

 Exercise caution with operational systems extracts because the data could contain many duplicates, inconsistencies, and errors and could skew the data mining results.

Data mining tools could theoretically access the operational databases and BI target databases directly without building data mining databases first, as long as the database structures are supported by the tool (e.g., relational like Oracle, hierarchical like IMS, or even a flat file like VSAM). However, this is not an advisable practice for several reasons.

- The data pool needs to be able to change for different data mining runs, such as dropping a sales region or restricting a product type for a specific mining purpose. Changing the data content of operational or BI target databases is not possible.

- The performance of operational as well as BI target databases would be impacted by the data mining operations. That is unacceptable for operational databases and not desirable for BI target databases.

- A data mining operation may need detailed historical data. Operational databases do not store historical data, and BI target databases often do not have the desired level of detail. Archival tapes may have to be restored and merged to extract the desired data.

Therefore, organizations often extract data for data mining as needed from their BI target databases and from their operational files and databases into special-purpose data mining databases (Figure 13.1).

DATA MINING TECHNIQUES

Data mining techniques are specific implementations of algorithms used in data mining operations. The five most common data mining techniques are described briefly below.

Associations Discovery

This data mining technique is used to identify the behavior of specific events or processes. Associations discovery links occurrences within a single event. An example might be the discovery that men who purchase premium brands of coffee are three times more likely to buy imported cigars than men who buy standard brands of coffee. Associations discovery is based on rules that follow this general form: "If item A is part of an event, then X percent of the time (confidence factor), item B is part of the same event." For example:

- If a customer buys snacks, there is an 85 percent probability that the customer will also buy soft drinks or beer.

- If a person buys vacation airline tickets for an entire family, there is a 95 percent probability that he or she will rent a full-size car at the vacation location.

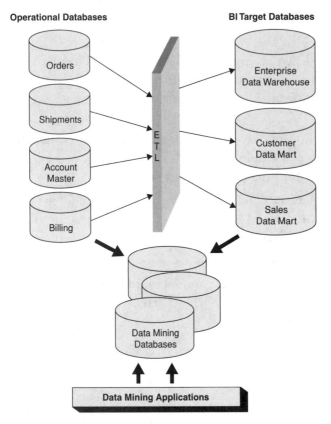

Figure 13.1: Data Sources for Data Mining Applications

With the help of scanners, retail stores use this data mining technique to find buying patterns in grocery stores. Because of the context of a grocery store, associations discovery is sometimes called *market basket analysis*.

Sequential Pattern Discovery

This data mining technique is similar to associations discovery except that a sequential pattern discovery links events over time and determines how items relate to each other over time. For example, sequential pattern discovery might predict that a person who buys a washing machine may also buy a clothes dryer within six months with a probability of 0.7. To increase the chances above the predicted 70 percent probability, the store may offer each buyer a 10 percent discount on a clothes dryer within four months after purchasing a washing machine.

Classification

The classification technique is the most common use of data mining. Classification looks at the behavior and attributes of predetermined groups. The groups might include frequent flyers, high spenders, loyal customers, people who respond to direct mail campaigns, or people with frequent back problems (e.g., people who drive long distances every day). The data mining tool can assign classifications to new data by examining existing data that has already been classified and by using those results to infer a set of rules. The set of rules is then applied to any new data to be classified. This technique often uses supervised induction, which employs a small training set of already classified records to determine additional classifications. An example of this use is to discover the characteristics of customers who are (or are not) likely to buy a certain type of product. This knowledge would result in reducing the costs of promotions and direct mailings.

Clustering

The clustering technique is used to discover different groupings within the data. Clustering is similar to classification except that no groups have yet been defined at the outset of running the data mining tool. The clustering technique often uses neural networks or statistical methods. Clustering divides items into groups based on the similarities the data mining tool finds. Within a cluster the members are very similar, but the clusters themselves are very *dis*similar. Clustering is used for problems such as detecting manufacturing defects or finding affinity groups for credit cards.

Forecasting

The forecasting data mining technique comes in two flavors: regression analysis and time sequence discovery.

- **Regression analysis** uses known values of data to predict future values or future events based on historical trends and statistics. For example, the sales volume of sports car accessories can be forecasted based on the number of sports cars sold last month.

- **Time sequence discovery** differs from regression analysis in that it forecasts only time-dependent data values. For example, it determines the rates of accidents during a holiday season based on the number of accidents that occurred during the same holiday season in prior years. The property of time can be:

- Work week versus calendar week
- Holidays
- Seasons
- Date ranges and date intervals

DATA MINING OPERATIONS

Data mining tools enable statisticians to build analytical models, which the tools then use during data mining operations. A predictive engine asks for a list of input criteria and follows the steps and relationships from the analytical model to determine the most likely predictions. The results of data mining operations are tables and files loaded with analysis data that can be accessed with query and reporting tools. The four main data mining operations are described below.

Predictive and Classification Modeling

This data mining operation is used to forecast a particular event. It assumes that the analyst has a specific question he or she wants to ask. The model provides the answer by assigning ranks that indicate the likelihood of certain classes. For example, if a bank analyst wants to predict which customers are likely to leave, he or she has to prepare for predictive modeling by feeding data about two types of customers into the data mining tool.

1. Customer data that indicates which customers have already left. This data is called "bad" data.

2. Customer data that indicates which customers stayed and are long-time customers. This data is called "good" data.

The tool then sifts through the data to uncover the variables that identify classes of profiles of typical customers who leave and classes of profiles of typical customers who stay. The analysis results might be, "A female customer over 40 years of age who has an income greater than $150,000 per year and owns her own home has a 35 percent chance of leaving the bank."

Typical probing questions for predictive data mining are those that look for associations, patterns, trends, and facts in order to make decisions. For example:

- Which offers will prompt customers to buy more? (Trend)
- Which customers should be targeted for a new product? (Association)

- What are the signs of fraudulent activity? (Pattern)
- Which customers are better credit risks? (Fact)

Link Analysis

The link analysis data mining operation is a collection of mathematical algorithms and visualization techniques that identify and visually present links between individual records in a database. It is related to the associations discovery and sequential pattern discovery data mining techniques. For example, link analysis can determine which items usually sell together (e.g., cereal and milk).

Database Segmentation

This data mining operation is a set of algorithms that group similar records into homogeneous segments. It is related to the clustering data mining technique. This grouping is often the first step of data selection, before other data mining operations take place. For example, database segmentation may group airline passengers as either frequent flyer passengers or occasional passengers.

Deviation Detection

The deviation detection data mining operation is a set of algorithms that look for records that fall outside some expectation or norm and then suggest reasons for the anomalies. While deviation detection is mainly used for fraud detection, other uses include tracing the potential reasons for declines in customer numbers or sales. For example, "Customers who used to make frequent purchases but have not purchased anything in a long time were either transferred by their companies or have moved away from the area."

APPLICATIONS OF DATA MINING

It is important to keep in mind that in spite of all the dazzling technologies, data mining has to be driven by strong business needs in order to justify the expenditure of time and money. One of the common business drivers for engaging in data mining is to gain market share. This can be accomplished by either introducing new products or by taking away market share from competitors. In either case, a data mining application can help you decide how best to achieve your goals.

There are many types of data mining applications. The five most common ones are briefly described below.

- **Market management**
  - *Cross-selling:* Identify cross-selling opportunities among existing customers, who are likely to buy as a result of direct mail campaigns and promotions (and thus minimize selling costs).
  - *Defecting customers:* Determine which customers are likely to switch brands by using vulnerability analysis that creates a predictive model of behavior, so that the company can craft strategies to retain these customers.
  - *Promotions and campaigns:* Distinguish natural groupings in the market, such as key sales periods for given items, by performing market segmentation analysis as a way to fine-tune promotions and campaigns.
  - *Prospecting:* Classify groups of prospects in order to find ways to perform target marketing for each group.
  - *Market basket analysis:* Evaluate which items people buy together during a visit to a supermarket or store, using market basket analysis on point-of-sale data. Then use the information to group products in store displays, to adjust inventory, and to price and promote items.

- **Fraud detection**
  - *Credit card fraud:* Isolate credit card fraud by identifying meaningful patterns of transactions as well as deviations from those patterns. Use this model to predict an applicant's trustworthiness.
  - *Calling card fraud:* Determine telephone calling card situations that look suspicious and are likely to indicate fraud.
  - *Insurance fraud:* Analyze large data pools of insurance claims to identify possible fraud related to health insurance, car insurance, or property and casualty insurance.

- **Risk management**
  - *Credit risk:* Assess the credit risk of potential loan applicants based on a predictive model of the database that looks for reasons and patterns affecting risk.
  - *Quality control:* Find patterns of quality problems on assembly lines to help reduce the number of products returned due to substandard quality.

- **Financial services**
  - *Customer retention:* Identify loyal bank customers who have many high-balance accounts and provide each of them a personalized fee structure. It is much cheaper to retain existing customers than to acquire new ones.

– *Stock performance:* Develop models of stock performance to aid portfolio management. Look for stocks that have performed in ways similar to certain high-performing securities.

• **Distribution**

– *Inventory control:* Improve inventory control and distribution by developing predictive models of which products or parts will be needed at various distribution points at various points in time.

One good indication of the value of data mining is the secrecy that surrounds its implementations. Many of the companies that have implemented data mining hesitate to talk about their successes. Some will not even confirm that they use this technology.

DATA MINING ACTIVITIES

The activities for data mining do not need to be performed linearly. Figure 13.2 indicates which activities can be performed concurrently. The list below briefly describes the activities associated with Step 13, Data Mining.

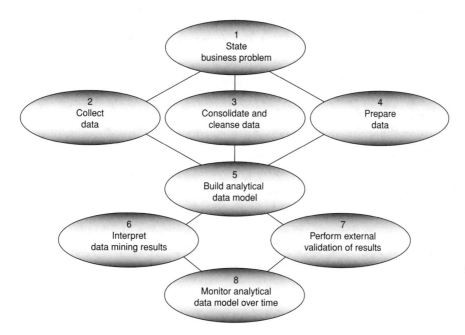

Figure 13.2: Data Mining Activities

1. **State the business problem.**

   Set goals before starting the data mining efforts, and prioritize the goals (such as increase profits, reduce costs, create innovative product strategies, or expand the market share). Time and money have to be invested in order to reach any of these goals. There also needs to be a commitment from management to implement a data mining solution at the organization.

2. **Collect the data.**

   One of the most time-consuming activities of data mining is the collection of the appropriate types and quantities of data. In order to have correct representation, first identify all the data needed for analysis. This includes data stored in the operational databases, data from the BI target databases, and any external data that will have to be included. Once you have identified the source data, extract all pertinent data elements from these various internal and external data sources.

3. **Consolidate and cleanse the data.**

   Redundantly stored data is more of a norm than an exception in most organizations. Therefore, the data from the various sources has to be consolidated and cleansed. If the internal data is to be supplemented by acquired external data, match the external data to the internal data, and determine the correct content.

4. **Prepare the data.**

   Before building an analytical data model, you need to prepare the data. Part of data preparation is the classification of variables. The variables could be discrete or continuous, qualitative or quantitative. Eliminate variables with missing values or replace them with *most likely* values. It provides great insight to know the maximum, minimum, average, mean, median, and mode values for quantitative variables. In order to streamline the preparation process, consider applying data reduction transformations. The objective of data reduction is to combine several variables into one in order to keep the result set manageable for analysis. For example, combine education level, income, marital status, and ZIP code into one profile variable.

5. **Build the analytical data model.**

   One of the most important activities of data mining is to build the analytical data model. An analytical data model represents a structure of consolidated, integrated, and time-dependent data that was selected and preprocessed from various internal and external data sources. Once implemented, this model must be able to continue "learning" while it is repeatedly used by the data mining tool and tuned by the data mining expert.

6. **Interpret the data mining results.**

Once the data mining operations are run and results are produced, the next major task is to interpret the results. Important things to consider during this interpretation are how easily the results can be acted upon and whether the results can be presented to business executives in a convincing, business-oriented way.

7. **Perform external validation of the results.**

Compare your results with published industry statistics. Identify the deviations from those statistics and determine the reasons for the deviations. Be sure you are using updated industry statistics since they change from time to time. Compare the selection criteria of your data to that of the industry statistics, and compare the time frame during which your data was selected to the time frame covered by the industry statistics. The selection criteria and time frame of your model and of the industry statistics must be similar.

8. **Monitor the analytical data model over time.**

Industry statistics are usually established by using very large samples. It is important to validate your analytical data model against industry statistics at regular intervals. Industry statistics change over time, and some industries have seasonal changes. In that case, adjust your internal analytical model.

DELIVERABLES RESULTING FROM THESE ACTIVITIES

1. **Data mining database**

The data mining database is designed and built for a specific analytical data model and a specific set of data mining operations. This database will be populated with data from either an operational system, a BI target database, or a combination of both.

2. **Analytical data model**

The analytical data model is developed and tested so it can be used by the algorithms of the data mining operations in the data mining tool.

ROLES INVOLVED IN THESE ACTIVITIES

◆ **Business representative**
In the end, it is the business representative (or his or her management) who will benefit from the results of data mining. Therefore, the business representative has to work very closely with the data mining expert (unless the business representative on this BI application *is* the data mining expert) in order to understand and interpret the data mining results.

◆ **Data mining expert**
The data mining expert is a statistician who really knows the data and is familiar with the data mining techniques. He or she is usually responsible for selecting the most appropriate data mining tool for the organization. He or she is also the primary person who builds the analytical data model and analyzes the data mining results.

◆ **Database administrator**
The database administrator must have a good understanding of the data content in order to design the data mining databases for the data mining activities. He or she works very closely with the data mining expert.

◆ **Subject matter expert**
The subject matter expert can help analyze, define, cleanse, and prepare the source data for the data mining databases. He or she will work under the direction of the data mining expert.

RISKS OF NOT PERFORMING STEP 13

Most organizations are sitting on top of a gold mine—the "gold" being all the data collected about their customers and the products their customers buy. Embedded in this data is information about their customers' spending styles, likes and dislikes, and buying habits. This data is a wasted resource if it is not mined to expose the hidden business intelligence. In addition, executive management must take notice of data mining performed by competitors. If the competitors end up increasing their profits, reducing their costs, creating more innovative product strategies, and expanding their market shares, the organization may lose customers at a very quick rate, which may put its survival in jeopardy.

BIBLIOGRAPHY AND ADDITIONAL READING

Abramowicz, Witold, and Jozef Zurada. *Knowledge Discovery for Business Intelligence Systems.* Kluwer Academic Publications, 2000.

Bajaj, Chandrajit. *Trends in Software: Data Visualization Techniques.* New York: John Wiley & Sons, 1999.

Bashein, Barbara, and M. Lynne Markus. *Data Warehouse: More Than Just Mining.* Morristown, NJ: Financial Executives Research Foundation, 2000.

Berson, Alex, and Stephen J. Smith. *Data Warehousing, Data Mining, and OLAP.* New York: McGraw-Hill, 1997.

Berson, Alex, Stephen Smith, and Kurt Thearling. *Building Data Mining Applications for CRM.* New York: McGraw-Hill, 1999.

Cabena, Peter, Pablo Hadjinian, Rolf Stadler, Jaap Verhees, and Alessandro Zanasi. *Discovering Data Mining: From Concept to Implementation.* Upper Saddle River, NJ: Prentice Hall, 1997.

Edelstein, Herb. *Introduction to Data Mining and Knowledge Discovery.* Potomac, MD: Two Crows Corporation, 1998.

———. *Data Mining: Products and Markets.* Potomac, MD: Two Crows Corporation, 1997.

Kudyba, Stephan, and Richard Hoptroff. *Data Mining and Business Intelligence.* Idea Group Publishing, 2001.

CRoss Industry Standard Process for Data Mining: *http://www.crisp-dm.org*

Data Management Association: *http://www.dama.org*

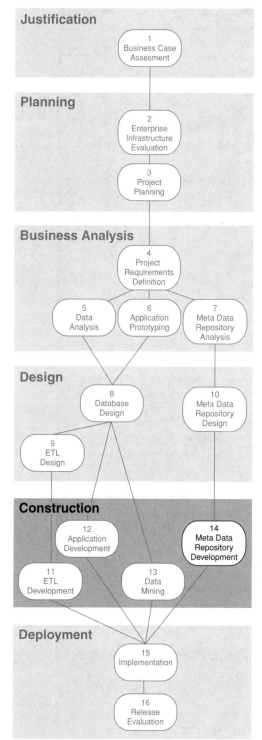

CHAPTER FOURTEEN

Step 14: Meta Data Repository Development

CHAPTER OVERVIEW

This chapter covers the following topics:

- Things to consider about meta data repository development

- The many potential sources of meta data and the difference between active and passive meta data repositories

- The need to develop two types of meta data repository interface processes: a tool interface process and an access interface process

- The four types of testing that apply to meta data repository development: unit testing, integration testing, regression testing, and acceptance testing

- Six activities to perform before the meta data repository goes into production

- How to organize a directory for the meta data repository

- Brief descriptions of the activities involved in meta data repository development, the deliverables resulting from those activities, and the roles involved

- The risks of not performing Step 14

Things to Consider

Meta Data Repository Product Support

✓ What interfaces are required for the meta data repository product?

✓ Will we need to contact the meta data repository vendor for assistance with writing these interfaces?

✓ Do we expect any problems with extracting meta data from the tools that originate it (e.g., computer-aided software [CASE] tool, extract/transform/load [ETL] tool, or online analytical processing [OLAP] tool)? Do we know if other companies experienced any problems?

✓ Will we need to contact the tool vendors and ask for their assistance?

✓ Can we embellish the meta data reports that are provided with the meta data repository product?

✓ Does the meta data repository product have a context-sensitive online help function?

Custom-Built Meta Data Repository

✓ Is our meta data repository design flexible enough to be expanded in the future?

✓ Do we need to build a meta data repository directory as part of the access interface for the business people and for the technicians?

✓ Do we need to build a context-sensitive online help function for the meta data repository?

✓ Do we need to write meta data reports? How will we distribute them? On paper? On the intranet?

✓ Will meta data be integrated with the queries and reports of the BI application? What type of process do we have to build to support that?

✓ How can we ensure that the meta data in the meta data repository does not get out of synch with the meta data in the other tools and the database management system (DBMS)?

Staffing

✓ How much can we modularize the coding and testing? Do we have enough developers and testers to speed up the development effort?

✓ Will the same developers work on the meta data repository online help function? Or can we develop the help function in parallel?

✓ Will we have full-time or part-time support from the database administrator? Will the same database administrator support the BI target databases?

> ✓ Who will continue to maintain the meta data repository? Do we have a full-time meta data administrator? Is one person enough?
>
> ✓ Are there any special training needs we have to consider? For the developers? For the business people?
>
> **Preparation for Production**
>
> ✓ Will the production meta data repository be installed on a dedicated production server? Who will install and test the server?
>
> ✓ Do we need to set up any regularly scheduled meta data repository programs on the job scheduler? Will the operations staff run and monitor them?
>
> ✓ Do we need to write operating procedures for the operations staff?
>
> ✓ Do we need to write a reference guide for the help desk staff and for the business people?

To navigate through the BI decision-support environment more efficiently, business people must have access to a meta data repository. There are only two options: license (buy) a meta data repository or build one. Once a meta data repository is implemented, it has to be maintained and expanded over time. It also has to be populated and updated during each ETL process cycle with load statistics, reconciliation totals, data reliability metrics, data rejection counts, and the reasons for the data rejections.

POPULATING THE META DATA REPOSITORY

Populating a meta data repository is usually not a manual effort. A meta data repository receives most of its meta data from many different meta data sources. These meta data sources are controlled by people other than the meta data administrator, as illustrated in Figure 14.1. A meta data migration process has to be developed to extract the meta data from these sources, associate (link) related meta data components, and populate the meta data repository. The different sources for the meta data are briefly discussed below.

- *Word processing files* can be manuals, procedures, and other less formal documents that contain data definitions and business rules. Embedded in these business rules could be policies about the data, processing rules, data domains (in code translation manuals), and sundry notes about the history and ownership of the data or the processes performed on the data. Some

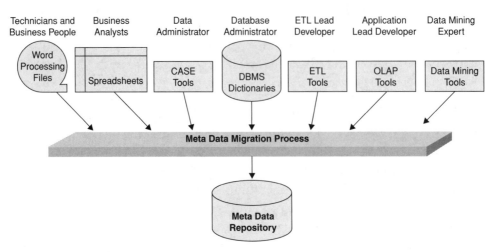

Figure 14.1: Sources for the Meta Data Repository

word processing files also contain valuable technical documentation describing data and process rules enforced by programs.

 Be cautious with word processing files. These files are rarely maintained, and the information contained in them could be out of date and no longer applicable.

- *Spreadsheets* contain calculations and macros, which are executed on the data in the private spreadsheets of business analysts after they have downloaded the data from the various operational systems. These calculations and macros could be the source for transformation rules, cleansing rules, derivations, aggregations, and summarizations.

- *CASE tools* contain the names, definitions, sizes, lengths, relationships, cardinality information, referential integrity rules, and notes about data that has been modeled either for an operational system or for a BI application. In addition, CASE tools usually can store the technical names of tables and columns, as well as primary keys and foreign keys. Some of the more sophisticated CASE tools have modules to include meta data for process components, such as programs, screen displays, and report layouts.

- *Internal DBMS dictionaries* are an integral part of all DBMSs since the dictionaries control the database structures. In relational databases, these are usually called SYSTABLES, and they store the names, definitions, sizes, lengths, relationships, and volumes of database structures, such as storage groups, tablespaces, tables, columns, primary keys, foreign keys, and indices.

- *ETL tools* would not function without instructions (technical meta data) for the required transformations. The internal dictionaries of ETL tools store the source-to-target mapping as well as all the transformation algorithms, which are applied to the source data during the ETL process.

- *OLAP tools* store specifications about data derivations (calculations), aggregations, and summarizations in their internal directories. These specifications allow the OLAP tool to perform its drill-down and roll-up functions. Some OLAP products have the capability to drill across into another database under the same DBMS or even into another database under a different DBMS to extract detailed data for a query.

- *Data mining tools* store the descriptions of the analytical data models against which the data mining operations are executed.

If any meta data contained in these meta data sources is about to change, the meta data administrator must be notified *before* the change occurs. He or she will then have to determine whether the meta data repository can accommodate that change or whether the meta data repository has to be modified or enhanced. Therefore, in order to maintain a healthy and useful meta data repository, the meta data administrator must collaborate with the ETL team, the OLAP team, the data mining expert, the data administrator, the database administrator, and the business people on the BI projects. In addition, and more importantly, the meta data administrator must have full cooperation from the operational systems people who maintain the operational source files and source databases.

 Changes made to operational source systems are frequently not communicated to the meta data administrator in time to make the necessary changes to the meta data repository. Because these changes also affect the ETL process, and in some cases the structures of the BI target databases, the ETL team is also impacted. This breakdown in communication between the operational systems people and the BI decision-support staff can cause severe delays.

Ideally, meta data repositories should be *active* repositories, similar to the DBMS dictionaries. In an active meta data repository, changes would be made only to the meta data repository, and the meta data repository would propagate the changes into the appropriate target tool or DBMS. However, currently the meta data repository products on the market are still *passive* repositories. That means changes must be made both to the meta data repository and to the appropriate target tool or DBMS, and these changes must be kept synchronized, either manually or with programs.

META DATA REPOSITORY INTERFACE PROCESSES

Every meta data repository must have two interfaces in order to function: a tool interface to accept meta data from other tools and an access interface to interact with business people and technicians. If the meta data repository is built in-house, the processes to provide both types of interfaces must be developed (Figure 14.2). If a meta data repository product is licensed, the access interface will be provided as part of the product, but a tool interface process must still be developed.

The Tool Interface Process

Most of the business meta data and the technical meta data is not entered directly into the meta data repository but is extracted from the tools that capture it and use it to support their own functionality. In order to exchange this meta data, the meta data repository and the tools where the meta data originates need to com-

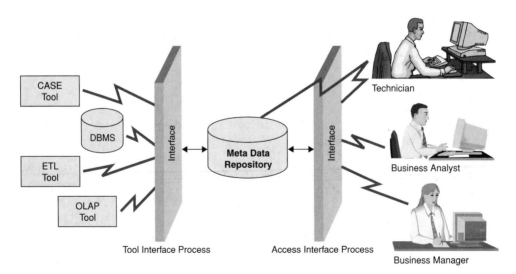

Figure 14.2: Meta Data Repository Interface Processes

municate with each other using common meta data standards. Unfortunately, these tools do not interact with each other very well outside of rudimentary import and export capabilities, and common meta data standards have not yet been agreed upon and ratified by the meta data repository vendors. Therefore, it is necessary to develop a tool interface process with several interface programs to extract the meta data from the various tools.

Meta data repository vendors are recognizing the lack of tool integration as a problem, and meta data standards are being debated by two authoritative groups: the Meta Data Coalition (MDC, influenced by Microsoft) and the Object Management Group (OMG, influenced by Oracle). At this time it is unclear which meta data standards will be adopted as the industry standards.

The Access Interface Process

A meta data repository must also have a common access interface for the people who need to access it. Business people and technicians will want to retrieve information (meta data) about the business data in the BI target databases, the load statistics from the ETL processes, and other process-related meta data. Because business people and technicians may have different requirements, some access interface screens and programs may have to be designed slightly differently for these two constituencies. Technicians and "power users" may also get authorization to access the meta data repository directly without going through the access interface.

If you have only one centralized meta data repository, building a common access interface process for it seems like an obvious requirement and relatively easy to do. But if you are implementing a decentralized meta data repository solution, or even a distributed one, building a common access interface process to all meta data repositories or tools may not be such an obvious requirement. It is definitely a lot harder to build a common access interface process for a decentralized or distributed meta data repository—with or without the help of Extensible Markup Language (XML). However, without that common access interface, everybody who wants to access meta data from multiple meta data repositories or tools would have to learn to use a different access interface for every meta data repository and tool. To avoid having to use multiple access interfaces, business people may well end up insisting on duplicating common meta data into their own "preferred" repositories. This can rapidly lead to redundant meta data repository silos, which is precisely what must be avoided.

META DATA REPOSITORY TESTING

Developing a meta data repository can be as complicated as developing any other application. Therefore, the same structured development guidelines should be followed, particularly the testing guidelines.

While most business managers and information technology (IT) managers demand quality in their applications, they often do not want to spend much time on testing. That does not work! In addition, many project managers constantly underestimate how long testing will take, and they do not allocate sufficient time for testing in the project plan. What is worse, when milestones are missed, the short time originally planned for testing is reduced further.

The point is that you must schedule sufficient time for meta data repository testing and reflect it in the project plan. In addition, plan to have a sufficient number of testers available at the appropriate time. Fortunately, testing is one of the few activities that can easily be modularized, and adding more testers will speed up the testing effort.

 Experience has shown that for every day of coding, you should plan three days of testing.

Of the various types of testing discussed in Step 11, ETL Development (unit testing, integration testing, regression testing, performance testing, quality assurance [QA] testing, and acceptance testing), only four types of testing are usually required for a meta data repository, as shown in Table 14.1.

- *Unit testing* for meta data repository programs is no different from unit testing for other types of application programs. The programs must compile without error; they must perform their functions according to the program specifications; and they must include the appropriate edit checks.

Table 14.1: Required Testing for a Meta Data Repository

Unit testing	Does the code compile without errors?
Integration testing	Do the deliverables meet the requirements?
Regression testing	Did the changes to the program cause damage to this or any other program?
Acceptance testing	Are all aspects of the deliverable acceptable?

- *Integration testing,* sometimes referred to as system testing, verifies that the original objectives of the meta data application are being met and that all meta data repository functions perform as expected. Integration testing should include the initial population of the meta data repository, periodic or intermittent updates to it, the access interface process, the tool interface process, scheduled reports, canned queries, and the online help function. This test is carried out according to a test plan (described in Step 11, ETL Development), and the test cases are run by testers rather than by the developers of the code. (Developers can test other developers' code, just not their own.)

- *Regression testing* is performed on different versions of the same software, which can be produced during the development cycle within one project or when the same software is revised during different subsequent projects. Each time changes are made anywhere in the existing programs, a full regression test cycle should be run to ensure that the changes did not inadvertently break some programming logic downstream in the program or somewhere in the entire stream of programs. Regression testing is a formal test activity and must be performed with a test plan. Since a complete meta data repository will probably not be built all at once but over time, regression testing is an important part of all projects that enhance the meta data repository.

- *Acceptance testing* is even more important than the other forms of testing. This test determines whether the meta data repository (new or enhanced) is ready to be rolled out. This final testing process for the meta data repository usually combines QA testing and acceptance testing. The business people and the technicians who will be using and supporting the meta data repository are involved in this testing. Similar to integration testing and regression testing, this test is executed with a test plan, predefined test cases, and expected test results; all test runs are documented in the test log.

PREPARING FOR THE META DATA REPOSITORY ROLLOUT

Moving a meta data repository into production requires preparation, as shown in Figure 14.3. This preparation should start early, not when all the coding and testing have been completed. Novice meta data repository teams often underestimate the time it takes to prepare the basic aspects of the production environment outlined below.

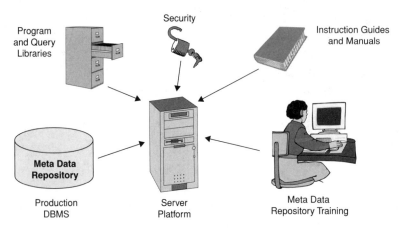

Figure 14.3: Preparation for Meta Data Repository Rollout

- *Server platform:* The meta data repository should reside on a production server and not on the development server. Therefore, the production server platform has to be installed and tested, which includes the hardware components, operating system, monitoring utilities, and network connectivity.

- *Production DBMS:* If the meta data repository is installed on a new production server, an instance of the DBMS has to be created, and parameters for it have to be set and tested under the operating system. If a meta data repository product is being licensed, all product components including the meta data repository database have to be installed and tested on the production server.

- *Program and query libraries:* All meta data migration programs (including the tool interface programs) and all meta data application programs (including the access interface programs, the online help function, the reports, and the queries) will reside in a version-controlled library. A library management product has to be installed and tested before the meta data repository programs can be moved into production.

- *Security:* The production server, the DBMS product, the meta data repository database, and all programs need to have the proper levels of security implemented. Security levels in a production environment are much stricter than in the development environment. Developers who could change the meta data repository database structures and its content at will in the development environment should not be granted the same authority in the production environment.

- *Instruction guides and manuals:* Once the meta data repository is in production, some of the meta data programs will be scheduled to run automatically with every ETL process cycle to capture the load statistics and data quality metrics and to load them into the meta data repository. Certain reports or queries may also be put on a schedule.

  Operations staff will monitor the scheduled runs and notify the meta data administrator if something goes wrong. Operating procedures should be prepared for them, listing the scheduled jobs, the order in which the jobs should be run, and what to do if a job fails. The help desk staff will mentor and support the business people with their meta data questions. Therefore, the help desk staff will need a reference guide to fall back on in case they get inquiries they need to investigate. This reference guide could also be given to business people since it contains helpful hints about where to locate specific meta data components and where to get additional help.

- *Meta data repository training:* Business people and technicians need to be trained differently on how to use the meta data repository either through the access interface or directly and interactively. Business analysts need to know how to access the meta data repository to help them select BI data for ad hoc queries. Technicians need to know how to use meta data to help them maintain the BI applications and how to retrieve meta data in order to deliver it as an integral part of the BI application reports and queries.

A best practice is to provide "just enough" training "just in time." The first training session, no longer than one day, should provide a review of the meta data repository, how it is organized, and how to extract some meta data components, as well as an introduction to one or two basic functions. Tell the trainees that the first training session is only an introduction to the meta data repository and that they will need additional training. After one or two weeks of hands-on practice while performing their job duties, the trainees should return for another one- or two-day training session to learn about more advanced features of the meta data repository.

Use the training session as an opportunity to introduce the business people to the help desk staff who will support them. Mention to the business people that the help desk staff will be mentoring them as they become proficient in navigating through the meta data repository and through the entire BI decision-support environment. Encourage the business people to establish their own network. In this network, they could help each other not only with using the meta data repository but also with learning about the business data and the application features of the BI decision-support environment as a whole.

Meta Data Repository Directory

Some thought should be given to the best way to organize and present the meta data repository contents to the business people and technicians. The meta data repository contents could be organized into a directory that serves as a map for easier navigation through the meta data repository. For example, the contents of a general meta data repository directory could be organized into three major groupings: business directory, information navigator, and technical directory, as shown in Table 14.2. These three groupings could list the meta data components contained within each grouping, or they could show a layer of lower-level subgroupings.

A meta data repository directory could be designed as fancy as a Web site map or as simple as a basic context-sensitive matrix. The directory could also be expanded and included as part of the online help facility of the BI decision-support environment as a whole to serve as a potential entry point into the meta data repository. If a meta data repository directory is developed, its use should be covered during the training sessions.

Table 14.2: Example of a Meta Data Repository Directory

	Business Directory	*Information Navigator*	*Technical Directory*
Audience	Business staff	Business staff	Technical staff
Meta Data Components and Functions	Business terms	Aggregations	Security
	Source of data	Transformations	BI target databases
	Currency of data	Query library	Indices
	Ownership	Drill-down functions	Data mapping
	Data quality	Roll-up functions	Quality metrics

Meta Data Repository Development Activities

The activities for meta data repository development do not need to be performed linearly. Figure 14.4 indicates which activities can be performed concurrently. The list below briefly describes the activities associated with Step 14, Meta Data Repository Development.

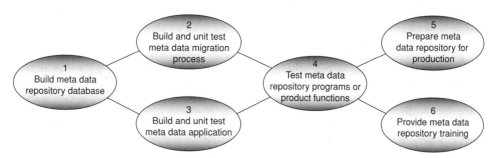

Figure 14.4: Meta Data Repository Development Activities

1. **Build the meta data repository database.**

   If you are building a meta data repository, regardless of whether it is based on an entity-relationship design or an object-oriented design, generate the data definition language (DDL) and run it to create the meta data repository database structures. Also, generate the data control language (DCL) and run it to establish create, read, update, and delete (CRUD) authority on the meta data repository database. If you are licensing a meta data repository product, install and test all product components, especially the meta data repository database. Set up CRUD authority on the meta data repository product to allow execution of the meta data migration process and the reports and to allow direct access to the meta data repository.

2. **Build and unit test the meta data migration process.**

   Once you have created the meta data repository database, you must develop the meta data migration process, including the tool interface process and the meta data transformation programs that will prepare the extracted meta data for the meta data repository. If you licensed a meta data repository product and if the import facility of the product is used to populate the meta data repository, test it to verify that it functions as expected.

3. **Build and unit test the meta data application.**

   If you are building the meta data repository, you must also develop the meta data application functions, including the access interface process and the online help function, as well as the meta data reports and queries. If the meta data repository is a licensed product, you must test its application functions (interfaces, reports, queries). If it is necessary to enhance the product with additional functionality, write and test the additional code.

4. **Test the meta data repository programs or product functions.**

Test all meta data repository programs or product functions from beginning to end through formal integration or regression testing. Every component of the meta data migration process as well as every component of the meta data application must be tested vigorously. Perform integration testing or regression testing with a formal test plan; run prepared test cases, log the actual test results on a test log, and compare them to the expected results. Once the meta data repository programs or product functions have been thoroughly integration or regression tested, the business people and the technicians can perform their combination QA/acceptance testing.

5. **Prepare the meta data repository for production.**

Install and test the server platform for the production meta data repository. Create the DDL and DCL for the production meta data repository database. Write operating procedures for the operations staff, with instructions for running regularly scheduled meta data repository programs. Also write a reference guide for the help desk staff and for the business people with instructions on how to use the meta data repository. Establish other procedures, such as monitoring of database performance and meta data usage.

6. **Provide meta data repository training.**

Since a meta data application can be as complicated as any business application, training is an important aspect. Business people and liaison personnel, such as "power users" and help desk staff, have to be trained in the use of the meta data repository database, the online help function, reports, and queries. Develop and present in-house training sessions or schedule training through the meta data repository vendor.

DELIVERABLES RESULTING FROM THESE ACTIVITIES

1. **Physical meta data repository database**

This is the physical database of the meta data repository. Its tables, columns, primary keys, foreign keys, and CRUD authorization are defined to the DBMS with Structured Query Language (SQL) instructions containing DDL and DCL statements.

2. **Meta data repository test plan**

   The test plan should state the purpose for each meta data repository test and show a schedule for running the tests in a predetermined sequence. It should also describe the test cases, including input criteria and expected output results. A test log should document when the tests were run, who ran them, and what the test results were.

3. **Meta data repository programs**

   All meta data migration programs, access interface programs, tool interface programs, report programs, query scripts, and online help function programs for the meta data repository should be coded and tested. If a meta data repository product is being used, all of the meta data repository product functions should be tested.

4. **Meta data repository program library**

   All meta data repository programs and scripts should reside in the meta data repository program library. The entire meta data migration process, as well as the meta data application functions, should have been integration or regression tested and QA/acceptance tested.

5. **Meta data repository production documentation**

   Meta data repository production documentation includes the following:
   - Operating procedures for operations staff covering all scheduled meta data repository jobs
   - Meta data repository reference guide for the help desk and the business people with instructions on how to use the meta data repository

6. **Meta data repository training materials**

   The training materials for internal meta data repository training should include presentation slides, instructor notes, student workbooks, exercises and their solutions, and any additional pertinent handouts.

ROLES INVOLVED IN THESE ACTIVITIES

◆ **Business representative**

   The business representative should participate in acceptance testing the meta data application functions the same way he or she participates in acceptance testing the ETL and access and analysis functions of the BI application. The business representative must also take part in the meta data repository training.

◆ **Database administrator**
The database administrator has to create the database structures (tables, columns, indices, and so on) for the meta data repository. He or she grants authority to technicians, business people, tools, and programs for accessing and writing to the meta data repository database. He or she also assists the meta data administrator with the meta data migration process and the database access calls for the meta data application functions.

◆ **Meta data administrator**
The meta data administrator must install the meta data repository product, if one is being licensed. If a meta data repository is being built from scratch, the meta data administrator must oversee the development effort. He or she must install and test the production server for the meta data repository. He or she also coordinates the meta data repository development activities with the database administrator, the meta data repository developers, and the testers.

◆ **Meta data repository developers**
The meta data repository developers should write the code for the meta data migration process, including the tool interface process, and for the meta data application, including the access interface process and online help function.

◆ **Testers**
Since developers should never test their own code, independent testers (other developers) should perform the integration and regression tests.

RISKS OF NOT PERFORMING STEP 14

Without a meta data repository you would have to develop a complicated custom meta data application to extract meta data from all the tools and DBMSs to produce meta data reports. That would be too difficult, too time consuming, too coding intensive, too convoluted, and too frustrating. Other meta data approaches, such as expanding the use of a CASE tool, may work as stopgap measures but not as long-term solutions. CASE tools are not equipped to accept meta data from ETL tools or OLAP tools, just as ETL tools are not equipped to accept meta data from CASE tools, and so on. A meta data repository is the only solution.

BIBLIOGRAPHY AND ADDITIONAL READING

Aiken, Peter H. *Data Reverse Engineering: Slaying the Legacy Dragon.* New York: McGraw-Hill, 1996.

Beck, Kent. *Extreme Programming Explained: Embrace Change.* Boston, MA: Addison-Wesley, 2000.

Dick, Kevin. *XML: A Manager's Guide.* Boston, MA: Addison-Wesley, 2000.

Hetzel, Bill. *The Complete Guide to Software Testing, Second Edition.* New York: John Wiley & Sons, 1993.

Humphrey, Watts S. *Winning with Software: An Executive Strategy.* Boston, MA: Addison-Wesley, 2002.

Marco, David. *Building and Managing the Meta Data Repository: A Full Lifecycle Guide.* New York: John Wiley & Sons, 2000.

Tannenbaum, Adrienne. *Metadata Solutions: Using Metamodels, Repositories, XML, and Enterprise Portals to Generate Information on Demand.* Boston, MA: Addison-Wesley, 2002.

Enterprise Warehouse Solutions: *http://www.EWSolutions.com*

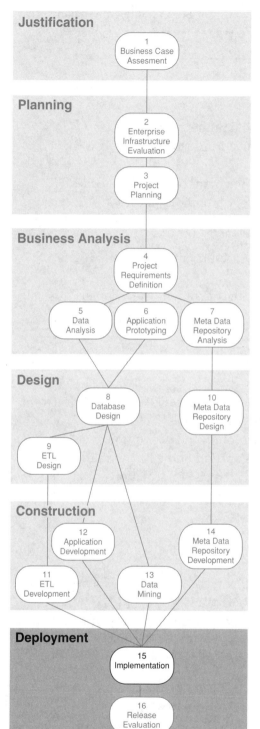

CHAPTER FIFTEEN

Step 15: Implementation

CHAPTER OVERVIEW

This chapter covers the following topics:

- Things to consider about implementation of BI applications

- The two types of security implementations: centralized security and decentralized security

- How to perform a security gap analysis

- The three types of backup procedures: incremental backup, high-speed mainframe backup, and partial backup

- Monitoring the utilization of computer, network, and personnel resources

- Managing growth in data, growth in usage, and growth in hardware

- Brief descriptions of the activities involved in implementation, the deliverables resulting from those activities, and the roles involved

- The risks of not performing Step 15

THINGS TO CONSIDER

Preparing for Production

✓ Have we defined all the production libraries and production databases?

✓ Are the daily, weekly, and monthly extract/transform/load (ETL) processes on the job scheduler?

✓ Are the regularly scheduled application report programs on the job scheduler?

✓ Are the regularly scheduled meta data repository programs on the job scheduler?

✓ Is the operations staff ready to take over?

✓ Have they approved the quality assurance (QA) test results? Do they have any concerns?

✓ Do we have to write operating procedures for the operations staff? For all components of the BI application? Or just for the ETL process?

✓ When will we copy all programs into the production libraries?

✓ When will we load the production databases?

Security Considerations

✓ What types of security measures do we need? What are we securing?

✓ How are we securing the data? The applications? The tools? The interfaces?

✓ Do the security measures have to include encryption and decryption, especially for the Web-enabled access and analysis portion of the BI application?

✓ Are single-user authentication services of an enterprise information portal part of this BI application?

Database Maintenance

✓ What is our backup and recovery procedure?

✓ What is our disaster recovery procedure?

✓ How will database performance monitoring take place? What tools will be used? Who is responsible for monitoring the databases?

✓ How will we know if we have met the service-level agreement (SLA) for performance?

✓ How will we monitor growth in usage and growth in data volume?

Training and Support

✓ Have the business people received training on using the BI application?

✓ Have the business people received training on using the meta data repository?

> ✓ Have the "power users" received training on writing efficient queries in Structured Query Language (SQL)?
> ✓ Is the help desk staff geared up to mentor the business people in their use of the BI application, including the meta data repository?
> ✓ Has the help desk staff received sufficient training?
> ✓ If there is no help desk, who will support the business people?

Now that the BI application is built and tested, it is ready to be implemented in the production environment. You can roll out the new BI application in two ways, all at once as is done traditionally or in increments as briefly described in the section below.

INCREMENTAL ROLLOUT

When planning the implementation, use the same iterative approach used when developing the BI application and the meta data repository. The iterative approach, or incremental rollout, works well because it reduces the risk of exposing potential defects in the BI application to the entire organization. In addition, it gives you the opportunity to informally demonstrate the BI concepts and the BI tool features to the business people who were not directly involved in the BI project. Here are some suggestions.

- Start with a small group of business people. This small group should consist of not only "power users" but also some less technology-savvy knowledge workers and business analysts, as well as the primary business representative who was involved in the development work as a member of the core team.

- Treat the business people as *customers*—keeping customer care in mind. Trouble-free implementation, interactive training, and ongoing support will help you get their buy-in. Always ask yourself, "What is in it for the customers?"

- Take the opportunity to test your implementation approach. You may consider adjusting your implementation approach or modifying the BI application prior to the full rollout (e.g., change cumbersome logon procedures).

- It may be necessary to duplicate implementation activities at multiple sites. Adding these sites slowly over time is easier than launching them all at the same time.

SECURITY MANAGEMENT

Security features must be tested early during the first rollout. Security is often overlooked in BI applications or is given superficial attention. Keep in mind that the data in the BI target databases is the same data contained in the operational systems. The common argument that security is not an issue for BI applications because the data is aggregated and summarized holds true only if detailed data is not available through drill-down features. In that case, the security measures for the BI data do not need to be as stringent as the security measures imposed on the same operational source data. However, most BI target databases store a fair amount of detailed data in addition to the summaries. Therefore, the security measures may be relaxed for some of the data but not for all.

Security Measures for BI Applications

Organizations that have strong security umbrellas on their mainframes are more likely to pay attention to security measures for their BI applications on multi-tier platforms. Organizations that have very lax security policies for their mainframes are usually prone to treating security casually for their BI applications as well. These organizations may unwittingly expose themselves to security breaches, especially if they plan to deliver information from the BI target databases over the Web.

The following is an example of a security requirement that may need to be imposed on a BI application. Suppose an organization wants to give its distributors the ability to analyze their orders and shipments via a multidimensional BI application. To prevent a distributor from searching through other distributors' sales data, there would have to be a mechanism for restricting each distributor's access to only the sales data pertaining to that particular distributor. In other words, some security lock is required to prevent access to the competitors' sales data. This is not as straightforward as it sounds.

- No off-the-shelf umbrella security solutions can impose this kind of security. This security requirement would have to be implemented through the various security features of the database management system (DBMS) and of the access and analysis tools used by the BI application.

- The solution of imposing security at a table level may not be granular enough. However, one possible way to achieve this type of security is to partition the tables either physically or logically (through VIEWs). Partitioning will restrict access solely to the appropriate distributor as long as both the fact tables and the dimension tables are partitioned. Therefore, this method could become too cumbersome.

• An alternative may be to enhance the meta data with definitions of data parameters, which could control access to the data. This form of security would be implemented with appropriate program logic to tell the meta data repository the distributor's identity, allowing the application to return the appropriate data for that distributor only. This type of security measure will be only as good as the program controlling it.

This example illustrates that the required security measures must be well considered and that the security features of the DBMS and of the access and analysis tools must be well understood and cross-tested. Complete reliance on one comprehensive security package that has the capability to implement any and all types of security measures is not a security solution because such a security package does not exist.

To get the security you need, you will most likely have to implement a number of different security measures, including purchased security packages. However, be sure to minimize the number of security packages you implement because one of two things may happen.

1. Business people will be logging in through multiple security packages, using multiple logon identifiers (IDs) and multiple passwords that expire at different times. They will get frustrated very quickly if they have to go through different logon procedures and remember different IDs and passwords for each procedure. Complaints will run high.

2. Business people will stop using the BI decision-support environment entirely because it is too cumbersome. You do not want this to happen.

A number of organizations avoid this problem by adopting a single-sign-on scheme, which keeps the frustration level to a minimum but still allows tracking of any security breaches, albeit in a less sophisticated way.

Security in a Multi-Tier Environment

Implementing security measures in a centralized environment is less complicated than in a multi-tier environment. In a centralized environment, all security measures can be implemented in one location because all the data is in one place. The goal of centralized security is "one entry point, one guard." It is much easier to guard a single door than multiple doors.

In a BI decision-support environment, keeping all the data in one central place is not always feasible or desirable. If data needs to be stored in a distributed fashion in a multi-tier environment, implementing security measures becomes much more complicated. The list below briefly describes the steps involved.

1. Identify the end points in your network architecture and the paths connecting the end points. Draw a diagram of your physical architecture, similar to Figure 15.1.

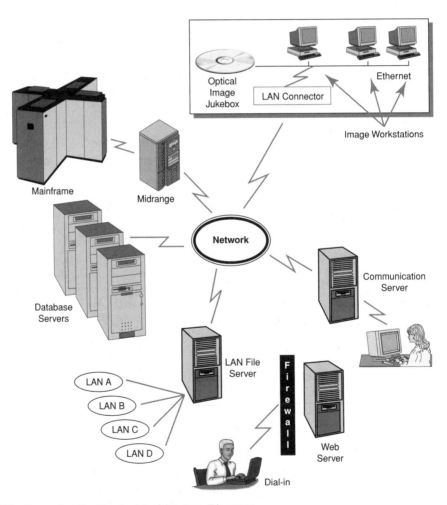

Figure 15.1: Example of a Physical Architecture Diagram

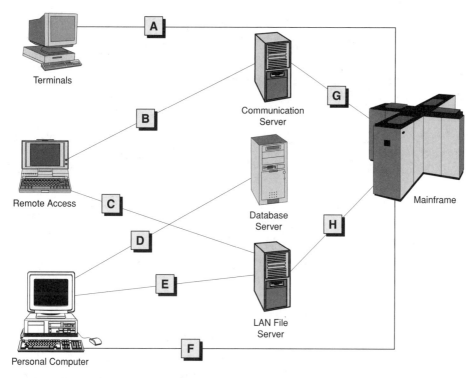

Figure 15.2: Example of a Connectivity Path Diagram

2. Determine the connectivity paths (from the entry points) used to get to the data. Draw a diagram with links and labels for the connectivity paths (Figure 15.2).

3. Compare the paths with your existing security measures. You may already have some security packages installed, and some of them may be sufficient to guard a subset of the data. Draw a matrix for security gap analysis purposes (Figure 15.3).

The security gap analysis matrix will help you identify where security is still needed and what type of security is needed. Keep in mind the following points:

- Password security may be the least expensive to implement, but it can be easily violated.

- DBMS security is the most important component of the security solution and should override all other security measures that may contradict the data access authority granted by the DBMS.

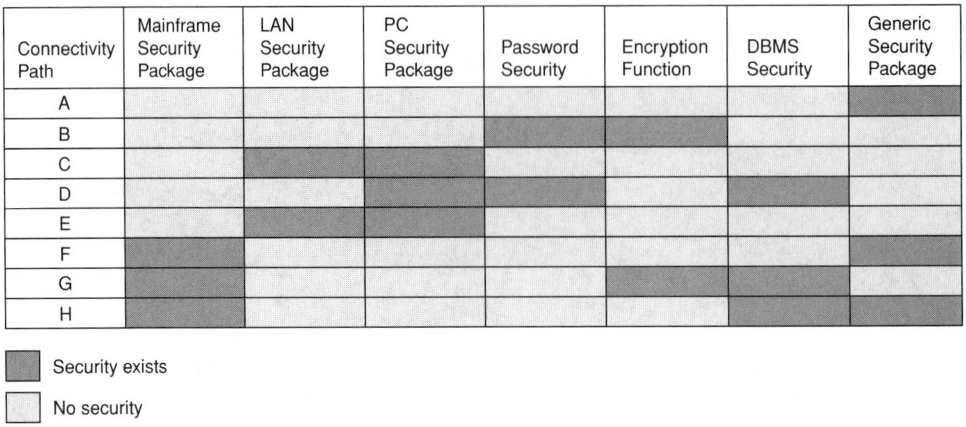

Connectivity Path	Mainframe Security Package	LAN Security Package	PC Security Package	Password Security	Encryption Function	DBMS Security	Generic Security Package
A							■
B				■	■		
C		■	■				
D			■		■	■	
E		■	■				
F	■						■
G	■				■		
H	■					■	■

■ Security exists

☐ No security

Figure 15.3: Example of a Security Gap Analysis Matrix

- Encryption is not that prevalent in BI decision-support environments because of the complicated encryption and decryption algorithms. Encryption and decryption processes also degrade performance considerably. However, with the frequent use of the Internet as an access and delivery mechanism, encryption should be seriously considered to protect the organization from costly security breaches.

Security for Internet Access

The Internet enables distribution of information worldwide, and the BI decision-support environment provides easy access to organizational data. Combining the two capabilities appears to be a giant leap forward for engaging in e-commerce. However, carefully consider the implications of combining these technologies before you decide to take the risk of potentially exposing sensitive organizational data (Figure 15.4).

Many product vendors are enabling Web access to databases in general, and some vendors are allowing access to BI target databases in particular. This complicates the concerns for:

- The security of the BI decision-support environment in general
- The security issues associated with allowing Web access to the organization's data

The bottom line on security is that you need to define your security requirements early in order to have time to consider and weigh all factors. If you opt to

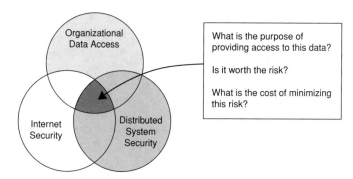

Figure 15.4: Security Considerations for Internet Access

display the data on the Web, spend extra time and money on authentication and authorization of internal staff and external customers. If you are transmitting sensitive data to and from external customers, consider investing in encryption and decryption software.

- *Authentication* is the process of identifying a person, usually based on a logon ID and password. This process is meant to ensure that the person is who he or she claims to be.

- *Authorization* is the process of granting or denying a person access to a resource, such as an application or a Web page. In security software, authentication is distinct from authorization, and most security packages implement a two-step authentication and authorization process.

- *Encryption* is the "translation" of data into a secret code. It is the most effective way to achieve data security. To read an encrypted file, you must have access to a secret key or password that enables you to decrypt it. Unencrypted data is usually referred to as *plain text*, while encrypted data is usually referred to as *cipher text*.

DATA BACKUP AND RECOVERY

After spending several million dollars on your BI decision-support environment, you want to make certain that you will never lose the content of the BI target databases and that you will never be deprived of the analytical capabilities of the BI applications for a long period of time.

There is a school of thought that says, "Don't worry about backing up your BI target databases because that data is derived from other systems—if the data is destroyed, simply rebuild it." This is a careless and expensive attitude when dealing with a very large database (VLDB). Although backing up a database is time-consuming and takes the database offline for several hours, the alternative of reloading years' worth of data into a VLDB will take much longer—if it can be done at all. Not every organization opts to keep all source extract files for years just in case it needs to reprocess them.

It is mandatory to back up the BI target databases on a regular basis, but the sheer size of VLDBs make this a technological challenge. Many of the hardware platforms on which BI applications reside often have limitations on the amount of data that can be backed up on a regular basis. These limitations are due to the slow speed of data transfers between the server and the backup device. Several backup strategies are available to mitigate this problem.

- **Incremental backup:** One strategy is to take advantage of the grow-only aspect of BI target databases (no updating of rows) by backing up only the actual changes to a database (new rows) since the last update rather than the entire database. This incremental ("net change") backup strategy is even possible for most daily backups. However, since there are usually multiple databases in the BI decision-support environment, and since the summarized data must stay synchronized with the detail data, no loads or refreshes can occur to any of these databases until the backups of *all* databases have completed successfully.

- **High-speed mainframe backup:** Another possibility is to use the mainframe transfer utilities to pass BI data back to the mainframe for a high-speed backup, which is supported only on the mainframe. Channel connects on the mainframe allow speeds that cannot yet be approached on most midrange servers. This is an expensive solution, but it is a robust one that usually works.

- **Partial backup:** Another strategy relies on partitioning the database tables by date to support partial backups. While one partition is being backed up, the other partitions can remain available. Considerations about this strategy are listed below.
  - Databases, which support parallelization of backups, have a major advantage with this strategy since multiple partitions can be backed up at the same time.
  - If your BI target databases are loaded daily, group multiple days into one partition rather than setting up a new partition for each day. During

backup, the data for all days in the partition being backed up would not be available.

– A big drawback of this strategy is that if the table is partitioned by a date column for backup purposes (which means it is clustered by the date column), it cannot be clustered in any other way for access purposes. This can affect performance when running the reports and queries, unless database parallelism is used.

MONITORING THE UTILIZATION OF RESOURCES

You must continuously monitor the utilization of various resources in a BI decision-support environment, especially the utilization of computers, networks, and personnel. If any one of these resources is neglected, it may potentially become a bottleneck for the BI applications.

Computer Utilization

Computer utilization includes the central processing unit (CPU), input/output (I/O) channels, random access memory (RAM), direct access storage devices (DASDs) or disk drives, and other related hardware. These devices should be dedicated for the BI decision-support environment and should not be shared by other applications. Since utilization of these devices increases over time, they should be monitored.

 It is vitally important to use appropriate monitoring and alert utilities that will detect any resource problem and sound an alarm in case of an actual or pending system failure or resource shortfall. Selecting an appropriate monitoring utility is especially critical in a distributed environment.

Network Utilization

Network utilization may be a relatively minor issue for the day-to-day execution of BI applications, but it may be a big issue for the ETL process. One large telecommunications organization found out that even with access to the latest and greatest communications technologies, it had insufficient bandwidth to transmit its source data from the mainframe to the database server to populate its BI target databases in a timely fashion.

When monitoring your network utilization, also consider the following points:

- Bandwidth may be a serious problem for BI applications that frequently involve several levels of drill-down access into detailed data. Queries after queries may be executed by many people from many locations, each potentially returning huge amounts of data across the network.

- If bandwidth is an ongoing problem, one potential solution is to move toward a distributed BI implementation and away from a centralized strategy. However, if a lot of communication and integration among the distributed BI target databases is required, this solution could make the situation worse.

Personnel Utilization

A BI decision-support environment is a high-maintenance environment. This is especially true during the initial development and deployment of the first few BI applications. It is also true to the extent that manual processes are used during or after the ETL cycles to validate and analyze load statistics produced by the ETL runs. A BI decision-support environment requires dedicated support from a number of IT personnel, such as:

- Application developers
- Data administrators
- Database administrators
- Hardware and operating system specialists
- Middleware specialists
- Network administrators

Good technicians are often hard to find. Many technicians want to work on BI applications, especially the multidimensional ones, because these challenging applications involve new technologies (and thus they look good on a résumé). However, because the operational systems still need to be supported— since they are more mission-critical than BI applications—a "tug of war" over available staff is often the result.

This is especially true for database administrators who already have a full plate supporting the operational systems. Some senior database administrators have to be released from those duties to become the chief designers and managers of the BI target databases. These database administrators are responsible for designing, building, monitoring, tuning, and maintaining the BI target databases and, to some extent, the database access calls from the BI application programs and access and analysis tools (e.g., writing passthrough queries). In addition, they have to be concerned with monitoring and managing the increasing data volumes and increasing database usage, which will require even more of their time. Redistributing the workload of database administrators is a culture shift and an issue in many organizations that perceive the database administrator's function as nothing more than running DBMS maintenance procedures on production databases.

GROWTH MANAGEMENT

By conservative estimate, the data in a BI decision-support environment doubles every two years. The good news is that the cost per query for most BI decision-support environments goes down with properly managed growth. The bad news is that the overall cost climbs, assuming that more and more business people use the BI decision-support environment as time progresses. The three key growth areas to watch are data, usage, and hardware.

Growth in Data

Growth in data means not only adding new rows to the tables but also expanding the BI target databases with additional columns and new tables. Adding new columns to a dimension table is not as involved as adding new dimension tables to an existing star or snowflake schema, which usually requires the following:

- Unloading the fact table
- Adding another foreign key to the fact table to relate to the new dimension table
- Recalculating the facts to a lower granularity (because of the new dimension)
- Reloading the fact table

BI target databases need a large amount of disk space, with workspace and indices taking up as much as 25 to 40 percent of that space. In the relational world, the data is only a fraction of the overall database size; a major portion of it is index space. Indexing is required to provide better response time when enormous volumes of data are read.

When calculating space requirements, it might be prudent to use the standard engineering maxim: Calculate how large the BI target databases will be (including indices), and then triple those numbers.

As data volumes increase, there needs to be a plan to aggregate and summarize the data as it ages. Business analysts rarely require the same level of granularity for very old data as they do for recent data. Therefore, the level of granularity should decrease with a moving calendar. For example, assume the business people want to store ten years of historical data. They require monthly summary data by department for two years but are satisfied with monthly summaries by region for the remaining eight years. Before a new month is loaded into the BI target database, the department-level data for the 24th month is summarized into regional totals and rolled off into another fact table so that the 23rd month becomes the 24th month, the 22nd month becomes the 23rd month, and so on.

The following list contains some of the new technologies available to support the massive data volumes and the analysis capabilities of these huge databases:

- Parallel technologies
- Multidimensional databases
- New indexing technologies
- Relational online analytical processing (ROLAP) tools
- Distributed database maintenance tools and utilities

Growth in Usage

Another key growth area is usage. Organizations that have built successful BI applications have often uncovered a pent-up need for information throughout the organization. This need translates to more business people using the existing BI applications and asking for new ones. The number of business people accessing the BI target databases can easily double or triple every year, which drives up growth in usage exponentially. Since different business people want to see different data and look at it in different ways, they want to slice and dice the data by new business dimensions, which increases the data volume. Although the data volume is a far more critical factor in determining processor requirements, the number of people accessing the BI target databases is equally important.

Technicians view growth in usage as something negative. Managers, however, think of growth in usage as something positive, as long as there is a return on investment (ROI). Purchasing new hardware or updating existing hardware to handle the growth may not be a concern if the organization is making a sizable profit due to better decision-making capabilities with the BI applications. Therefore, growth in usage may mean that the BI strategy is working.

 BI target databases are by nature read-only and grow-only. Therefore, the key is to stop trying to conserve disk space if the BI applications and BI data are helping the organization make a profit.

Growth in Hardware

Given the information about the growth in data and the growth in usage, it should be obvious that scalability of the BI hardware architecture is key. But before you plan five years ahead, remember that the hardware cost is only one part of the total BI cost. Look at a planning horizon of 12 to 24 months; it is best to start small but also plan for long-term growth. Consider the following factors.

- Keep in mind the capacity threshold of your BI platform. If you exceed that capacity, you have to add more processors, I/O channels, independent disk controllers, and other high-speed components to keep the BI decision-support environment at an acceptable level of performance.

- Of all the BI hardware, the BI server platform is the most important. When ordering new hardware of any kind, there must be enough lead time to have the equipment delivered, tested, and prepared for the development and production environments.

- Parallel technology is an absolute must for VLDBs. The ability to store data across striped disks and the ability to have multiple independent disk controllers play an enormously important role in the performance of processes running against the BI target databases.

- The Transmission Control Protocol/Internet Protocol (TCP/IP) is appropriate for most hardware platforms. TCP/IP is rapidly becoming a standard for scalability, growth considerations, and multiplatform environments.

- Consider the advantages of a data mart approach with separate BI target databases. This approach permits scalability in smaller and less expensive increments.

IMPLEMENTATION ACTIVITIES

The activities for implementation do not need to be performed linearly. Figure 15.5 indicates which activities can be performed concurrently. The list below briefly describes the activities associated with Step 15, Implementation.

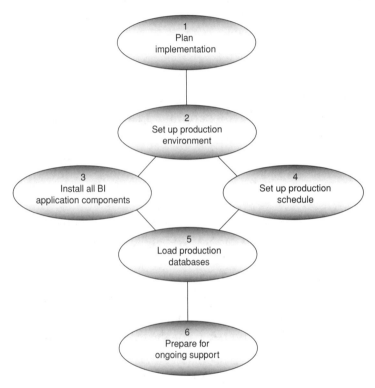

Figure 15.5: Implementation Activities

1. Plan the implementation.

Set the implementation date and make sure that all the resources needed for the implementation will be available. Depending on the progress you have made, the lessons you have learned, and the difficulties you have encountered, you may want to roll out the BI application to the business community in phases. Start with a small group of business people, learn from the experience, and modify your approach if necessary (e.g., increase the time for training or change the security measures) before making the BI application available to more people.

If the BI application has any organizational impact, prepare to make those organizational changes (e.g., business process improvement changes or shifted roles and responsibilities).

2. **Set up the production environment.**
   In most large organizations, strict procedures have to be followed to prepare the production environment.
   - Set up the production program libraries (ETL, application, meta data repository).
   - Create the production databases (BI target databases, meta data repository database).
   - Grant appropriate access authority on the production databases.
   - Grant appropriate access authority to developers, operations staff, and business people to execute programs from production program libraries.
   - Write operating procedures for the operations staff with instructions for running the ETL process, as well as the regularly scheduled application report jobs.
   - Prepare a reference guide for the help desk staff and the business people with instructions on how to use the BI application.
   - Determine production security levels for all components of the BI application.

3. **Install all the BI application components.**
   Move all ETL programs, application programs, and meta data repository programs to their respective production libraries.

4. **Set up the production schedule.**
   All ETL programs, application report programs, and meta data repository programs that will run on a regular basis have to be set up on the job scheduler. The ETL job schedule has to include the meta data programs that are part of the ETL process (e.g., capture load statistics, reconciliation totals, data reliability factors).

5. **Load the production databases.**
   Load the BI target databases by running the initial load process, followed by the historical load process. Also load the meta data repository with meta data from your various meta data sources such as spreadsheets, computer-aided software engineering (CASE) tool, ETL tool, and online analytical processing (OLAP) tool.

6. **Prepare for ongoing support.**
   Establish a schedule for on-call emergency support. Schedule regular backups as well as occasional database reorganizations for all production databases.

Plan to use the DBMS-provided utilities for these database maintenance activities. In addition, plan to monitor performance, growth, usage, and quality as part of the ongoing database maintenance activities. Periodically review and revise capacity plans for processors, disk storage, network, and bandwidth.

DELIVERABLES RESULTING FROM THESE ACTIVITIES

1. **Production ETL program library**
   All fully functioning ETL programs and scripts should reside in the production ETL program library.

2. **Production application program library**
   All fully functioning access and analysis programs and scripts should reside in the production application program library.

3. **Production meta data repository program library**
   All fully functioning meta data repository programs and scripts should reside in the meta data repository program library.

4. **Production BI target databases**
   The data definition language (DDL) and data control language (DCL) SQL statements are run in the production environment to build the production BI target databases. The ETL initial load process and the ETL historical load process are run to populate these production BI target databases.

5. **Production meta data repository database**
   The DDL and DCL statements for the meta data repository are run in the production environment to build the production meta data repository database. The meta data migration programs and tool interface programs are run to populate the production meta data repository database with business meta data, technical meta data, and ETL meta data (load statistics, reconciliation totals, data quality metrics) from the initial load and historical load processes.

6. **Production documentation**
   Production documentation for the BI application includes:
   – Operating procedures for operations staff covering the ETL process and all scheduled application report jobs
   – Reference guide for the help desk staff and the business people with instructions on how to use the BI application

ROLES INVOLVED IN THESE ACTIVITIES

◆ **Application developers**

The application developers work with the operations staff to move the report programs, query scripts, interface programs, and online help function programs into the production application program library.

◆ **Application lead developer**

The application lead developer supervises the implementation activities of the access and analysis portion of the BI application. He or she is in charge of setting up the production application program library and writing the access and analysis portion of the operating procedures and the reference guide. He or she also has the responsibility of setting up the application report programs on the job scheduler.

◆ **Data mining expert**

The data mining expert works with the database administrator to create, revise, and maintain the data mining databases for the planned data mining activities. Data mining is an iterative and ad hoc endeavor that requires ongoing changes to the data mining databases, the analytical data models, and the data mining operations.

◆ **Database administrator**

The database administrator creates the production BI target databases and the production meta data repository database and grants appropriate access authority for these production databases. He or she must run the initial load process and the historical load process to load the BI target databases. He or she schedules database maintenance activities (backups, reorganizations) as well as ongoing database monitoring activities (for performance, growth, usage). He or she also reviews the capacity plans for processors, disk storage, and network bandwidth.

◆ **ETL developers**

The ETL developers work with the operations staff to move the ETL programs into the production ETL program library.

◆ **ETL lead developer**

The ETL lead developer supervises the implementation activities of the ETL portion of the BI application. He or she works with the operations staff to prepare the production environment and set up the production ETL program library. He or she should write the ETL portion of the operating procedures and the reference guide. He or she is also responsible for setting up the ETL process on the job scheduler.

◆ **Meta data administrator**
The meta data administrator is responsible for moving all the meta data repository programs into the production meta data repository program library. He or she also has to run the meta data migration (load) process and schedule ongoing data quality monitoring activities, such as gathering meta data metrics and performing data quality spot checks.

◆ **Meta data repository developers**
The meta data repository developers assist the meta data administrator with moving all the meta data repository programs into the production meta data repository program library.

◆ **Web developers**
The Web developers are responsible for moving their Web pages and scripts from their local servers to the production Web server.

◆ **Web master**
The Web master is responsible for setting up the production Web server. He or she also has to work with the staff of security services and network services to install and test the firewall and other required security features.

RISKS OF NOT PERFORMING STEP 15

If you got this far, you will obviously deploy your BI application. If you perform this step with diligence, you can be reasonably assured that the BI decision-support environment will be as stable, robust, and secure as any other production environment. If you perform this step hastily, you run the risk that your BI decision-support environment will not be the robust and secure environment the business people expect it to be.

BIBLIOGRAPHY AND ADDITIONAL READING

Bischoff, Joyce, and Ted Alexander. *Data Warehouse: Practical Advice from the Experts.* Upper Saddle River, NJ: Prentice Hall, 1997.

Corey, Michael J., and Michael Abbey. *Oracle Data Warehousing: A Practical Guide to Successful Data Warehouse Analysis, Build, and Roll-out.* Berkeley, CA: Osborne McGraw-Hill, 1997.

Imhoff, Claudia, Lisa Loftis, and Jonathan G. Geiger. *Building the Customer-Centric Enterprise: Data Warehousing Techniques for Supporting Customer Relationship Management.* New York: John Wiley & Sons, 2001.

Inmon, William H. *Building the Data Warehouse.* New York: John Wiley & Sons, 1996.

Inmon, William H., Claudia Imhoff, and Greg Battas. *Building the Operational Data Store.* New York: John Wiley & Sons, 1996.

Inmon, William H., Claudia Imhoff, and Ryan Sousa. *Corporate Information Factory.* New York: John Wiley & Sons, 1998.

Inmon, William H., J. D. Welch, and Katherine L. Glassey. *Managing the Data Warehouse: Practical Techniques for Monitoring Operations and Performance, Administering Data and Tools and Managing Change and Growth.* New York: John Wiley & Sons, 1997.

Kimball, Ralph, and Richard Merz. *The Data Webhouse Toolkit: Building the Web-Enabled Data Warehouse.* New York: John Wiley & Sons, 2000.

Kimball, Ralph, Laura Reeves, Margy Ross, and Warren Thornthwaite. *The Data Warehouse Lifecycle Toolkit: Expert Methods for Designing, Developing, and Deploying Data Warehouses.* New York: John Wiley & Sons, 1998.

The Information Systems Audit and Control Association & Foundation: *http://www.isaca.org*

Information Systems Control Journal: *http://www.isaca.com*

MIS Training Institute: *http://www.misti.com*

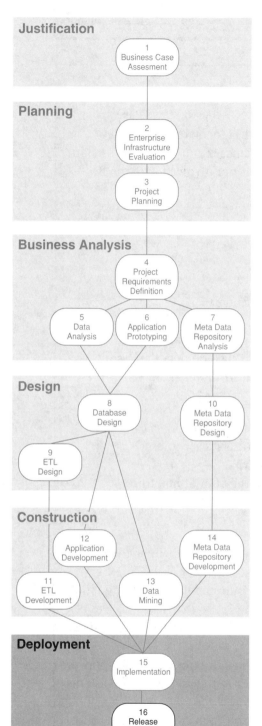

Justification

1
Business Case
Assesment

Planning

2
Enterprise
Infrastructure
Evaluation

3
Project
Planning

Business Analysis

4
Project
Requirements
Definition

5
Data
Analysis

6
Application
Prototyping

7
Meta Data
Repository
Analysis

Design

8
Database
Design

10
Meta Data
Repository
Design

9
ETL
Design

Construction

12
Application
Development

14
Meta Data
Repository
Development

11
ETL
Development

13
Data
Mining

Deployment

15
Implementation

16
Release
Evaluation

CHAPTER SIXTEEN

Step 16: Release Evaluation

CHAPTER OVERVIEW

This chapter covers the following topics:

- Things to consider about release evaluation

- Guidelines for using the application release concept when developing BI applications

- How to organize a post-implementation review meeting, including when and where to schedule the session, who to invite, and what to discuss

- The process flow of a post-implementation review session, including responsibilities for conducting the meeting

- Brief descriptions of the activities involved in release evaluation, the deliverables resulting from those activities, and the roles involved

- The risks of not performing Step 16

THINGS TO CONSIDER

Post-Implementation Review

✓ How soon after the rollout should we schedule a formal project review?
✓ Should the business sponsor or the project manager run the review session? Or should we ask a trained facilitator who was not involved with the BI project to facilitate the review session?
✓ Who should attend the review session?
✓ Should it be held offsite? Where?
✓ Who will prepare and distribute the agenda?
✓ What topics should appear on the agenda?
✓ Who will be responsible for taking notes?
✓ Will we invite stakeholders from other departments?
✓ Will we invite the data owners?
✓ Who will track the assigned action items? The project manager?
✓ How will we communicate to other teams and stakeholders the lessons we learned from the review? Who else can benefit from this review?

Measures of Success

✓ Is the business sponsor satisfied with the BI application?
✓ Do the business people like the BI application? Is it easy to use?
✓ What do they like? What do they dislike? Why?
✓ Are they using the meta data repository? Do they find it helpful?
✓ Is the business sponsor willing to support another BI application?

Plans for the Next Release

✓ Do we have leftover requirements that did not get implemented due to time constraints or other project constraints?
✓ Do we know how we want to address these requirements? Will they go into the next release? Will they be reprioritized?
✓ Are we planning another release of this BI application for the same business area?
✓ Are we switching to a different department and a different business sponsor?
✓ Do we want to invite the new business sponsor to the review session as one of the stakeholders?
✓ Are we prepared to split the core team into two groups the next time so we can work on two BI projects at the same time?
✓ Who will continue with the next release of this BI application?
✓ Who will lead the new BI project for the new business sponsor?

Building a BI decision-support environment is a never-ending process. Unlike most operational systems, which have sharply defined functionalities, BI applications must evolve to handle emerging information needs. As the needs and goals of your organization change, so must the BI decision-support environment. There is no practical way to anticipate all possible questions in the initial design of the BI decision-support environment or of any BI application. The best you can do at any given time is to have an environment that supports the current organizational goals and that can be easily adapted to new goals. Plan to design flexible and easy-to-change BI applications so that you have the ability to modify them when the organization's goals change. This applies to all BI initiatives, from small departmental data marts to large industrial-strength enterprise data warehouses. Be prepared to modify all BI applications and BI target databases in future releases in order to provide new query and reporting capabilities and more data.

THE APPLICATION RELEASE CONCEPT

BI projects introduce many new practices: new techniques for business analytics, new prototyping techniques, new design techniques, new architectures, and new technologies. These practices are relatively new not only to organizations but also to the information technology (IT) industry as a whole. In addition, BI projects usually involve a significant level of capital investment. All of these factors add up to make IT managers and business executives quite anxious. When a BI application does not turn out flawless or is not complete on its initial implementation, some IT managers and business executives get very unnerved.

A major shift must occur in how IT managers and business executives approach BI projects. The approach of "get it right the first time" has never worked, even though people have pretended for years that it does—or that it should. That misconception should have been put to rest long ago. No major invention or significant endeavor has ever worked right the first time. Usually, good things evolve over time. Nature evolves. This fact is generally accepted. Technology evolves (Figure 16.1), and this fact is also accepted. But the truth that software evolves as well is usually not accepted, at least not when the software is developed in-house.

When software is purchased from a vendor, it seems to be more palatable to accept an imperfect and evolving product because a software vendor never promises that the first product release will be the last. Vendors also never claim that

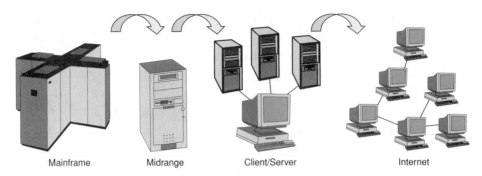

Figure 16.1: Evolving Technologies

their software products will not have to be enhanced; on the contrary, we want them to be enhanced. Why, then, do we have exact opposite expectations of internally developed software?

For example, when vendors publish a new release of their products, they include new functionality, new screens, new modules—and of course some fixes to defective parts of the prior release. Sometimes, the new software release is completely redesigned and is not even compatible with the previous release. We do not hesitate to pay good money to upgrade purchased software products under those conditions. But when the in-house IT technicians have to redesign a BI target database or portions of a BI application after the third or fourth release, the situation is treated like a disaster. Organizations must accept the fact that internally developed applications evolve over time, just as vendor software products do. Hence, it is high time to embrace the application release concept.

Guidelines for Using the Release Concept

When developing BI applications under the release concept, IT and business management must agree on and follow some basic guidelines (Table 16.1). When following these guidelines, there should never be any concern about the completeness of a BI application on its initial release. Any incomplete functionality that was negotiated out of the scope due to unforeseen roadblocks will be bundled with new functionality in the next release or some future release. Business management gets to decide how long to defer the functionality, and the decision will probably be based on the priorities of outstanding requirements.

Table 16.1: BI Application Release Guidelines

Dos and Don'ts of Application Releases
• Releases should be delivered every three to six months (the first release will take longer).
• Releases must have very small and manageable deliverables.
• Expectations regarding deliverables must be managed continuously and must remain realistic.
• A release does not have to equal a completed BI application. It may take several releases to complete a BI application.
• The first release of a BI application should deliver only the basics.
• Business management must be willing to accept a partial delivery of a BI application (e. g., the basics).
• Nothing is cast in concrete. Everything is negotiable. That includes scope, schedule, budget, resources, and quality.
• The enterprise infrastructure, both technical and nontechnical, must be robust.
• Meta data must be an integral part of each release; otherwise, the releases will not be manageable.
• The development process must be sound and flexible. Developing releases feels like prototyping, but the effort is more disciplined and controlled because the results are treated as production-worthy deliverables.
• Designs, programs, and tools must be flexible to allow for occasional redesigns of BI target databases and BI applications.
• New requirements must be triaged and prioritized; scope is strictly controlled and kept small for every BI release.
• Small errors or defects are addressed under strict change-control procedures during the development of the release.
• Large errors or defects are deferred to another release by removing the function or data associated with the problem.
• When deferred functions or data are implemented in a future release, business management must prioritize the sequence of delivering the deferred requirements.

If time is a critical project constraint, using the release concept to deliver a partial application of high quality is much better than delivering a completed application with many defects and dirty data.

POST-IMPLEMENTATION REVIEWS

A post-implementation review should be conducted after every BI project, regardless of whether the BI application runs perfectly or has problems. It is imperative to learn from each project in order to improve the quality as well as the speed of the development process for future BI applications.

A post-implementation review session is also an excellent forum for IT managers and business executives to become comfortable with the dynamic development process and the release concept of BI applications. In addition, the review session is an ideal venue for sharing the lessons learned with other project teams as well as with other business managers in the organization. This goes a long way toward making the necessary culture shift more natural and acceptable.

Topics to be reviewed can include schedule, budget, satisfaction, scope, negotiation skills, staffing, skills and training, project planning and reporting, and development approach (methodology), as well as contractors, consultants, and vendors or any other general topic. Table 16.2 lists some suggested review questions for those topics.

Table 16.2: Suggested Post-Implementation Review Questions

Post-Implementation Review Topics
Schedule
• Did the project come in on time?
• If not, why not? Was the schedule realistic? What slowed us down?
• How can we prevent delays next time?
Budget
• Did the project come in within budget?
• If not, why not? Was the budget realistic?
• How can we prevent cost overruns next time?

(Continued)

Table 16.2: *(Continued)*

Post-Implementation Review Topics

Satisfaction
- Are we achieving the benefits we expected in terms of the return on investment (ROI)?
- Are the online analytical processing (OLAP) tool and other access and analysis tools satisfying the analytical business needs?

Scope
- Were scope changes requested during the project? Were scope changes made as a result of prototyping?
- Was the impact analyzed and measured? What was the impact? Could it have been avoided?
- What did we learn about scope changes and the existing change-control procedure?

Negotiation Skills
- Were all requested functions and data implemented? Did the scope have to be renegotiated?
- Did other project constraints have to be renegotiated (time, quality, resources, budget)?
- Was the renegotiating process painless, or did it create friction between the business people and IT staff?
- What needs to be done to improve the renegotiating process?

Staffing
- Did we lose any key people during the project?
- Why did they leave? What was the impact of their departure?
- How can we avoid that type of loss in the future?
- Was the core team staffed properly? Were there too few or too many team members?
- Were the roles and responsibilities assigned appropriately?
- Did the team members work well together? Was there friction? If so, what was the reason for the friction?
- How can we increase team spirit and team morale in the future?

Skills and Training
- Were the skills of the team members sufficient? Was "just enough and just in time" training provided or was "emergency training" required during the project?
- Was the provided training effective? What should be done differently next time?

(Continued)

Table 16.2: *(Continued)*

Post-Implementation Review Topics

Project Planning and Reporting
- Did the team report "actual time" truthfully? If not, why not?
- Were the activities estimated correctly? If not, do we know why they were overestimated or underestimated?
- Does our procedure for tracking time and reporting project status work? How can we improve it?
- What other lessons did we learn about project planning, tracking, and reporting?

Development Approach
- Did we select the appropriate steps, activities, and tasks from *Business Intelligence Roadmap*? If not, why not?
- Were important tasks left out? Were unnecessary tasks included?
- Did we use the operational prototype approach for application development? Did it work? What were the benefits?

Contractors, Consultants, and Vendors
- Did we effectively use outside consultants or contractors?
- Did they transfer their knowledge to our staff?
- What lessons did we learn from negotiating with vendors?
- Did the vendors follow the rules or try to go around them? How can we control that situation in the future?

General
- Was communication effective?
- Were business people available when needed?
- What other lessons did we learn? What should be done differently next time?

Organizing a Post-Implementation Review

Consider the following items when organizing a project review.

- **How to prepare for the review:** The project manager has to take some time to prepare for the review by:
  - Examining the issues log to see which issues were effectively resolved and which were not
  - Assessing the change-control procedure for its effectiveness
  - Reviewing the project plan to determine whether all the appropriate tasks were included

- Studying the estimated and actual task completion times on the project plan to determine which tasks were underestimated and which were overestimated
- Noting any problems with the technology platform, such as problems with tools or their vendors, hardware, network, and so on
- Reviewing the budget to see if the actual expenditures came close to the estimated ones
- Assessing the effectiveness of the training sessions

All of these items are potential topics for discussion at the review.

- **When to schedule the review:** It is advisable to wait for two months after going into production before holding a formal review of the BI application. This will give the project team time to iron out all the glitches that are common during the first few weeks after "going live." It will also give the project manager and the business sponsor time to:
  - Review the project charter, project plan, project reports, project activities, and budget
  - Collect information and metrics about the usage of the BI application, the BI target databases, and the meta data repository
  - Organize the meeting

- **Where to hold the review:** The review session should be held offsite. Pagers and cell phones should be used for emergencies only; they should not ring during the session. The room should be set up as a conference room supplied with:
  - Several flipcharts
  - An overhead or data projector
  - Markers and masking tape
  - Two laptops, one for the facilitator and one for the scribe
  - Coffee—lots of strong coffee

- **How long the review should last:** A well-organized, thorough review usually lasts two full days, especially for the first release of a new BI application. However, if time is in short supply, or if the release was small in scope and effort with no significant hurdles, one full day could be scheduled with the option of a follow-up session within two weeks if necessary.

- **Who should attend the review:** All team members from the core team and the extended team should be invited to participate in the review. They must be prepared to contribute. That means they must review the agenda and prepare to discuss the topics listed on it. They must also review any documents sent to them ahead of time and be prepared to discuss them. In short, every project team member should be an active participant!

- **What to discuss during the review:** A preliminary agenda should be published about four weeks before the scheduled review session.
  - The preliminary agenda should list all topics, including introduction and wrap-up, with estimated time allocations for each topic.
  - The time estimates must take into account the complexity of the topic and the number of people participating.
  - Everyone who is invited should be given the opportunity to add to the agenda and submit any pertinent documents to be reviewed.
  - About two weeks before the review session, the final agenda and all documents should be sent to the attendees.

Post-Implementation Review Session Flow

Post-implementation reviews are very structured and follow a prescribed procedure by which the group must abide. Figure 16.2 illustrates the typical flow of a review session.

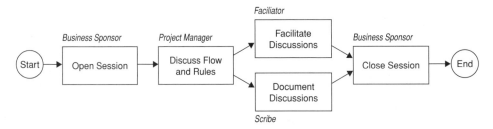

Figure 16.2: Post-Implementation Review Session Flow

Certain people conduct certain parts of the meeting (Figure 16.3), as described briefly below.

- The *business sponsor* should open the meeting and give an introduction before turning the meeting over to the project manager. At the end of the session, the business sponsor should close the meeting.

- The *project manager* should discuss the flow, the rules, and the expectations of the review, then turn the meeting over to a skilled facilitator.

- The *facilitator* should lead the group through the topics on the agenda. The facilitator's responsibilities include the following:
  - Asking the person who owns a topic on the agenda to introduce the topic
  - Soliciting comments and feedback from the other participants

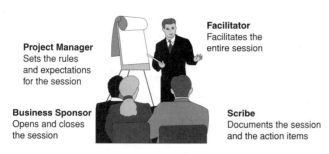

Project Manager
Sets the rules
and expectations
for the session

Facilitator
Facilitates the
entire session

Business Sponsor
Opens and closes
the session

Scribe
Documents the session
and the action items

Figure 16.3: Conducting a Post-Implementation Review

- Assuring that the meeting does not get bogged down on any given topic
- Monitoring the allocated time for each topic and interrupting the discussion when the time limit has been reached, at which point the facilitator must temporarily turn the meeting over to the project manager for a decision (see below)
- The "*scribe*" is a person who was not involved with the BI project. The main purpose for having a third-party scribe is to have a knowledgeable but neutral note taker who:
  - Documents the highlights of all conversations and comments
  - Documents identified action items and to whom they were assigned

If more time is required for a topic, the project manager and the business sponsor must decide whether to continue the discussion beyond its allocated time or to cut the topic short and discuss the remaining topics on the agenda. In either case, a second meeting has to be called to either finish the discussion on the interrupted topic or to cover the other topics that had to be dropped from the agenda during this meeting.

At the end of the review session, all action items are reviewed, and the person to whom an action item was assigned estimates a completion date or a reply date (the date on which an estimate will be provided for the effort to complete the action item). The group must decide who will get the task to follow up on the action items and whether another meeting is necessary (and if so, how soon).

RELEASE EVALUATION ACTIVITIES

The activities for release evaluation do not need to be performed linearly. Figure 16.4 indicates which activities can be performed concurrently. The list below briefly describes the activities associated with Step 16, Release Evaluation.

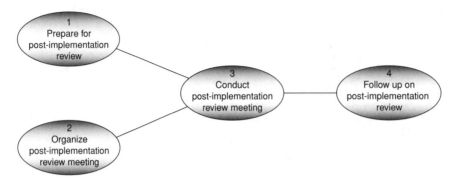

Figure 16.4: Release Evaluation Activities

1. **Prepare for the post-implementation review.**
   All aspects of the completed project are subject to review. That includes strategies, plans, documents, designs, deliverables, procedures, and infrastructure. The goal of the review is to get an accounting of what worked well on the project and what did not, and to produce a list of action items to implement changes to the development process.

2. **Organize the post-implementation review meeting.**
   Prepare a list of discussion topics and an agenda, and distribute them to all attendees. The agenda should list the date, time, place, attendees, and topics to be discussed. Appoint a facilitator and scribe, and find a venue for the session.

3. **Conduct the post-implementation review meeting.**
   The business sponsor should open and close the review session. The project manager should explain the agenda, the rules of the meeting, and the roles of the facilitator and the scribe. The scribe should document all discussion points, which must be reviewed at the end of the session. Assign any action items that come up during the session.

4. **Follow up on the post-implementation review.**
   Action items are usually assigned to the attendees, but they can occasionally be delegated to staff other than the attendees. In either case, someone must follow up on the action items to ensure that they are performed. Action items can include updating the standards or the methodology, revising estimating guidelines, seeking resolution to a business problem, or repairing an urgent problem that cannot wait for the next release. Prioritize functions or data dropped from the scope due to constraints on the BI project so you can bundle them with future releases.

Deliverables Resulting from These Activities

1. **Post-implementation review agenda**

   The agenda is the "program" for the review session. It lists the date, time, and place of the meeting; invited attendees; topics for review; and questions to be discussed.

2. **Post-implementation review meeting minutes**

   This short document highlights all the discussions, suggestions, and resolutions regarding the topics and questions on the agenda.

3. **Action item list**

   The action item list briefly describes each action item, noting to whom an action item was assigned and showing a projected completion date (or response date) for each action item.

Roles Involved in These Activities

◆ **Application lead developer**

   The application lead developer should be prepared to discuss access and analysis issues on the review agenda. He or she may also actively participate in discussions regarding database design, tool selection, and technical infrastructure. Topics such as OLAP tools, ease of use, reports, and the extraction of data into private data sets require input from the application lead developer as well.

◆ **BI infrastructure architect**

   The BI infrastructure architect should be prepared to discuss the technical infrastructure components, such as servers, network, the database management system (DBMS), and the various tools. In addition, the BI infrastructure architect should be able to address the scalability of the current platform and the plans for expanding the platform for future BI application releases.

◆ **Business representative**

   The business representative who was involved in the BI project provides his or her opinions—from a business person's perspective—about the development process. He or she may comment on budgetary issues, the project plan, the overall management of the project, the effectiveness of his or her own contribution to the project, testing activities, or on any other topic he or she feels could be improved.

◆ **Business sponsor**

The business sponsor spearheads the BI project from its inception to its implementation and initiates the post-implementation review. He or she sends the invitation to the attendees, prepares opening remarks for the review, and closes the session.

◆ **Data administrator**

The data administrator must be prepared to discuss the data requirements and the business decisions made during the requirements and analysis activities. The data administrator should review the procedure used for resolving data disputes and make recommendations for improving it. He or she can also contribute to discussions about the nontechnical infrastructure.

◆ **Data mining expert**

The data mining expert should be prepared to suggest any necessary improvements to the BI application (or the BI decision-support environment as a whole) that could enhance the use of the data mining tool. These suggestions could involve discussions about the extract/transform/load (ETL) process, the cleanliness of the data, and the completeness of the data, as well as any limitations the current technologies impose on data mining activities.

◆ **Data quality analyst**

The data quality analyst should be a very active participant on the topics of source data analysis and data cleansing. He or she must be prepared to present a summary of data quality problems. This summary should include the impact of the bad data on the BI application as well as on the operational systems. The data quality analyst must also explain what type of cleansing is being performed in the ETL process. He or she should send out a document before the meeting that lists the data elements not being cleansed, indicating whether they are being rejected or moved into the BI target databases as is. He or she should also be able to discuss the current triage procedure for prioritizing the source data for cleansing.

◆ **Database administrator**

The database administrator must be prepared to discuss the design and content of the BI target databases and how to navigate through them. If one of the session topics is database design or database performance, it is the database administrator's responsibility to explain the database design decisions made during the project.

◆ **Developers**

All developers, whether ETL developers, application developers, meta data repository developers, or Web developers, should be encouraged to share their experiences with the development process. This could include discussions about methodology, status reporting, technical infrastructure components, testing procedures, and any other topics directly related to their development activities.

◆ **ETL lead developer**

The ETL lead developer should be prepared to discuss the data transformations being performed in the ETL process. He or she must be able to explain how the data from the source systems is being reconciled to the BI target databases and where the reconciliation totals can be viewed. On the technical side, the ETL lead developer may actively participate in platform scalability and tool discussions.

◆ **Facilitator (not on the BI project team)**

The facilitator must be someone who was not directly involved with the project. This person must have training in facilitation. His or her responsibilities include time-boxing questions and discussion topics, halting runaway discussions, keeping on schedule with the agenda, giving turns to attendees to speak, and in general "directing traffic" at the review meeting.

◆ **Meta data administrator**

The meta data administrator must be prepared to discuss what meta data is available and how to access it. He or she should send out a document with meta data examples prior to the meeting. The meta data administrator should also walk through the ETL load metrics that are being captured in the meta data repository, such as ETL reconciliation totals, trapped data error totals, and data quality (reliability) statistics.

◆ **Project manager**

The project manager is primarily responsible for organizing the review session. This includes finding a venue, creating the agenda, shipping documents to be reviewed during the session, scheduling the session, arranging for a facilitator and a scribe, and following up on action items.

◆ **Scribe (not on the BI project team)**

The scribe's main responsibility is to document the review discussions. The scribe writes and distributes the minutes of the meeting, prepares and distributes the action item list, and helps with other administrative activities.

◆ **Stakeholders** (including data owners)

Occasionally other stakeholders may want to participate in the post-implementation review. Stakeholders could be business people from other departments, the data owners of the operational source data, or IT staff from other BI applications who want to benefit from the lessons learned. Stakeholders could also be staff from operations, technical support, or the help desk. In general, stakeholders (with the exception of the data owners) do not actively participate in the review discussions.

◆ **Subject matter expert**

The subject matter expert is an active participant who represents the business view during the review discussions. Topics of data quality, meta data, ease of use, and problem resolution procedures should be of particular interest to this person. The subject matter expert may also contribute to the discussions regarding cost justification, the measurement of ROI, the impact on operational systems, and potential improvements to business processes.

◆ **Web master**

The Web master must be prepared to review the Web application issues and to answer questions regarding data access capabilities through the Web, as well as data security on the Web server. If some data is accessible globally through the Internet, the Web master should invite the security officer to the meeting to answer global security and privacy questions raised during the review session.

RISKS OF NOT PERFORMING STEP 16

As George Santayana once said, "Those who cannot remember the past are condemned to repeat it."[1] This statement applies to BI projects as much as it does to life and politics. In order to know how to improve the next project, you have to learn from the mistakes made on the last project. The post-implementation review is the vehicle for discovering the mistakes and correcting them. Excluding this step would result in repeating the same mistakes in a rapidly growing environment that affects more people with each release. We have learned from experience that correcting mistakes on small systems is much easier than correcting mistakes on large systems. The BI decision-support environment can quickly become a very large system!

---

1. Santayana, George. *Life of Reason, Reason in Common Sense.* Scribner's, 1905, p. 284.

BIBLIOGRAPHY AND ADDITIONAL READING

Adelman, Sid, and Larissa Terpeluk Moss. *Data Warehouse Project Management.* Boston, MA: Addison-Wesley, 2000.

Beck, Kent. *Extreme Programming Explained: Embrace Change.* Boston, MA: Addison-Wesley, 2000.

Cockburn, Alistair. *Agile Software Development.* Boston, MA: Addison-Wesley, 2002.

DeMarco, Tom. *Slack: Getting Past Burnout, Busywork, and the Myth of Total Efficiency.* New York: Broadway Books, 2001.

English, Larry P. *Improving Data Warehouse and Business Information Quality: Methods for Reducing Costs and Increasing Profits.* New York: John Wiley & Sons, 1999.

Humphrey, Watts S. *Winning with Software: An Executive Strategy.* Boston, MA: Addison-Wesley, 2002.

Inmon, William H., J. D. Welch, and Katherine L. Glassey. *Managing the Data Warehouse: Practical Techniques for Monitoring Operations and Performance, Administering Data and Tools and Managing Change and Growth.* New York: John Wiley & Sons, 1997.

Kuan-Tsae, Huang, Yang W. Lee, and Richard Y. Wang. *Quality Information and Knowledge.* Upper Saddle River, NJ: Prentice Hall, 1999.

Yourdon, Edward. *Death March.* Upper Saddle River, NJ: Prentice Hall, 1997.

PART II

At a Glance

CHAPTER SEVENTEEN

Human Resource Allocation Matrix

 Listed in this matrix are roles, not people! Multiple roles can and probably will be assigned to one individual; occasionally, one role may be assigned to multiple individuals.

Development Step [a]	Vital Roles Involved in the Step [b]
1. Business Case Assessment	◆ Business representative ◆ Business sponsor ◆ Data quality analyst ◆ Project manager ◆ Subject matter expert
2. Enterprise Infrastructure Evaluation	
Section A. Technical Infrastructure Evaluation	◆ BI infrastructure architect ◆ Database administrator
Section B. Nontechnical Infrastructure Evaluation	◆ BI infrastructure architect ◆ Data administrator ◆ Data quality analyst ◆ Meta data administrator

a. Steps that can be performed in parallel are boxed together to indicate potential overallocation of resources, depending on how the roles are assigned (if different overlapping roles are assigned to the same person).

b. Only the roles that perform vital development work are listed. Supporting roles, such as data owner, IT auditor, network services, technical support, and so on are not listed in this matrix.

Human Resource Allocation Matrix

Development Step	Vital Roles Involved in the Step
3. Project Planning	◆ Application lead developer ◆ Business representative ◆ Data administrator ◆ Data quality analyst ◆ Database administrator ◆ ETL lead developer ◆ Meta data administrator ◆ Project manager ◆ Subject matter expert
4. Project Requirements Definition	◆ Application lead developer ◆ Business representative ◆ Data administrator ◆ Data quality analyst ◆ Meta data administrator ◆ Subject matter expert

Human Resource Allocation Matrix

Development Step	Vital Roles Involved in the Step
5. Data Analysis	◆ Business representative
	◆ Data administrator
	◆ Data quality analyst
	◆ ETL lead developer
	◆ Meta data administrator
	◆ Stakeholders (including data owners)
	◆ Subject matter expert
6. Application Prototyping	◆ Application lead developer
	◆ Business representative
	◆ Database administrator
	◆ Stakeholders
	◆ Subject matter expert
	◆ Web master
7. Meta Data Repository Analysis	◆ Data administrator
	◆ Meta data administrator
	◆ Subject matter expert

Human Resource Allocation Matrix

Development Step	Vital Roles Involved in the Step
8. Database Design	◆ Application lead developer ◆ Data administrator ◆ Database administrator ◆ ETL lead developer
9. Extract/Transform/Load Design[c]	◆ Data quality analyst ◆ Database administrator ◆ ETL lead developer ◆ Subject matter expert
10. Meta Data Repository Design	◆ BI infrastructure architect ◆ Data administrator ◆ Meta data administrator

c. Although all design activities can be started and performed in parallel, the design of the BI target databases must be finalized before the design of the ETL process can be completed. This mainly affects the time allocation for the database administrator, who must actively participate in both steps.

Human Resource Allocation Matrix

Development Step	Vital Roles Involved in the Step
11. Extract/Transform/Load Development	◆ Business representative
	◆ Database administrator
	◆ ETL developers
	◆ ETL lead developer
	◆ Subject matter expert
	◆ Testers
12. Application Development	◆ Application developers
	◆ Application lead developer
	◆ Business representative
	◆ Database administrator
	◆ Subject matter expert
	◆ Testers
	◆ Web developers
	◆ Web master
13. Data Mining	◆ Business representative
	◆ Data mining expert
	◆ Database administrator
	◆ Subject matter expert
14. Meta Data Repository Development	◆ Business representative
	◆ Database administrator
	◆ Meta data administrator
	◆ Meta data repository developers
	◆ Testers

Human Resource Allocation Matrix

Development Step	Vital Roles Involved in the Step
15. Implementation	◆ Application developers ◆ Application lead developer ◆ Data mining expert ◆ Database administrator ◆ ETL developers ◆ ETL lead developer ◆ Meta data administrator ◆ Meta data repository developers ◆ Web developers ◆ Web master

Human Resource Allocation Matrix

Development Step	Vital Roles Involved in the Step
16. Release Evaluation	◆ Application lead developer
	◆ BI infrastructure architect
	◆ Business representative
	◆ Business sponsor
	◆ Data administrator
	◆ Data mining expert
	◆ Data quality analyst
	◆ Database administrator
	◆ Developers (ETL, application, meta data repository, and Web)
	◆ ETL lead developer
	◆ Facilitator (not on the BI project team)
	◆ Meta data administrator
	◆ Project manager
	◆ Scribe (not on the BI project team)
	◆ Stakeholders (including data owners)
	◆ Subject matter expert
	◆ Web master

CHAPTER EIGHTEEN

Entry & Exit Criteria and Deliverables Matrix

Development Step	Entry Criteria	Exit Criteria	Deliverables

1. Business Case Assessment	1. Strategic business goals of the organization
	2. Strategic plan for the overall BI decision-support initiative
	3. Objectives of the BI application
	4. Business problem or business opportunity
	5. Unfulfilled application requirements from a prior release
	6. Request for infrastructure changes (technical as well as nontechnical)
		1. Project endorsement (from IT and business executive management)
		2. Identified business sponsor (and an alternate sponsor, if possible)
		3. Identified business representative for the core team
		4. Requirements for the next release (new requirements or those deferred from a prior release)
			1. Business case assessment report documenting:
			  – Executive summary
			  – Strategic business goals of the organization
			  – Objectives of the proposed BI application
			  – Statement of the business need (business problem or business opportunity)
			  – Explanation of how the BI application will satisfy that need
			  – Ramifications for *not* addressing the business need and not committing to the proposed BI solution
			  – Cost-benefit analysis results
			  – Risk assessment
			  – Recommendations

Entry & Exit Criteria and Deliverables Matrix   —   Development Step 2:   Enterprise Infrastructure Evaluation

Development Step	Entry Criteria	Exit Criteria	Deliverables
2. Enterprise Infrastructure Evaluation Section A. Technical Infrastructure Evaluation	1. Objectives of the BI application 2. Statement of the business problem or business opportunity 3. Project endorsement (from IT and business executive management) 4. Identified business sponsor (and an alternate sponsor, if possible) 5. Request for technical infrastructure changes 6. Proposed BI solution	1. Compatibility issues and solutions for them 2. Product and vendor evaluations 3. Licensed (purchased) products or upgrades	1. Technical infrastructure assessment report, covering: – Servers and operating systems – Client workstations – Middleware (especially DBMS gateways) – Custom interfaces – Network components – Bandwidth – DBMS functionality and utilities (backup and recovery, performance monitoring) – Development tools (ETL, OLAP) – Meta data repository – Product evaluation scores – Vendor evaluation scores – Recommendations for product licensing (purchase) 2. Installation of selected products

Entry & Exit Criteria and Deliverables Matrix   —   Development Step 2: Enterprise Infrastructure Evaluation (continued)

Development Step	Entry Criteria	Exit Criteria	Deliverables
2. Enterprise Infrastructure Evaluation *(continued)*			
Section B. Nontechnical Infrastructure Evaluation	1. Objectives of the BI application 2. Statement of the business problem or business opportunity 3. Project endorsement (from IT and business executive management) 4. Identified business sponsor (and an alternate sponsor, if possible) 5. Request for nontechnical infrastructure changes 6. Proposed BI solution	1. Improved nontechnical infrastructure 2. Development guidelines for project core team	1. Nontechnical infrastructure assessment report with proposed improvements to: – Standards – Use of a development methodology – Estimating guidelines – Scope management (change control) procedure – Issues management procedure – Roles and responsibilities – Security process – Meta data capture and delivery process (business and technical meta data) – Process for merging logical data models into a single enterprise view – Data quality measures and triage process – Testing standards and procedures – Service-level agreements – Support function – Dispute resolution procedure – Communication process

Entry & Exit Criteria and Deliverables Matrix   —   Development Step 3:   Project Planning

Development Step	Entry Criteria	Exit Criteria	Deliverables
3. Project Planning	1. Objectives of the BI application 2. Statement of the business problem or business opportunity 3. Identified business sponsor (and an alternate sponsor, if possible) 4. Cost-benefit analysis 5. Risk assessment 6. Technical infrastructure gap analysis assessment 7. Nontechnical infrastructure gap analysis assessment 8. Requirements for the next release (new requirements or those deferred from a prior release)	1. Identified project team members and their levels of participation 2. Critical success factors 3. Measures of success 4. Approved BI project 5. Approved budget	1. Project charter with the sections: – Goals and objectives – Statement of the business problem – Proposed BI solution – Results from the cost-benefit analysis – Results from the infrastructure gap analysis (technical and nontechnical) – Functional project deliverables – Historical requirements – Subject area to be delivered – High-level logical data model – Items not in scope (originally requested but subsequently excluded) – Condition of source files and databases – Availability and security requirements – Access tool requirements – Roles and responsibilities – Team structure – Communication plan – Assumptions – Constraints – Risk assessment – Critical success factors 2. Project plan

Entry & Exit Criteria and Deliverables Matrix — Development Step 4: Project Requirements Definition

Development Step	Entry Criteria	Exit Criteria	Deliverables
4. Project Requirements Definition	1. Approved BI project 2. Project charter 3. Project plan 4. Identified business sponsor (and an alternate sponsor, if possible) 5. Business (process) ownership defined 6. Unfulfilled requirements from previous BI project 7. New requirements 8. Request for infrastructure changes (technical as well as nontechnical) 9. Critical success factors 10. Measures of success	1. Detailed project requirements (data and process) 2. Detailed infrastructure requirements (technical as well as nontechnical) 3. Selected internal and external data sources (operational files and databases)	1. Application requirements document, with the following sections: – Technical infrastructure requirements – Nontechnical infrastructure requirements – Reporting requirements – Ad hoc and canned query requirements – Requirements for source data, including history – High-level logical data model – Data-cleansing requirements – Security requirements – Preliminary service-level agreements

Entry & Exit Criteria and Deliverables Matrix — Development Step 5: Data Analysis

Development Step	Entry Criteria	Exit Criteria	Deliverables

5. Data Analysis	1. Approved project
	2. Project charter
	3. Project plan
	4. Business (process) ownership defined
	5. Data ownership defined
	6. Full-time availability of business representative, part-time availability of other business people, especially data owners
	7. Trained data modeler
	8. Application requirements document with detailed project requirements
	9. High-level logical data model (if available)
	10. List of data elements as well as source files and source databases
		1. Logically integrated data view from a business perspective
		2. Source data quality assessment
		3. Standardized business meta data for:
		  – Data names
		  – Data definitions
		  – Data relationships
		  – Data identifiers
		  – Data types
		  – Data lengths
		  – Data content (domain)
		  – Data rules
		  – Data policies
		  – Data ownership
			1. Normalized and fully attributed logical data model (project-specific) with:
			  – Kernel entities
			  – Associative entities
			  – Characteristic entities
			  – Cardinality and optionality
			  – Unique identifiers
			  – Attributes
			2. Business meta data:
			  – Data names and definitions
			  – Data relationships
			  – Unique identifiers
			  – Data types and lengths
			  – Domains
			  – Business rules and policies
			  – Data ownership
			3. Data-cleansing specifications
			4. Expanded enterprise logical data model*
			
			*Note: This deliverable is typically created by data administration behind the scenes of the BI project.

Entry & Exit Criteria and Deliverables Matrix   —   Development Step 6: Application Prototyping

Development Step	Entry Criteria	Exit Criteria	Deliverables
6. Application Prototyping	1. Project charter 2. Project plan 3. Application requirements document with detailed project requirements 4. Approval for prototyping 5. Sample reports that currently exist and are actively used 6. Sample mock-up report layouts for new reports 7. New or existing tools (report writers and query tools) 8. Full-time availability of business representative, part-time availability of other business people	1. Gap analysis of reporting needs and current reporting capabilities 2. Justification, benefits, and feasibility for BI application 3. Tool demo and verified tool functionality 4. Decision whether to license (buy) a new access and analysis tool (OLAP, report writer) 5. OLAP (or report writer) product and vendor evaluation 6. Installation of OLAP tool (or report writer)	1. Prototype charter with the following sections: – Primary purpose for the prototype (what requirement is being prototyped and why) – Prototype objectives (what type of prototype will be used, what will be proven or tested) – Prototype participants (IT and business people) – Data to be used for the prototype – Hardware and software platforms for the prototype – Measures of success (how you will know it was worth it) – Application interface agreement (standards, skills, ease of use) 2. Completed prototype 3. Revised application requirements document with detailed project requirements (data and functions) 4. Skills survey matrix 5. Issues log

Entry & Exit Criteria and Deliverables Matrix — Development Step 7: Meta Data Repository Analysis

Development Step	Entry Criteria	Exit Criteria	Deliverables

7. Meta Data Repository Analysis	1. Approved meta data repository project
	2. Requirements for a new meta data repository or for new functionality of the existing meta data repository
	3. Requirements for new meta data components
	4. Gap analysis of meta data already available versus meta data needed and not available
		1. Identified new meta data repository functionality
		2. Mapping between business meta data and technical meta data
		3. Updates to the revised application requirements document with detailed meta data repository requirements
			1. Logical meta model (new or enhanced) showing:
			  – Kernel entities
			  – Associative entities
			  – Characteristic entities
			  – Relationships
			  – Cardinality and optionality
			  – Unique identifiers
			  – Attributes
			2. Meta-meta data:
			  – Meta data names
			  – Meta data definitions
			  – Meta data relationships
			  – Unique identifiers
			  – Types and lengths
			  – Domains
			  – Business rules and policies
			  – Meta data ownership

Entry & Exit Criteria and Deliverables Matrix — Development Step 8: Database Design

Development Step	Entry Criteria	Exit Criteria	Deliverables
8. Database Design	1. Revised application requirements document with detailed project requirements (data and functions) 2. List of data elements as well as source files and source databases 3. Normalized and fully attributed logical data model (project-specific) 4. Expanded enterprise logical data model 5. Standardized business meta data	1. Database design schema: Entity-relationship design for: – Operational data store (ODS) – Enterprise data warehouse (EDW) – Data marts with detailed data for ad hoc reporting Multidimensional design for: – Data marts with aggregations and summarizations – Oper marts (operational data marts for patterned reporting) – Web warehouse with summarized click-stream data	1. Physical data model: – Tables and columns – Primary and foreign keys – Cardinality – Referential integrity rules – Indices 2. Physical design of BI target databases: – Dataset placement – Index placement – Partitioning – Clustering – Indexing 3. Data definition language (DDL) 4. Data control language (DCL) 5. Physical BI target databases 6. Database maintenance procedures

Entry & Exit Criteria and Deliverables Matrix — Development Step 9: Extract/Transform/Load Design

Development Step	Entry Criteria	Exit Criteria	Deliverables

9. Extract/Transform/Load Design	1. Revised application requirements document with detailed project requirements (data and functions)
	
	2. List of data elements as well as source files and source databases (both internal and external)
	
	3. Business meta data
	
	4. Data-cleansing specifications
	
	5. Physical BI target databases
		1. Expected performance of ETL process
		
		2. Identified meta data to be produced by the ETL process:
		  – Load statistics
		  – Data quality metrics
		  – Reconciliation totals
		
		3. Decision whether to license (buy) an ETL tool
		
		4. ETL product and vendor evaluation
		
		5. Installation of ETL tool
			1. Source-to-target mapping document with transformation specifications for:
			  – Data transformations
			  – Data cleansing
			  – Referential integrity checking
			  – Reconciliation and error handling
			  – Algorithms for aggregations and summarizations
			
			2. ETL process flow diagram showing process dependencies among:
			  – Program modules
			  – Temporary and permanent work files and tables
			  – Sort, merge, and load utilities
			
			3. ETL program design document for three sets of ETL programs:
			  – Initial load
			  – Historical load
			  – Incremental load
			
			4. Staging area with:
			  – Program libraries
			  – Allocated disk space for temporary and permanent work files and tables

Entry & Exit Criteria and Deliverables Matrix   —   Development Step 10: Meta Data Repository Design

Development Step	Entry Criteria	Exit Criteria	Deliverables

10. Meta Data Repository Design	1. Revised application requirements document with detailed meta data repository requirements
	
	2. New or enhanced logical meta model for the meta data repository
	
	3. Identified new meta data repository functionality
	
	4. Mapping (link) between business meta data and technical meta data
		1. New or enhanced meta data repository design
		
		2. Decision whether to license (buy) or build a meta data repository
		
		3. Meta data repository product and vendor evaluation
		
		4. Installation of meta data repository product
			1. Physical meta model:
			  – Tables and columns
			  – Primary and foreign keys
			  – Cardinality
			  – Referential integrity rules
			2. DDL for the meta data repository
			3. DCL for the meta data repository
			4. Meta data repository programming specifications for:
			  – Meta data extract and transformation programs
			  – Meta data load programs
			  – Tool interfaces
			  – Meta data reports and queries
			  – Access interfaces
			  – Online help function

Entry & Exit Criteria and Deliverables Matrix   —   Development Step 11: Extract/Transform/Load Development

Development Step	Entry Criteria	Exit Criteria	Deliverables

11. Extract/ Transform/Load Development	1. Source-to-target mapping document
	2. ETL process flow diagram showing process dependencies
	3. ETL program design document
	4. Staging area
		1. Fully functioning ETL process
		2. Fully tested ETL programs or ETL tool modules:
		  – Integration tested or regression tested
		  – Performance tested
		  – Quality assurance tested
		  – Acceptance tested
			1. ETL test plan with test cases
			2. ETL programs or instructions for the ETL tool to:
			  – Extract source data
			  – Transform source data
			  – Load data into BI target databases (unless a DBMS utility is used)
			3. ETL program library with fully functioning ETL programs and scripts (or ETL tool library with fully functioning ETL tool modules)

Entry & Exit Criteria and Deliverables Matrix   —   Development Step 12: Application Development

Development Step	Entry Criteria	Exit Criteria	Deliverables
12. Application Development	1. Completed prototype with partial application functionality (optional) 2. Revised application requirements document with detailed project requirements (data and functions) 3. Sample reports that currently exist and are actively used 4. Sample mock-up report layouts for new reports 5. New or existing tools (report writers and query tools) 6. Physical BI target databases	1. Fully functioning access and analysis components of the BI application (application programs) 2. Fully tested application programs or OLAP functions: – Integration or regression tested – Performance tested – Quality assurance tested – Acceptance tested	1. Application design document containing: – Report layouts – Screen designs – Interface designs – Programming specs – Calculations for reports and queries – Online help function 2. Application test plan with test cases 3. Application programs or OLAP functions for the access and analysis components of the BI application 4. Application program library with fully functioning application programs and scripts (or OLAP tool library with fully functioning OLAP tool modules) 5. Training materials: – Presentation slides – Instructor notes – Student workbooks – Exercises and their solutions – Other pertinent handouts

Entry & Exit Criteria and Deliverables Matrix — Development Step 13: Data Mining

Development Step	Entry Criteria	Exit Criteria	Deliverables

13. Data Mining	1. Approved data mining initiative
	
	2. Objectives of the BI application
	
	3. Statement of the business problem or business opportunity
	
	4. Identified business sponsor (and an alternate sponsor, if possible)
	
	5. Data mining activities of the competition
	
	6. Dedicated data mining expert (statistician) to interpret the data mining results
	
	7. Data mining tool
		1. Requirements for pattern discovery in the data
		
		2. Data mining algorithms and operations
		
		3. Plan for measuring the results of data mining activities
		
		4. Knowledge discovery from data mining
		
		5. New marketing strategies to:
		  – Increase revenue
		  – Increase profit
		  – Decrease costs
		  – Increase market share
		  – Increase customer satisfaction
		
		6. New business strategies based on knowledge discovery
			1. Data mining database
			2. Analytical data model

Entry & Exit Criteria and Deliverables Matrix — Development Step 14: Meta Data Repository Development

Development Step	Entry Criteria	Exit Criteria	Deliverables

14. Meta Data Repository Development	1. Physical meta model (database design) for the meta data repository
	2. Meta data repository program specifications for:
	  – Populating the meta data repository
	  – Access and tool interfaces to the meta data repository
	  – Reporting from the meta data repository
	  – Online help function for the meta data repository
		1. Fully functioning meta data repository
		2. Fully tested meta data repository programs or meta data repository product modules:
		  – Integration or regression tested
		  – Acceptance tested (and quality assurance tested)
			1. Physical meta data repository database
			2. Meta data repository test plan with test cases
			3. Meta data repository programs or meta data repository product functions for:
			  – Meta data migration process (including tool interfaces)
			  – Meta data application (including access interfaces)
			  – Meta data repository online help function
			4. Meta data repository program library with fully functioning meta data repository programs and scripts (or fully functioning meta data repository product modules)
			5. Meta data repository production documentation:
			  – Operating procedure
			  – Reference guide
			6. Meta data repository training materials
			  – Presentation slides
			  – Instructor notes
			  – Student workbooks
			  – Exercises and their solutions
			  – Other pertinent handouts

Entry & Exit Criteria and Deliverables Matrix — Development Step 15: Implementation

Development Step	Entry Criteria	Exit Criteria	Deliverables

15. Implementation	1. ETL programs or instructions for the ETL tool
	
	2. Application programs (access and analysis) or OLAP functions
	
	3. Meta data repository programs or meta data repository product functions
	
	4. Physical BI target databases
	
	5. Physical meta data repository database
		1. Fully functioning production ETL process
		
		2. Fully functioning production BI application
		
		3. Fully functioning production meta data repository process
		
		4. Metrics for measuring success
			1. Production ETL program library with fully functioning ETL programs and scripts
			
			2. Production application program library with fully functioning application programs (access and analysis)
			
			3. Production meta data repository program library with fully functioning meta data repository programs
			
			4. Production BI target databases fully populated with initial and historical source data
			
			5. Production meta data repository database populated with business meta data, technical meta data, and ETL meta data (load statistics, reconciliation totals, data quality metrics)
			
			6. Production documentation:
			  – Operating procedures
			  – Reference guides

Entry & Exit Criteria and Deliverables Matrix — Development Step 16: Release Evaluation

Development Step	Entry Criteria	Exit Criteria	Deliverables

16. Release Evaluation	1. Project charter
	2. Project plan
	3. Issues log
	4. Availability of all project team members
	5. Measurements for:
	  – Data quality
	  – Ease of use
	  – Training effectiveness
	  – Business satisfaction
	  – Performance
	  – Return on investment
	6. Honest observations and assessments of project development approach
	7. Suggestions for improvement
		1. Evaluation of business satisfaction
		2. Lessons learned
		3. Process improvement items
		4. Repeatable success
			1. Post-implementation review agenda listing:
			  – Date and time of the meeting
			  – Place of the meeting
			  – Invited attendees
			  – Topics for review
			  – Questions to be discussed
			2. Post-implementation review meeting minutes recording:
			  – Highlights of discussions
			  – Suggestions and resolutions of agenda topics
			3. Action item list

CHAPTER NINETEEN

Activity Dependency Matrix

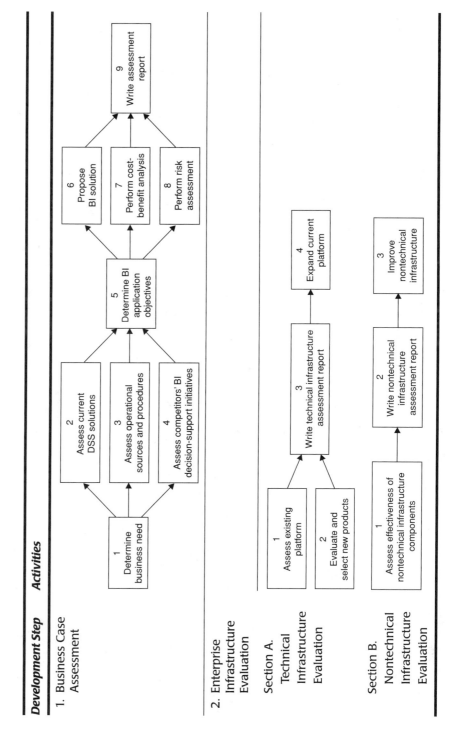

Development Step	Activities

1. Business Case Assessment

2. Enterprise Infrastructure Evaluation

Section A. Technical Infrastructure Evaluation

Section B. Nontechnical Infrastructure Evaluation

Activity Dependency Matrix

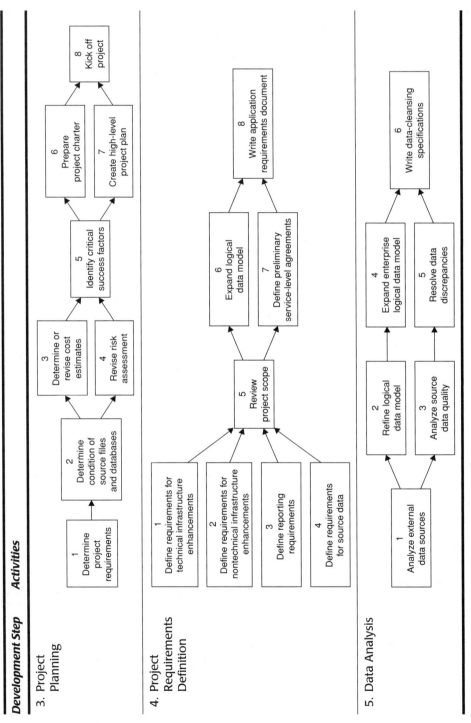

Activity Dependency Matrix

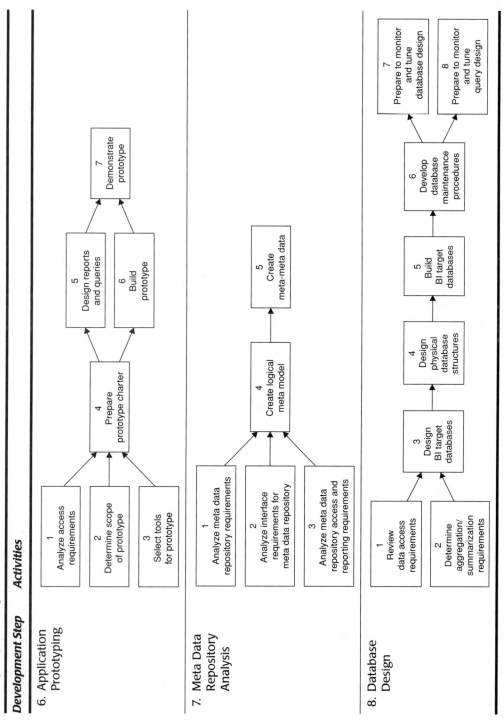

Activity Dependency Matrix

Development Step	*Activities*

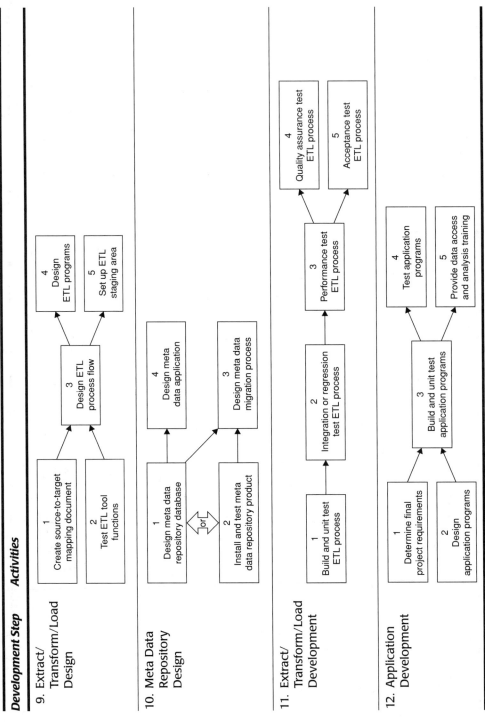

Activity Dependency Matrix

Development Step	*Activities*

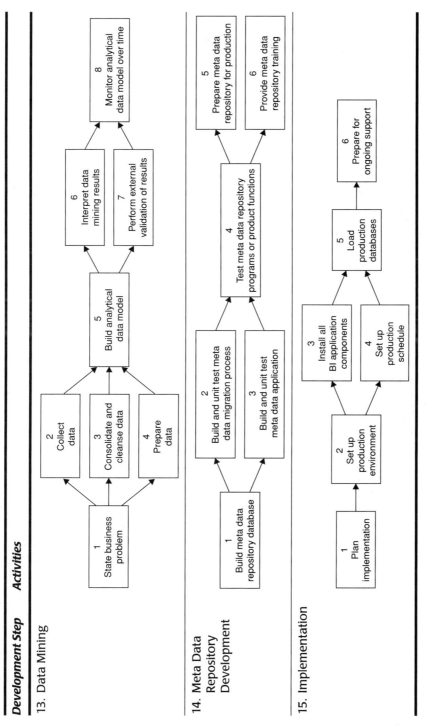

13. Data Mining

14. Meta Data Repository Development

15. Implementation

Activity Dependency Matrix

Development Step	**Activities**

16. Release Evaluation

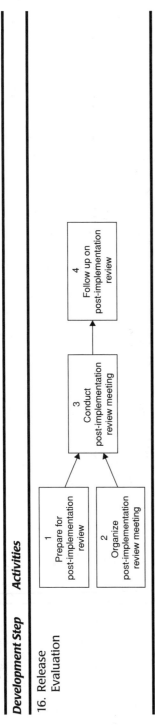

CHAPTER TWENTY

Task/Subtask Matrix

Development Step	Activities	Tasks/Subtasks
1. Business Case Assessment	1. Determine the business need	• Identify the business need (business problem or business opportunity) • Determine current financial consequences of the business need (lost revenue, lost opportunity, competition, obsolescence, cost overrun)
	2. Assess the current decision-support system (DSS) solutions	• Assess current usage of the existing DSS • Determine the shortcomings of the existing DSS (different keys, data redundancy, inconsistencies, difficult to access) • Perform gap analysis, identifying which business questions are being answered by the existing DSS and which ones are not

	3. Assess the operational sources and procedures	• Assess the data quality of operational systems in terms of:
		  – File structures and database structures
		  – Content (domain) of source data elements
		• Assess the current data movement in terms of:
		  – Data entry
		  – Data extraction
		  – Data manipulation
		  – Data duplication
		• Assess current operational procedures in terms of:
		  – Poor data entry practices
		  – Lack of edit checks
		  – Defective program code
		  – Lack of training

Task/Subtask Matrix   —   Development Step 1: Business Case Assessment

Development Step	Activities	Tasks/Subtasks
	4. Assess the competitors' BI decision-support initiatives	• Determine the competitors' successes and failures with their BI decision-support initiatives, especially their data mining initiatives • Determine whether your competitors gained market advantages, such as more sales, new customers, or innovative products
	5. Determine the BI application objectives	• Identify the strategic business goals of the organization • Define the overall BI decision-support objectives • Define the project-specific BI application objectives • Match the overall BI decision-support objectives to the strategic business goals • Match the project-specific BI application objectives to the strategic business goals
	6. Propose a BI solution	• Review current DSS solutions • Review DSS gap analysis • Determine how the BI application will lessen the business pain • Create a high-level architecture for the proposed BI solution • Consolidate and prioritize unfulfilled requirements from previous BI projects with new requirements • Create a high-level (conceptual) logical data model

	7. Perform a cost-benefit analysis	• Determine costs
		• Determine benefits:
		  – Identify tangible benefits
		  – Identify intangible benefits
		  – Identify short-term benefits to the organization
		  – Identify long-term benefits to the organization
		• Calculate the projected return on investment (ROI)

Task/Subtask Matrix — Development Step 1: Business Case Assessment

Development Step	Activities	Tasks/Subtasks
	8. Perform a risk assessment	• Create a risk assessment matrix, listing all possible BI project risks in terms of technology, complexity, integration, organization, project team, and financial investment • Assign weights to the risks • Rank the risks: low, medium, or high • Determine the risks (ramifications) of not addressing the business need and not implementing a BI solution

	9. Write the assessment report	• Write the assessment report to describe:
		  – Business need (business problem or business opportunity)
		  – Lost opportunities (ramifications of not addressing the business need)
		  – Proposed BI solution (and alternative solutions)
		  – Cost justification and expected ROI
		  – Risk assessment
		  – Recommendations (include operational business process improvements)

Task/Subtask Matrix — Development Step 2: Enterprise Infrastructure Evaluation

Development Step	Step Activities	Tasks/Subtasks
2. Enterprise Infrastructure Evaluation		
Section A. Technical Infrastructure Evaluation	1. Assess the existing platform	• Review hardware • Review operating systems • Review middleware, especially DBMS gateways • Review custom interfaces • Review network components and bandwidth • Review the DBMS • Review tools (CASE, ETL, OLAP, report writers, data mining tool) • Review the meta data repository (if one exists) • Perform gap analysis, identifying which platform components seem adequate and which ones seem inadequate
	2. Evaluate and select new products	• Identify the product categories you need to evaluate (for example, hardware, middleware, DBMS, tools) • List all products being considered for each category • Itemize your requirements for the products • Weigh each product requirement on a scale of 1 to 10 • Rank each product against the weighted requirements on a scale of 0 to 10 (0 means the product cannot satisfy the requirement) • Determine the total score for each product by multiplying the rank by the requirement weight factor • List all vendors of all products • Itemize your requirements for the vendors • Weigh each vendor requirement on a scale of 1 to 10 • Rank each vendor against the weighted requirements on a scale of 0 to 10 (0 means the vendor cannot satisfy the requirement) • Determine the total score for each vendor by multiplying the rank by the requirement weight factor

Task/Subtask Matrix   –   Development Step 2: Enterprise Infrastructure Evaluation

Development Step	Step Activities	Tasks/Subtasks
	2. Evaluate and select new products *(continued)*	• Evaluate the product scores and vendor scores • Create a short list of products and vendors in each category • Have the products demonstrated by the vendors • Choose the final product in each product category • Obtain business sponsor approval to license the products

	3. Write the technical infrastructure assessment report	• Fill in the following sections of the assessment report:
		  – Executive summary
		  – Findings about servers, operating systems, middleware, interfaces, network and bandwidth, DBMS, tools, and meta data repository
		  – List of weighted requirements
		  – Product scores
		  – Vendor scores
		  – Product costs
		  – Products on the short list
		  – Rationale for selecting or rejecting products
		  – Final selection criteria

	4. Expand the current platform	• Order new products • Install new products • Test new products • Train technical staff on new products

Task/Subtask Matrix — Development Step 2: Enterprise Infrastructure Evaluation

Development Step	Step Activities	Tasks/Subtasks
Section B. Nontechnical Infrastructure Evaluation	1. Assess the effectiveness of existing nontechnical infrastructure components	• Review standards for data naming, abbreviations, logical data modeling, testing, and reconciliation • Review the use of the development methodology • Review estimating guidelines • Review change-control procedures • Review issues management procedures • Review roles and responsibilities • Review security processes and guidelines • Review meta data capture and delivery processes for business meta data as well as technical meta data • Review meta data repository functionality • Review the process for merging logical data models into the enterprise data model • Review data quality measures and the cleansing triage process • Review the service-level agreement (SLA) process • Review the BI support function • Review the dispute resolution process • Review the communication process • Perform gap analysis, identifying which standards, guidelines, and procedures are adequate and which ones are inadequate

	2. Write the nontechnical infrastructure assessment report	• Fill in the following sections of the assessment report:
		  – Executive summary
		  – Findings about inadequate standards, guidelines, procedures, and processes
		  – Recommendations for nontechnical infrastructure changes
		  – Prioritized nontechnical infrastructure requirements to be implemented within the BI project
		  – Prioritized nontechnical infrastructure enhancements to be implemented outside the BI project

Task/Subtask Matrix — Development Step 2: Enterprise Infrastructure Evaluation

Development Step	Step Activities	Tasks/Subtasks
	3. Improve the nontechnical infrastructure	• Create time estimates for creating or modifying new standards, guidelines, and procedures
		• Change the guidelines for using the development methodology before the BI project begins, if necessary
		• Modify the roles and responsibilities before the BI project begins, if necessary
		• Create new processes as needed, or modify any process that appears to be inadequate or not working

Task/Subtask Matrix   —   Development Step 3:   Project Planning

Development Step	Step Activities	Tasks/Subtasks
3. Project Planning	1. Determine the project requirements	• Define data requirements • Define functional requirements (reports, queries, online help function) • Define infrastructure requirements (technical and nontechnical) • Expand or create the high-level logical data model • Validate the requirements with other business people • Obtain sponsor approval for the requirements

	2. Determine the condition of the source files and databases	• Review the content of each potential source file and source database (internal and external)
		• Assess source data violations to the:
		  – Technical data conversion rules
		  – Business data domain rules
		  – Business data integrity rules
		• Determine which data elements are critical to the business, which are important (but not critical), and which are insignificant
		• Estimate how long it would take to cleanse the critical source data elements and extrapolate an estimate (make an educated guess) for cleansing the important source data elements
		• Review data-cleansing estimates with the business sponsor and have the business sponsor prioritize the cleansing effort

	3. Determine or revise the cost estimates	• Review the technical infrastructure assessment report • Review the nontechnical infrastructure assessment report • Review the project requirements • Review the project constraints (time, scope, budget, resources, quality) • Review the need for consulting, contracting, and training • Revise the original cost estimates, if necessary

Task/Subtask Matrix — Development Step 3: Project Planning

Development Step	Step Activities	Tasks/Subtasks
	4. Revise the risk assessment	• Review and revise the original risk assessment matrix • For every risk, determine the likelihood of it materializing: low, medium, high • Determine the impact of every risk: low, medium, high • Define triggers (indications that a risk is about to materialize) • Define a risk mitigation plan, listing actions to prevent or circumvent each risk • Define a contingency plan, listing alternative actions to take when a risk materializes • Identify your assumptions because they may become risks • Include assumptions in the contingency plan (list alternatives) • Review the project constraints (time, scope, budget, resources, quality) as they relate to risk
	5. Identify critical success factors	• Define the success criteria for the BI project (what would be considered a "success") • Determine critical success factors (what must be in place in order for the project to meet the success criteria) • Review critical success factors with the business sponsor • Obtain agreement and cooperation on the critical success factors from the business sponsor (for example, provide one full-time business representative for the project)

Task/Subtask Matrix — Development Step 3: Project Planning

Development Step	Step Activities	Tasks/Subtasks
	6. Prepare the project charter	• Write the project charter with information about the BI project collected up to this point: – Purpose and reason for the BI project – Costs and benefits – Infrastructure and business process improvements – High-level scope (data and functions) – Items not in the scope (originally requested but subsequently excluded from the scope) – Expectations from the business people in terms of availability, security, response time (performance), data cleanliness, ongoing support – Team structure, roles, and responsibilities – Risks, assumptions, and constraints – Critical success factors
	7. Create a high-level project plan	• Create a work breakdown structure (list of appropriate tasks) • Determine base estimates for all tasks (using estimates provided by the team members who will do the work) • Identify task dependencies • Revise the base estimates for assigned resources, based on: – Skill level – Subject matter expertise – Additional administrative activities – Non-work-related activities • Identify resource dependencies (resource leveling) • Create a critical path method (CPM) or Pert chart • Create a Gantt chart

Task/Subtask Matrix — Development Step 3: Project Planning

Development Step	Step Activities	Tasks/Subtasks
	8. Kick off the project	• Prepare an agenda for the kickoff meeting • Call a kickoff meeting (include the business sponsor and the business representative) • Assign roles and responsibilities to core team members • Identify extended team members and review their responsibilities • Discuss the project charter • Walk through the project plan • Discuss the concept of self-organizing teams (core team members monitoring and redistributing [sharing] their workload)

Task/Subtask Matrix   —   Development Step 4:   Project Requirements Definition

Development Step	Step Activities	Tasks/Subtasks
4. Project Requirements Definition	1. Define the requirements for technical infrastructure enhancements	• Define the requirements for additional hardware • Define the requirements for additional middleware • Define the requirements for a new DBMS or upgrades to the existing DBMS • Define the requirements for the network or upgrades to it • Define the security requirements and decide whether to buy a security package • Define the requirements for development tools (CASE, ETL) • Define the requirements for data access and reporting tools (OLAP, report writers) • Define the requirements for a new data mining tool • Determine whether to license (buy) or custom build a meta data repository • If a meta data repository already exists, determine how to enhance it

	2. Define the requirements for nontechnical infrastructure enhancements	• Define the requirements for creating or changing standards, guidelines, and procedures for:
		  – Governance standards and procedures for prioritizing requirements and deliverables (functions, data, meta data)
		  – Use of the development methodology
		  – Estimating guidelines
		  – Scope management (change control) process
		  – Issues management process
		  – Roles and responsibilities
		  – Security process
		  – Meta data capture and delivery process
		  – Logical data modeling
		  – Data quality measures and triage process
		  – Testing process
		  – SLA process
		  – Support functions
		  – Dispute resolution process
		  – Communication process

Task/Subtask Matrix — Development Step 4: Project Requirements Definition

Development Step	Step Activities	Tasks/Subtasks
	3. Define the reporting requirements	• Collect or create sample report layouts • Collect or create sample queries • Define business rules for the reports • Define aggregation and summarization rules • Define reporting dimensions • Define query libraries • Identify stewards of the libraries • Get samples of the types of ad hoc queries the business analysts may want to write • Define access interfaces (GUI front end, Web display, portal)
	4. Define the requirements for source data	• Define all source data elements (for reporting dimensions, for report fields, for queries, for data mining) • Classify data elements as critical, important, insignificant • Define the data domains (allowable values) • Define the significant and obvious business rules for the data • Analyze the source files and source databases in more detail to determine data-cleansing requirements • Define the historical data requirements (how much history to load and from how many years back, or accumulate history from this point forward)
	5. Review the project scope	• Compare the detailed project requirements to the high-level scope in the project charter • Review the project constraints (time, scope, budget, resources, quality) • Determine whether the scope is still realistic under those constraints • Renegotiate the scope, if necessary • Create a change-control document for managing changes to the requirements • Create an issues log for tracking and resolving issues

Task/Subtask Matrix — Development Step 4: Project Requirements Definition

Development Step	Step Activities	Tasks/Subtasks
	6. Expand the logical data model	• Add newly discovered entities and their relationships to the high-level (conceptual) logical data model • Refine the logical data model by resolving the many-to-many relationships • Add unique identifiers to each entity • Attribute the logical data model with critical data elements
	7. Define preliminary service-level agreements	• Identify or revise the expectations (outermost acceptable limits) of the business people in terms of: – Availability – Security – Response time – Data cleanliness – Ongoing support
	8. Write the application requirements document	• Fill in the following sections of the application requirements document: – Technical infrastructure requirements – Nontechnical infrastrucure requirements – Reporting requirements – Ad hoc and canned query requirements – Requirements for source data, including history (include the high-level logical data model) – Data-cleansing requirements – Security requirements – Preliminary SLAs

Task/Subtask Matrix   —   Development Step 5: Data Analysis

Development Step	Step Activities	Tasks/Subtasks
5. Data Analysis	1. Analyze the external data sources	• Identify the entities and relationships from each external data source • Merge the new entities and relationships from the external data sources into the logical data model
	2. Refine the logical data model	• Fully attribute the logical data model to include all required source data elements from internal as well as external data sources • Create new entities and relationships where needed to store the new attributes (data elements) • Analyze the *layout* of all identified source files and source databases, and normalize overused data elements, which are *explicitly* redefined; for example, a "redefines" clause or an "occurs" clause in a program • Analyze the *content* of all identified source data elements in the source files and source databases, and normalize overused data elements, which are *implicitly* redefined; for example, when a data element is used for multiple purposes • Create the data-specific business meta data components for all attributes (data name, definition, domain, length, type, and so on)

	3. Analyze the source data quality	• Apply business data domain rules and business data integrity rules to find data elements with invalid domains, such as:
		  – Default values
		  – Missing values
		  – Cryptic values
		  – Contradicting values (between two dependent data elements)
		  – Values that violate the business rules
		  – Missing primary keys
		  – Duplicate primary keys
		• Determine the severity of the problem: how many data elements have invalid domains and how many records are affected; for example, 140 data elements out of 260 and 609,772 records out of 2,439,087
		• Determine the criticality of the problem (how the dirty data will affect the BI application if not corrected)

Task/Subtask Matrix   —   Development Step 5: Data Analysis

Development Step	Step Activities	Tasks/Subtasks
	4. Expand the enterprise logical data model **Note:** *This activity is typically performed by data administration behind the scenes of the BI project. However, if the core team member who plays the role of the project data administrator must also play the role of the enterprise data administrator, the BI project schedule may be affected.*	• Merge the project-specific logical data model into the enterprise logical data model • Identify data discrepancies and inconsistencies between the logical data models
	5. Resolve data discrepancies	• Discuss the discrepancies and inconsistencies with the BI project team, the data owners, and the business executives who use the data in question for their business decisions • Adjust either the project-specific logical data model or the enterprise logical data model, as appropriate • Notify other project teams that are affected by the changes • If changes cannot be implemented, document the discrepancies and inconsistencies as meta data, and schedule a time for the changes to be implemented
	6. Write the data-cleansing specifications	• Review the classification of data elements: critical, important, insignificant • Write data-cleansing specifications for all critical data elements • Write data-cleansing specifications for selected important data elements (let the business representative make the selection) • Unless there is sufficient time on the project and the business representative specifically requests it, do not write data-cleansing specifications for the insignificant data elements

Task/Subtask Matrix — Development Step 6: Application Prototyping

Development Step	Step Activities	Tasks/Subtasks
6. Application Prototyping **Note:** *Prototyping is an iterative process, and activities in this step will be repeated multiple times.*	1. Analyze the access requirements	• Review the application requirements document with the subject matter expert and the business representative, and together analyze: – Report requirements; for example, how many reports look similar and can therefore be combined due to a pattern in the reports or use of the same facts and dimensions – Query requirements; for example, do the business people want parameterized queries and if so, what are the parameterized variables and who will maintain the query library – Ad hoc requirements; if possible, try to determine what type of ad hoc questions the business people may want to ask based on what types of questions they currently ask – Interface requirements; for example, a GUI front end or a Web portal • Communicate all your findings to the database administrator • Create a skill set matrix for each business person participating in the prototyping activities: – Indicate computer skill level as beginning, advanced, expert – Indicate application knowledge as beginning, advanced, expert
	2. Determine the scope of the prototype	• Determine the objective and the primary use of the prototype • Decide which type of prototype to build: – Show-and-tell – Mock-up – Proof-of-concept – Visual-design – Demo – Operational • Select a subset of functions (reports, queries, ETL, interface) • Select a subset of sample data from the source files and source databases • Create a change-control document for managing scope changes during the prototype • Create an issues log for tracking and resolving issues during the prototype • Determine the number of prototype iterations

Task/Subtask Matrix — Development Step 6: Application Prototyping

Development Step	Step Activities	Tasks/Subtasks
	2. Determine the scope of the prototype *(continued)*	• Determine the number of prototype participants (IT and business people) • Determine the time limits for each prototype iteration (time-box) • Estimate the cost and benefit for each prototype iteration • Determine the point of diminishing returns for the prototyping effort
	3. Select tools for the prototype	• Review existing in-house tools and find out who uses them • Review the availability of new reporting and querying tools • Review existing or new graphical tools • Review existing or new report distribution tools • Review existing DBMS options for the prototype • Select the platform on which the prototype will be developed • Select one of the installed and tested DBMSs • Select one or more existing or new tools • Determine training needs for the new tools • Schedule training sessions as soon as possible
	4. Prepare the prototype charter	• Write the prototype charter with information about: – Why you are building the prototype (purpose) – What type of prototype you selected (show-and-tell, mock-up, proof-of-concept, visual-design, demo, operational) – Who will participate (IT and business people) – What the rules are (scope, time, iterations) – How you will measure your degree of success

Task/Subtask Matrix   –   Development Step 6: Application Prototyping

Development Step	Step Activities	Tasks/Subtasks
	5. Design the reports and queries	• Design the reports based on existing reports or mock-up report layouts
		• Design the queries based on existing spreadsheets or reports or on mock-up samples
		• Design the interfaces: GUI or Web front end
		• Create a physical data model (database design) for the prototype database
		• Identify the data to be used for the prototype: either a representative sample of source data or new test data
		• Map sample source data or new test data into the prototype database
	6. Build the prototype	• Create the physical prototype database (tables, columns, indices)
		• Create sample test data (extract sample source data or create new data)
		• Load the prototype database with sample source data or sample test data
		• Write a selected subset of reports
		• Write a selected subset of queries
		• Write a selected subset of interfaces or other functions
		• Test reports, queries, interfaces, or other functions
		• Document any problems with the tool
		• Document any issues with the reports or queries
		• Document any issues with the interfaces or other functions
		• Document any issues with dirty source data (do not waste time resolving them unless you are prototyping an ETL function)
		• Using the prototype as a yardstick, validate the time and cost estimates for the BI application

Task/Subtask Matrix — Development Step 6: Application Prototyping

Development Step	Step Activities	Tasks/Subtasks
	7. Demonstrate the prototype	• Review reports and queries with the business people
		• Review problems and issues with the business sponsor and the business representative on the core team
		• Review the project requirements with the subject matter expert and the business representative
		• Document requested changes in the change-control document
		• Analyze the impact of requested changes in terms of:
		– Time
		– Quality
		– Cost
		– Additional skills or resources required
		• Review the impact of requested changes with the business sponsor and the business representative
		• Revise the application requirements document to include approved changes
		• Review lessons learned with the entire *project* core team and in particular with the ETL *step* core team
		• Use prototype demonstrations to promote the BI application
		• Perform the next prototype iteration, if applicable

Task/Subtask Matrix — Development Step 7: Meta Data Repository Analysis

Development Step	Step Activities	Tasks/Subtasks
7. Meta Data Repository Analysis	1. Analyze the meta data repository requirements	• Review the technical infrastructure assessment report for requirements to license (buy), build, or enhance a meta data repository • Perform a cost-benefit analysis for licensing versus building a meta data repository • Make the decision to license or build a meta data repository • Review the nontechnical infrastructure assessment report for new meta data requirements (business and technical) • Determine the scope of the meta data repository deliverables • Prioritize the meta data repository deliverables, indicating whether the meta data components are mandatory, important, or optional • Update the application requirements document to reflect any changes

	2. Analyze the interface requirements for the meta data repository	• Analyze the meta data sources from which the meta data components will be extracted:
		  – Word processing files and spreadsheets
		  – DBMS dictionaries
		  – CASE, ETL, OLAP tools
		  – Report writers and query tools
		  – Data mining tool
		• Determine what import and export features are available in these tools as well as in the meta data repository product

	3. Analyze the meta data repository access and reporting requirements	• Review the original meta data repository access and reporting requirements • Review the meta data security requirements • Identify the access interface media for displaying meta data ad hoc query results (for example, PDF, HTML) • Analyze the feasibility of a context-sensitive help function • Determine what reports should be produced from the meta data repository

Task/Subtask Matrix   —   Development Step 7: Meta Data Repository Analysis

Development Step	Step Activities	Tasks/Subtasks
	4. Create the logical meta model	• Create business meta data entities • Create technical meta data entities • Determine the relationships between the meta data entities • Create attributes for business and technical meta data entities • Draw an entity-relationship diagram

	5. Create the meta-meta data	• Describe all meta data entities with:
		  – Name
		  – Definition
		  – Relationships
		  – Security
		  – Physical location
		  – Timeliness
		  – Volume
		• Describe all meta data attributes with:
		  – Name
		  – Definition
		  – Type and length
		  – Domain (content)
		  – Security
		  – Ownership
		• Define the business rules for meta data entities, attributes, and relationships

Task/Subtask Matrix — Development Step 8: Database Design

Development Step	Step Activities	Tasks/Subtasks

8. Database Design	1. Review the data access requirements	• Review the data-cleansing specifications
		• Review the prototyping results with the application lead developer
		• Review detailed access and analysis requirements with the application lead developer and the subject matter expert or business representative:
		  – Reporting requirements
		  – Querying requirements
		  – Ad hoc querying requirements
		• Review data security requirements
		• Determine projected data volumes and growth factors
		• Determine the projected number of concurrent database usages
		• Determine the location of business people
		• Determine the frequency of report and query executions
		• Determine the peak and seasonal reporting periods
		• Determine platform limitations
		• Determine tool limitations (ETL, OLAP, report writers)

	2. Determine the aggregation and summarization requirements	• Review the measures (facts) used by the prototype (how they were derived through aggregation and summarization) • Review the dimensions used by the prototype • Review the drill-down and roll-up functions of the prototype • Review common reporting patterns among existing reports and among business people from various departments • Determine the most frequently used reporting dimensions • Review the logical data model with the data administrator • Determine the level of detail (granularity) needed • Determine how the detailed data will be accessed (drill-down or ad hoc) • Determine how many business relationships (entity relationships) among detailed data will be needed, if any

Task/Subtask Matrix — Development Step 8: Database Design

Development Step	Step Activities	Tasks/Subtasks

	3. Design the BI target databases	• Determine the appropriate database design schemas:
		  – Multidimensional star schema
		  – Multidimensional snowflake schema
		  – Entity-relationship-based relational schema
		  – Hybrid design schema (mixture)
		• Create the physical data models (database design diagrams)
		• Create the technical meta data for the physical data models (for example, names and definitions for tables, columns, keys, indices)
		• Map the physical data models to the logical data model

	4. Design the physical database structures	• Determine how to cluster the tables • Determine the placement of datasets • Determine how to stripe disks • Determine how to partition the tables across multiple disks • Determine how much free space to choose • Determine how much buffer space to declare • Determine how large to set the blocksize • Determine the most appropriate indexing strategy • Determine whether referential integrity will be enforced by the DBMS or by the ETL programs

	5. Build the BI target databases	• Create the data definition language (DDL) defining:
		  – Storage groups
		  – Databases
		  – Partitions
		  – Tablespaces
		  – Tables
		  – Columns
		  – Primary keys
		  – Foreign keys
		  – Indices

Task/Subtask Matrix — Development Step 8: Database Design

Development Step	Step Activities	Tasks/Subtasks

	5. Build the BI target databases (*continued*)	• Create the data control language (DCL) to:
		  – Define parameters for the security SYSTABLE
		  – Set up group IDs
		  – Grant CRUD (create, read, update, delete) authority to the group IDs
		  – Assign developers, business analysts, and programs to the appropriate group IDs
		• Run the DDL to create the physical database structures
		• Run the DCL to grant CRUD authority to the physical database structures
		• Build the indices

	6. Develop database maintenance procedures	• Define database maintenance activities for:
		  – Database backups (full backups and incremental backups)
		  – Disaster recovery procedures
		  – Reorganization procedures for fragmented tables
		• Define the frequency of and procedure for performance monitoring activities

	7. Prepare to monitor and tune the database designs *Note:* *This is an ongoing post-implementation activity.*	• Plan to monitor the performance of ETL loads, reports, and queries at runtime • Plan to use a performance-monitoring utility to diagnose performance degradation • Plan to refine the database design schemas • Plan to add additional indices, if necessary
	8. Prepare to monitor and tune the query designs *Note:* *This is an ongoing post-implementation activity.*	• Plan to review and streamline all SQL calls in ETL programs and application programs • Plan to write pass-through queries for OLAP tools, if necessary • Plan to utilize parallel query execution

Task/Subtask Matrix — Development Step 9: Extract/Transform/Load Design

Development Step	Step Activities	Tasks/Subtasks
9. Extract/ Transform/ Load Design	1. Create the source-to-target mapping document	• Review the record layouts for the source files • Review the data description blocks for the source databases • Review the data-cleansing specifications for source data elements with the data quality analyst, the subject matter expert, and the business representative • Create a matrix for all target tables and target columns • List all applicable source files and source databases for every target table • List all relevant source data elements for every target column • List data type and length for every target column • List data type and length for every source data element • Write transformation specifications for populating the columns: 　– Combine data content from multiple sources (if needed) 　– Split data content from one data element across multiple columns if source data was used for multiple purposes 　– Include aggregation and summarization algorithms 　– Include data-cleansing specifications for each column 　– Include logic for checking referential integrity (if not performed by the DBMS) 　– Include logic for error messages and record rejection counts 　– Include logic for reconciliation totals (record counts, domain counts, amount counts)
	2. Test the ETL tool functions	• Review the transformation specifications in the source-to-target mapping document • Determine whether the ETL tool functions can perform the required transformation logic • Determine what supplementary custom code must be written for transformations that cannot be handled by the ETL tool
	3. Design the ETL process flow	• Determine the most efficient sequence in which source data can be extracted from the source files and source databases • Determine the most efficient sequence in which the extracted source data can be transformed, cleansed, and loaded • Determine the sort and merge steps in the ETL process

Task/Subtask Matrix — Development Step 9: Extract/Transform/ Load Design

Development Step	Step Activities	Tasks/Subtasks

	3. Design the ETL process flow (continued)	• Identify all temporary and permanent work files and tables
		• Determine what components of the ETL process can run in parallel
		• Determine what tables can be loaded in parallel
		• Draw the process flow diagram showing process sequence and process dependencies for:
		  – Extracts from source files and source databases
		  – Temporary and permanent work files and tables
		  – Sorting and merging performed on the temporary and permanent work files and tables
		  – Transformation programs (program modules)
		  – Error rejection files and error reports
		  – Load files and load utilities

	4. Design the ETL programs	• Design three sets of ETL programs for:
		  – Initial load
		  – Historical load
		  – Incremental load
		• Modularize the ETL programs as much as possible
		• Translate the transformation specifications from the source-to-target mapping document into programming specifications for each ETL program module (or for each ETL tool module)

	5. Set up the ETL staging area	• Determine whether the entire ETL process can run in one central staging area or whether it has to be distributed (some ETL programs running on the mainframe, some on the ETL server) • Set up the ETL server (if a dedicated server is used) • Allocate space for temporary and permanent work files and tables • Create program libraries • Establish program-versioning procedures

Task/Subtask Matrix — Development Step 10: Meta Data Repository Design

Development Step	Step Activities	Tasks/Subtasks
10. Meta Data Repository Design	1. Design the meta data repository database	• Review the logical meta model for the meta data repository • Design the meta data repository database (entity-relationship or object-oriented) • Draw the physical meta model diagram (entity-relationship or object-oriented) • Map the physical meta model to the logical meta model • Create the DDL for the meta data repository database • Create the DCL for the meta data repository database • Design backup and recovery procedures • Design versioning and archival procedures
	2. Install and test the meta data repository product	• Compile a list of meta data repository products and vendors • Compare the meta data repository products to the meta data repository requirements in the revised application requirements document and in the logical meta model • Create a scorecard for each evaluated meta data repository product • Create a scorecard for each evaluated meta data repository vendor • Narrow the list of meta data repository products and vendors to a short list • Arrange for meta data repository product demos • Check the vendors' client references • License (buy) the meta data repository product • Install and test the meta data repository product

Task/Subtask Matrix — Development Step 10: Meta Data Repository Design

Development Step	Step Activities	Tasks/Subtasks
	3. Design the meta data migration process	• Analyze all sources for extracting business meta data (for example, CASE tool, word processing documents, spreadsheets)
		• Analyze all sources for extracting technical meta data (for example, ETL tool, OLAP tool, data mining tool)
		• Design the tool interface process
		• Design the transformations for the extracted meta data
		• Design the load programs for the meta data repository
		• Write the programming specifications for the meta data migration process:
		– Tool interface process
		– Transformation process
		– Load process
	4. Design the meta data application	• Design the meta data repository report programs
		• Design the context-sensitive online help function
		• Design the media for displaying meta data ad hoc query results (for example, PDF, HTML)
		• Design the access interface process (Web display, GUI front end, meta data repository directory)
		• Write the programming specifications for the meta data application:
		– Reports
		– Queries
		– Access interface process
		– Online help function

Task/Subtask Matrix — Development Step 11: Extract/Transform/Load Development

Development Step	Step Activities	Tasks/Subtasks
11. Extract/ Transform/Load Development	1. Build and unit test the ETL process	• Code the ETL programs by following the programming specifications in the ETL program design document • If using an ETL tool, write instructions (technical meta data) for the ETL tool modules • Capture the ETL technical meta data for the meta data repository • Write code in the ETL programs to produce reconciliation totals, data quality metrics, and load statistics • Unit test each individual program module • If using an ETL tool, unit test each ETL tool module • Write the scripts to execute the ETL programs and the sort, merge, and load utilities in the proper sequence
	2. Integration or regression test the ETL process	• Create a test plan with test cases for the ETL process • Create test data (a representative subset of source data) for the ETL programs • Integration or regression test the entire ETL process from beginning to end using the test plan • Log the actual test results and document any test issues • Compare actual test results with expected test results • Revise the ETL programs (or the instructions for the ETL tool) • Retest the entire ETL process from beginning to end until it produces the expected results
	3. Performance test the ETL process	• Test individual ETL programs and ETL tool modules that read or write to high-volume tables • Test the parallel execution of ETL programs and ETL tool modules against high-volume tables • Test the ETL programs and ETL tool modules that perform complicated operations • Use full-volume data for performance testing • If using a stress test simulation tool, define the test components (programs, databases, tables, volumes, and so on) to the simulation tool and run a simulation test before testing with full-volume data

Task/Subtask Matrix — Development Step 11: Extract/Transform/Load Development

Development Step	Step Activities	Tasks/Subtasks
	4. Quality assurance (QA) test the ETL process	• Move all ETL programs into the QA environment • QA test the entire ETL process from beginning to end with the operations staff • Obtain approval from the operations staff to move the ETL process into production

	5. Acceptance test the ETL process	• Acceptance test the entire ETL process from beginning to end with the subject matter expert and the business representative:
		  – Validate all cleansing transformations
		  – Validate error-handling routines
		  – Validate reconciliation totals
		• Obtain certification for the ETL process from the business representative

Task/Subtask Matrix — Development Step 12: Application Development

Development Step	Step Activities	Tasks/Subtasks
12. Application Development	1. Determine the final project requirements	• Review the results of the prototype • Review the prototyping programs and scripts • Review the change-control document • Review the issues log • Review existing and mock-up report layouts • Review existing spreadsheets • Review the latest version of the application requirements document • Agree on the final project requirements; renegotiate the final scope if necessary • Update the application requirements document to reflect any changes

	2. Design the application programs	• Design the final reports
		• Design the final queries
		• Design the front-end interface (GUI, Web portal)
		• Design the online help function
		• Write the programming specifications for:
		  – Reports
		  – Queries
		  – Front-end interface process
		  – Online help function
		• Create a test plan with test cases and a test log

	3. Build and unit test the application programs	• Create sample test data • Load the development databases with sample test data • Rewrite or enhance prototyping programs and scripts • Code the final report programs • Code the final query scripts • Code the final front-end interface programs • Code the online help function programs • Unit test each individual program module

Task/Subtask Matrix — Development Step 12: Application Development

Development Step	Step Activities	Tasks/Subtasks
	4. Test the application programs	• Integration test (first release) or regression test (subsequent releases) all programs and scripts from beginning to end, using the test cases from the test plan: – Report programs – Query scripts – Front-end interface programs – Online help function programs • Log the actual test results and document any test issues • Compare actual test results with expected test results • Revise the application programs and scripts • Retest the application programs and scripts from beginning to end until they perform as expected • Performance test those programs that have many JOINs, require complicated calculations, and read high-volume tables • Use full-volume data for performance testing • If using a stress test simulation tool, define the test components (programs, databases, tables, volumes, and so on) to the simulation tool and run a simulation test before testing with full-volume data • Move databases, programs, and scripts into the QA environment • QA test the entire application from beginning to end with the operations staff • Obtain approval from the operations staff to move the application programs into production • Acceptance test the entire application from beginning to end with the subject matter expert and business representative • Obtain certification for the application from the business representative

Task/Subtask Matrix — Development Step 12: Application Development

Development Step	Step Activities	Tasks/Subtasks

	5. Provide data access and analysis training	• Identify help desk staff to be trained
		• Identify "power users" or other business liaison personnel to be trained
		• Identify business people to be trained
		• Create training materials:
		  – Presentation slides and instructor notes
		  – Student workbooks with exercises
		  – Exercise solutions and other pertinent handouts
		• Schedule training sessions
		• Conduct training sessions
		• Measure training effectiveness

Task/Subtask Matrix — Development Step 13: Data Mining

Development Step	Step Activities	Tasks/Subtasks
13. Data Mining	1. State the business problem	• Define the business problem • Obtain commitment for a data mining solution • Set realistic expectations for the data mining tool • Identify preliminary algorithms relevant to the business problem
	2. Collect the data	• Identify available data sources (operational as well as BI) • Extract pertinent data from various internal data sources • Acquire (purchase) pertinent data from external data sources
	3. Consolidate and cleanse the data	• Merge data from various internal data sources • Match and merge internal data with external data • Review the structure of the merged data • Select a sample of data for each analytical data model • Select related meta data from the meta data repository • Review the data domains (content) and measure the quality and reasonability of the data values • Validate domain reasonability across active variables
	4. Prepare the data	• Review the frequency distribution of categorical variables • Review maximum, minimum, mean, mode, and median for quantitative variables • Use statistical distribution parameters to filter noise in the data • Eliminate variables with missing values or replace the missing values with "most likely" values • Convert data formats to suit the particular data mining algorithm used • Derive new variables from original input data, where appropriate • Consolidate customers by assigning a household number to related customers • Relate customers with products and services • Apply data reduction, where appropriate

Task/Subtask Matrix   —   Development Step 13:   Data Mining

Development Step	Step Activities	Tasks/Subtasks

	4. Prepare the data *(continued)*	• Apply data mining transformation techniques, where appropriate:
		  – "Discretization" technique to convert quantitative variables into categorical variables
		  – "One-of-N" technique to convert a categorical variable to a numeric representation for input to a neural network

	5. Build the analytical data model	• Create the analytical (informational) data model • Select data mining operations with the appropriate algorithms • Test accuracy of the analytical data model using confusion matrices and input sensitivity analyses • Repeat prior steps (if necessary) to train and retrain the model (beware of overtraining the model)
	6. Interpret the data mining results ***Note:*** *This is an ongoing activity.*	• Review the data mining results • Look for results that are interesting, valid, and actionable • Present the new findings in a convincing, business-oriented way using visualization technology • Formulate ways in which the new information can best be exploited
	7. Perform external validation of the results ***Note:*** *This is an ongoing activity.*	• Compare data mining results to published industry statistics • Validate the selection of variables and time frame of your data against the variables and time frame of the industry statistics • Identify the variations between your analysis results and the industry statistics • Determine the reasons for the variations
	8. Monitor the analytical data model over time ***Note:*** *This is an ongoing activity.*	• Keep validating your analytical data model against industry statistics at regular time intervals • When industry statistics change, change your analytical data model and retrain it • Research the data mining capabilities of your competitors • Monitor your competitors' market share and adjust your analytical data model accordingly

Task/Subtask Matrix — Development Step 14: Meta Data Repository Development

Development Step	Step Activities	Tasks/Subtasks
14. Meta Data Repository Development	1. Build the meta data repository database	• Run the DDL to create the physical meta data repository database structures • Run the DCL to grant CRUD authority on the meta data repository database structures • If licensing a meta data repository product, set up CRUD authority on the meta data repository product • Test all meta data repository product components, especially the meta data repository database

	2. Build and unit test the meta data migration process	• Code the tool interface programs or use the export facility of the various tools; (for example, ETL tool, CASE tool)
		• Code the meta data transformation programs
		• Code the meta data load programs or use the import facility of the meta data repository product or the DBMS load utility
		• Code the meta data programs that will run during the ETL process to capture:
		   – Load statistics
		   – Reconciliation totals (record counts, domain counts, amount counts)
		   – Data-cleansing (reliability) metrics
		   – Data rejection counts and reasons for rejections
		• Unit test the meta data migration programs (or meta data repository product modules):
		   – Tool interface programs
		   – Meta data transformation programs
		   – Meta data load programs
		• Unit test the meta data programs that will run during the ETL process

Task/Subtask Matrix — Development Step 14: Meta Data Repository Development

Development Step	Step Activities	Tasks/Subtasks
	3. Build and unit test the meta data application	• Code the access interface programs (GUI or Web front end) • Code the meta data report programs • Code the meta data query scripts • Code the meta data repository online help function programs • Unit test the meta data application programs (or meta data repository product modules): – Access interface programs – Report programs – Query scripts – Online help function programs
	4. Test the meta data repository programs or product functions	• Create a test plan with test cases for: – Meta data migration process – Meta data repository application programs or product modules – Meta data programs that run during the ETL process • Create test data for meta data repository testing: – Meta data migration process – Meta data repository application or product modules – Meta data programs that run during the ETL process • Integration or regression test the meta data repository: – Meta data migration process – Meta data repository application or product modules – Meta data programs that run during the ETL process • Log the actual test results and document any test issues • Compare actual test results with expected test results • Revise the meta data repository programs • Retest the meta data repository programs from beginning to end until they perform as expected • Conduct QA testing with operations staff • Conduct acceptance testing with the subject matter expert and the business representative (QA and acceptance testing may be conducted at the same time)

Task/Subtask Matrix — Development Step 14: Meta Data Repository Development

Development Step	Step Activities	Tasks/Subtasks
	5. Prepare the meta data repository for production	• Install and test the server platform for the production meta data repository
		• Create DDL and DCL for the production meta data repository database
		• Write operating procedures for the operations staff with instructions for running meta data repository reports at predetermined dates and times
		• Write a reference guide for the help desk staff and the business people with instructions on how to use the meta data repository
		• Develop performance monitoring and tuning procedures for the meta data repository database
		• Develop meta data repository usage monitoring procedures
	6. Provide meta data repository training	• Identify help desk staff to be trained on the content and use of the meta data repository
		• Identify "power users" or other business liaison personnel to be trained
		• Identify business people to be trained
		• Create meta data repository training materials:
		– Presentation slides and instructor notes
		– Student workbooks with exercises
		– Exercise solutions and other pertinent handouts
		• Schedule meta data repository training sessions
		• Conduct meta data repository training sessions
		• Measure meta data repository training effectiveness

Task/Subtask Matrix — Development Step 15: Implementation

Development Step	Step Activities	Tasks/Subtasks
15. Implementation	1. Plan the implementation	• Select an implementation strategy (gradual rollout or entire BI application at once to all business people) • Set the implementation date • Determine the number of business people who will be using the BI application (initially and eventually) • Schedule the necessary resources to participate in implementation activities • Schedule the functions to be rolled out • Prepare for organizational impact
	2. Set up the production environment	• Set up the production ETL program library • Set up the production application program library • Set up the production meta data repository program library • Create the production BI target databases (including data mining databases) • Create the production meta data repository database • Grant appropriate authority on the production BI target databases • Grant appropriate authority on the production meta data repository database • Grant appropriate authority to developers, operations staff, and business people to execute programs from production program libraries • Write operating procedures for operations staff with instructions for running ETL programs and application report programs at predetermined dates and times • Write reference guides for the help desk staff and the business people with instructions for how to use the BI application • Implement production security levels for all BI application components

Task/Subtask Matrix – Development Step 15: Implementation

Development Step	Step Activities	Tasks/Subtasks
	3. Install all the BI application components	• Move ETL programs into the production ETL program library: – Initial load – Historical load – Incremental load • Move application programs into the production application program library: – Reports – Queries – Front-end interface process – Online help function • Move meta data repository programs into the production meta data repository program library: – Meta data migration programs – Meta data application programs or product modules (including meta data repository online help function programs)
	4. Set up the production schedule	• Set up the ETL process on the job scheduler • Add to the job scheduler the meta data programs that run during the ETL process • Set up on the job scheduler the regularly scheduled application report programs • Set up on the job scheduler the regularly scheduled meta data repository programs: – Meta data migration process – Meta data repository application
	5. Load the production databases	• Run the initial load process • Run the historical load process • Run the meta data migration process

Task/Subtask Matrix — Development Step 15: Implementation

Development Step	Step Activities	Tasks/Subtasks
	6. Prepare for ongoing support	• Establish a schedule for on-call emergency support
		• Schedule database maintenance activities for the BI target databases and the meta data repository database:
		– Database backups
		– Disaster recovery testing
		– Database reorganizations
		• Schedule database monitoring activities for the BI target databases and the meta data repository database:
		– Performance
		– Growth
		– Usage
		• Schedule data quality monitoring activities for the BI target databases:
		– Meta data metrics
		– Quality spot checks
		• Develop or review capacity plans for the BI platform:
		– Processors
		– Disk storage
		– Network components (including bandwidth)
		• Start production processing (go live)

Task/Subtask Matrix   —   Development Step 16: Release Evaluation

Development Step	Step Activities	Tasks/Subtasks
16. Release Evaluation	1. Prepare for the post-implementation review	• Review budget expenditures • Review the original project plan and final schedule • Review the estimated and actual task completion times • Review the issues log (resolved and unresolved issues) • Review the change-control procedure and scope changes • Review unfulfilled requirements (dropped from scope) • Review the effectiveness of the development approach • Review the effectiveness of the team structure • Review the effectiveness of the organizational placement • Review the existing infrastructure (technical and nontechnical) • Identify missing infrastructure pieces (technical and nontechnical) that hindered progress on the BI project • Assess the performance of the BI application • Review the effectiveness of training • Review the implementation (rollout) strategy • Review the effectiveness of the release concept

	2. Organize the post-implementation review meeting	• Create the preliminary post-implementation review agenda:
		  – List date, time, and place
		  – List invited attendees
		  – List topics for discussion
		  – List and assign topics for research
		  – List questions to be discussed and answered
		• Solicit additional topics and questions from attendees
		• Send out the preliminary agenda to attendees
		• Schedule the meeting at an off-site location
		• Arrange facilitation by a third party
		• Arrange for a third-party scribe to take notes during the meeting
		• Revise and send the final meeting agenda
		• Send out documentation to be discussed during the review

Task/Subtask Matrix   —   Development Step 16: Release Evaluation

Development Step	Step Activities	Tasks/Subtasks
	3. Conduct the post-implementation review meeting	• Introduce the attendees • Explain the rules for the facilitated session • Discuss each item on the agenda • Document discussions, suggestions, resolutions • Document action items • Assign action items • Establish a completion or response date for each action item
	4. Follow up on the post-implementation review	• Document unfulfilled requirements (dropped from scope), which should be bundled with new requirements for the next (or a future) BI release • Write the meeting minutes • Publish the meeting minutes • Work on assigned action items • Monitor the work performed on action items, especially those that were assigned to people outside the BI project team • Document the action item results • Publish the action item results • Implement nontechnical infrastructure improvements to: – Development approach – Use of the development methodology – Processes and procedures – Guidelines – Standards

CHAPTER TWENTY-ONE

Practical Guidelines Matrix

Development Step	Dos
1. Business Case Assessment	• Identify your organization's strategic business goals. Understand the impact of the external drivers. A common cause of failure for BI decision-support initiatives is that the objectives of these BI initiatives do not align with the strategic business goals of the organization. • Let the business representative work with a number of business managers and business executives to define the business value of the BI application. Help him or her differentiate between the needs of different business people. The level of detail, timeliness, accuracy, security, and external data needs will differ for senior managers, knowledge workers, business analysts, sales and marketing personnel, and external clients. • Concentrate your efforts on defining the business case with business people from the marketing arm of the organization. In many industries, marketing personnel often serve on the forefront of BI decision-support initiatives. Use their business savvy to help identify business benefits, and call upon their influence to sell the value of the BI initiative throughout the organization. • Have a clear business driver. You cannot justify BI costs (many range up to $25 million or more) unless you have very specific business reasons to create your BI application. • Keep it simple. Start with one business need (business problem or business opportunity) that you would like the BI application to satisfy. With a flexible design, you can add more functionality later, once the initiative has proven itself profitable and once some comfort level has been attained. • Clearly state the financial consequences of the current business problems and how these problems could be resolved with a BI solution. Include this in the cost-benefit analysis.

Practical Guidelines Matrix   —   Development Step 1: Business Case Assessment

Development Step	Don'ts
	• Don't depend on any single business unit to completely fund the BI initiative. The true business potential for BI usually lies in delivering information that is used across the lines of business. • Don't get maneuvered into promising a specific dollar-value return on investment that the BI information is supposed to offer. For example, if a business benefit is the potential for cross-selling, the amount that could be generated from cross-selling is pure guesswork. One selling experience could generate a minute amount, while another could generate enough revenue to cover the entire cost of the first BI application release. • Never work alone. Realize that business managers would like to profit from any competitive advantage they can get in this increasingly competitive marketplace. Business managers are quite willing to work with IT on business justification for a BI decision-support initiative.

Tips and Rules of Thumb

• Chances to succeed or fail:

  – If the BI decision-support initiative is driven by a business problem, it has a very good chance of success.

  – If the BI decision-support initiative is driven only by the latest trend in technology, it has a very good chance of failure.

• Keep complexity and integration to a minimum on every BI decision-support project to avoid a higher risk of failure.

• As early as possible, assess the risk for the six categories of technology, complexity, integration, organization, staffing, and financial investment in order to gain a better understanding of the BI initiative.

• Usage: 20 percent of the business people will be using the BI decision-support environment 80 percent of the time. Initially address the needs of those people who form that 20 percent.

Practical Guidelines Matrix — Development Step 2: Enterprise Infrastructure Evaluation

Development Step	Dos
2. Enterprise Infrastructure Evaluation	
Section A. Technical Infrastructure Evaluation	• Pay attention to scalability; avoid any components that scale poorly. Scalability is one of the most important factors to be considered.
	• Watch out for products that offer unnecessary technical elegance. The price you will pay for this elegance is either needing more staff training or requiring more resources.
	• Use tools whenever possible instead of writing your own custom code.
	• Understand the types of analyses the business people need to perform so that you can choose the appropriate tool set.
	• Keep current with technology.
	Don'ts
	• Don't jump to implement a very large database (VLDB) unless the vendor's VLDB features are delivered and have proven themselves.
	• Don't expect to buy a BI decision-support turnkey solution. A BI decision-support environment evolves over time.
	• Don't select a tool without participation by the business people; otherwise they may not buy into it and may not use it.
	• Never assume that because a software product is labeled "OLAP" it will satisfy the analytical reporting needs of the business community.
	• Don't select an OLAP tool just because it is popular. First and foremost, it must have functionality that matches the analytical requirements of the business community, and it must be easy to use.

Practical Guidelines Matrix   —   Development Step 2:   Enterprise Infrastructure Evaluation

Tips and Rules of Thumb

- Hardware: One of the main features required to support the BI decision-support environment is scalability. Therefore, monitor the rapid changes in:
  - Data volume
  - Load frequencies
  - Data access patterns
  - Number of reports and queries
  - Number of tools
  - Number of people accessing the BI target databases
  - Number of operational systems feeding the BI target databases

- DBMS functions: The necessary and important functions of the selected DBMS for the BI decision-support environment are:
  - Degree of parallelism in handling queries and data loads
  - Intelligence in handling dimensional database designs (optimizers)
  - Database scalability
  - Internet integration
  - Availability of advanced index schemes
  - Replication on heterogeneous platforms
  - Unattended operations

- DBMS workload: The BI decision-support environment is an unpredictable mix in workload demand. It is common for a BI application to support hundreds of knowledge workers, business analysts, and business managers performing data access requests that range from simple indexed retrievals to more complex comparative analysis queries. Such an environment requires that the DBMS not only provide efficient complex JOIN processing but also manage and balance the overall workload effectively.

Practical Guidelines Matrix — Development Step 2: Enterprise Infrastructure Evaluation

Development Step	Dos
Section B. Nontechnical Infrastructure Evaluation	• Identify the missing or ineffective nontechnical infrastructure components. These components provide the glue for cross-organizational integration. • Pay attention to meta data. Meta data is much more than documentation. It facilitates navigation through the BI decision-support environment and is an integral part of every BI project. • Provide standards for your formal project documents. For example, specify that each document must have a title, description, purpose, author, owner, creation date, latest update date, latest version number, revision history, page numbers, and sign-off space.

Don'ts

• Don't attempt to build all components of the nontechnical infrastructure at once. Start with standards, then model the common business data architecture, and go from there. This is an iterative refinement process.

• Don't forget to allocate time and resources on the project plan for working on noninfrastructure activities.

• Don't skip data standardization because you think it is too difficult or takes too much time. One of the main reasons for a BI decision-support initiative is to address data quality and data standardization.

Tips and Rules of Thumb

• Use a meta data repository if you have one. If you do not have one, but you have a fairly sophisticated CASE tool, use that CASE tool in the interim until a more permanent repository solution is established. At a minimum, document the source-to-target data mapping and the transformation rules in some format that can be accessed by the business people and that can later be used to populate a meta data repository.

• Determine what types of standards, guidelines, and procedures already exist in the organization— what is useful, what is not, and what is missing. The fastest way to assess this is to talk to the staff of the following groups: data administration, strategic architecture, quality assurance, security, audit, standards, training, and even operations.

• Include at least one nontechnical infrastructure requirement with every BI project. Implement at least 80 percent of its functionality, and plan to revise it in future BI projects.

• As much as possible, reuse the standards, guidelines, procedures, and so on that already exist in the organization. Try not to reinvent the wheel. Get input from as many people in IT and on the business side as you can to develop a practical and useful nontechnical infrastructure at your organization.

Practical Guidelines Matrix — Development Step 3: Project Planning

Development Step	Dos
3. Project Planning	• Use *Business Intelligence Roadmap* to create your work breakdown structure and project plan. If you have Microsoft Project, copy and modify the work breakdown structure on the CD included with this book.
	• Insist on having a full-time business representative matrixed into your project. Development work will go much faster because issues can be resolved on the spot. Also, knowledge transfer will occur because the business representative will be part of the project core team. This will also go a long way toward eliminating the "us versus them" syndrome between IT and the business.
	• Create a detailed project charter and use it as your baseline for change control.
	• Have stringent change-control procedures. Never change the scope without renegotiating the constraints of time, budget, resources, and quality. If your project plan was doable before the scope change, it will no longer be doable unless you renegotiate all constraints.
	• Plan to keep an issues log. Be aware that some issues may not get resolved during the project. This may result in a scope change, and some deliverables may have to be deferred to a future release.
	• Perform a detailed risk analysis. Be sure to weigh the risks and provide recommendations and a plan to mitigate them. Also, include a contingency plan in case the risks cannot be avoided.
	• Consider all your assumptions as potential risks, and manage them accordingly.
	• Assess the quality of source data early so that you can have confidence in your estimates for the project completion date.

Don'ts
• Never build the BI application "by the seat of the pants" because you will miss tasks, and you will underestimate the effort.
• Never make any assumptions about knowing intuitively what tasks have to be performed and how long they will take. Document your estimates in a detailed project plan.
• Don't assemble a large team. Although BI projects are big and complicated, communication and coordination among the team members will slow down the project. Keep the *project* core team down to about four or five people (never more than seven). Keep each *step* core team down to two or three people. Remember that multiple roles can be assigned to one person, and that multiple people can share one role.
• Don't plan to perform all tasks or all activities in *Business Intelligence Roadmap*. Select only the ones you need and add any additional tasks that may be unique to your BI decision-support project.
• Don't forget to allocate time to be spent on other common project-related or organizational activities not listed as tasks on your project plan (for example, troubleshooting other systems, attending department meetings, and dealing with computer downtime).

Practical Guidelines Matrix — Development Step 3: Project Planning

- Don't forget to allocate time for vacations, sick leave, jury duty, and so on.
- Don't spend too much time on tuning your estimates, only enough to have confidence in them.

Tips and Rules of Thumb

- Review the stages and determine at which stage your project needs to begin. For example, some projects will begin with justification, others will begin with planning, and some short enhancement releases may even begin with design. Then, in a similar vein, review the steps and determine which ones are appropriate for your project. Finally, review the activities as well as the tasks and subtasks, and extract only those you need to perform on your project. Most projects require 90 percent of the activities to be performed for the selected steps.

- Be prepared to answer the four questions that are always asked about every project:
  - What will be delivered?
  - How much will it cost?
  - When will it be done?
  - Who will be doing it?

- Project failures: A very high percentage of BI projects are aborted because of inadequate or non-existent project planning and because of inadequate resources. Don't become one of the casualties.

- One of the critical success factors is having a very strong business sponsor who understands the release concept of BI projects and who is agreeable to keeping the scope small and the quality high.

- Skills: It takes one week to acquire a basic skill in a seminar and six months to master it. Be sure you understand the skill set of your BI project team members.

- Estimates of time required for data cleansing are often missed by a factor of three or four. Estimate the time you think you will require and multiply it by three if your source data is stored in relational databases; multiply it by four if your source data is stored in old flat files.

- Data quality: Find out in how many places the data is stored and how many variations of the data exist.
  - If the same customer record is stored in no more than two places and the data is consistent, you have a minor problem.
  - If the same customer record is stored in three to five places and the data is consistent, you have a medium-sized problem.
  - If the same customer record is stored in six or more places and the data is inconsistent, you have a serious problem!

  Work with several important business people who will be using the BI data and discuss your findings with them.

Practical Guidelines Matrix — Development Step 4: Project Requirements Definition

Development Step	Dos
4. Project Requirements Definition	• Prioritize the functional requirements into mandatory, important, and nice-to-have. Concentrate on the mandatory functions and add important functions as time allows. Nice-to-have requirements should be dropped from the project scope.
	• Prioritize data requirements into mandatory, important, and nice-to-have. Identify the exact business needs that will be met by each category. Concentrate on the mandatory and important data, and don't include the nice-to-have data. Remember to keep data scope to a minimum because that is where all the effort is.
	• Determine whether the required source data has ever been gathered and stored in an operational system. You cannot create new data with a BI decision-support application.
	• Try to determine the types of ad hoc queries the business people may want to write. Although "ad hoc" implies that those queries are not yet defined, most business people have a pattern of questions they usually ask on a regular basis. This information will have bearing on the design of the BI target databases.
	• Be prepared to negotiate and renegotiate the final deliverables throughout the project. Unexpected roadblocks can derail a project if the scope is not renegotiated with the business representative and the business sponsor. Keeping the business representative involved in all decisions increases your chances for success despite the obstacles.

Don'ts

• Don't work without a business representative. Project requirements must come from business people, not from IT systems analysts.

• Don't spend too much time in this step on source data analysis. Investigate suspected data quality problems only enough to get a better understanding of the cleansing complexity. Conversely, don't wait until design or testing to discover dirty source data. Preliminary source data analysis must be performed in this step, and rigorous source data analysis will be performed in Step 5, Data Analysis.

• Don't spend too much time in this step on refining the logical data model, only enough to take it beyond the conceptual level and to add the significant attributes (data elements).

• Never accept a wish list of data elements and a stack of mock reports as the final requirements. Requirements need to be negotiated.

• This is not the time to commit to service-level agreements because it is too early to know if they can be met. However, you *can* document the outer limits of what will be acceptable and what will not be acceptable to the business sponsor and to the business people.

Practical Guidelines Matrix — Development Step 4: Project Requirements Definition

Tips and Rules of Thumb

- Always review the scope to see if it is still doable within the constraints of time, budget, resources, and quality. Always balance the constraints and renegotiate them when necessary with the business sponsor and the business representative.

- Defining requirements is a different activity than designing a solution. Don't let the technicians jump into designing the solution at this time, as many like to do.

- Try to conduct as many group interviews as possible. The synergy created during these sessions often brings new requirements to the surface, uncovers definitional and quality problems, clears up misunderstandings, and occasionally even resolves disputes.

- In regards to source data for the BI target databases, going after too much operational data "just in case they'll need it some day" leads to more complex data models and more time and money spent for data extraction, cleansing, and maintenance. Not all data is created equal. Keep in mind that in most cases, only 20 percent of the BI data is regularly used 80 percent of the time.

- Ask the IT staff to help identify which source data is seldom or never used by the business people. This means that it most probably does not have to be included in the BI project scope. However, let the business representative make the final decision, not the technicians.

Practical Guidelines Matrix   —   Development Step 5: Data Analysis

Development Step	Dos
5. Data Analysis	• Ensure that the logical data model reflects the cross-organizational understanding of data and is not an isolated view of one business representative or one department. For example, if the desire is to study customer profiles that cross all product lines in the organization, common customer and product definitions are critical components.
	• Understand the kinds of external data that will be used in the BI decision-support environment. Determine what the basis will be to synthesize the external information with the internal information.
	• Review all business meta data with the data owners and with the information consumers (business managers and business analysts in other departments who use that data) to obtain their concurrence on data definitions, data domains, business rules, and data usage.
	• Establish a dispute resolution procedure to resolve differences among business people from different departments regarding data definitions, data domains, business rules, and data usage. These procedures should suggest the involvement of a BI arbitration board as a last resort.
	• Urge the data owners to accept responsibility and accountability for the quality of their data. Ask them to clean up their operational source data, if feasible.
	• Identify the critical data elements that have real business value. These critical data elements have to be cleansed to meet the business expectations of data reliability.

	Don'ts
	• Never develop a logical data model in isolation. Business people must drive the data requirements: what information they need, how they need it, when they need it, and how clean it has to be.
	• When reviewing the business meta data with business people from other departments, resist including their data requirements in your scope. Remind those other business people that you only want them to validate the correctness of your data definitions, domains, business rules, and so on.
	• Don't ask programmers or systems people to create the business meta data. (Technicians generally do not enjoy analysis, just as business analysts generally do not enjoy programming.) Find people who enjoy detailed business analysis, such as data administrators, business analysts, and subject matter experts.
	• Don't assume that the more current the data, the higher the accuracy. If quality processes are not enforced at an organization, new data can get corrupted within months.
	• Don't underestimate the time it will take to resolve the many battles among the business people to arrive at a consensus on valid data definitions, data domains, business rules, and interpretations of data.

Practical Guidelines Matrix — Development Step 5: Data Analysis

- Never suck and plunk! In other words, don't plan to move all the source data as is. One of the main reasons for a BI decision-support initiative is gaining access to reliable and clean data. Simply giving access to dirty data through a BI application will not help business executives make better decisions.
- Don't attempt to cleanse every piece of data because the cleansing task can become overwhelming without providing real business value. Triage your data-cleansing activity.

Tips and Rules of Thumb

- The most effective techniques for both data integration and source data analysis are normalization rules and logical data modeling. Involve a data administrator on your project to create the logical data model. Data administration should then compare and merge your project-specific logical data model with the enterprise logical data model to find and resolve data discrepancies.
- In regards to business rules, use top-down logical data modeling to *define* the business rules and bottom-up source data analysis to discover where the source data *violates* the business rules.
- While the data is being modeled, have the source data analyzed. Since there is never enough time to analyze each data element, prioritize the data elements, and concentrate on the most critical ones.
- The data analysis effort on BI projects can be greatly reduced if logical data models and business meta data already exist for the operational source systems. Unfortunately, these models and meta data are rarely created for operational systems and, therefore, they rarely exist. The business representative and business sponsor should urge the owners of the operational systems (line-of-business managers) to consider creating logical data models and collecting business meta data for their operational systems in the future.
- Business managers (and many IT managers) who have not been through data cleansing before and who are unfamiliar with the effort often underestimate the time required by a factor of four.
- Source data analysis is primarily an intensive manual effort. Although tools can help with the effort, they cannot eliminate it.
- Solicit help from the IT staff when needed. Systems analysts, developers, and database administrators often know the technical aspects of the data more intimately than the business representative or the data owners do. The IT staff knows how and where the data is stored, processed, and used. They often have in-depth knowledge of the accuracy, the relationships, and the history of the data.

Practical Guidelines Matrix   —   Development Step 5: Data Analysis

- Be sure that you have a mechanism for capturing the business meta data during this step. At a minimum, capture:
  - Data names
  - Definitions
  - Relationships
  - Cardinality
  - Data domains
  - Business rules
- Source data quality will only be as good as the enforcement of quality processes in the operational systems. Quality enforcement should include data entry rules, edit checks, and training. Improving the organization's quality of data is a holistic approach and cannot be achieved through data cleansing alone.

Practical Guidelines Matrix   —   Development Step 6: Application Prototyping

Development Step	Dos

6. Application Prototyping	• Decide on the type of application prototype to create:
	  – Show-and-tell
	  – Mock-up
	  – Proof-of-concept
	  – Visual-design
	  – Demo
	  – Operational
	
	• Get business people to participate in the prototype from the beginning, especially during needs assessment and graphical user interface construction. Remember, it is *their* definition of success and failure that counts, not yours.
	
	• Make sure that time limits are set and followed for each prototype iteration.
	
	• Limit each prototype to a specific subject area or a specific application function.
	
	• Review and renegotiate the project constraints whenever the scope of the prototype changes.
	
	• Communicate daily with the project core team members, especially the database administrator and the ETL lead developer.
	
	• Make sure that the business people realize that only a *prototype* is being built, not a full-scale, production-worthy BI application.
	
	• Learn about the reporting dimensions, the level of aggregation needed, and the variety of data accessed. Test the database design during the prototype.
	
	• Stop prototyping when you reach the point of diminishing returns.

Don'ts
• Don't promise what you cannot deliver. Unfulfilled promises can damage your reputation. • Don't include all the project requirements in the scope of the prototype. Even when using the operational prototype as a development method for the access and analysis portion of the BI application, each prototype should deliver only a small piece of the final BI application. • Don't keep adding new functionality to the end of the prototype when the original objectives of the prototype have been reached. If you want to continue prototyping, set new objectives, and revise the project plan.

Practical Guidelines Matrix   —   Development Step 6:   Application Prototyping

- It is best not to use an arbitrary sample of source data. Source data is usually voluminous, and an arbitrary sample may not necessarily represent all the possible combinations that need to be tested in that particular prototype.

- Don't contaminate the prototype with poor-quality data, and don't spend any time cleansing the data unless you are testing an ETL function.

- Don't address too many data integration requirements. The more integration, the higher the complexity, and the longer the prototype will take. Data integration requirements should be kept to a minimum.

- Don't ignore the front-end interface design. Be sure to have the business people involved.

- Don't work only with the business people who are vocal or who are your favorites. You need to have some nonbelievers as well because they will tell you more readily when something is not working. You want to find out during prototyping what is working and what is not. Most importantly, include the business people who "sign the check" for the prototype since the funding is coming out of their budget and they form the core group for whom the prototype is being built.

- Don't underestimate the time required to implement suggested changes.

- Don't use the prototype to test technology *performance*. This is not a stress-testing environment.

Tips and Rules of Thumb

- To test ease of use, let the business people have as much hands-on experience with the prototype as possible so that you can see whether the application will be easy to use the way you are planning to build it.

- Use the prototype activity to build and maintain a coalition comprised of line-of-business managers, IT managers, and senior business executives.

- Ensure that an appropriate number of business people participate in the prototype (more than one but no more than eight).

- Avoid using a large project team to build the prototype. Don't add to the team size if deadlines are missed. Instead, *shrink* the team size! "Bloating" the team will increase the time required for staff communication and *slow things down* even more. Shrinking the team size will reduce required communication among team members and will enable the team to get things done faster.

- Business managers often think they need only summary data, but sooner or later they end up asking for detailed data. Depending on your design and the tools you are using, providing detailed data may not be as trivial as it sounds. Be sure to test it in the prototype.

Practical Guidelines Matrix — Development Step 6: Application Prototyping

- Consider building an operational prototype for the access and analysis portion of the BI application. Operational prototypes are robust enough, and access and analysis tools are flexible enough, that this type of prototype could naturally evolve into the final access and analysis application after several tightly controlled iterations. The activities of Step 12, Application Development, could be applied to the final iteration of the operational prototype.

- Define ease of use. When is a system considered easy to use? Some measurements include the following:

  - Learning curve: One or two days is the maximum that a business person can usually set aside for learning a new application.

  - Speed of task accomplishment: By using the new BI application, knowledge workers and business analysts have to be able to finish their analysis tasks at least 25 percent faster.

  - Subjective satisfaction: The business people should be looking forward to using the new BI application and not avoiding it.

  - The help function: The business people should be using the help function at least once a day for the first month rather than avoiding it because it is too complicated or too confusing.

  - Difference in usage and needs: Not all business people are created equal. Understand the different needs of executive managers versus business analysts.

Practical Guidelines Matrix — Development Step 7: Meta Data Repository Analysis

Development Step	Dos
7. Meta Data Repository Analysis	• Have the business representative participate in the meta data requirements definition process. Meta data is an important part of every BI project and needs to be given the same amount of attention as business data.
	• Establish data ownership and allow those data owners to control the meta data for the business data over which they have authority. Data ownership can be assumed by business managers individually or by a representative committee.
	• Work with the data administrators to develop or revise cross-organizational data standards and publish those standards.
	• Plan to consolidate all existing meta data from various tools into one enterprise meta data repository.
	• Capture and validate the meta data requirements through a logical meta model using the entity-relationship modeling technique, even if you later decide to license a meta data repository or to build one based on an object-oriented design.
	• Pay equal attention to business meta data and technical meta data.

Don'ts

• Don't try to do everything at once, but don't forget the big picture either. The meta data repository will evolve over time just like the other components of the BI decision-support environment.

• Don't forget to analyze the interface requirements for the meta data repository. There are two types of interfaces to consider: the access interface for business people and technicians, and the tool interface to the ETL, OLAP, CASE, and other tools.

• Don't consider meta data to be just documentation. Meta data provides the context for business data and is used as a navigation tool in the BI decision-support environment. It is therefore an integral deliverable of every BI application.

Tips and Rules of Thumb

• If your organization has no meta data solution and this is the first time you are addressing meta data, triple your time estimates for the development steps in the Meta Data Repository track.

Practical Guidelines Matrix   —   Development Step 7: Meta Data Repository Analysis

- Prioritize the meta data components into three categories:
  - Mandatory
  - Important
  - Optional

  All mandatory meta data components should be captured and stored. Also try to capture as many important components as you can, and postpone the optional ones if you run out of time.

- When creating the logical meta model, draw the entity-relationship diagram for the most critical meta data components:
  - Entity
  - Attribute
  - Relationship rules (cardinality and optionality)
  - Table
  - Column
  - Keys (primary and foreign)
  - Domain
  - Data type and length
  - Definition
  - Transformation rules

  Add additional components to your logical meta model as time allows.

Practical Guidelines Matrix — Development Step 8: Database Design

Development Step	Dos
8. Database Design	• Work with multiple business people to understand the types of analyses they need to perform and the ways they will access the data. Choose the appropriate database design schema based on those requirements and access patterns. • Use the entities on the logical data model and the business meta data as a starting point for designing the conformed dimensions and the normalized snowflake dimensions. • Review the lessons learned from the prototyping activities. See how many reports and queries can be run in parallel, what dimensions are needed, and what security is needed. • Identify similar reporting patterns among business analysts in order to minimize the number of star schemas needed. • Plan to monitor the performance of queries and reports on a regular basis. • Expect to continually refine the BI target database designs. • Make decisions about clustering tables, partitioning, data placement, and indexing with performance in mind. • Index those columns that are searched on frequently and that have a high distribution in values.

	Don'ts
	• Never attempt to implement a fully normalized logical data model! The purpose for a normalized logical data model in any environment (operational or BI) is to facilitate business analysis. Even if an entity-relationship design schema is chosen, the logical data model must still be *denormalized* into a physical data model (database design). • Don't assume that one size fits all. Different business people have different access requirements; they need different levels of detail and summarization; and they have different requirements for timeliness, availability, and quality. • Don't assume that all BI target databases must be multidimensional. There are occasions where an entity-relationship design is appropriate. Be sure to let the *requirements* drive the database design decision, not the latest technology or design trends. • Don't count on being able to reload your BI target databases from scratch after a catastrophic database failure. It would take a very long time, if it could be done at all. Plan on taking frequent backups (full, partial, or incremental).

Practical Guidelines Matrix — Development Step 8: Database Design

- Don't blindly use a physical data model (database design) developed for a different organization. Often those models reflect compromises made for a given organization, which could easily lead to having to redesign your database later.

Tips and Rules of Thumb

- Database administrators—not programmers—should design databases. Do not use database administrators as "data entry clerks" who simply type up and run DDL handed to them by the programmers. The job description of database administrators includes database design for the main reason that database administrators are or should be trained in the DBMS-specific optimizers as well as in multidimensional design techniques.

- Understand the differences between operational databases and BI target databases. Key features in well-designed operational databases are normalization, utilization of DBMS referential integrity, and judicious use of indexing. Key features in BI target databases are just the opposite: denormalization, reliance on program-enforced referential integrity, and heavy indexing.

- Many BI target databases will almost inevitably fall into the VLDB category.
  - Small databases are in the range of 10 to 100 GB
  - Medium databases are in the range of 100 to 300 GB
  - Large databases are in the range of 300 to 800 GB
  - VLDBs are in the range of 800 GB to many terabytes

  Since a BI target database is grow-only, today's small database is next year's medium (or large) database.

- Clustering is a very useful technique for sequential access of large amounts of data. Since sequential access of data is the norm in BI applications, using this technique can dramatically improve performance.

- Physically co-locate related tables on the disk drive.

- When indexing the dimension tables, either of two extreme approaches may pay off.
  - Index everything in sight.
  - Leave the table as a heap (no physical index or ordering whatsoever).

  The decision depends on the makeup, usage, size, and distribution of data values in the dimension tables.

Practical Guidelines Matrix — Development Step 8: Database Design

- When should an index *not* be built?
  - When value entries in the index are more than 15 percent, building an index does not pay off. For example, if an index is built on the column Gender_Code there will be about 50 percent entries in the index for the value "female" and 50 percent entries for the value "male."
  - When the index database is searched sequentially.
  - When performance still does not improve.
  - Or worse, when as a result of building the index, performance is degraded even further because of the additional adding and dropping of indices and maintaining the index database.

- When should the databases be reorganized?
  - When 5 percent of the records are inserted or deleted. Removing fragmentation improves performance.

Practical Guidelines Matrix — Development Step 9: Extract/Transform/Load Design

Development Step	Dos
9. Extract/ Transform/Load Design	• Remember that the more data elements you include in the scope, the more transformations will need to be coded, and the longer the ETL process will run.
	• Let your transformation requirements drive the selection of an ETL tool, not marketing hype from the vendors.
	• Create the load files for all BI target databases for the same ETL process. Loading one BI target database only to turn around and read it again to extract, transform, and load another BI target database is too time consuming and unnecessary.
	• Share *one* ETL process and staging area. Do not allow each data mart to have its own ETL process because that produces stovepipe systems. While a staging area can be decentralized (running different ETL functions on different platforms), the only valid reasons for decentralizing are due to different types and locations of source files and source databases, as well as the functions, capabilities, and licensing terms of the ETL tool. Nevertheless, the ETL staging area should be managed as one logical unit.
	• Include data quality metrics and reconciliation totals in the ETL process design for every program that moves or manipulates data.

Don'ts

• Don't develop the ETL process flow without the assistance and participation of the database administrator. Database administrators often know about tricks of the trade that can help streamline the ETL process flow.

• Never limit the ETL process to the technical conversion rules. ETL is much more than converting the data type and length of your source data structures to your target data structures. It also includes transformation logic for business data domain rules and business data integrity rules.

• Don't automatically delete rows from the BI target databases after discovering that an operational record was deleted from a source file or source database. Develop business rules for the ETL process, which specify when to propagate operational record deletions into the BI target databases and when not to propagate them.

• Don't overlook aggregations and summarizations for the data marts. These need to be incorporated toward the end of the ETL process flow.

• No matter how advanced the ETL tool is, don't rely on it to know exactly how to populate the BI target databases by following standard conversion rules. Only the business people and IT understand the business rules that are buried in the source data and in the operational programs.

Practical Guidelines Matrix   —   Development Step 9:   Extract/Transform/Load Design

Tips and Rules of Thumb

- About 80 percent of ETL work is in the "T" (transform). It is the most complicated process of any BI decision-support application. Be sure to allocate enough time for designing the ETL processes. The success of your BI initiative may depend on it.

- At a minimum, transformations should reconcile different expressions of the same data from different sources. Transformations should also enforce business data domain rules and business data integrity rules.

- The biggest challenge in determining the correct transformation and cleansing specifications is finding people who understand the origin and history of the source data. Do not limit yourself to the business people. Look for programmers who have been around for many years and who know the history of some of the source files and source databases.

- If loading past history is not required with the initial implementation of the BI application, try to postpone building the historical load process until the next release. That will reduce the scope of the project and speed up delivery of the BI application release.

- Turn off referential integrity during the ETL load cycle, and turn it back on after the load has completed to allow the DBMS to find referential integrity violations. Look for tables in "check pending."

- Drop all indices during the ETL load cycle, and recreate them after the load has completed.

Practical Guidelines Matrix — Development Step 10: Meta Data Repository Design

Development Step	Dos
10. Meta Data Repository Design	• Review and expand (if necessary) the meta data repository design with every BI project. Be sure your design can accommodate expansion.
	• Evaluate off-the-shelf meta data repository products, which have the capability to integrate business meta data with technical meta data. It may be easier and faster to install a product than to build custom software, especially when the schedule is tight.
	• Follow up with client references provided by vendors when licensing (buying) a meta data repository product. Ask the vendors' clients what the vendor products cannot do and what they don't like about the products.
	• Design a reusable interface between the meta data repository and other tools (CASE, ETL, OLAP, report writers, other access and analysis tools)
	• Provide a context-sensitive online help function for meta data. This feature is invaluable to business people, who will use it to help them navigate not only through the meta data repository but also through the BI decision-support environment as a whole.

Don'ts

• Don't shortcut the meta data repository design by modeling only the most common meta data entities. When building a customized solution, design it to be fully functioning, even though you may not implement all of the features at once.

• Don't fail to automate the integration process of linking the business meta data with the technical meta data. Linking (relating) those two types of meta data manually is a labor-intensive process.

• Don't forget to include meta data components for capturing metrics, such as data reliability factors, reconciliation totals, and load statistics.

• Don't even consider any meta data repository products that do not satisfy your *mandatory* meta data requirements.

• Don't forget to evaluate the vendors in addition to their products. Vendor stability is important for sustaining a meta data repository solution.

Practical Guidelines Matrix   —   Development Step 10: Meta Data Repository Design

Tips and Rules of Thumb

- Since the meta data repository is a database, many tips and rules of thumb that are applicable to database design are also applicable to meta data repository design.

- Start with a central meta data repository database because distributed meta data repositories and XML-enabled meta data solutions are more difficult to build and maintain.

- Start with an entity-relationship design rather than an object-oriented design. They are easier to implement and easier to comprehend.

- About 90 percent of direct access to the meta data repository will be from the business people and only about 10 percent from the technicians. Meta data helps business people understand the meaning of the data, the quality of the data content, where the data came from (source system), and how to use it. Therefore, spend time on designing an easy-to-use access interface to the meta data repository.

Practical Guidelines Matrix — Development Step 11: Extract/Transform/Load Development

Development Step	Dos
11. Extract/Transform/Load Development	• Run as many ETL programs in parallel as possible to cut down on runtime. Since the ETL staging window at most large organizations is very short (often only a few hours per night), be prepared to run your ETL process over several nights.
	• Produce reconciliation totals for record counts, domain counts, and amount counts. These totals should be stored in the meta data repository for every load cycle.
	• Produce a detailed error accounting for source data that failed the edit rules and was rejected, as well as for source data that failed the edit rules but was accepted. Errors should be categorized, such as number of missing values, number of domain violations, number of business rules violations, and so on.
	• Perform rigorous testing with formal test plans, test cases, and expected test results.
	• Involve the business representative in writing the test cases and expected test results.
	• Use a stress test simulation tool to project estimated performance numbers before running an actual performance (stress) test with real data.
	• Use peer reviews or XP programming techniques for quality control.

	Don'ts
	• Developers should not test their own code; however, they can test the code of other developers.
	• Don't limit the business representative and the subject matter expert to testing only the access and analysis portion of the BI application. Be sure they are also involved in testing the ETL process.
	• Don't consider integration or regression testing completed until all programs in the ETL process run as expected from beginning to end. In other words, don't just test individual modules until they are error free, but test and retest the entire job stream until it runs error free.
	• Never skip testing because you think you can fix problems in the next release. If the BI target databases are not loaded properly with correct data, the BI application is of no use to the business people.
	• Don't expect to cleanse the source data in the operational systems. The operational systems staff actually expect their dirty data to run successfully! In many cases, modifying an operational system is not cost-effective. On the other hand, old practices and bad habits that produce these data quality problems should be addressed. Ask your business sponsor to make the owners of the operational systems and the business executives aware of the cost and effort it takes to cleanse their bad data for the BI decision-support environment. Some general data quality standards should be implemented across the entire organization to avoid perpetuating data quality problems.

Practical Guidelines Matrix — Development Step 11: Extract/Transform/Load Development

Tips and Rules of Thumb

- Organizations devote close to 80 percent of the BI project time to back-end efforts, including labor-intensive data cleansing. Although tools can help with assessing the extent of data quality problems in the operational systems, they cannot magically turn bad data into good data.

- Cleansing data is a time-intensive and expensive process. Analyze, prioritize, and then choose your battles since cleansing 20 percent of the enterprise data may solve 80 percent of the information needs.

- About 80 percent of the data transformation effort is spent on enforcing business data domain rules and business data integrity rules, and only about 20 percent of the effort is spent on technical data conversion rules.

- The most common symptoms of dirty source data are data inconsistencies and overuse of data elements, especially in old flat files, where one data element can explicitly be redefined half a dozen times or can implicitly have half a dozen different meanings.

- Why use automated software tools for data transformation? Data-profiling tools can significantly shorten the time it takes to analyze data domains. ETL tools can perform data type and length conversions and code translations in minutes, rather than hours when done manually. However, note that writing data-cleansing algorithms is still a manual effort and must be performed before the ETL tool can be utilized.

- The ETL process will run into fewer problems if extensive source data analysis is performed ahead of time. Source data rules are usually discovered *proactively* during requirements gathering, data analysis, and meta data repository analysis. They are discovered *reactively* during prototyping, application development, ETL development, and when loading the BI target databases during implementation.

Practical Guidelines Matrix — Development Step 12: Application Development

Development Step	Dos
12. Application Development	• Let the business people define what types of analyses they will perform. Let their analysis needs drive the choice of tools to be deployed. And, let the requirements of the tools define the schema in which the data should be stored.
	• Keep abreast of the latest BI tools. Standards and tools are evolving constantly, and new tools and features leapfrog each other. The features that used to clearly delineate OLAP strengths and weaknesses (for example, indexing approaches, size barriers and scalability, API standardization) have become less important as tools mature and add features.
	• Determine and communicate the strengths and weaknesses of each access and analysis tool, whether it is a report writer, an OLAP tool, or another query tool.
	• Consider selecting a product suite that combines querying, reporting, and analysis capabilities for multidimensional analysis. Querying, reporting, and analysis are interrelated, interactive, and iterative and can be implemented with one tool. A business person should not have to switch between tools for different types of analyses, such as from the "what" analysis (query and reporting) to the "why" analysis (OLAP).

Don'ts

• Don't start with every possible dimension to satisfy every conceivable multidimensional query. Keep in mind that the more dimensions you have, the bigger the database, the more granular the facts, the longer it will take to precalculate the facts, the longer the ETL process will run, and the longer it will take to run reports and queries.

• Don't plan to store every possible computation and ratio (fact) just because you can.

• Don't forget to stress test the access and analysis components of the BI application. OLAP tools have their limitations, and you must find those limitations early in order to adjust your design before moving the BI application into production.

• Avoid having completely different production and development platforms. In many organizations, the development platform is very "rich" in resources, but the production machines are very "meager." As a result, performance is outstanding during development and terrible in production.

Practical Guidelines Matrix — Development Step 12: Application Development

Tips and Rules of Thumb

- Find out how many dimensions the business people commonly use for slicing and dicing.
  - Two or three dimensions are easily grasped.
  - Four dimensions require training and practice for comprehension (the fourth dimension is usually the time dimension).
  - Five and six dimensions get difficult to comprehend and to use effectively.
  - Seven should be the maximum number of dimensions used.
- In order to optimize performance, store and use precalculated facts for slicing-and-dicing analysis. A simple query should be able to run in less than 5 seconds. Business people are not interested in knowing about the delay in response time because of the sizes of the tables or because of inefficient indexing. They expect *reasonable* performance, even for complex queries.
- The complexity of queries run against the BI target databases generally breaks down as follows:
  - About 80 percent of the queries are simple.
  - About 20 percent of the queries are complex.
- The breakdown of the complexity of reports run against the BI target databases is generally the opposite of that for queries.
  - About 20 percent of the reports are simple.
  - About 80 percent of the reports are complex.
- Knowledge workers and business analysts executing simple queries are like farmers—they harvest their crops on a regular basis. In order to get better performance, prebuild tables to satisfy these routines.
- Knowledge workers and business analysts executing complex queries are like gold miners—they dig many mines before they strike gold, so they need a powerful platform to let them look for their data and manipulate it.

Practical Guidelines Matrix — Development Step 13: Data Mining

Development Step	Dos
13. Data Mining	• Plan to incorporate data mining into the BI decision-support environment. Although data mining can use data from operational files and databases, BI target databases usually provide the only place where data has been cleansed and consolidated across functional boundaries. • Work with sales or marketing groups to bring in data mining technology. These groups are the most likely groups to understand the business value of data mining and may champion the data mining effort. • Spend some time and effort researching data mining and knowledge discovery techniques and methods before selecting products or hiring consultants. The technology itself takes various approaches and employs high-level applied mathematics, advanced statistics, and artificial intelligence. Since few vendors offer a full range of data mining techniques and methods, most will be biased toward whatever is used in their products. • Hire consultants specializing in data mining to help set up your data mining environment and to help interpret the data mining results. Data mining is difficult; it requires a statistical background to interpret data mining results. • Start the data mining efforts with realistic expectations. Setting expectations too high may result in disappointment. It is commonly known that your satisfaction depends on your expectations.
	Don'ts
	• Don't forget to work with other departments to find additional potential applications for data mining. Sales and marketing are not the only departments that can benefit; credit risk, manufacturing, acquisition, billing, and human resources can also utilize data mining. • Don't get fooled by software vendors who claim to have data mining capabilities in their products, when their tools are just query tools that require the business analyst to be the analytical engine. • Don't believe software vendors who say that data mining does not offer any real advantages. • Don't assume that you must have a BI decision-support environment in order to implement data mining. Also, don't assume that every BI target database will be a suitable source for data mining. • Don't run data mining directly against operational files and operational databases. The performance impact on the operational systems would be enormous.

Practical Guidelines Matrix — Development Step 13: Data Mining

Tips and Rules of Thumb

- Beware of using operational data for data mining. Operational data is often full of duplicates, inconsistencies, and errors. Using this data could throw off your data mining results.

- Before building an analytical data model you have to prepare the data by classifying the variables. Variables could be discrete or continuous, qualitative or quantitative. If you find variables that have missing values, either eliminate the variables or replace the missing values with "most likely" values.

- Compare your data mining results with industry statistics on a regular basis. Industry statistics are established periodically by using very large samples of data.

- When using data mining, one or more of the following marketing opportunities should be realized in order to cost-justify the activity:

  - Cross-selling should be enabled or enhanced as a result of data mining efforts.

  - A large percentage of customers should be retained. These customers would have left if a defection pattern had not been noticed through data mining.

  - Marketing costs should be reduced as a result of data mining efforts.

  - New customers should be acquired as a result of data mining efforts.

  However, it is challenging to know when to attribute these changes to the data mining efforts and when these changes would have occurred naturally without the data mining efforts.

Practical Guidelines Matrix — Development Step 14: Meta Data Repository Development

Development Step	Dos
14. Meta Data Repository Development	• Provide interactive and context-sensitive meta data query capabilities. Using the meta data repository should be easy and intuitive. • Keep the meta data repository in synch with the meta data contained in other tools and in the DBMS. Unfortunately, meta data repositories are still passive, which means that the synchronization has to be performed manually or through custom-written programs. • Actively maintain the meta data repository. If the content of the meta data repository becomes stale, it will affect the business people who are relying on the completeness and accuracy of the meta data. It will make the meta data repository questionable, and the business people may stop using it.

Don'ts

• Don't underestimate the effort required to build and maintain a meta data repository, especially if you choose a decentralized or distributed approach. Building gateways and portals are not trivial activities.

• Don't attempt to develop a meta data repository with part-time people who will leave after the meta data repository is implemented. You need at least one dedicated person to maintain the meta data repository on an ongoing basis.

• Don't overlook existing sources of meta data. Organizations are sometimes drowning in documentation. The challenge will be to separate the valuable current information from outdated information that is no longer valid.

Tips and Rules of Thumb

• Developing a meta data repository solution is not an event—it is an evolution. It starts with the first BI decision-support initiative and continues to evolve on an ongoing basis. Whenever new business data is added to the BI target databases, new meta data is added to the meta data repository (for example, names, definitions, and domains of the new business data). Whenever new functionality is added to the BI applications, new meta data is added to the meta data repository (for example, calculations and reconciliation totals for the new functions).

• Be prepared to develop two types of meta data repository interfaces:
 – Access interface for business people and technicians
 – Tool interface for sharing meta data between the meta data repository and the tools where meta data is originated

Practical Guidelines Matrix — Development Step 14: Meta Data Repository Development

- Be sure to understand the import/export features of the tools from which you will extract meta data, for example, CASE, ETL, OLAP. Depending on how much or how little commonality there is among the tools, you may have to write several different tool interface programs.

- The estimated size of a meta data repository could reach 5 percent of the total size of BI target databases, if done correctly and diligently.

- Keeping the meta data repository up to date and synchronized with other tools, databases, and programs is a challenge. It will require collaboration from all stakeholders on all BI projects. The bigger challenge is to get the operational systems people to communicate any changes to their source data *immediately*. Changes to source data may also affect the ETL process and the design of the BI target databases.

- Remember that for every day of coding, you will probably spend at least three days on testing.

Practical Guidelines Matrix — Development Step 15: Implementation

Development Step	Dos
15. Implementation	• Work closely with the operations staff in creating the production program libraries and moving all programs into the production environment.
	• Include regular database maintenance activities in the job schedule, such as database backups and reorganizations.
	• Use appropriate monitoring and alert utilities to detect and diagnose resource problems early.
	• Work with your organization's security officer to prepare a security gap analysis matrix, and make sure that only authorized persons can access the data that is intended for their use.

Don'ts

• Don't try to roll out a BI application to the entire organization all at once. Use an incremental implementation approach, learn as you go, and make adjustments where needed (for example, provide training earlier in the process or change the log-on procedures).

• Don't skimp on support staff. A BI decision-support environment is very complex, and the business people will need mentoring.

• Don't offer open Internet access to the BI target databases without properly tested security measures. Improper security measures could allow competitors to view sensitive organizational data, allow unauthorized people to see customer data, or allow someone to misuse or abuse displayed information. In the worst case, you may also be liable for fines, legal consequences, and so on.

Tips and Rules of Thumb

• The standard engineering maxim for sizing databases is to estimate the volume of your business data, then triple it to get a realistic size (if a lot of indices are created, quadruple it). The allocation of space is often distributed as follows:

  – 30 percent business data
  – 30 percent indices
  – 30 percent summaries, aggregates
  – 10 percent miscellaneous

• Based on the experience of other organizations, you can assume that your BI decision-support environment will double in size every two years. Some believe this is a conservative estimate.

Practical Guidelines Matrix   –   Development Step 15: Implementation

- Many BI target databases are by their nature VLDBs. Therefore, stop conserving disk space if the BI application is helping the organization to make a profit.
- Because of the immense size of VLDBs, backing up entire tables all at once may not be possible. Consider incremental ("net change") backups, high-speed mainframe backups, or partial backups of partitions.
- Monitor computer utilization, network utilization, and personnel utilization closely to avoid unexpected bottlenecks.

Practical Guidelines Matrix — Development Step 16: Release Evaluation

Development Step	Dos
16. Release Evaluation	• Conduct the post-implementation review meeting offsite to eliminate interruptions. • Invite all project team members (from the core team as well as the extended team). You may invite additional stakeholders as observers if they have a vested interest in the lessons learned from the BI project. • Stay focused on the agenda during the meeting. Schedule a second meeting if the topics cannot be covered adequately in the time allocated. • Send out a preliminary agenda early and invite attendees to add items to it. • End on a positive note and with assigned action items for future development improvements and possible business process improvements.

Don'ts

• Don't pretend you are using the release concept if you don't follow the BI application release guidelines. To simply hurry an incomplete project to implementation with little thought, no structure, and poor quality is not in the spirit of the release concept.

• Never accept the excuse that "nobody has time for a one-day post-implementation review." This indicates a lack of commitment from management to improve the quality and speed of the development process, which they claim they want.

• Don't review voluminous documentation because that is unproductive. However, if some documents will be referenced during the meeting, send those documents out ahead of time so that the attendees can read them before the meeting.

• Don't let the meeting deteriorate into a "finger-pointing" session.

• Don't postpone the meeting beyond two to three months after implementation because people will become disinterested and will forget the issues.

• Don't use anyone from the core team to be the facilitator or the scribe. Core team members are major players and contributors during the post-implementation review. Their level of participation would be diminished if they had to lead the session or take notes. Have a trained third-party facilitator conduct the meeting, and have a third-party scribe take notes during the meeting.

Practical Guidelines Matrix   —   Development Step 16:   Release Evaluation

Tips and Rules of Thumb

- Implement your BI applications using the release concept. It is much better to deliver high-quality, partially functioning application releases over time than to deliver a low-quality, completed application that is fraught with many defects and with dirty data. If the first release is successful, new requirements will emerge as the business people get used to the iterative development process.

- Post-implementation reviews should always be performed after each BI project. The purpose for these reviews is to document "lessons learned" and to improve the BI development approach. These lessons could also be shared with other project teams and business managers.

Work Breakdown Structure

The work breakdown structure in this appendix reflects the contents of the enclosed CD-ROM.

TASK_DATA

ID	Task_Name	Predecessors
1	**Your Project Name**	
2	**Step 1: Business Case Assessment**	
3	**Determine the business need**	
4	Identify the business need	
5	Determine current financial consequences of the business need	
6	**Assess the current decision-support system (DSS) solutions**	3
7	Assess current usage of the existing DSS	
8	Determine the shortcomings of the existing DSS	
9	Perform gap analysis	
10	**Assess the operational sources and procedures**	3
11	**Assess the data quality of operational systems**	
12	Review file structures and databases	
13	Review content (domain) of source data elements	
14	**Assess the current data movement**	
15	Review data entry practices	
16	Review data extraction practices	
17	Review data manipulation practices	
18	Review data duplication practices	
19	**Assess current operational procedures**	
20	Identify poor data entry practices	

ID	Task_Name	Predecessors
21	Identify lack of edit checks	
22	Identify defective program code	
23	Identify lack of training	
24	**Assess the competitors' BI decision-support initiatives**	3
25	Determine the competitors' successes and failures	
26	Determine whether competitors gained market advantages	
27	**Determine the BI application objectives**	6, 10, 24
28	Identify the strategic business goals of the organization	
29	Define the overall BI decision-support objectives	
30	Define the project-specific BI application objectives	
31	Match the overall BI decision-support objectives to the strategic business goals	
32	Match the project-specific BI application objectives to the strategic business goals	
33	**Propose a BI solution**	27
34	Review current DSS solutions	
35	Review DSS gap analysis	
36	Determine how the BI application will lessen the business pain	
37	Create a high-level architecture for the proposed BI solution	
38	Consolidate and prioritize unfulfilled requirements from previous BI projects	
39	Create a high-level (conceptual) logical data model	
40	**Perform a cost-benefit analysis**	27
41	Determine costs	
42	**Determine benefits (tangible and intangible)**	
43	Identify short-term benefits to the organization	
44	Identify long-term benefits to the organization	
45	Calculate the projected return on investment (ROI)	41, 42
46	**Perform a risk assessment**	27
47	**Create a risk assessment matrix**	
48	List the technology risks	
49	List the complexity risks	

ID	Task_Name	Predecessors
50	List the integration risks	
51	List the organization risks	
52	List the project team risks	
53	List the financial investment risks	
54	Assign weights to the risks	47
55	Rank the risks: low, medium, or high	54
56	Determine the risks (ramifications) of not implementing a BI solution	54
57	**Write the assessment report**	33, 40, 46
58	Describe the business need	
59	Describe lost opportunities	
60	Describe the proposed BI solution	
61	State the cost justification and expected ROI	
62	Include risk assessment results	
63	Write recommendations (include operational business process improvements)	
64	Obtain project approval from business sponsor	57
65	**Step 2: Enterprise Infrastructure Evaluation**	
66	**Section A: Technical Infrastructure Evaluation**	
67	**Assess the existing platform**	64
68	Review hardware	
69	Review operating systems	
70	Review middleware, especially DBMS gateways	
71	Review custom interfaces	
72	Review network components and bandwidth	
73	Review the DBMS	
74	Review tools (CASE, ETL, OLAP, etc.)	
75	Review the meta data repository	
76	Perform gap analysis	
77	**Evaluate and select new products**	64
78	Identify the product categories you need to evaluate (hardware, DBMS, tools)	

ID	Task_Name	Predecessors
79	List all products being considered for each category	
80	Itemize your requirements for the products	
81	Weigh each product requirement (scale of 1 to 10)	
82	Rank each product against the weighted requirements (scale of 0 to 10)	81
83	Determine the total score for each product	82
84	List all vendors of all products	
85	Itemize your requirements for the vendors	
86	Weigh each vendor requirement (scale of 1 to 10)	
87	Rank each vendor against the weighted requirements (scale of 0 to 10)	86
88	Determine the total score for each vendor	87
89	Evaluate the product scores and vendor scores	83, 88
90	Create a short list of products and vendors in each category	89
91	Have the products demonstrated by the vendors	90
92	Choose the final product in each product category	91
93	Obtain business sponsor approval to license the products	92
94	**Write the technical infrastructure assessment report**	67, 77
95	Itemize findings about servers, operating systems, middleware, etc.	
96	List the weighted requirements	
97	List the product scores	
98	List the vendor scores	
99	List the product costs	
100	List the products on the short list	
101	Explain the rationale for selecting or rejecting products	
102	Explain the final selection criteria	
103	Write the executive summary	
104	**Expand the current platform**	94
105	Order new products	
106	Install new products	105
107	Test new products	106

ID	Task_Name	Predecessors
108	Train technical staff on new products	106
109	**Section B: Nontechnical Infrastructure Evaluation**	
110	**Assess the effectiveness of existing nontechnical infrastructure components**	57
111	Review standards for data naming, abbreviations, modeling, etc.	
112	Review the use of the development methodology	
113	Review estimating guidelines	
114	Review change-control procedures	
115	Review issues management procedures	
116	Review roles and responsibilities	
117	Review security processes and guidelines	
118	Review meta data capture and delivery processes	
119	Review meta data repository functionality	
120	Review the process for merging logical data models into the enterprise data model	
121	Review data quality measures and the cleansing triage process	
122	Review the service-level agreement (SLA) process	
123	Review the BI support function	
124	Review the dispute resolution process	
125	Review the communication process	
126	Perform gap analysis	
127	**Write the nontechnical infrastructure assessment report**	110
128	Itemize findings about inadequate standards, guidelines, procedures, etc.	
129	Write recommendations for nontechnical infrastructure changes	
130	Prioritize nontechnical infrastructure requirements for the BI project	
131	Prioritize nontechnical infrastructure requirements for outside the BI project	
132	Write the executive summary	
133	**Improve the nontechnical infrastructure**	127
134	Create time estimates for creating or modifying new standards, guidelines, procedures	
135	Change the guidelines for using the development methodology	
136	Modify the roles and responsibilities	

ID	Task_Name	Predecessors
137	Create new processes as needed	
138	**Step 3: Project Planning**	
139	**Determine the project requirements**	94, 127
140	Define data requirements	
141	Define functional requirements (reports, queries, online help function)	
142	Define infrastructure requirements (technical and nontechnical)	
143	Expand or create the high-level logical data model	140
144	Validate the requirements with other business people	140, 141, 142
145	Obtain sponsor approval for the requirements	144
146	**Determine the condition of the source files and databases**	139
147	Review the content of each potential source file and source database (internal and external)	
148	**Assess source data violations**	
149	Review technical data conversion rules	
150	Review business data domain rules	
151	Review business data integrity rules	
152	Determine which data elements are critical, important, insignificant	
153	Estimate the time needed for cleansing of critical source data	152
154	Estimate the time needed for cleansing of important source data	152
155	Review data-cleansing estimates with the business sponsor and prioritize the cleansing effort	153, 154
156	**Determine or revise the cost estimates**	146
157	Review the technical infrastructure assessment report	
158	Review the nontechnical infrastructure assessment report	
159	Review the project requirements	
160	Review the project constraints (time, scope, budget, resources, quality)	
161	Review the need for consulting, contracting, training	
162	Revise the original cost estimates	161
163	**Revise the risk assessment**	146
164	Review and revise the original risk assessment matrix	
165	Determine the likelihood of the risks materializing: low, medium, high	

ID	Task_Name	Predecessors
166	Determine the impact of every risk: low, medium, high	
167	Define triggers	
168	Define a risk mitigation plan	
169	Define a contingency plan	
170	Identify your assumptions	
171	Include assumptions as risks on the contingency plan	
172	Review the project constraints as they relate to risk	
173	**Identify critical success factors**	156, 163
174	Define the success criteria for the BI project	
175	Determine critical success factors	174
176	Review critical success factors with the business sponsor	175
177	Obtain agreement and cooperation on the critical success factors from the business sponsor	176
178	**Prepare the project charter**	173
179	State the purpose and reason for the BI project	
180	State costs and benefits	
181	Describe infrastructure and business process improvements	
182	Describe the high-level scope (data and functions)	
183	List items not in the scope	
184	List expectations from the business people (preliminary SLA)	
185	Define team structure, roles, and responsibilities	
186	List risks, assumptions, and constraints	
187	List critical success factors	
188	**Create a high-level project plan**	173
189	Create a work breakdown structure	
190	Determine base estimates for all tasks	
191	Identify task dependencies	
192	**Revise the base estimates for assigned resources**	191
193	Address skill level	
194	Address subject matter expertise	

ID	Task_Name	Predecessors
195	Address additional administrative activities	
196	Address non-work-related activities	
197	Identify resource dependencies (resource leveling)	192
198	Create a critical path method (CPM) or Pert chart	197
199	Create a Gantt chart	197
200	**Kick off the project**	178, 188
201	Prepare an agenda for the kickoff meeting	
202	Call a kickoff meeting	201
203	Assign roles and responsibilities to core team members	202
204	Identify extended team members and review their responsibilities	202
205	Discuss the project charter	202
206	Walk through the project plan	202
207	Discuss the concept of self-organizing teams	202
208	**Step 4: Project Requirements Definition**	
209	**Define the requirements for technical infrastructure enhancements**	200
210	Define the requirements for additional hardware	
211	Define the requirements for additional middleware	
212	Define the requirements for a new DBMS or upgrades to the existing DBMS	
213	Define the requirements for the network or upgrades to it	
214	Determine the security requirements	
215	Define the requirements for development tools (CASE, ETL)	
216	Define the requirements for data access and reporting tools (OLAP, report writers)	
217	Define the requirements for a new data mining tool	
218	Determine whether to license or build a meta data repository	
219	Determine how to enhance an existing meta data repository	
220	**Define the requirements for nontechnical infrastructure enhancements**	200
221	Define the requirements for governance (prioritizing) standards and procedures	
222	Define the requirements for the development methodology	
223	Define the requirements for estimating guidelines	

ID	Task_Name	Predecessors
224	Define the requirements for the scope management process	
225	Define the requirements for the issues management process	
226	Define the requirements for roles and responsibilities	
227	Define the requirements for the security process	
228	Define the requirements for the meta data capture and delivery process	
229	Define the requirements for logical data modeling	
230	Define the requirements for the data cleansing process	
231	Define the requirements for the testing procedures	
232	Define the requirements for the SLA process	
233	Define the requirements for the BI support function	
234	Define the requirements for the dispute resolution process	
235	Define the requirements for the communication process	
236	**Define the reporting requirements**	200
237	Collect or create sample report layouts	
238	Collect or create sample queries	
239	Define business rules for the reports	
240	Define aggregation and summarization rules	
241	Define reporting dimensions	
242	Define query libraries	
243	Identify stewards of the libraries	
244	Get samples of ad hoc queries (if possible)	
245	Define access interfaces	
246	**Define the requirements for source data**	200
247	Define all source data elements	
248	Classify data elements as critical, important, insignificant	
249	Define the data domains (allowable values)	
250	Define the significant and obvious business rules for the data	
251	Determine the data-cleansing requirements	
252	Define the historical data requirements	

ID	Task_Name	Predecessors
253	**Review the project scope**	209, 220, 236, 246
254	Compare the detailed project requirements to the high-level scope in the project charter	
255	Review the project constraints (time, scope, budget, resources, quality)	
256	Determine whether the scope is realistic under those constraints	
257	Renegotiate the scope, if necessary	256
258	Create a change-control document	
259	Create an issues log	
260	**Expand the logical data model**	253
261	Add newly discovered entities and relationships	
262	Refine the logical data model by resolving the many-to-many relationships	261
263	Add unique identifiers to each entity	262
264	Attribute the logical data model with critical data elements	262
265	**Define preliminary service-level agreements**	253
266	Identify or revise the expectations for availability	
267	Identify or revise the expectations for security	
268	Identify or revise the expectations for response time	
269	Identify or revise the expectations for data cleanliness	
270	Identify or revise the expectations for ongoing support	
271	**Write the application requirements document**	260, 265
272	Describe the technical infrastructure requirements	
273	Describe the nontechnical infrastructure requirements	
274	Describe the reporting requirements	
275	Describe the ad hoc and canned query requirements	
276	Describe the requirements for source data, including history	
277	Describe the data-cleansing requirements	
278	Describe the security requirements	
279	List the preliminary SLAs	

ID	Task_Name	Predecessors
280	**Step 5: Data Analysis**	
281	**Analyze the external data sources**	271
282	Identify entities and relationships from each external data source	
283	Merge the new entities and relationships from the external data sources into the logical data model	
284	**Refine the logical data model**	271, 281
285	Fully attribute the logical data model to include all required source data elements	
286	Create new entities and relationships where needed to store the new attributes	
287	Analyze the layout of all identified source files and source databases	
288	Analyze the content of all identified source data elements	
289	Create the data-specific business meta data components	
290	**Analyze the source data quality**	271, 281
291	**Apply business data domain rules and business data integrity rules**	
292	Look for default values	
293	Look for missing values	
294	Look for cryptic values	
295	Look for contradicting values	
296	Look for values that violate the business rules	
297	Look for missing primary keys	
298	Look for duplicate primary keys	
299	Determine the severity of the problem	
300	Determine the criticality of the problem	
301	**Expand the enterprise logical data model**	284, 290
302	Merge the project-specific logical data model into the enterprise logical data model	
303	Identify data discrepancies and inconsistencies between the logical data models	
304	**Resolve data discrepancies**	290
305	Discuss the discrepancies with data owners and other business executives	
306	Adjust either the project-specific logical data model or the enterprise logical data model	
307	Notify other affected project teams	

ID	Task_Name	Predecessors
308	Document the discrepancies as meta data and schedule time for resolutions	
309	**Write the data-cleansing specifications**	304
310	Review the classification of data elements: critical, important, insignificant	
311	Write data-cleansing specifications for all critical data elements	
312	Write data-cleansing specifications for selected important data elements	
313	**Step 6: Application Prototyping**	
314	**Analyze the access requirements**	271
315	**Review the application requirements document with the subject matter expert and the business representative**	
316	Analyze the report requirements	
317	Analyze the query requirements	
318	Analyze the ad hoc requirements	
319	Analyze the interface requirements	
320	Communicate all your findings to the database administrator	
321	**Create a skill set matrix for each business person participating in the prototyping activities**	
322	Indicate computer skill level: beginning, advanced, expert	
323	Indicate application knowledge: beginning, advanced, expert	
324	**Determine the scope of the prototype**	271
325	Determine the objective and the primary use of the prototype	
326	Decide which type of prototype to build (show-and-tell, demo, etc.)	
327	Select a subset of functions (reports, queries, ETL, interface)	
328	Select a subset of sample data from source files and source databases	
329	Create a change-control document for the prototype	
330	Create an issues log for the prototype	
331	Determine the number of prototype iterations	
332	Determine the number of prototype participants	
333	Determine the time limits for each prototype iteration	331
334	Estimate the cost and benefit for each prototype iteration	331
335	Determine the point of diminishing returns for prototyping	331

ID	Task_Name	Predecessors
336	**Select tools for the prototype**	271
337	Review existing in-house tools and find out who uses them	
338	Review the availability of new reporting and querying tools	
339	Review existing or new graphical tools	
340	Review existing or new report distribution tools	
341	Review existing DBMS options for the prototype	
342	Select the platform on which the prototype will be developed	
343	Select one of the installed and tested DBMSs	
344	Select one or more existing or new tools	
345	Determine training needs for the new tools	
346	Schedule training sessions	345
347	**Prepare the prototype charter**	314, 324, 336
348	State the purpose of the prototype	
349	State what type of prototype you selected	
350	List who will participate (IT and business people)	
351	Define what the rules are (scope, time, iterations)	
352	Define how you will measure the success of the prototype	
353	**Design the reports and queries**	347
354	Design the reports	
355	Design the queries	
356	Design the interfaces	
357	Create a physical data model (database design) for the prototype database	
358	Identify the data to be used for the prototype	
359	Map sample source data or new test data into the prototype database	358
360	**Build the prototype**	347
361	Create the physical prototype database	
362	Create sample test data	
363	Load the prototype database with sample data	
364	Write a selected subset of reports	

ID	Task_Name	Predecessors
365	Write a selected subset of queries	
366	Write a selected subset of interfaces or other functions	
367	Test reports, queries, interfaces, or other functions	364, 365, 366
368	Document any problems with the tool	367
369	Document any issues with the reports or queries	367
370	Document any issues with the interfaces or other functions	367
371	Document any issues with dirty source data	367
372	Validate the time and cost estimates for the BI application	367
373	**Demonstrate the prototype**	353, 360
374	Review reports and queries with the business people	
375	Review problems and issues with the business sponsor and the business representative	
376	Review the project requirements with the subject matter expert and the business representative	
377	Document requested changes in the change-control document	
378	Analyze the impact of requested changes on other constraints (time, quality, cost, resources)	377
379	Review impact of requested changes with the business sponsor and the business representative	378
380	Revise the application requirements document to include approved changes	379
381	Review lessons learned with the entire project core team and in particular with the ETL step core team	380
382	Use prototype demonstrations to promote the BI application	380
383	Perform the next prototype iteration, if applicable	373
384	**Step 7: Meta Data Repository Analysis**	
385	**Analyze the meta data repository requirements**	271
386	Review the technical infrastructure assessment report	
387	Perform a cost-benefit analysis for licensing versus building a meta data repository	
388	Make the decision to license or build a meta data repository	387
389	Review the nontechnical infrastructure assessment report	
390	Determine the scope of the meta data repository deliverables	

ID	Task_Name	Predecessors
391	Prioritize the meta data repository deliverables	390
392	Update the application requirements document to reflect any changes	391
393	**Analyze the interface requirements for the meta data repository**	271
394	**Analyze the meta data sources**	
395	Analyze word processing files and spreadsheets	
396	Analyze DBMS dictionaries	
397	Analyze CASE, ETL, OLAP tools	
398	Analyze report writers and query tools	
399	Analyze the data mining tool	
400	Determine what import and export features are available in these tools	
401	Determine what import and export features are available in the meta data repository product	
402	**Analyze the meta data repository access and reporting requirements**	271
403	Review the original meta data repository access and reporting requirements	
404	Review the meta data security requirements	
405	Identify the access interface media (PDF, HTML)	
406	Analyze the feasibility of a context-sensitive help function	
407	Determine what reports should be produced from the meta data repository	
408	**Create the logical meta model**	385, 393, 402
409	Create business meta data entities	
410	Create technical meta data entities	
411	Determine the relationships between the meta data entities	
412	Create attributes for business and technical meta data entities	
413	Draw an entity-relationship diagram	
414	**Create the meta-meta data**	
415	**Describe all meta data entities**	408
416	Name the meta data entities	
417	Define all meta data entities	
418	Define the relationships between all meta data entities	

ID	Task_Name	Predecessors
419	Define the security for meta data entities	
420	Define the physical location for meta data entities	
421	Define timeliness for meta data	
422	Define volume for meta data entities	415
423	**Describe all meta data attributes**	
424	Name the meta data attributes	
425	Define all meta data attributes	
426	Define type and length for meta data attributes	
427	Define the domain for meta data attributes	
428	Define the security for meta data attributes	
429	Define ownership for meta data attributes	
430	Define the business rules for meta data entities, attributes, and relationships	423
431	**Step 8: Database Design**	
432	**Review the data access requirements**	309, 373
433	Review the data-cleansing specifications	
434	Review the prototyping results	
435	**Review detailed access and analysis requirements**	
436	Review detailed reporting requirements	
437	Review detailed querying requirements	
438	Review known ad hoc querying requirements	
439	Review data security requirements	
440	Determine projected data volumes and growth factors	
441	Determine the projected number of concurrent database usages	
442	Determine the location of business people	
443	Determine the frequency of report and query executions	
444	Determine the peak and seasonal reporting periods	
445	Determine platform limitations	
446	Determine tool limitations (ETL, OLAP, report writers)	

ID	Task_Name	Predecessors
447	**Determine the aggregation and summarization requirements**	309, 373
448	Review measures (facts) used by the prototype	
449	Review the dimensions used by the prototype	
450	Review the drill-down and roll-up functions of the prototype	
451	Review common reporting patterns among existing reports	
452	Determine the most frequently used reporting dimensions	
453	Review the logical data model with the data administrator	
454	Determine the level of detail (granularity) needed	
455	Determine how the detailed data will be accessed (drill-down or ad hoc)	
456	Determine how many business relationships (entity relationships) will be needed	
457	**Design the BI target databases**	435, 447
458	Determine the appropriate database design schemas (multidimensional or entity-relationship)	
459	Create the physical data models (database design diagrams)	
460	Create the technical meta data for the physical data models	459
461	Map the physical data models to the logical data model	459
462	**Design the physical database structures**	457
463	Determine how to cluster the tables	
464	Determine the placement of datasets	
465	Determine how to stripe disks	
466	Determine how to partition the tables across multiple disks	
467	Determine how much free space to choose	
468	Determine how much buffer space to declare	
469	Determine how large to set the blocksize	
470	Determine the most appropriate indexing strategy	
471	Determine whether referential integrity will be enforced by the DBMS	
472	**Build the BI target databases**	462
473	**Create the data definition language (DDL)**	
474	Define storage groups	

ID	Task_Name	Predecessors
475	Define databases	
476	Define partitions	
477	Define tablespaces	
478	Define tables	
479	Define columns	
480	Define primary keys	
481	Define foreign keys	480
482	Define indices	480
483	**Create the data control language (DCL)**	473
484	Define parameters for the security SYSTABLE	
485	Set up group IDs	
486	Grant CRUD (create, read, update, delete) authority to group IDs	
487	Assign developers, business analysts, and programs to the appropriate group IDs	
488	Run the DDL to create the physical database structures	473
489	Run the DCL to grant authority to the physical database structures	483
490	Build the indices	488
491	**Develop database maintenance procedures**	483
492	**Define database maintenance activities**	
493	Define database backups (full and incremental backups)	
494	Define disaster recovery procedures	
495	Define reorganization procedures for fragmented tables	
496	Define the frequency of and procedure for performance monitoring activities	
497	**Prepare to monitor and tune the database designs**	491
498	Plan to monitor the performance of ETL loads, reports, and queries at runtime	
499	Plan to use a performance-monitoring utility to diagnose performance degradation	
500	Plan to refine the database design schemas	
501	Plan to add additional indices, if necessary	
502	**Prepare to monitor and tune the query designs**	491
503	Plan to review and streamline all SQL calls in programs	

ID	Task_Name	Predecessors
504	Plan to write pass-through queries for OLAP tools, if necessary	
505	Plan to utilize parallel query execution	
506	**Step 9: Extract/Transform/Load Design**	
507	**Create the source-to-target mapping document**	491
508	Review the record layouts for the source files	
509	Review the data description blocks for the source databases	
510	Review the data-cleansing specifications for source data elements	
511	Create a matrix for all target tables and target columns	
512	List all applicable source files and source databases for every target table	
513	List all relevant source data elements for every target column	
514	List data type and length for every target column	
515	List data type and length for every source data element	
516	**Write transformation specifications for populating the columns**	514, 515
517	Combine data content from multiple sources (if needed)	
518	Split data content from one data element across multiple columns (if needed)	
519	Include aggregation and summarization algorithms	
520	Include data-cleansing specifications for each column	
521	Include logic for checking referential integrity (if not performed by the DBMS)	
522	Include logic for error messages and record rejection counts	
523	Include logic for reconciliation totals (record counts, domain counts, amount counts)	
524	**Test the ETL tool functions**	491
525	Review the transformation specifications in the source-to-target mapping document	516
526	Determine whether the ETL tool functions can perform the required transformation logic	525
527	Determine what supplementary custom code must be written	526
528	**Design the ETL process flow**	507, 524
529	Determine the most efficient sequence to extract source data	
530	Determine the most efficient sequence to transform, cleanse, and load the data	
531	Determine the sort and merge steps in the ETL process	
532	Identify all temporary and permanent work files and tables	

ID	Task_Name	Predecessors
533	Determine what components of the ETL process can run in parallel	
534	Determine what tables can be loaded in parallel	
535	**Draw the process flow diagram**	533, 534
536	Show the extracts from source files and source databases	
537	Indicate temporary and permanent work files and tables	
538	Show the sort and merge processes	
539	Show the transformation programs	
540	Show the error rejection files and error reports	
541	Show the load files and load utilities	
542	**Design the ETL programs**	528
543	**Design three sets of ETL programs**	
544	Design the initial load programs	
545	Design the historical load programs	
546	Design the incremental load programs	
547	Modularize the ETL programs	
548	Translate the transformation specifications into programming specifications	547
549	**Set up the ETL staging area**	528
550	Determine whether and how to distribute the ETL process	
551	Set up the ETL server	
552	Allocate space for temporary and permanent work files and tables	551
553	Create program libraries	551
554	Establish program-versioning procedures	551
555	**Step 10: Meta Data Repository Design**	
556	**Design the meta data repository database**	414
557	Review the logical meta model for the meta data repository	
558	Design the meta data repository database (entity-relationship or object-oriented)	
559	Draw the physical meta model diagram (entity-relationship or object-oriented)	
560	Map the physical meta model to the logical meta model	
561	Create the DDL for the meta data repository database	

ID	Task_Name	Predecessors
562	Create the DCL for the meta data repository database	
563	Design backup and recovery procedures	
564	Design versioning and archival procedures	
565	**Install and test the meta data repository product**	414
566	Compile a list of meta data repository products and vendors	
567	Compare the meta data repository products to the meta data repository requirements	
568	Create a scorecard for each evaluated meta data repository product	
569	Create a scorecard for each evaluated meta data repository vendor	
570	Narrow the list of meta data repository products and vendors to a short list	568, 569
571	Arrange for meta data repository product demos	
572	Check the vendors' client references	
573	License the meta data repository product	572
574	Install and test the meta data repository product	573
575	**Design the meta data migration process**	556, 565
576	Analyze all sources for extracting business meta data	
577	Analyze all sources for extracting technical meta data	
578	Design the tool interface process	
579	Design the transformations for the extracted meta data	
580	Design the load programs for the meta data repository	
581	**Write the programming specifications for the meta data migration process**	
582	Write tool interface programming specifications	578
583	Write transformation programming specifications	579
584	Write meta data repository load programming specifications	580
585	**Design the meta data application**	556
586	Design the meta data repository report programs	
587	Design the media for displaying meta data ad hoc query results	
588	Design the access interface process	
589	Design the context-sensitive online help function	

ID	Task_Name	Predecessors
590	**Write the programming specifications for the meta data application**	586
591	Write report programming specifications	587
592	Write query script specifications	588
593	Write access interface programming specifications	589
594	Write online help function programming specifications	
595	**Step 11: Extract/Transform/Load Development**	
596	**Build and unit test the ETL process**	542, 549
597	Code the ETL programs	
598	If using an ETL tool, write instructions for the ETL tool modules	
599	Capture the ETL technical meta data for the meta data repository	
600	Write code to produce reconciliation totals, quality metrics, and load statistics	
601	Unit test each individual program module	597, 600
602	If using an ETL tool, unit test each ETL tool module	598, 600
603	Write the scripts to execute the ETL programs and the sort, merge, and load utilities	601, 602
604	**Integration or regression test the ETL process**	596
605	Create a test plan with test cases for the ETL process	
606	Create test data for the ETL programs	
607	Integration or regression test the entire ETL process	605, 606
608	Log the actual test results and document any test issues	605, 606
609	Compare actual test results with expected test results	605, 606
610	Revise the ETL programs (or the instructions for the ETL tool)	609
611	Retest the entire ETL process from beginning to end	610
612	**Performance test the ETL process**	604
613	Test individual ETL programs and tool modules that read or write to high-volume tables	
614	Test the parallel execution of ETL programs and tool modules against high-volume tables	
615	Test the ETL programs and ETL tool modules that perform complicated operations	
616	Use full-volume data for performance testing	
617	If using a stress test simulation tool, define test components and run a simulation test	

ID	Task_Name	Predecessors
618	**Quality assurance (QA) test the ETL process**	612
619	Move all ETL programs into the QA environment	
620	QA test the entire ETL process from beginning to end	619
621	Obtain approval from the operations staff to move the ETL process into production	620
622	**Acceptance test the ETL process**	612
623	**Acceptance test the entire ETL process from beginning to end**	
624	Validate all cleansing transformations	
625	Validate error-handling routines	
626	Validate reconciliation totals	
627	Obtain certification for the ETL process from the business representative	623
628	**Step 12: Application Development**	
629	**Determine the final project requirements**	491
630	Review the results of the prototype	
631	Review the prototyping programs and scripts	
632	Review the change-control document	
633	Review the issues log	
634	Review existing and mock-up report layouts	
635	Review existing spreadsheets	
636	Review the latest version of the application requirements document	
637	Agree on the final project requirements	
638	Update the application requirements document to reflect any changes	637
639	**Design the application programs**	491
640	Design the final reports	
641	Design the final queries	
642	Design the front-end interface (GUI, Web portal)	
643	Design the online help function	
644	**Write programming specifications**	
645	Write report programming specifications	640
646	Write query script specifications	641

ID	Task_Name	Predecessors
647	Write front-end interface programming specifications	642
648	Write online help function programming specifications	643
649	Create a test plan with test cases and a test log	645, 646
650	**Build and unit test the application programs**	639
651	Create sample test data	
652	Load the development databases with sample test data	
653	Rewrite or enhance prototyping programs and scripts	
654	Code the final report programs	
655	Code the final query scripts	
656	Code the final front-end interface programs	
657	Code the online help function programs	
658	Unit test each individual program module	654, 655, 656, 657
659	**Test the application programs**	650
660	**Integration or regression test all programs and scripts from beginning to end**	
661	Integration or regression test report programs	
662	Integration or regression test query scripts	
663	Integration or regression test front-end interface programs	
664	Integration or regression test online help function programs	
665	Log the actual test results and document any test issues	
666	Compare actual test results with expected test results	
667	Revise the application programs and scripts	666
668	Retest the application programs and scripts from beginning to end	667
669	Performance test complex high-volume programs	668
670	Use full-volume data for performance testing	668
671	If using a stress test simulation tool, define test components and run a simulation test	668
672	Move databases, programs, and scripts into the QA environment	669
673	QA test the entire application from beginning to end	672
674	Obtain approval from the operations staff to move the application programs into production	673
675	Acceptance test the entire application from beginning to end	669

ID	Task_Name	Predecessors
676	Obtain certification for the application from the business representative	675
677	**Provide data access and analysis training**	650
678	Identify help desk staff to be trained	
679	Identify "power users" or other business liaison personnel to be trained	
680	Identify business people to be trained	
681	**Create training materials**	
682	Create presentation slides and instructor notes	
683	Create student workbooks with exercises	682
684	Create exercise solutions and other pertinent handouts	683
685	Schedule training sessions	684
686	Conduct training sessions	685
687	Measure training effectiveness	686
688	**Step 13: Data Mining**	
689	**State the business problem**	491
690	Define the business problem	
691	Obtain commitment for a data mining solution	690
692	Set realistic expectations for the data mining tool	691
693	Identify preliminary algorithms relevant to the business problem	691
694	**Collect the data**	689
695	Identify available data sources (operational as well as BI)	
696	Extract pertinent data from various internal data sources	
697	Acquire pertinent data from external data sources	
698	**Consolidate and cleanse the data**	689
699	Merge data from various internal data sources	
700	Match and merge internal data with external data	
701	Review the structure of the merged data	
702	Select a sample of data for each analytical data model	
703	Select related meta data from the meta data repository	
704	Review the data domains and measure the quality and reasonability of data values	702

ID	Task_Name	Predecessors
705	Validate domain reasonability across active variables	702
706	**Prepare the data**	702
707	Review the frequency distribution of categorical variables	
708	Review maximum, minimum, mean, mode, and median for quantitative variables	
709	Use statistical distribution parameters to filter noise in the data	
710	Eliminate or replace variables with missing values	
711	Convert data formats to suit the particular data mining algorithm used	
712	Derive new variables from original input data	
713	Consolidate customers by assigning a household number to related customers	
714	Relate customers with products and services	
715	Apply data reduction	
716	**Apply data mining transformation techniques**	715
717	Apply "discretization" technique	
718	Apply "one-of-N" technique	
719	**Build the analytical data model**	694, 698, 706
720	Create the analytical (informational) data model	
721	Select data mining operations with the appropriate algorithms	
722	Test accuracy using confusion matrices and input sensitivity analyses	
723	Repeat prior steps to train and retrain the model	722
724	**Interpret the data mining results**	719
725	Review the data mining results	
726	Look for results that are interesting, valid, and actionable	
727	Present the new findings using visualization technology	726
728	Formulate ways in which the new information can be exploited	726
729	**Perform external validation of the results**	719
730	Compare data mining results to published industry statistics	
731	Validate the selection of your variables and time frame against the variables and time frame of the industry statistics	
732	Identify the variations between your analysis results and the industry statistics	

ID	Task_Name	Predecessors
733	Determine the reasons for the variations	
734	**Monitor the analytical data model over time**	724, 729
735	Keep validating your analytical data model against industry statistics at regular time intervals	
736	When industry statistics change, change your analytical data model and retrain it	735
737	Research the data mining capabilities of your competitors	
738	Monitor your competitors' market share and adjust your model	
739	**Step 14: Meta Data Repository Development**	
740	**Build the meta data repository database**	575, 585
741	Run the DDL to create the physical meta data repository database structures	
742	Run the DCL to grant CRUD authority on the meta data repository database structures	
743	If licensing a meta data repository product, set up CRUD authority on the meta data repository product	
744	Test all meta data repository product components, especially the meta data repository database	
745	**Build and unit test the meta data migration process**	740
746	Code the tool interface programs or use the export facility of the various tools	
747	Code the meta data transformation programs	
748	Code the meta data load programs or use the import facility of the meta data repository product or the DBMS load utility	
749	**Code the meta data programs that will run during ETL**	
750	Code the meta data programs to capture load statistics	
751	Code the meta data programs to capture reconciliation totals	
752	Code the meta data programs to capture data-cleansing metrics	
753	Code the meta data programs to capture rejection counts and reasons for rejections	
754	**Unit test the meta data migration programs**	
755	Unit test the tool interface programs	746
756	Unit test the meta data transformation programs	747
757	Unit test the meta data load programs	748
758	Unit test the meta data programs that will run during the ETL process	749

ID	Task_Name	Predecessors
759	**Build and unit test the meta data application**	740
760	Code the access interface programs	
761	Code the meta data report programs	
762	Code the meta data query scripts	
763	Code the meta data repository online help function programs	
764	**Unit test the meta data application programs (or meta data repository product modules)**	
765	Unit test the access interface programs	760
766	Unit test the meta data report programs	761
767	Unit test the meta data query scripts	762
768	Unit test the meta data repository online help function programs	763
769	**Test the meta data repository programs or product functions**	745, 759
770	**Create a test plan with test cases**	
771	Create test cases for the meta data migration process	
772	Create test cases for the meta data repository application programs or product modules	
773	Create test cases for the meta data programs that run during the ETL process	
774	**Create test data for meta data repository testing**	
775	Create test data for the meta data migration process	
776	Create test data for the meta data repository application or product modules	
777	Create test data for the meta data programs that run during the ETL process	
778	**Integration or regression test the meta data repository**	770, 774
779	Integration or regression test the meta data migration process	
780	Integration or regression test the meta data repository application or product modules	
781	Integration or regression test the meta data programs that run during the ETL process	
782	Log the actual test results and document any test issues	778
783	Compare actual test results with expected test results	778
784	Revise the meta data repository programs	783
785	Retest the meta data repository programs from beginning to end	784
786	Conduct QA testing with operations staff	785
787	Conduct acceptance testing with the subject matter expert and the business representative	785

ID	Task_Name	Predecessors
788	**Prepare the meta data repository for production**	769
789	Install and test the server platform for the production meta data repository	
790	Create DDL and DCL for the production meta data repository database	
791	Write operating procedures for the operations staff for running the meta data repository reports	
792	Write a reference guide for the help desk staff and the business people	
793	Develop performance monitoring and tuning procedures for the meta data repository database	
794	Develop meta data repository usage monitoring procedures	
795	**Provide meta data repository training**	769
796	Identify help desk staff to be trained	
797	Identify "power users" to be trained	
798	Identify business people to be trained	
799	**Create meta data repository training materials**	
800	Create meta data repository presentation slides and instructor notes	
801	Create meta data repository student workbooks with exercises	800
802	Create exercise solutions and other pertinent handouts	801
803	Schedule meta data repository training sessions	802
804	Conduct meta data repository training sessions	803
805	Measure meta data repository training effectiveness	804
806	**Step 15: Implementation**	
807	**Plan the implementation**	618, 622, 659, 719, 788
808	Select an implementation (rollout) strategy	
809	Set the implementation date	
810	Determine the number of business people for the initial rollout	
811	Schedule the necessary resources to participate in implementation activities	
812	Schedule the functions to be rolled out	
813	Prepare for organizational impact	

ID	Task_Name	Predecessors
814	**Set up the production environment**	807
815	Set up the production ETL program library	
816	Set up the production application program library	
817	Set up the production meta data repository program library	
818	Create the production BI target databases	
819	Create the production meta data repository database	
820	Grant appropriate authority on the production BI target databases	818
821	Grant appropriate authority on the production meta data repository database	819
822	Grant appropriate authority on all production program libraries	815, 816, 817
823	Write ETL operating procedures for operations staff	
824	Write application reference guides for help desk staff and the business people	
825	Implement production security levels for all BI application components	
826	**Install all the BI application components**	814
827	**Move ETL programs into the production ETL program library**	
828	Move initial load programs	
829	Move historical load programs	
830	Move incremental load programs	
831	**Move application programs into the production application program library**	
832	Move report programs	
833	Move query scripts	
834	Move front-end interface programs	
835	Move online help function programs	
836	**Move meta data repository programs into the production meta data repository program library**	
837	Move meta data migration programs	
838	Move meta data application programs or product modules	
839	**Set up the production schedule**	814
840	Set up the ETL process on the job scheduler	
841	Add to the job scheduler the meta data programs that run during the ETL process	

ID	Task_Name	Predecessors
842	Set up on the job scheduler the regularly scheduled application report programs	
843	**Set up on the job scheduler the regularly scheduled meta data repository programs**	
844	Set up the meta data migration process	
845	Set up the meta data repository application	
846	**Load the production databases**	826, 839
847	Run the initial load process	
848	Run the historical load process	
849	Run the meta data migration process	
850	**Prepare for ongoing support**	846
851	Establish a schedule for on-call emergency support	
852	**Schedule database maintenance activities for the production databases**	
853	Schedule database backups	
854	Schedule disaster recovery testing	
855	Schedule database reorganizations	
856	**Schedule database monitoring activities for the production databases**	
857	Schedule performance monitoring activities	
858	Schedule growth monitoring activities	
859	Schedule usage monitoring activities	
860	**Schedule data quality monitoring activities for the BI target databases**	
861	Schedule activities for reviewing meta data metrics	
862	Schedule quality spot checks	
863	**Develop or review capacity plans for the BI platform**	
864	Develop capacity plans for processors	
865	Develop capacity plans for disk storage	
866	Develop capacity plans for network components (including bandwidth)	
867	Start production processing (go live)	850
868	**Step 16: Release Evaluation**	
869	**Prepare for the post-implementation review**	850FS+30 days
870	Review budget expenditures	

ID	Task_Name	Predecessors
871	Review the original project plan and final schedule	
872	Review the estimated and actual task completion times	
873	Review the issues log (resolved and unresolved issues)	
874	Review the change-control procedure and scope changes	
875	Review unfulfilled requirements (dropped from scope)	
876	Review the effectiveness of the development approach	
877	Review the effectiveness of the team structure	
878	Review the effectiveness of the organizational placement	
879	Review the existing infrastructure (technical and nontechnical)	
880	Identify missing infrastructure pieces (technical and nontechnical)	879
881	Assess the performance of the BI application	
882	Review the effectiveness of training	
883	Review the implementation (rollout) strategy	
884	Review the effectiveness of the release concept	
885	**Organize the post-implementation review meeting**	
886	**Create the preliminary post-implementation review agenda**	
887	List date, time, and place	
888	List invited attendees	
889	List topics for discussion	
890	List and assign topics for research	
891	List questions to be discussed and answered	
892	Solicit additional topics and questions from attendees	
893	Send out the preliminary agenda to attendees	
894	Schedule the meeting at an off-site location	
895	Arrange facilitation by a third party	
896	Arrange for a third-party scribe to take notes during the meeting	
897	Revise and send the final meeting agenda	893
898	Send out documentation to be discussed during the review	897

Task 885 has predecessor 850FS+30 days

ID	Task_Name	Predecessors
899	**Conduct the post-implementation review meeting**	869, 885
900	Introduce the attendees	
901	Explain the rules for the facilitated session	
902	Discuss each item on the agenda	
903	Document discussions, suggestions, resolutions	
904	Document action items	
905	Assign action items	
906	Establish completion or response date for each action item	
907	**Follow up on the post-implementation review**	899
908	Document unfulfilled requirements to be bundled with the next BI release	
909	Write the meeting minutes	
910	Publish the meeting minutes	
911	Work on assigned action items	
912	Monitor the work performed on action items	
913	Document the action item results	911
914	Publish the action item results	913
915	**Implement nontechnical infrastructure improvements**	
916	Improve the development approach	
917	Improve use of the development methodology	
918	Improve processes and procedures	
919	Improve guidelines	
920	Improve standards	

Index

CD-ROM Warranty

Addison-Wesley, Larissa T. Moss, and Shaku Atre warrant the enclosed disc to be free of defects in materials and faulty workmanship under normal use for a period of ninety days after purchase. If a defect is discovered in the disc during this warranty period, a replacement disc can be obtained at no charge by sending the defective disc, postage prepaid, with proof of purchase to:

Editorial Department
Addison-Wesley Professional
Pearson Technology Group
75 Arlington Street, Suite 300
Boston, MA 02116
Email: AWPro@awl.com

Addison-Wesley, Larissa T. Moss, and Shaku Atre make no warranty or representation, either expressed or implied, with respect to this software, its quality, performance, merchantability, or fitness for a particular purpose. In no event will Addison-Wesley, its distributors, dealers, Larissa T. Moss, or Shaku Atre be liable for direct, indirect, special, incidental, or consequential damages arising out of the use or inability to use the software. The exclusion of implied royalties is not permitted in some states. Therefore, the above exclusion may not apply to you. This warranty provides you with specific legal rights. There may be other rights that you may have that vary from state to state. The contents of this CD-ROM are intended for personal use only.

More information and updates are available at:

http://www.awprofessional.com